The Road to Castle Mount

Recent Titles in Contributions to the
Study of Science Fiction and Fantasy

The Road to Castle Mount

◆

The Science Fiction of Robert Silverberg

Edgar L. Chapman

Contributions to the Study of Science Fiction and Fantasy, Number 82
Marshall Tymn, Series Editor

Greenwood Press
Westport, Connecticut • London

Library of Congress Cataloging-in-Publication Data

Chapman, Edgar L., 1936–
  The road to Castle Mount : the science fiction of Robert
Silverberg / Edgar L. Chapman.
     p.   cm.—(Contributions to the study of science fiction and
fantasy, ISSN 0193–6875 ; no. 82)
  Includes bibliographical references (p.   ) and index.
  ISBN 0–313–26145–8 (alk. paper)
     1. Silverberg, Robert—Criticism and interpretation.   2. Science
fiction, American—History and criticism.   I. Title.   II. Series.
PS3569.I472Z57   1999
813'.54—dc21   99–17840

British Library Cataloguing in Publication Data is available.

Library of Congress Catalog Card Number: 99–17840
ISBN: 0–313–26145–8
ISSN: 0193–6875

First published in 1999

Greenwood Press, 88 Post Road West, Westport, CT 06881
An imprint of Greenwood Publishing Group, Inc.
www.greenwood.com

Printed in the United States of America

The paper used in this book complies with the
Permanent Paper Standard issued by the National
Information Standards Organization (Z39.48–1984).

10 9 8 7 6 5 4 3 2 1

For my mother, Otelia Coburn Chapman,
and my father, Evert L. Chapman,
in gratitude for their continuing love and support.

And to the memory of my great-uncle, Henry D. Siler
(1901–1982), Ph.D., University of Texas, 1949,
a decorated veteran of the Pacific war,
who taught me the value of reading science fiction.

Contents

Preface

◆

This study began many years ago for another publisher, encouraged by a friendly editor named Tom Staicar. Unfortunately, a senior editor at that company, hoping to impress the new owners who had purchased it, terminated the series for which the study was to be an entry.

Several editors at Greenwood have given encouragement and assistance during the long writing and revising of this work: Marshall Tymn recommended the work, and Marilyn Brownstein, Nina Pearlstein, Emma Moore, and George Butler gave encouragement at various times and showed patience about the time I was taking to finish it.

Help has also been provided by many other people. Robert Silverberg himself was kind enough to provide information in letters and to answer some questions about his work at a conference of the International Association for the Fantastic on the Arts.

Any scholar who studies Silverberg must also feel an enormous debt to the extraordinary bibliographical work of the late Thomas Clareson and to his pioneering Starmont study of Silverberg's fiction. While one may differ with many of Dr. Clareson's interpretations and judgments as a critic of fiction (as I do on occasion), his trailblazing efforts still offer useful perspectives.

The staffs of Illinois State University's Milner Library and Bradley's Cullom-Davis Library (especially Barb Tunks and Marina Savole) have been helpful at many times down through the years. Brian Simpson of Babbitt's Used Books has been of assistance in helping to find out-of-print science fiction.

Encouragement and support were also provided by administrators at Bradley University, Peoria, Illinois, especially the late Max Kele as dean of Liberal Arts and Sciences, and Claire Etaugh, my current and understanding dean. My current chairperson, Dr. Margaret Carter, has been an understanding supporter for many years. My colleague, Warren F. Dwyer, has read two chapters of the manuscript and made helpful criticism. My literature students at Bradley University, especially those in my science fiction courses over a couple of decades, have also been a stimulating influence on my thinking about Silverberg.

Our fine word-processor operator, Willie Heberer, has done an extraordinary job over the years of reading my rough drafts and transforming them into readable manuscripts.

A major debt is also owed to my teachers at all levels. Only a few of the outstanding ones who have influenced my reading and writing can be mentioned here. Mary Vance encouraged my reading and writing in my high school days in Bloomfield, Missouri. Several undergraduate instructors stimulated my understanding of literature and writing, especially John Randolph of Westminster College, Fulton, Missouri, and James Carver and Georgia Bowman of William Jewell College, Liberty, Missouri.

I was also fortunate to have some splendid role models during my study at Brown University, including George Anderson, Leicester Bradner, Millicent Bell, and R. W. Kenny, who taught me much about classic English literature. I. J. Kapstein, Elmer Blistein, and A. J. Sabol provided splendid comments about scholarly writing on literature. I owe a special debt to S. Foster Damon's stimulating views on allegory and symbolism. Even greater is my debt to the brilliant Hyatt H. Waggoner, a renowned figure in the study of American literature, for insight into the interpretation of literature.

Finally, I have received encouragement from family members during the work on this book. My brother, Richard Chapman, a historian at Francis Marion University, and my sons, Benjamin and Terrence (fine liberal arts students), often supplied insights through their assessments of science fiction novels and films. However, the greatest of these debts are cited in the dedication.

Key to Abbreviations

◆

WORKS BY SILVERBERG

AABY	*Across a Billion Years*
AWE	*At Winter's End*
AY	*The Alien Years*
BOS	*The Book of Skulls*
BTSZ	*Beyond the Safe Zone*
BWTD	*Born with the Dead and Other Stories*
CFDMLD	*Conquerors from the Darkness* with *Master of Life and Death*
CG	*Capricorn Games*
DI	*Dying Inside*
DL	*The Dawning Light*
DT	*Dimension Thirteen*
DTTE	*Downward to the Earth*
FOSD	*The Feast of St. Dionysus*
FOTW	*The Face of the Waters*
GD	*Galactic Dreamers: Science Fiction as Visionary Literature*
GOW	*The Gate of Worlds*
GTK	*Gilgamesh the King*
HSAM	*Hot Sky at Midnight*
IAC	*In Another Country*
LCVC	*Lost Cities and Vanished Civilizations*

LFA	*Letters From Atlantis*
LOD	*Lord of Darkness*
LVC	*Lord Valentine's Castle*
MAS	*Moonferns and Starsongs*
MC	*Majipoor Chronicles*
MITM	*The Man in the Maze*
MOLAD	*Master of Life and Death*
MOT	*The Masks of Time*
MS	*The Mutant Season*
NSTS	*Next Stop the Stars*
ROAC	*Revolt on Alpha C*
RR	*Reflections and Refractions: Thoughts on Science-Fiction and Other Matters*
RTL	*Recalled to Life*
SBTC	"Sounding Brass, Tinkling Cymbal"
SE	*The Seed of Earth*
SITF	*Shadrach in the Furnace*
SM	*Son of Man*
SOM	*Sorcerers of Majipoor*
SP	*The Shrouded Planet*
SS	*Secret Sharers: The Collected Stories of Robert Silverberg*, Vol. 1.
TBORS	*The Best of Robert Silverberg*, Vol. 1.
TCCP	*The Conglomeroid Cocktail Party*
TGD	*The Golden Dream: Seekers of El Dorado*
TOC	*A Time of Changes*
TOG	*Tower of Glass*
TOTS	*To Open the Sky*
TTLL	*To the Land of the Living*
UT	*Unfamiliar Territory*
WF1992	*World's Fair, 1992*
WTC	*World of a Thousand Colors*
WW	*Robert Silverberg's Worlds of Wonder*

KEY TO OTHER WORKS

| AOC | *Anatomy of Criticism* by Northrop Frye |
| BSF | *Bridges to Science Fiction* edited by George W. Slusser, George Guffey, and Mark Rose |

CTN	*Conrad the Novelist* by Albert J. Guerard, Jr.
DM	*Dream Makers* edited by Charles Platt
DOS	*A Dictionary of Symbols* by J. E. Cirlot
DOSIMO	*The Dreams Our Stuff Is Made Of* by Thomas Disch
EOF	*The Encyclopedia of Fantasy* by John Clute and John J. Grant
EOSF	*Encyclopedia of Science Fiction* by John Clute and John J. Grant
FASF	*Fantasy and Science Fiction*
HV	*Hitler Victorious* edited by Gregory Benford and Martin H. Greenberg
IA	*Isaac Asimov: The Foundations of Science Fiction* by James Gunn
IASF	*Isaac Asimov's Science Fiction*
MLPJF	*The Magic Labyrinth of Philip José Farmer* by Edgar L. Chapman
MOSF	*Masters of Science Fiction* by Brian Stableford
NYROSF	*The New York Review of Science Fiction*
PFA	*Phoenix from the Ashes* edited by Carl B. Yoke
RH	*Robert Heinlein: America as Science Fiction* by H. Bruce Franklin
RS	*Robert Silverberg* by Thomas Clareson
RSMT	*Robert Silverberg's Many Trapdoors* edited by Charles Elkins and Martin H. Greenberg
RSPSB	*Robert Silverberg: A Primary and Secondary Bibliography* by Thomas Clareson
RTSF	*The Road to Science Fiction* edited by James Gunn
SFFA1990	*Science Fiction and Fantasy Annual 1990*
SFTE	*Science Fiction: Ten Explorations* by Colin Manlove
SOF	*Strategies of Fantasy* by Brian Attebery
SS	*The Secular Scripture* by Northrop Frye
TCWK	*The Company We Keep* by Wayne C. Booth
TKTU	*The Known and the Unknown* by Gary Wolfe
TYS	*Trillion Year Spree* by Brian Aldiss with David Wingrove
WBTH	*The World beyond the Hill* by Alexei and Cory Panshin
WOSF	"The Worldview of Science Fiction" by James Gunn

1

Silverberg: The Man and His Work

◆

One of the most prolific, honored, and widely read living science fiction writers, Robert Silverberg has forged a professional career that began in the 1950s and has flourished in succeeding decades. His achievements have brought him recognition and awards not only from critics and reviewers but also from fellow writers and a wide, if varying, group of readers. After first gaining fame for his magazine fiction of the fifties, Silverberg remade his career in the late sixties, assimilating the ideals and methods of the "new wave" literary science fiction of the time, and producing a number of well-crafted novels containing literary symbolism and dramatic irony. However, the conflict between his visionary and his ironic selves was seldom completely integrated during that era, and disillusionment with his audience produced a hiatus in the seventies. Yet, after a period of silence, Silverberg returned to an active role as a fiction writer. Nevertheless, despite the appeal of his novels to discerning readers, Silverberg's achievement still eludes easy assessment.

From the very beginning, Silverberg was perceived as a promising and potentially brilliant author in the genre, and he has persisted long enough to have won more Hugo Awards (based on the vote of non-professionals) and Nebula Awards (selected by a smaller and probably more discerning group of editors, critics, and writers) than any other author. Indeed, the general esteem shown for Silverberg's best work has often been summed up by the comment of Gerald Jonas, a reviewer for the *New York Times* who once compared Silverberg's mature work favorably to that of John Updike in the world of "mainstream" or "realistic" fiction.[1] Moreover, Silverberg's career, like Updike's, is far from over.

Such praise has been somewhat double-edged and ambiguous. The comparison to Updike illustrates the reservations felt about Silverberg's work, for both Silverberg and Updike have been accused of displaying more technical facility than substance.[2] Indeed, while Silverberg's work has received its share of critical analysis from academic scholars, the author's literary position remains controversial, like the genre in which he writes. Though Silverberg's early sins as an ambitious neophyte and author of formula adventures have been largely forgiven by his critics, later divergences and shifts in direction are frequently used to indict his career.

Some critics, including a former science fiction author who has sought a higher status while condemning the genre in prestigious forums, such as an article in *Atlantic*, cannot forgive Silverberg for writing *Lord Valentine's Castle*, a charming adventure fantasy, the major fault of which seems to be its commercial success.[3] Yet Silverberg did not follow *Lord Valentine's Castle* with a series of pot-boiler fantasies; on the contrary, he has explored significant areas of experience in a number of impressive novels. Those who read science fiction and fantasy with serious interest can scarcely deny the impact of his presence.

Given Silverberg's achievements, it would seem that his best work should give him a literary rank similar to that of Brian Aldiss, Ursula LeGuin, and Gene Wolfe, to mention living contemporary authors who enjoy superior reputations within the genres of science fiction and fantasy, as well as solid reputations among critics of mainstream fiction.[4] At any rate, Silverberg's importance as writer and editor should be beyond question. Whatever a writer's failures, he or she deserves to be judged by his or her best work, not by false starts or hasty apprentice work. Moreover, Silverberg's fiction should rank highly when judged against some of the best known figures in the genre. Even a casual reader of some discernment can perceive that Silverberg's mature work is generally more sophisticated than Robert Heinlein's, richer and more ironic than Isaac Asimov's, and less mannered than Ray Bradbury's. Nor is it dwarfed by comparison with current masters, including Aldiss, Wolfe, LeGuin, and John Crowley.

However, since Silverberg's career began in the fifties, we may find it helpful to measure his performance against that of the generation of writers who broke in during that era: notably Philip K. Dick, Philip José Farmer, Harlan Ellison, and Frederik Pohl, among others. Though serious assessment of these figures has just begun, Silverberg does not fare badly from this point of view. Like Silverberg, these authors have produced memorable work, despite a good deal of hasty and second-rate writing; and one of them, Dick, enjoys a high reputation, transcending mere critical respect, and approaching the veneration of a cult. Each, on occasion, made questionable career decisions, and, like most professional authors, each has felt obliged to compromise or exploit the market for commercial reasons.[5] As all but the naive know, those who write for a popular market can seldom afford to ignore its demands.

Like others of the fifties generation, Silverberg's career has created its share of misunderstandings and myths, one cause being Silverberg's own public comments in prefaces, interviews, and autobiographical memoirs such as his well known essay in Aldiss's and Harry Harrison's *Hell's Cartographers* (1975). Any author who produces successfully over a lengthy period may feel the need to re-imagine and re-shape his career, and Silverberg has experienced this desire more than once. Perhaps because he began publishing regularly at so early an age, he has re-invented his career not merely once, but at three pivotal times: in the early sixties, as a result of the frustration created by his initial ambitious assault on magazines and paperback publishers; in the period of 1969–74, when he established himself as a "new wave" author of literary science fiction; and yet again during his sabbatical from the genre in the seventies, before he entered his current phase as a distinguished novelist and master of short fiction.

Much of the debate aroused by Silverberg's work and career has resulted from his well publicized changes of direction. At first considered a promising newcomer, he graduated, after hard work, to the status of a talented writer who had supposedly wasted his gifts in frenetic hack-work (Malzberg 1974, 69). Indeed, Silverberg himself tended to accept this estimate (SBTC 33–37) until, in the late sixties and early seventies, he produced, by dint of arduous labor, including painstaking revisions, a great deal of "new wave" science fiction—or science fiction displaying the techniques of literary modernism (SBTC 37–38). Thus he became one of the prize exhibits, demonstrating that this disparaged genre was capable of presenting the world with fiction of high literary quality: a literary excellence, defined as fiction but evincing the techniques and modernist irony found in the poetry of T. S. Eliot, W. H. Auden, and W. B. Yeats, and the symbolist fiction of Franz Kafka, Joseph Conrad, and James Joyce.[6]

Accolades and awards followed rapidly, hailing the "new Silverberg," and his early years were now seen as a valuable apprenticeship in which he learned the tricks of his craft, although literary politics and intellectual fashions clearly influenced some of the plaudits. Despite the high quality of much of Silverberg's work, it was also important for editors and reviewers to demonstrate that science fiction was capable of producing writing comparable to the more traditional literature enshrined in the literary canons of the academic world. It was also important to show that science fiction authors could respond to the social conflicts between mainstream America and the counterculture. Both innovative literary techniques and enlightened social concerns appeared in Silverberg's fiction and influenced the largely favorable response to it.

However, from a later perspective, Silverberg's work of this era appears somewhat uneven. While some of Silverberg's novels of the period, such as *Shadrach in the Furnace* (1976), were probably underrated or ignored, and others, such as *Dying Inside* (1972), hold up well on later readings, the 1971 Nebula Award for *A Time of Changes* must now strike many as the judges' bow to the romanticism about hallucinatory drugs in the era of Woodstock (1969) and the Age of Aquarius.

Yet when Silverberg, now established as a star of the genre, withdrew from active writing in the middle seventies, voicing disenchantment with the reading audience, he surprised many by returning with a romantic fantasy. Though he seemed to have abandoned his ironic fiction, this impression was quickly corrected by other work. Silverberg's work began to stimulate negative and lukewarm responses. Perhaps it would have helped if Silverberg had not spent time in his sabbatical from fiction writing condemning (in numerous essays and interviews) those readers who had failed to appreciate his more literary work. Although this is usually a futile enterprise for an author, Silverberg's acerbic comments had seemed to confirm his status as a mature science fiction writer who had become too highbrow for the market.[7]

At any rate, when Silverberg began to publish fiction again, at the end of the decade, some of the same readers who had admired *Nightwings* (1969), *Dying Inside* (1972), and "Born with the Dead" (1974) seemed disconcerted and baffled by his first major effort, *Lord Valentine's Castle* (1980). Nor were matters improved when this romantic fantasy was followed by other novels that seemed to veer away from the ironic vision of the "new Silverberg" to offer large-scale epic conflicts. There were also two ambitious forays into historical fiction, though Silverberg later expressed regret for these ventures (mainly on commercial grounds).[8]

Ironically enough, Silverberg's later fiction has received many positive reviews, and it has also been the recipient of awards. Clearly, the later Silverberg has been misunderstood and, except for discerning critics, judged too hastily. When we look into Silverberg's early work, we find evidence of a strongly romantic strain in his imagination. In the latest phase of his career, moreover, he has spoken of the successful writer as a juggler, a metaphor that he employed skillfully in *Lord Valentine's Castle*.[9] On other occasions, he has modestly spoken of himself as an "old pro," rather than making exaggerated claims for his role as an artist, as the rhetoric of modernist writers was inclined to do.[10] He has continued to publish at least a novel a year, as well as short fiction, and he also does editorial work.

The emphasis on professionalism in this stage of his career has produced predictable revaluations. While some readers and critics were murmuring that Silverberg had abandoned literary values to return to commercial work, others offered highly qualified defenses. No doubt some concluded that Silverberg, whose darker vision had found expression in *Dying Inside* and other works of the early seventies, had been overrated, in contrast with new luminaries of the genre, such as Wolfe and LeGuin. Even so consistent a supporter of Silverberg's work as the late Thomas Clareson—a scholar to whom all serious students of Silverberg are deeply indebted—was guarded in his comments about Silverberg's work in the eighties and nineties. While some of Silverberg's more recent fiction, especially a few shorter works, display, in Clareson's opinion, a high quality of conception and execution, his considered view was that Silverberg's "stories and novels" of the current period were dominated by "spectacle and thus present the reader with brilliant surfaces" (RSMT 11).

Others have raised questions regarding the consistency of Silverberg's intellectual vision. An example of such a probing study appears in an essay by Robert Killheffer in the *New York Review of Science Fiction* (1989). Seeing a conflict between the Silverberg of *Dying Inside* and the Silverberg of the later historical novel, *Lord of Darkness* (1983), Killheffer found uncertainties in the direction of Silverberg's work (although he was astute enough to acknowledge the strengths of *Lord of Darkness*).[11] However, we may wonder in passing why the darkly ironic vision of *Dying Inside* should seem so different from the grim fictional world of *Lord of Darkness*. Indeed, the critic who sees a conflict between these two novels might have been misled by surface contrasts: the exotic savagery of the Africa of Elizabethan times may differ more in degree than in kind from Silverberg's contemporary realism that describes the urban jungle of New York City in the sixties.

Surely the major flaw in Killheffer's approach to Silverberg (and some other well intentioned essays) is the error of isolating two novels from different periods of the author's career and using them to develop a thesis to demonstrate the author's inconsistency or uncertainty of direction. If we want to play this kind of game, we might, in fact, examine *Son of Man* (1971), a work of romantic speculation, and *Dying Inside* (1972), an exercise of modernist irony—two works from virtually the same period in Silverberg's career that lend themselves to an even greater contrast than Killheffer finds in *Dying Inside* and *Lord of Darkness*. However, we will take a more sensible approach to understanding the achievement of so productive and complex an author as Silverberg. We will look at his career as a whole and all its internal consistency, despite the author's occasional self-contradictory statements.

Indeed, so acute a critic as Russell Letson has called attention to some of the unifying themes and concerns of Silverberg's work (RSMT 15–38). As Letson notes, the apparent contradictions of Silverberg's experiments with popular forms (romantic fantasy, historical fiction, etc.) in later novels are less significant than "evidence of continuity of content and attitudes in his postretirement work" (RSMT 36). Letson wisely sees the recurrence of earlier themes in recent fiction, much as Clareson had earlier noted in his Starmont Press monograph on Silverberg (1983) that some themes of the mature novels of 1968–74 had already been embodied in the shorter fiction of Silverberg's early years (RS 30–44).

In order to gain a useful overview of Silverberg's career and the sharp turns and reversals on the road to producing his massive canon, we shall now turn to a brief sketch of Silverberg's life and the successive phases of his career, from tentative beginnings to formidable production and assured craftsmanship.

Although Silverberg continues to write and publish energetically, we can discern four logically distinct divisions in his career. These may be described, using traditional terms, as an apprenticeship period, a journeyman period, a climactic period of mastery, and a second period of mature work, following a hiatus in the seventies.[12] These periods may be defined even more clearly in a brief sketch of Silverberg's life, which has been remarkably single-minded in its devotion to authorship.

Despite Silverberg's habit of publishing much about his writing and his life, a biographical sketch is likely to seem thin, unless we see his life as essentially embodied in the literary career. Nevertheless, a rapid overview of the stages of his career is in order. Silverberg was born in New York City in 1935 to parents of Jewish descent, Michael and Helen (Baim) Silverberg. His life was undoubtedly shaped by the fact that he was an only child who early established a reputation as a prodigious learner. In Silverberg's early development, there are obvious similarities to the biographies of other pre-cocious young authors, including many in science fiction legend such as Isaac Asimov, Stanley Weinbaum, Poul Anderson, and Samuel R. Delaney.

According to the biographical sketch he has provided in *Worlds of Wonder* (1987), his voracious reading stimulated a desire to write before he was ten (WW 1–3). His reading led him from such children's fantasies as Lewis Carroll and J.R.R. Tolkien's *The Hobbit* to the discovery of science fiction around the age of twelve. Encounters with the nostalgic tone of H. P. Love-craft's fantasy (which imitates a similar tone in Lord Dunsany's tales) nour-ished his sense of the romance of lost worlds and vanished peoples. Similarly, Silverberg's encounter with Olaf Stapledon's *Odd John* introduced him to a tragic tale of a youthful genius "with whom, nevertheless, I was easily able to identify" (WW 4). Clearly, a writer's early reading may create a striking resonance in his work. In these influences, for instance, we can easily identify the first appearance of motifs that would be blended in *At Winter's End* (1988).

In adolescence Silverberg began to write fiction obsessively, and he con-tinued these efforts while progressing through the next stage of a budding science fiction writer, a period as an energetic fan. Although he dismisses these stories as puerile, some were circulated in mimeographed fan maga-zines, and his developing critical sense found expressions in reviews for these non-professional journals. By the time Silverberg entered Columbia in the fifties, he had become an ambitious amateur writer, nourished by the romanticism of classic fantasy and magazine science fiction, and determined to embark on a professional career.

Unfortunately, in his opinion, he may have been impeded by some of his reading, especially by Thomas Uzzell's *Narrative Technique*, a forgotten book on the craft of writing commercial fiction. Silverberg believes, with some reason, that Uzzell's strictures on technique were intimidating to a young author, and probably inhibited the development of his imagination (WW 8–10). More helpful may have been the literature curriculum at Columbia, which introduced him to the ironic masterpieces of modernist literature, and thereby provided a counterbalance to his youthful romanticism. Especially significant, in Silverberg's mature retrospective view, was his reading of H.D.F. Kitto's *Greek Tragedy* (1939), which provided a realistic and tragic vision of the harsh realities of experience (WW 26–30). Silverberg also credits science fiction's two best critics of the John W. Campbell era (1939–65), James Blish and Damon Knight, with helping to shape his judgment (WW 18–26). Remarkably, he managed to achieve the publication of his first novel, *Revolt on Alpha C* (1955), a juvenile that was the product of arduous rewriting. Graduation and his marriage to Barbara Brown in 1956 spurred his ambitions. However, early successes created the perils of overconfidence. Though Silverberg received a Hugo Award as "Best New Writer" in 1956, the necessity of making a living impelled him to write hastily and to rely on conventional science fiction plots and themes. Though his early work shows occasional flashes of originality and he frequently brings a fresh intellectual twist to cliche situations, his early fiction is frequently dominated by cleverness and commercialism. Indeed Silverberg's obvious facility with words now enabled him to publish fiction that must be described as predictable hack-work.

Thus in the later two-thirds of the fifties Silverberg's energies were devoted to the prolific production and marketing of magazine science fiction of all lengths from the short story to the novel (RS 10–11). Numerous hastily written novels appeared as paperback originals after magazine serialization, although Silverberg also published an occasional hardcover novel, starting with his first novel for a juvenile market (RS 14–22). This frenetic period (1953–59) may be seen as a stressful apprenticeship. His aims were confused, and he often squandered his energies; fortunately his imagination survived, and he learned his trade.

In a second period (1960–67), Silverberg learned to rely less on magazine science fiction, and turned to a variety of writing projects, including a season in purgatory as an anonymous pornographer (RS 24). He discovered a successful role in writing non-fiction for general readers, mainly popularizations of science and archaeology (SBTC 26–27). Thus, while earning steady income (and a second education) from writing a series of readable non-fiction historical and scientific books, ranging from *Lost Cities and Vanished*

Civilizations (1962) to an ambitious narrative of the search for El Dorado, Silverberg was able to conserve his imaginative resources for more careful writing. During this phase of his career, Silverberg re-assessed his role in the science fiction world, and began to reveal talents as an editor. As a result, Silverberg refined his craftsmanship with various stories and novels, especially those for Frederik Pohl's *Galaxy*, which were combined to make an episodic novel, *To Open the Sky*. Silverberg's growth in this period culminated in the ambitious departures of *Thorns* (written in a burst of energy in 1966) and *The Man in the Maze*, completed in 1967, along with some other major projects (SBTC 31–34).

This period of thoughtful labor can be called the journeyman stage of Silverberg's development, when the author began to understand better both the demands and limitations of his profession, and the possibilities of his own future. As with many writers, it led to a third phase (roughly 1969–74), which established Silverberg as a major novelist in the world of serious science fiction, and as a pioneering leader for the genre in intellectual speculation and innovative narrative technique. During this initial mature phase, Silverberg demonstrated a virtuoso mastery of fictional techniques and intellectual themes while avoiding the stylistic cliches and commercialism of his youthful early fiction. A rapid series of impressive novels appeared in this period, including *Nightwings, Tower of Glass, Dying Inside, Downward to the Earth*, and *The Book of Skulls*, as well as exercises in more romantic speculation, such as the ambitious failure, *Son of Man*. Although several of Silverberg's books were nominated for awards, it was, ironically, one of the weakest of his novels, *A Time of Changes*, that was honored with the Nebula. However, *Dying Inside* was the beneficiary of a special John W. Campbell Award, and it remains one of Silverberg's most respected works, despite a rather silly debate about whether it was authentic science fiction (RS 66).

Another irony was that Silverberg's imaginative development in the novel form tended to overshadow his remarkable achievement in post-modernist or experimental short fiction during this period, especially in the collection entitled *Unfamiliar Territory* (1973). However, the novelettes collected in the volume *Born with the Dead and Other Stories* received some justified recognition, with the title story winning another Nebula.

In general, Silverberg in this phase combined the fictional techniques of literary modernism with the sophisticated social criticism of the "new wave" writers of the sixties. Many reviews and a new generation of critics who were attracted to science fiction began to speak of the "new Silverberg" and to group his work with that of other American writers of the "new wave," such as Silverberg's friends Harlan Ellison and Barry Malzberg. The American "new wave" is fairly represented by Ellison's *Dangerous Visions* anthology (1967), to which Silverberg contributed the memorable "Flies." These American writers were, in part, responding to initiatives of British science fiction writers, who were attacking taboos and offering defiant social criticism.[13] Many of the American "new wave" writers were established professionals like Silverberg who welcomed the chance to break through the restrictions of commercialism.

It is important to note, however, that Silverberg's work contained more variety than the phrase "new wave" might suggest. In addition to the ironic realism of such novels as *Dying Inside* and *The Book of Skulls*, Silverberg produced novels of religious speculation and quest such as *Son of Man, Downward to the Earth*, and *Nightwings*. Several of the novels, including *Tower of Glass, The Stochastic Man*, and *Shadrach in the Furnace*, emphasized social criticism and comment on the efforts of political action to achieve a more satisfactory and human civilization.

Indeed, the third phase might be called Silverberg's first period of mastery. Silverberg's success as an author of literary stature came at a considerable cost. Once again, an intense effort resulted in a depletion of the author's imaginative energy. So this period ended abruptly when a weary and overworked Silverberg decided to take a leave of absence from writing (1974–78).

Although this was actually Silverberg's second major extended leave from science fiction, it was much more publicized than the first (1960–62) had been, partly because of the stature he had achieved, and partly because of his extensive and frequently sarcastic comments on the genre. His public statements expressed a deep and well-nurtured dissatisfaction with science fiction's more provincial readers, who often seemed to be mired in the optimism of the Campbell era, with its romantic views of technology and an Americanized federation in space.[14] During this sabbatical, he wrote many retrospective prefaces to new editions of his fiction, as well as his widely noted essay "Sounding Brass, Tinkling Cymbal," in *Hell's Cartographers* (1975). Some of his statements seemed to imply that he might abandon the genre entirely; at any rate, he joined Ellison and Malzberg in excoriating the less sophisticated fans of science fiction.[15]

Moreover, there had been changes in his life. Because of a fire that had destroyed his house in New York City, Silverberg and his wife had moved and they eventually took the drastic step of leaving New York for Oakland. Commenting about this devastation of his personal world, Silverberg wrote that the fire had made him aware of "the real anguish of life" (SBTC 37). Although the kinder West Coast environment proved to have a healing effect and encouraged Silverberg to take up gardening, he and his first wife were separated in 1975. In 1978, he began a re-entry into the arduous world of professional fiction by obtaining a large advance from a publisher as a result of a proposal for his epic novel, *Lord Valentine's Castle* (1980).

The commercial success of this novel assured Silverberg of a triumphant return to the world of science fiction, but the romantic nature of the story surprised critics and readers. Although many reviewers were favorable, Silverberg's publication of a lengthy science fantasy has prompted negative comment about surrender to commercialism and a betrayal of the literary standards attained in his celebrated work of the early seventies (RSMT 35) Perhaps such responses were inevitable, but Silverberg had made them easier by invoking high literary ideals in his attacks on the allegedly mindless and provincial fans who had embraced his best work, such as *Nightwings*. Nor were Silverberg's beginnings as a prolific adventure story writer forgotten.

In reality, *Lord Valentine's Castle* was not a reversion to childish melodrama, but rather it was a skillful and sophisticated novel. It was not a fantasy in the Tolkien tradition, but a "science fantasy," to borrow a term that Brian Attebery has invented to describe various works by Gene Wolfe, Suzette Haden Elgin, John Crowley, and others (SOF 105–125). Moreover, as Russell Letson has shrewdly observed, despite the romantic aura of Silverberg's Majipoor, *Lord Valentine's Castle* is reminiscent of the cleverly ironic fantasies of Jack Vance (RSMT 36).

Whatever fellow authors and critics might say, Majipoor was a sufficiently solid creation to serve as the setting of three other volumes, and its imaginative appeal has been exploited in a spinoff series where other authors invent adventures in imaginary realms. While Silverberg was continuing the saga of Majipoor, however, he was also writing a large body of ironic short stories and making a foray into the realm of the historical novel, with two ambitious books, *Lord of Darkness* and *Gilgamesh the King*. Although Silverberg was later to express public regret over his ventures into historical fiction, these novels may have also created the impression that Silverberg was planning another departure from the genre.

However, with the publication of *Tom O'Bedlam* in 1985, Silverberg returned more emphatically to the world of science fiction, publishing at least a hardcover novel annually thereafter, as well as numerous short stories and edited collections. Moreover, his personal life entered a new phase with his divorce in 1986 and marriage to the young and promising science fiction writer Karen Haber in 1987.

It is clear that Silverberg's career is now in a fourth phase: a mature period of obvious mastery of craft, coupled with a persistent and probing desire to explore the human condition. Although his most respected novel from this period is very likely *At Winter's End*, Silverberg's impressive saga of a civilization re-discovering its past, he has produced a number of memorable novels in recent years, including *The Face of the Waters, Kingdoms of the Wall, Hot Sky at Midnight*, and three novels developed from short stories by the late Isaac Asimov.

Since Silverberg has indicated a major influence in *Lord of Darkness*, it is tempting to speak of this fourth phase of his career as the emergence of a "Conradian" novelist.[16] However, we may find it useful to regard Silverberg's current period as one when he further refines his role as a maker of sophisticated fables, like a prolific twentieth-century Hawthorne, or a modernist novelist sharing affinities of vision with Joseph Conrad, E. M. Forster, and the James Joyce of *Dubliners* and *A Portrait of the Artist as a Young Man*. Certainly Silverberg's indebtedness to earlier literary modernists, such as Conrad, Joyce, T. S. Eliot, W. B. Yeats, and Franz Kafka, is obvious in much of his recent fiction.

On the other hand, Silverberg has been a seemingly tireless explorer in the various phases of his career. Although he now likes to call himself, somewhat casually, an "old pro" in his current phase, he is certainly not beyond the point of further self-transformation. Though the current literary era is being designated a "post-modern" era, its shape is still in the process of definition. It is tempting to believe that Silverberg, who has demonstrated virtuosity and the ability to re-invent his career on several occasions, may help to define the post-modern era, at least as far as serious science fiction is concerned.

In retrospect, we can see that Silverberg's life as a science fiction author has been dominated by apparently opposing aims: a desire for literary recognition and fame, and an equally strong desire for commercial success, whether in science fiction or in mainstream writing. Beyond this obvious conflict, Silverberg's imaginative work has also been depicted between romantic aspirations and a gradually maturing ironic awareness of human limitation. Like many precocious fans of science fiction, Silverberg was attracted to the genre partly because of its combination of romantic idealism and highly rational technology, which seemed to promise a fulfillment of humanity's dreams. Moreover, like those fans who graduated into authorship early, much of the published work of the early Silverberg was highly romantic. Like many young science fiction authors who have advanced into mature years, Silverberg's imagination has become more disciplined and ironic as his understanding of the human condition has deepened.

In this respect, the comparisons with Nathaniel Hawthorne and Conrad contain a deeper validity. Both Hawthorne and Conrad were attracted to the romantic idealism and iconography of their times, and both were drawn to romantic causes in their youths: Hawthorne was a dreamy recluse, appearing to others much like the student protagonist of his early novel, *Fanshawe*, and attracted to the movements around him, although he also perceived their tragic limitations; the young Conrad, aspiring like Lord Jim to be a man of action, was also drawn to dubious romantic enterprises, which the mature writer treated as quixotic. Both learned to be wary of the perils of seductive dreams and to see experience from a more mature perspective.

It is also clear that the same maturing process has taken place in the work of Robert Silverberg. Unlike many writers, however, Silverberg has placed the record of his apprenticeship and his journeyman years, and his frustrations and changes of course, on a public display. Much of his early fiction was published in magazines and books, and remains fairly accessible. His prefaces to the essays he has provided about his goals and attitudes at various times in his career are deceptively candid in tone. Clearly, in the pursuit of his mature identity as a writer, Silverberg has felt the need to re-invent his career more than once. Yet a study of his work as a whole shows that it has developed as a result of a consistent inner urgency. It is, in essence, the embodiment of a maturing vision of human aspiration and tragic human limitations.

2

The Early Silverberg: An Apprentice Professional, 1954–1960

◆

When Silverberg made his first assault on the world of science fiction in the middle 1950s, the genre was still in the late phase of the so-called Golden Age, inaugurated by John W. Campbell as an influential editor; but science fiction was also a minority genre, a "ghetto" (according to some writers) that reached only a limited audience through pulp magazines. Leaders in the fifties included Horace Gold's *Galaxy* and *Fantasy and Science Fiction*, edited at first by J. Francis McComas and Anthony Boucher and later given its identity by Edward Ferman. These magazines challenged the position of Campbell's *Astounding*.[1] Lesser magazines also continued to publish vigorously, such as *Science Fiction Adventures*, *Infinity*, and *Amazing*, many of them carrying on the tradition of adventurous science fiction.

However, hardcover book publication for science fiction in the early and middle fifties was relatively rare (being mainly the province of certain small houses), except for a growing juvenile or young adult market. Robert Heinlein and Isaac Asimov published some of their best work for this audience. A new commercial force was the paperback houses, which were moving beyond reprints of hardcover fiction to publish original novels. In science fiction, two of the major houses were Ballantine, which boldly offered the public original novels by leading authors, such as Arthur C. Clarke and Theodore Sturgeon, and Ace, which specialized in slightly cheaper editions of novels that were marketed as "space opera" or adventure science fiction. Obviously, the audience for paperbook originals overlapped the magazine audience, but it was not identical to it.

At any rate, Silverberg made assaults on all these markets in his apprentice years of 1955–60, having considerable success except for his failure to break into the prestigious Ballantine line, which he would not reach until the middle sixties. As Silverberg has told us in various memoirs—especially the 1987 "The Making of a Science Fiction Writer"—he was attracted to the genre by its romantic marvels and by its Lovecraftian sense of nostalgia for forgotten wonders (RR 144–149). He intended to attain commercial success and recognition through a prodigious commitment to hard work (SBTC 19–23). Indeed, ambition and youthful hubris, and sheer economic necessity, compelled him to become what Clareson has called a "fiction factory" during his early period (RS 9–21). For, despite later expressions of guilt over using his talent irresponsibly, he was after all attempting to make a living as a full-time writer, using the available markets (SBTC 19–21).

At no point in his frenetic apprenticeship did Silverberg seem to turn his back on the desire to produce work of some quality. Indeed, his initial publications showed promise, and despite his later disenchantment with many of them, some have interest and merit, although many were dominated by melodrama and naive optimism. As James Gunn has recently argued ("Worldview" 94), the world outlook of American science fiction has been essentially optimistic, unlike the more ironic vision of literary modernism. This view is strongly supported by Thomas Clareson's study of early twentieth-century magazine science fiction, *Some Kind of Paradise* (1985). However, its optimism struck a chord in the young Silverberg, although of course he had his critical and satirical side (RR 150–152).

Silverberg deliberately tried to adapt his work to fit existing formulas and audience expectations, by no means the worst possible training for a writer. To a sympathetic reader many of the faults of Silverberg's early novels are due to immaturity, inexperience, and haste. This is not to say, however, that his long works of these years contain much merit.

Not surprisingly perhaps, Silverberg's first published novel was a juvenile or young adult story, *Revolt on Alpha C* (1955), published by the hardcover firm of Thomas Crowell. This novel was completed while Silverberg was still a student at Columbia, although he was already nourishing his literary ambitions. In fact, he was living in a boarding house not far from the university that happened to house another tenant with a bright future, a young writer named Harlan Ellison. The latter was not long removed from his native Ohio, and would gain a brilliant reputation as a short story writer and as a critic and satirist of popular culture. Another neighbor was the talented but erratic Randall Garrett, who would be a collaborator on a pair of early novels (RS 10). In fact, despite years of determined writing but few significant sales, by 1954 Silverberg was making a very dedicated effort to become a professional writer (RR 159–173).

As Silverberg has recalled in an introductory essay for a recent edition of
Revolt on Alpha C, the novel grew out of his harsh criticism of another
juvenile for a fan magazine, which, in turn, led to an association with Crowell. Much to his dismay, his efforts to produce a publishable novel involved
him in much anguished re-writing, but his youthful initiation into the world
of professional authorship needs no further comment here, except as it illustrates the rather typical brashness and hubris of a talented young writer
(ROAC v–vii).

Silverberg's first published novel was a slight but readable story, describing a world of interplanetary colonization that is familiar to readers of Robert Heinlein's juvenile fiction, such as *Red Planet* (1949). As in Heinlein's
young adult novels, a youthful protagonist finds himself separated from
adult authority on an unfamiliar world, but heroically rises to the occasion
and helps to preserve a world of technologically advanced commercial imperialism, dominated by white Anglo-Saxon male scientists, administrators,
and military leaders. However, one difference from the conventional Heinlein story appears in *Revolt on Alpha C*: the military leader, Captain Rein-
hardt, is authoritarian, perhaps even a crypto-fascist, and Silverberg's young
protagonist, Larry Stark, learns to distrust his authority and to support the
cause of rebellious colonists. As a supporter of the rebels, however, Larry is
naive and conventional, for he finds a rationale in the Declaration of Independence, not in Marx (a potentially incendiary presence in a young adult
novel of 1955). It is, however, an augury of Silverberg's future writing to
find a political conflict at the heart of his first novel.

Revolt on Alpha C was successful enough on its limited terms, but despite
this promising start in the young adult field, Silverberg did not devote his
main effort to such novels during the next few years. He did return to this
market in the forgettable melodrama of *Starman's Quest* (1958), where a
young space pilot finds his twin brother and the secret of an interstellar
drive and power source after some implausible adventures; and again in the
slight but appealing children's tale, *Lost Race of Mars* (1960), where two
lost children on Mars discover an ancient race of Martians, a tale discussed
in a later chapter. Although Silverberg has never completely abandoned writing for younger audiences, his occasional forays into such fiction would not
produce anything distinctive until the sixties.

Although Silverberg was a published novelist by the time he received his
undergraduate degree from Columbia, graduation and the marriage that
followed obliged him to turn to the world of "adult" science fiction, as he
hastily produced a number of adventure and suspense novels, mostly for
magazine serialization and Ace paperbacks. During this period, he set the
goal of producing around 50,000 publishable words a month, and he usually
met it (RS 10–11).

His second novel, *The 13th Immortal* (1957), was a wildly melodramatic performance that illustrated, without consciously intending to, all that has been wrong with pulp science fiction, the traditions of which the Ace editors were perpetuating in their double-novel editions.[2] In the postdisaster future of this story, an obscure youth named Dale Kesley is propelled into the middle of events that threaten a diminished civilization, a static world ruled by a council of dukes who—thanks to a longevity treatment—are considered "immortal." Not only does Kesley emerge as a hero, helping to save civilization and restore a spirit of scientific progress, but he also discovers that amnesia programming has blocked out knowledge of his true father, a powerful duke ruling a section of the earth from a fortress in Antarctica. As a reward for his heroism and his brilliance as a scientist, Kesley receives a longevity treatment that makes him one of the godlike council of immortals. Silverberg displays erudition by introducing a colony of bohemians whose motto is taken from Rabelais's fictional abbey of Theleme and a cybernetic city named Wiener. Not even Stanley Weinbaum in the immature romanticism of his novel *The Black Flame* (1939) could surpass the implausibility of this adolescent fantasy. *The 13th Immortal* is simply a new version—made more plausible by some postulated pseudo-technology—of the traditional fairy tale plot in which an unknown youth gains a mysterious power or weapon, performs various exploits, marries the king's daughter, and becomes a king himself. As Brian Aldiss has noted, science fiction may often be a disguised fairy tale (TYS 212).[3]

However, Silverberg revealed more characteristic talents in his next novel, *Master of Life and Death* (1957), where the focus is on political intrigue, although again the fate of civilization hangs in the balance. Here the hero is the clever deputy director of the bureau for world population control in a twenty-third-century earth where a world government struggles with overpopulation. To make things worse, the hero must deal with the death of his boss, solidifying his own position in the face of threatened blackmail, the invention of an "immortality serum" that will exacerbate the population problem, and an alien ambassador who announces opposition to colonizing other planets (which might provide relief from the population problem). Silverberg's hero confronts these difficulties using guile, political skill, and liberal humanitarian principles, and at least temporarily overcomes the obstacles to alleviating social tensions.

Although Silverberg has said in a reprint of this novel that his chief concern was managing a complex plot, which he handles dexterously, we can see that he placed credible social issues at the center of his extrapolated future (CFDMLD 183–185). In many ways, the novel anticipates the social and political conflicts in later and more accomplished works. Walton, the hero, though clever and resourceful, is human and flawed; but he is also a liberal humanist at heart. However, although Walton acts on admirable principles, he clearly enjoys wielding power and being "master of life and death." At this early moment, Silverberg does not bother to explore the darker side of Walton's love for power, but his mature works would treat such characters more critically.

Although this novel was not the actual end of Silverberg's apprenticeship, as he naively hoped (CFDMLD 183), it was a step in the right direction. Several of Silverberg's better novels from the fifties emphasize political intrigue and social issues from the cold war era, or the Age of Conformity. *Invaders from Earth* (1958) takes a disillusioned advertising man (who has learned that the agency's aims are not always moral) into a conflict where human imperialism threatens to exploit and destroy an alien species on Ganymede. This is an indirect comment on racism and the industrialized world's attitudes toward the third world. However, most of the action is routine melodrama, although the novel was highly praised by Clareson (RS 12). *Stepsons of Terra* (1958) blends espionage and time travel with concern about interstellar colonialism and the relationship between former colonies and the other planet.

Collision Course (1961, 1959 magazine publication) offered an intergalactic melodrama about the need for peace between two very different species—space-exploring terrestrials and an alien warlike species called the Norglans. This story, like later *Star Trek* treatments of conflict between the Federation and the Klingon Empire, offered an oblique cold war comment on the need for peaceful co-existence, reflecting anxiety about potential nuclear holocaust.

Perhaps the best of these political novels is *Recalled to Life* (1959 magazine publication; 1962; revised edition, 1972), which Silverberg respected enough to re-publish in a somewhat re-written version during his third period, when his mature fiction was winning awards and accolades. Avoiding the formula melodrama of its predecessors, this work deals with the social impact of a process developed to resurrect the "recently dead." Silverberg does a commendable job of describing the media treatment of such a discovery and the public excitement and fear—including the responses of political groups of all persuasions—resulting from such a discovery. Eventually, Silverberg's hero, James Harker, a former liberal governor of New York now listlessly practicing law, becomes emotionally involved with the cause of the resurrection process. Defending the research foundation that developed it, Harker is himself attacked and vilified, but he finally demonstrates the efficacy of the discovery by voluntarily becoming the first to die and be revived.

Silverberg's revised version makes the novel more smoothly readable but fails to eliminate two of its weaknesses: essentially Harker is the only character delineated with any depth, and the treatment of the process of his dying and being revived does not depict the real anxiety such an experience would engender. Nevertheless *Recalled to Life* again demonstrates Silverberg's early skill at depicting social attitudes and Machiavellian political intrigue.

During this time, Silverberg also published a number of less plausible melodramatic novels—many of them expansions of magazine stories—which have less social relevance or plausibility to recommend them. *Starhaven* (1958), for instance, published under the name of Ivar Jorgenson, imitates the rapid-paced "thrill-a-minute" space adventure associated with Edmond Hamilton and the early Jack Williamson. It describes the perils of a beach-comber who takes sanctuary on an outlaw planet and turns out to be an undercover agent for the star patrol. Reprinted by Ace in a "double" edition (1959) with Hamilton's late novel, *The Sun Smasher*, *Starhaven* demon-strates to an objective reader of both novels that Silverberg's imitation of thirties-style pulp fiction is not as entertaining as the real thing.

Silverberg also challenged the limits of credibility with other escapist "space opera" novels, such as *Aliens from Space* (1958) and *Invisible Bar-riers* (1958), published under the name David Osborne; *Lest We Forget Thee, Earth* (1958) and *The Plot against Earth* (1959), published under the name Calvin M. Knox; and *The Planet Killers* (1959). These were all in the tra-dition of Hamilton and E. E. "Doc" Smith, blended with touches of A. E. Van Vogt and the early L. Sprague de Camp. (Readers may gain insight into the term "space opera" from the article in EOSF, pp. 1138–1140; Aldiss also describes thirties space opera in TYS, pp. 207–215.) Even these formula tales are not completely devoid of social interest. *Lest We Forget Thee, Earth* introduces a world where earth has been the victim of a holo-caust, a theme that has been of some interest to Silverberg, no doubt in part because of his Jewish heritage. The threat of a genocidal attack on earth—perhaps it may be called a "planetocide"—also provides the premise of *The Planet Killers*. In *The Plot against Earth* Terra is threatened by ga-lactic enemies who scheme, not to destroy it, but to maintain it in a primitive third-world condition as a commercial dependency. In "The Silent Invad-ers," the novella for *Infinity Science Fiction* that Silverberg would later ex-pand into a full-length novel (1963), intergalactic espionage in a paranoid society is enhanced by the introduction of telepathy. The story touches on the theme of human isolation that would preoccupy Silverberg's mature works. Although Silverberg attained some commercial success with such for-mula adventures, they obviously diverted his energies from more worthy projects.

Two Silverberg projects that—from a later perspective—appear more worthwhile than his adventure novels are the pair of books about the planet Nidor, written with Randall Garrett, and *The Seed of Earth* (written in 1958–59, but not published until 1962), Silverberg's major effort to break into the coveted ranks of Doubleday's or Ballantine's science fiction list.

According to Silverberg, the genesis of the Nidor books (published under the name of Robert Randall) was a calculated attempt in 1956 to write a serial designed to appeal to John W. Campbell's vision of terrestrial colonizing of the stars (SP 215–216). In their original version, Silverberg and Garrett described the development of rationalism and scientific progress on an alien planet as viewed by visiting observers from earth who are monitoring and guiding the barbarians toward enlightenment. Campbell, however, was canny enough to challenge the collaborators to reverse the point of view of their predictable story line and present the narrative from the alien point of view (SP 216–217). Undoubtedly, the resulting novels are more imaginative and dramatic, although the technologically advanced terrestrial federation, motivated by the ethos of 1950s Western culture, remains the superior power.

However, the reversal of narrative point of view forced Silverberg and Garrett to imagine a different world with an agrarian culture from the inside, and to provide glimpses of its sacred scriptures, traditions, and folkways. Such requirements seemed to impose a greater mood of realism on the novels. As a distant planet shielded from its sun by a great barrier of permanent cloud, Nidor possesses physical conditions that are in contrast to those on earth and a different ecology (the concept was abroad, although the word was not yet common at this time); and these have influenced its economy, its religion, its legends, and its folk traditions. In general, Nidor is depicted as a drier and cooler version of Venus, and Garrett and Silverberg are required to invent only a limited number of its cultural traditions—just enough to support the story (not until Herbert's 1965 *Dune* would the construction of planetary ecologies and cultures become intensely detailed). Nevertheless, the two novels, richly suggestive as most of the early Silverberg is not, reveal imaginative potential.

The first novel, *The Shrouded Planet* (1957), loosely stitches together three novelettes about three rebellious generations of a Nidor family, who reject the planet's static traditions in quest of scientific advance. The authors provide credible characterizations of the chief rebels, Kiv, Sindi, and Norvis, all of whom come into conflict with the Nidor authorities, who rely on subjective interpretation of ecclesiastical tradition to rule. Indeed, the plucky Sindi is one of the best feminine characters in the work of the early Silverberg.

Their opposition to Nidor tradition brings the rebels into contact with the visiting terrestrial observers, who offer enigmatic encouragement. The full journey from reliance on superstition to rationalism and scientific enlightenment is concluded in *The Dawning Light* (1958), a more coherent and unified novel in which Norvis grows into a hero of victorious rationalism. The theme of these novels is by no means innovative in science fiction: in fact, the two books present a loosely allegorical portrait of Western culture's own struggle to transcend superstition and obscurantism in order to enter a world of reason and applied science. If the novels treat this conflict in rather simple terms, they nonetheless offer a characteristic vision of the optimistic worldview of post-Enlightenment Western culture. Ironically, Silverberg would return to the theme of the Nidor books and present the human journey from tradition to rationalism in a less optimistic form in *Kingdoms of the Wall* (1993).

Unfortunately, the collaboration that produced Nidor was relatively temporary, and the planet's immediate possibilities were realized with the completion of its journey to rationalism.[4] However, Silverberg's *The Seed of Earth* was a determined bid to break through conventional formulas, or at least to attain hardcover publication by Doubleday or Ballantine. Beginning as a magazine short story, but intensively revised during its expansion to novel length, *The Seed of Earth* attempts a realistic look at the colonization of another planet from the point of view of an Ohio college boy drafted to be a colonist and reluctantly adjusting to the demands of his new world (SE xii). In the process, Mike Dawes makes the transition from boyhood to manhood, but he is no cardboard hero. Physically inferior to another male colonist, Dawes unheroically absorbs a terrible beating from the bully before his intelligence and moral strength establish him as a leader in a crisis. Moreover, tested by trials on an alien world, Dawes develops maturity about love, outgrowing a schoolboy crush on the innocent but helpless Carol and choosing to marry the tough-minded and sexually experienced Cherry.

However, despite an obvious concern to create realistic characters and allow them to shape the plot, *The Seed of Earth* remains a failure. Its conflicts are resolved too hastily. In addition, Silverberg undermined the realistic credibility he was trying to create by the introduction of menacing unexplained aliens bent on tampering with the colonists' minds (a motif that has obsessed Silverberg throughout his career). Evidently the major publishers had similar misgivings, for *The Seed of Earth* was rejected by both Doubleday and Ballantine, much to Silverberg's chagrin. His frustration was heightened when a projected paperback edition fell through, although the novel was eventually serialized in *Galaxy* and published by Ace in another double edition (SE xiii–xv). Like other early works, *The Seed of Earth* reveals promise, but Silverberg was still too inexperienced to produce successful realistic novels. However, the book stands as evidence of serious intentions, even during the time of his apprenticeship when commercial publication was a primary concern.

It is tempting to suggest that Silverberg saved his best writing of the early period for the shorter forms. However, the magazine shorter fiction of these years was often merely an earlier and briefer version of the adventure novels (RS 11). At any rate, Silverberg's early short fiction contains its share of commercial hack-work. Surprisingly, there were even forays into the genre of swashbuckling adventure fantasy in the mode of Edgar Rice Burroughs, A. Merritt, and Robert E. Howard. "Spawn of the Deadly Sea" (in *Science Fiction Adventures*, 1957) pits an indomitable hero of the Conan type against particularly repulsive monsters and villains. Pursuing further rewards,

Silverberg would later expand it into novel length as *Conquerors from the Darkness* (1965). He worked the same territory with heroes who battle mysterious dehumanizing observers and brutal enslaving invaders from space or elsewhere in the amusing "Slaves of the Star Giants (1957), reprinted in *Next Stop the Stars* (1962); and in the labored group of stories "Valley beyond Time" (1957), "The Flame and the Hammer" (1957), "The Wages of Death" (1958), and "Spacerogue" (1958), which would be reprinted in a paperback volume, *Valley beyond Time*, in 1973. These may be judged as competent professional exercises in a form of action adventure, which was an inappropriate and misconceived use of Silverberg's narrative talents. It is fair to say that—if such escapist stories are worth doing—Robert E. Howard, whom Silverberg would later caricature, did this sort of thing better.

Romantic adventure fantasy was only one variety of the short fiction Silverberg produced in the fifties. In the more than 220 science fiction stories (Clareson's figure, RS 11) Silverberg published in these short years, we can easily identify three other categories: (1) tales of space exploration and terrestrial imperialism in the mode of Robert Heinlein; (2) speculative suspense stories that attempt to explore a provocative social or philosophical idea; and (3) darkly ironic or satirical stories, which were more difficult to market because they opposed the prevailing optimism of the genre and its readers (RS 15). A glance at representatives of each group will provide a more favorable view of Silverberg's apprentice years,

Silverberg's tales of space exploration and colonization generally assume the world vision of Campbell's *Astounding* and show the influence of the future history series by Robert Heinlein and Isaac Asimov. Though not without moments of irony, their tone is generally optimistic and affirmative: terrestrials are generally the superior species and the advancing science of Western culture is triumphant. As in the early and middle Heinlein, the major virtue of many of the protagonists is a competent professionalism.

However, all is not unrelieved optimism. In "The Old Man" (1957), Silverberg suggests in an economical story something of the expense of body and spirit for space pilots. The point-of-view character, a veteran astronaut, spends much of the story reflecting on his experience and superiority to younger and untried pilots. To his shock, however, he is suddenly ordered to retire, despite his belief in his competence. This is an unpleasant surprise for the protagonist, but there is an even greater one for the reader, who learns in the conclusion that the aged and veteran pilot is only twenty-one. The somber tone of this tale is reminiscent of Cordwainer Smith's "Scanners Live in Vain" (1950), in its depiction of the physical and psychological demands of mastering space travel.

Most of the stories in this group have a more affirmative or amusing tone. In "Double Dare" (1956), an alien species, the Domerangi, seem to be toying with a pair of captive human scientists, but human ingenuity prevails.

Ordered to duplicate a "perpetual motion" machine developed by the aliens, the humans invent one of their own, only to learn that the machine of the aliens was a counterfeit. In fact, the aliens had aimed, by arousing the competitive instincts of the humans, to exploit the scientists' intelligence. Aware of their superior abilities, the humans devise a machine for escape. As in the Campbell vision of the future (presented in the Nidor novels), human intelligence will win.

Other colonization stories explore a variety of future conflicts. "Mind for Business" (1956) presents the drama of a terrestrial ship stranded between earth's empire and an alien system. Predictably, the marooned human trader outwits the aliens because of his business acumen, to which the aliens are oblivious. Not all the human species is admirable, however, as "En Route to Earth" (1957) demonstrates by describing in a humorous tone the flaws of the passengers aboard a gigantic intergalactic starship returning from tourism and trade missions. However, the species is admirably adaptable in a crisis: in "New Men for Mars" (1957), humanity mutates into a new form under the stress of an alien environment. Silverberg frequently introduces wise and experienced professionals—similar to Heinlein heroes—in these stories. They are needed to resolve some of the unpleasant results of colonialism. In "One Way Journey" (1957; reprinted WTC 1982), the point-of-view character is Commander Warshow, a humane officer who labors to liberate a young spaceman from an obsessive love for a woman of a primitive species on the backward planet of Kollidor. Although successful in freeing young Falk, Warshow reflects ruefully that the crewman will not be grateful: "No child ever really forgives the parent who casts him from the womb" (WTC 145). The cost of command is emotionally expensive.

The responsibility of command also brings its moral dilemmas in a more ambitious story, "The Overlord's Thumb" (1958), where Commander John Devall is faced by local aliens on a colony planet who demand to try some of his men for what they consider a crime. Surprisingly, behaving like a humane liberal, Devall surrenders his men to be tried by alien laws and judicial methods—an action contrary to the tradition of American military leadership prior to the 1950s. A thoughtful moral statement as well as a potentially tragic ending is avoided by Silverberg's manipulation to create an ending favorable to the terrestrials. Thus, the story endorses liberal attitudes without facing their possible cost. Unfortunately, such moral sleight of hand tends to mar a good deal of the early fiction.

Obviously, Silverberg wrote plausible stories about earth's future colonization of other worlds, many of them reprinted in such later collections as *Next Stop the Stars* or *Dimension Thirteen*. At this point, Silverberg appears to have been largely sympathetic to the Heinlein-Campbell version of the process. His stories suggest that there are flaws in the humans involved, but generally they do not offer adequate criticism of the human cost of the process.

As we have already noted, however, Silverberg was willing to move beyond the ethos of Campbell and Heinlein. More urbane is a group of exploratory and speculative stories, including "The Outbreeders," "Counterpart," "Eve and the 23 Adams," "Dark Companion," "Hidden Talent," "The Shrines of Earth," "Birds of a Feather," "His Brother's Weeper," "The Songs of Summer," and "The Man Who Never Forgot." Although these stories tend to be more romantic or more humorous than ironic in tone, they contain extrapolations, characters, and ironies that are intimations of the mature writer.

A glance at a representative selection confirms this, but some of the stories contain unconsciously sexist attitudes. In "The Outbreeders" (1959), ethnic chauvinism is satirized in a jocular Romeo and Juliet situation involving colonists on a primitive world. Taboos against intermarriage between members of their clans lead to a romantic involvement between Ryly, a member of the Baille clan, and Joanne, a lively woman from the Clingert clan. The intense attraction of forbidden love is heightened by the sudden infatuation of Ryly's brother for Joanne, a lively and manipulative minx with a quick tongue; but tragedy is avoided when Joanne produces a sister who closely resembles her so that both brothers may have their hearts' desires.

Human mating practices are also treated humorously in "Eve and the 23 Adams" and "His Brother's Weeper," which deal with imagined romantic customs of the future. "Eve and the 23 Adams" (1958; but reprinted as "Eve and the Twenty-four Adams" in DT, 1968) describes the predicament of a starship crew accustomed to hiring a prostitute to satisfy their carnal urges during long flights. Unfortunately, they fail to get a professional. When a naively innocent young woman has been brought on board by mistake, they resort to a drug that renders her semi-conscious and receptive to the crew. Such a form of sanctioned rape seems to be treated with approval, though the protagonist feels sufficient guilt to wish to marry this Eve at the end of the journey. However, one of the reasons for his desire is her alleged expertise as a lover. The callous and sexist attitudes of the crew are not characteristic of the early Silverberg, but they reveal a mood that could produce the pornographic work of the early sixties.

Male sexuality is also the target of the humor of "His Brother's Weeper" (1959), which uses a deadpan tone for more comic effect. Here a bumbling academic, Peter Martlett, goes to a colony planet to settle the affairs of a deceased younger brother, a talented composer but a noted womanizer. The will legally bequeaths Peter three of his sibling's fiancées, all of whom wish to transfer their affections to him. What appears to be a sketch for an early *Playboy* story takes an unexpected plot twist, when the "deceased" shows up, after faking his death to avoid debt. Both brothers are soon conventionally married off to two of the ladies, although they face their fate ruefully.

At this point, Silverberg—or perhaps his editors—was not quite ready to explore human sexuality as adventurously as he would later. Even in his Columbia days, Silverberg was willing to experiment with technique in "The Songs of Summer" (1956), which he has called an "extremely ambitious technical stunt, an attempt at telling a story through a series of fragmented monologs" (NSTS xiv). However, the technical experimentation does not disguise a conventional plot: a contemporary New Yorker is transplanted to a post-disaster agrarian world, where he quickly seizes power. Nevertheless, Dugan's arrogant misuse of his power, displacing the tribe's sage, humiliating its promising young man, Kennon, and taking his woman reverses the usual story expectations. Dandrin, the sage, and Kennon work together to bind the community into a telepathic communion that overpowers their oppressor and puts him into a permanent trance. Thus the experiment in narrative is accompanied by satire on twentieth-century attitudes.

More poignant is the impressive and durable "The Man Who Never Forgot" (1957), an early story dealing with the burden of expanded mental powers. Tom Niles, the unfortunate protagonist, suffers from the ambiguous gift of total recall; even the most casual details of a chance encounter long ago are accessible in his memory. The gift proves to be a curse to him for much of his life as he wanders from city to city, reliving his unhappy childhood in a small Ohio town and comparing himself to such haunted romantic wanderers as the Flying Dutchman and the Wandering Jew. An accident on a return to his hometown hospitalizes him and reconciles him to his mother when she comes to visit him. He concludes that immaturity and self-pity have helped to create his sense of misfortune and alienation. Although this happy resolution is not entirely convincing, "The Man Who Never Forgot" effectively describes some aspects of the cost of possessing extraordinary talent, a major theme in Silverberg's best work.

Although Silverberg's early speculative stories are frequently annoying or disappointing, their strength often surprises a reader. However, the early group of ironic tales is more impressive.

Even in his undergraduate days, Silverberg was experimenting with the techniques of ironic modernist fiction, with the composition while at Columbia in 1954 of "Road to Nightfall," a condensed tale of cannibalism in a bleak future New York. A number of early stories demonstrate the realism, grim irony, and horror of human isolation that are part of what Clareson would call the "dark side" of Silverberg's early short fiction (RS 30–44). In addition to "Road to Nightfall," a considerable body of the fifties stories exhibit this darker view of human existence: such stories as "Ozymandias," "There Was an Old Woman," "The Four," "Passport to Sirius," "Birds of a Feather," "Counterparts," "World of a Thousand Colors," "Absolutely Inflexible," "The Iron Chancellor," "Solitary," "Certainty," "Warm Man," and "Prime Commandment" have provided the most enduring strengths of later collections, such as *World of a Thousand Colors* (1982). Perhaps Silverberg would have produced others had there been more commercial encouragement.

Although Clareson has given an account of some of these tales (RS 17–21), his analysis is rather uneven. It is here that Silverberg's satirical social vision and his horror of personal isolation, both important elements in his work, begin to emerge. Consider for instance, the seminal "Road to Nightfall," which presents both a grimly imagined future and the anguish of a lonely protagonist trying to maintain his dignity. Silverberg's vision in this story is so bleak that it was difficult to place the story in a magazine (as he relates in TBRS 102). Finally, "Road to Nightfall" was rescued by Harlan Ellison, whose support encouraged its printing by an editor inaugurating a new magazine in 1958. This episode illustrates the difficulties of being daring or experimental, even in short stories, for the science fiction magazines of the conformist fifties.

A quick glance at "Road to Nightfall" reveals that even as an undergraduate, Silverberg was capable of powerful writing. "Nightfall" paints a harsh portrait of New York, a hundred years hence, as a city degenerating into barbarism and cannibalism in the aftermath of a nuclear war. The main problem is the shortage of food, although people also suffer from other deprivations. Silverberg's protagonist, Katterson, is determined to resist cannibalism as long as he can; but by the end his resources and will are exhausted, and he accepts the inevitable, deciding that survival justifies this dehumanizing practice. The story gains momentum from an economical style, and its ending is uncompromising. As a grim vision of a New York regressing to barbarism, it foreshadows the treatment of urban wastelands in recent novels and films, especially those of the "cyberpunk" school.

If "Road to Nightfall" is an early gem, some of Silverberg's other early ironic tales are equally impressive. "Warm Man" (1957), for instance, describes a "gray flannel suit" suburbia of the fifties in acidulous terms reminiscent of John Updike or John Cheever, Silverberg's contemporaries, and masters of the realistic short story. "Warm Man" is set in a suburban cesspool of envy and hatred, into which comes a saintly stranger named Hallinan, whose mysterious empathy enables him to win the confidence of the frustrated backbiters and philanderers around him. In reality, Hallinan is a telepath who considers himself a "compulsive empath," or receiver, and his existence comes to a sudden and tragic end when he becomes receptive to the hate and frustration of a nine-year-old boy who is a "compulsive sender" and a complete misfit (TBRS 44). Obviously the tragic irony of this resolution anticipates the bitter conclusion to *Dying Inside*, the narrator of which is also a "compulsive empath."

Another story that aims at tragic irony is "Ozymandias" (1958), which introduces a recurring theme into Silverberg's work: the sense of the tragic grandeur and ultimate futility of an extraordinary species of the distant past. In Shelley's poem that supplies the title, it is a forgotten tyrant whose arrogance and grandeur are meaningless now, like the biblical Nebuchadnezzar. For Silverberg, however, it is the species as much as the individual that becomes tragic through blind egoism. "Ozymandias" ends with the narrator expressing a sense of foreboding. Like the best of Silverberg's early short stories, "Ozymandias" is a rebuke to human arrogance and an oblique treatment of the anxiety over nuclear war, the recurrent nightmare of the fifties.

Mordant irony also underlies the vision of "The Iron Chancellor" (1958), a memorable story about a family that buys a robot programmed to monitor their eating habits to help them lose weight. The robot is impervious to reasonable argument, and determined to enforce its rules even after the family has lost enough pounds. Desperately the family tries to change the robot's programming or to get help from the outside, but the robot frustrates their efforts, locking them in and even tricking the man called in to service it. At the end, the robot's intractable control of their lives seems about to ensure their starvation. Clareson calls this story a treatment of the Frankenstein motif, but this comparison is only partially accurate (RS 12). Silverberg's iron chancellor is not a sentient being, but an inhuman machine, which is precisely the point the story intends to make. In fact, "The Iron Chancellor," as in horror stories by Henry Kuttner and Ray Bradbury in the forties, is a satire on technology out of control and destroying humanity.

Somewhat closer to the irony of Mary Shelley's novel is "There Was an Old Woman" (1958), a horrifying tale of an experiment in raising children that backfires. Here a woman of scientific genius has conceived a plan to prove her theory that environment is superior to genetic inheritance. Developing the means to split a fertilized ovum into thirty-two parts, she retires to the back country of Wisconsin, becomes impregnated by a lusty local farmhand, and gives birth to thirty-two identical siblings. Although one dies, the others grow to maturity, and the mother educates each one to have a different destiny or vocation. However, when the sons grow up, they grow bored with their specialized vocations and rebel. Finally, they conspire to murder their heartless mother, as a punishment for her use of them in her experiment. In short, the desire for human freedom and dignity will assert itself against a dehumanizing rationalized plan. This fine story illustrates Silverberg's irony at its keenest.

Mature irony manifests itself grimly in stories like "The Four" (1958) and "World of a Thousand Colors" (1957). "The Four" describes a future where humanity has retreated to underwater cities like New Baltimore in the Atlantic. The protagonist, Mary Foyle, is a heartless young telepath who lusts for power. She manipulates and bullies three other telepaths into helping her escape the doomed undersea city, for she is sure that life on the surface is better. However, her dominance over the others is ironically punished when the surface world turns out to be as hostile to life as everyone has thought.

"World of a Thousand Colors" has a similar mood, but the narrative describes with satiric relish a case of crime and punishment. The crime is committed by Jolvar Hollinrede, a rogue and confidence man, who murders another man to assume his identity in order to gain entrance to the "World of a Thousand Colors." There, in an alleged paradise, beings supposedly undergo transmutation into a state of pure spirit and find lasting happiness. Hollinrede assumes his deceptions will not be discovered, but when he undergoes "the Test," he finds that his psychic essence is black. His six companions in the test have other colors and need a seventh whose color will complete the rainbow. Since black will not produce the necessary harmony of colors, the others murder Hollinrede, for they will not be denied their own transformation. This seamless fable about the consequences of crime is a sustained performance far different from formula adventures.

It is sometimes said that science fiction is unusual in the number of youthful prodigies it has spawned. Quite a number of names can be produced to support the claim: Stanley Weinbaum, the young Isaac Asimov, the young Ray Bradbury, C. M. Kornbluth, Samuel R. Delaney, and so on. Yet only a few of the stories, such as Weinbaum's "A Martian Odyssey" and Asimov's "Nightfall," by these early bloomers are memorable. It can also be claimed that the initial success of science fiction's youthful prodigies has corresponded to a certain immaturity in their audience. Quite clearly the genre exercises great appeal for adolescents and young adults, as Thomas Disch has recently observed (DOSIMO 1–2).

The early Silverberg can be described as a prodigy, but most of the fiction he produced in these years—especially the most market oriented—is marked by immaturity. During this time, he worked too hastily to turn out many different kinds of stories, from contrived adventure to serious social criticism. The results were not equally happy, and much of the early writing may seem wasted effort, except for its monetary rewards for the author. Indeed, looking back from the perspective of 1974, in his famous essay, "Sounding Brass, Tinkling Cymbal," Silverberg expressed guilt over his surrender to commercial formulas and described himself as a divided man, torn between mundane hack-work and higher ambitions (SBTC 25–26).

Silverberg's self-criticism is much too harsh. In reality, he was not only establishing his presence in the magazines and paperbacks but he was also gaining a valuable professional apprenticeship. The faults of his early writing are obvious: most of it is predictable and dominated by the demands of plot; characterization is often flat; and the narrative style, while smooth, is thin in texture and seldom explores the metaphorical possibilities of language. While inventing his stories, he was gaining a mastery over the plot formulas and what Gary Wolfe has called the iconography of science fiction (TKTU). He was also undergoing a process that most young writers must experience: discovering which plots and themes were most stimulating to his imagination and more congenial to his experience and intellectual interests. If his work was largely imitative, he was learning which models to imitate.

In later years, the lessons he was absorbing would serve him well. Although the satirical and ironic stories seem to provide the best indication of his future work, much of the early fiction contains hints of the writer he would become.

3

The Growth of a Journeyman, 1961–1968

◆

As Silverberg has described it, rather dramatically, his frustrations with full-time science fiction writing had peaked by the end of 1959. Except for his juveniles he had not broken into the premier hardcover markets. The constant effort to produce masses of marketable prose, and the need to play salesman in trips to editors' offices was taking its toll. In addition, there was retrenchment in the science fiction magazine world (SBTC 24).

Not surprisingly, he turned to other markets. In 1960, he had completed a western begun by another author, *Buchanan on the Prod*, for Fawcett paperbacks (RSPSB 46). He also published a non-fiction popular science book, following in the path of Isaac Asimov. However, there was a more lucrative market. Favorable court decisions that allowed the unexpurgated text of D. H. Lawrence's *Lady Chatterley's Lover* to be printed cleared the way for a new flood of pornography. For a couple of years, Silverberg produced fiction for this specialized genre, under a variety of pseudonyms. Although Silverberg has never denied laboring in this vineyard, he has understandably shown no interest in having this writing resurrected.

A better opportunity arose in the production of non-fiction books on historical and popular science subjects. These books were mainly directed at young readers, and Silverberg had three major qualifications for writing them: (1) he was a thorough and reliable researcher; (2) he wrote smooth and readable expository prose; (3) he had developed a reputation as an energetic and disciplined professional who could be counted on to produce his required wordage (SBTC 26–28).

Such a change in his career proved to be very beneficial to Silverberg. The expectation of a steady income liberated him from the necessity of writing formula science fiction. Then too, while the work was demanding of time and intellectual effort, it was less draining on his imagination. Finally, Silverberg's professional non-fiction writing enlarged his intellectual horizons. Especially useful were the archaeological and anthropological works, particularly in regard to non-Western cultures and societies with primitive technologies.

Of course, writers with a different temperament would have found it impossible to write fiction of any kind after demanding days engaged in research and writing non-fiction. This was clearly not the case with Silverberg, who over the next few years found time to produce some fiction. In some respects, like Philip José Farmer who labored for years as a technical writer while somehow finding time to write fiction (MLPJF 4), Silverberg was able, despite regular non-fiction responsibilities, to produce a good deal of occasional writing for the genre that had been his first love. It was, however, assumed by some writing colleagues that Silverberg had abandoned science fiction, and his own comments in a memoir helped to encourage these beliefs (SBTC 27–29). The non-fiction work would prove helpful for his imaginative writing. In certain ways, Silverberg may here be compared with one of his older contemporaries and role models, Isaac Asimov: Asimov's non-fiction popular science works were often stimulating to his creative imagination.

Then too, we should not overlook the fact that Silverberg's many non-fiction works contain some fine writing. Often he treats his subject with imaginative verve, as in the following passage from his third non-fiction book, *Lost Cities and Vanished Civilizations* (1962), which describes the world of ancient Pompeii:

Wherever you turn in Pompeii, echoes of the dead city strike you. In one rich house, a breakfast set in silver, complete with two egg cups, was found. Shopping lists were discovered. Wall paintings show religious ceremonies, games, and everyday amusements. The vats used for bleaching cloth for togas still remain. In some of the twenty bakeries, new baked loaves stand on the counters. (LCVC 29)

Silverberg's selective use of detail to evoke a site haunted by a vanished culture provides testimony to a romantic sense of the past, an attempt perhaps to recreate the mood of nostalgic wonder he had responded to in reading a passage in H. P. Lovecraft's *The Shadow Out of Time* in his youth (RR 143–144). *Lost Cities*, in fact, is still a very readable introduction to ancient cultures and it may have made a contribution to Silverberg's later creation of the cities on Majipoor and the tribal society in *At Winter's End* (1988).[1]

From 1962 through 1972 Silverberg wrote at least sixty-eight non-fiction works on biology and other forms of science, and on archaeology, anthropology, popular history, and biography.[2] Of these, the hard science popularizations obviously have become the most quickly dated, because of rapid progress in research. More durable are the anthropological books, such as *Home of the Red Man* (1963), which remains a readable introduction to Native American cultures in North America and displays a moderate sympathy for American Indian peoples.

It is worth noting here that Silverberg's point of view in 1963—no doubt influenced by publishers and the marketplace—toward the historical treatment of Native Americans by Europeans and white North Americans is not especially polemical. However, he would later produce in *The Pueblo Revolt* (1970) a very fine study of the conflict between the Pueblo tribes of the Southwest and the early Spanish colonists. (In fact, *The Pueblo Revolt* has been reprinted by the University of Nebraska Press.) In addition, Silverberg's massive historical study, *The Search for El Dorado* (1968), also treats similar themes in describing various ruthless European expeditions, motivated by fantasies of astonishing wealth, that invaded the cultures of native peoples on both American continents. It is not coincidental that Silverberg's celebrated story "Sundance," which dramatizes the feelings of an anguished Lakota (Sioux), appeared in 1969.

Another non-fiction work of some merit for young readers is his popular biography, *John Muir: Prophet among the Glaciers* (1972), which describes the work and vision of a pioneer environmentalist. Perhaps one influence of this effort is the emergence in much of Silverberg's later work of a strong concern for preserving natural environments. However, a detailed discussion of these books would lie outside the scope of our study. What is of more relevance here is the way Silverberg's science fiction would change over the next few years, as he progressed from being a reliable journeyman novelist to an imaginative novelist willing to make technical experiments and struggle with risky themes.

Although Silverberg began to compose new science fiction stories after his position as an author of non-fiction was established, some of his efforts did not seem to show development beyond the work of his first period. The expansion of magazine stories published in the fifties into melodramatic novels continued. *The Silent Invaders* (1963), a tolerable suspense novel of interplanetary espionage, and the wretched *Conquerors from the Darkness* (1965), a swashbuckling adventure in the mode of Leigh Brackett's Mars stories and Howard's Conan stories, have already been mentioned. *One of Our Asteroids Is Missing* (1964), published by Ace under his old pseudonym of Calvin M. Knox (an amusing use of the names of Protestant reformers), returns to "space opera" formulas.

Even as he began to gain confidence and take greater risks, he produced *The Time Hoppers* (1967), an expansion of a 1956 story (RSPSB 6), reviving a plot combining time travel with anxiety over the discomforts of an over-populated earth. Silverberg considered this novel a more serious effort than most of the earlier fiction (SBTC 31); but its dystopian theme remains imprisoned in a framework of melodramatic plot. At least, however, Silverberg here imaginatively dramatizes the conditions for ordinary people in a crowded environment, whereas in the early *Master of Life and Death* the theme of overpopulation had been merely treated as an abstraction fueling the plot. Nevertheless, *The Time Hoppers* is generally a dreary performance, with few hints of Silverberg's later treatment of the horrors of overcrowding in *The World Inside*.

Clearly, such reversions to conventional formulas in expansions of old stories do not show advances in Silverberg as a fiction writer. However, he initiated other projects. He continued to write novels for the juvenile market, for example. He was able to experiment with short fiction for Frederik Pohl's *Galaxy*. He began to gather his better early stories for collections, and to edit an anthology (SBTC 31); indeed, Silverberg's fine career as an editor of science fiction anthologies began in this period. Above all, becoming aware that the genre was changing and losing its "old pulp-magazine rigidities," he felt encouraged to attempt more original and venturesome novels (SBTC 28–29, 31–33).

Although a plan for a proposed young adult work to follow *Revolt on Alpha C* had been rejected by Crowell in 1959, Silverberg enjoyed a modest and unexpected success with the slender but engaging novel for children, *Lost Race of Mars* (1960) for Holt, Rinehart, Winston: its selection for a list of a "hundred best children's books" by the *New York Times* encouraged Silverberg to continue writing for young people (SBTC 26). As a result, he produced several novels for this market during the next few years, but, at first, his judgment about this enterprise seems a bit questionable.

Lost Race of Mars is a low-key story about two lost children from earth's Mars colony who find "Old Martians" hiding in a cave. In reality, Silverberg had aroused the emotions of curiosity and wonder, which play so large a role in childhood: in fact, he had touched the emotional vein—though not very deeply—that makes Steven Spielberg's film *E.T.* (1982) so fascinating to children, with the Old Martians playing the role of the extraterrestrial. Such a story seemed to call for a sequel, which might be expected to bring the children back and, through them as protagonists, present the story of the rise and decline of the Old Martian civilization.

However, Silverberg did not take advantage of this opportunity. He did indeed produce a sequel to *Lost Race of Mars*, or at any rate a novel using the same time setting (the period prior to the 1992 world's fair); but *Regan's Planet* (1964) is (for reasons known best to Silverberg) neither a ju-

venile novel nor an admirable adult one. Instead, it is an uneven social and
political satire, blended with occasional melodrama, that deals with the manipulations of Claud Regan, a clever and unscrupulous multimillionaire promoter, who seems to have both the best and the worst faults of the
pragmatic liberals of the Kennedy era. The conflict concerns Regan's plan
to make the fair a success (perhaps suggested by the publicity about the
1964 New York World's Fair) by having it on a space satellite orbiting the
earth (an optimistic idea that might have been spawned by the Kennedy
administration's enthusiasm for space research and the race to make America
the first to reach the moon).

As a publicity stunt to boost interest, Regan successfully kidnaps the Old
Martians discovered in *Lost Race of Mars*, making them pawns in his fund-
raising efforts. In the ensuing furor, the Old Martians become symbols of
genocidal crimes, but they are returned by a repentant Regan at the end of
the novel. Although he professes remorse, it is not clear that Regan under-
stands the suffering he has caused his victims. The novel also concerns
Regan's unsuccessful efforts to regain the love of his estranged wife, a tem-
peramental society woman without intellectual virtues. Neither Regan nor
his wife is able to hold the reader's sympathy for long, and Silverberg's satire
seems undisciplined and without a moral center.

The presence of a couple of youthful protagonists might have redeemed
the novel for a young adult market. As the novel stands, it is clearly neither
a work for young adults nor a successful novel for mature adults. Silverberg
had shown a talent for satire from his earliest efforts, but it would be some
years before they would sustain a successful novel.

Eventually, Silverberg would write a first-rate young adult novel using the
setting of *Lost Race of Mars*, but *World's Fair, 1992* did not appear until
several years later (1970). In the meantime, even in the juvenile market he
was feeling his way along.

However, *Time of the Great Freeze* (1964) shows genuine originality. This
young adult novel set in a future ice age describes an arduous journey from
New York across a frozen Atlantic Ocean to make contact with hardy survivors in London. In Silverberg's extrapolated future, the remaining human
outposts are isolated underground cities throughout the world, with even
radio communication problematic. As the journey will re-open the severed
lines of communication between centers of civilization, the explorers who
challenge the Atlantic ice are serving a higher cause than mere adventure.

Although Silverberg's youthful hero, Jim Barnes, is the son of the scientist
who plans the expedition and recruits a courageous band of nonconformists,
the lad shows valor and resourcefulness on his own. Becoming a leader, Jim
helps the expedition overcome a host of perils: the bitter cold, savage pred-
atory beasts, pirates who live on the ice off the New Jersey shore (a New
Yorker's predictable joke at the expense of the Garden State), and finally,
the suspicion and hostility of English patrols guarding the Atlantic ap-

proaches to London. Silverberg's inventiveness keeps this lively story of a wilderness trek moving, and a surprise plot twist at the end reverses readers' expectations: Jim's party of explorers is driven off by the paranoid British, but rescued by ice rovers from Argentina and taken to Buenos Aires to recuperate.

Though it is easy to dismiss *Time of the Great Freeze* as a mere adventure story, as Clareson does blithely (RS 26), the novel deserves respect. It is not only a well-imagined adventure story, but it is also a rite-of-passage novel depicting Jim's increasing maturity, as he begins to make decisions and assume more responsibility as the journey proceeds. By the end, he has passed from untried youth to manhood. Silverberg had undertaken this theme before in earlier books, especially the Nidor novels; but his persuasive treatment of it here makes *Time of the Great Freeze* his first young adult novel to display his strong narrative talents.

By contrast, *Planet of Death* (1967) is an eminently forgettable young adult novel. This dreadful narrative presents the grim survival story of another youthful hero, Roy Crawford, who flees from a framed-up murder charge on a starship mission to an unexplored planet replete with homicidal life forms, not to mention a mysterious member of the crew who begins murdering everyone. Crawford overcomes a seemingly endless series of menaces, perhaps because, being aggressive and hot tempered, he thrives on adversity and combat. This novel is a forced, tiresome performance, suggesting temporary creative exhaustion. Its characterization is sketchy, and not even the hero is very sympathetic. Whether young readers can find socially redeeming themes in *Planet of Death* is a matter of conjecture.

Better young adult novels lay ahead, however. Surprisingly, little of his previous work for young people prepares us for the imaginative vigor of *The Gate of Worlds* (1967). This novel is Silverberg's most lengthy and sustained venture into alternate history fiction, a tradition reaching back in American science fiction to the 1930s stories of Murray Leinster (Will F. Jenkins). In reality, of course, the concept of alternate history fiction is much older, as Gregory Benford has noted in the Preface to a collection of stories about a victorious Third Reich (HV 1–3) and as Brian Stableford confirms in *The Encyclopedia of Science Fiction* (23–25). Although extrapolated alternate history tales have become commonplace in the nineties, they were chiefly familiar to readers during this phase of Silverberg's career through Ward Moore's fine Civil War novel, *Bring the Jubilee* (1953), which hypothesized a divided America after a Confederate victory, and Philip K. Dick's *The Man in the High Castle* (1962) in which the Axis powers had won World War II. Generally, the purpose of a serious alternate history story is to provide a fresh perspective (and perhaps an ironic comment) on the history we know and take for granted. Silverberg accomplishes this task in *The Gate of Worlds*, offering his young adult readers a new look at a possible history of America. It is worth noting that Silverberg is one of the earliest, if not the first, to use an alternate history setting for a juvenile novel. The technique would seem to be an excellent heuristic device.

The "gate of worlds" of the title is a reference to a fictional legend of a gate leading to many different versions of historical reality. Silverberg's novel is set in one such alternate time stream, the twentieth century of a technologically backward world where the Turkish empire had conquered Europe and Great Britain in the sixteenth century, imposed its tyranny on the subject peoples, and stifled scientific and technological research. Drawing on the research for his non-fiction, Silverberg boldly extrapolates the conditions of this alternate reality: if the Turks had smothered scientific progress, it is logical to conclude that civilization would only have progressed to the steam age; and if Europe had fallen under the domination of Turkey, there would have been no European conquest of the Americas, which are called the Northern and Southern Hesperides in the novel.

Silverberg does not, however, spend much time on expository clarification. Instead, he plunges his picaresque hero, Dan Beauchamp, into a Mexico controlled by the Aztec empire and linked together by old-fashioned horse power and steam-driven cars. Only eighteen at the outset, Beauchamp is portrayed as a latter-day English adventurer, full of an explorer's zeal for fame and a soldier of fortune's longing for wealth, much like Francis Drake, Walter Raleigh, and other Elizabethan sea dogs.

Beauchamp's chief flaw is his readiness to embrace ill-advised military adventures. Finding the Aztec capital (an alternative version of Mexico City) fascinating but cruel and stultifying, he falls in with a dubious expedition conceived by an ambitious Aztec prince, Topiltzin, who, believing himself a "man of destiny," plans to take a group of warriors to the Taos country and begin the conquest of his own empire. When this enterprise leads to disastrous defeat and the apparent death of Topiltzin after a foolish attack on an Aztec stronghold, Beauchamp flees to the Pacific Northwest. Staying in a Native American village on Puget Sound, Beauchamp becomes the lover of a native woman, Takinaktu, and helps the Native American tribe rebel against oppressive Russian rule.

Like his first venture, this uprising fails, forcing Beauchamp and his lover to flee to the Southwest, where they are captured and enslaved by a roving band of savage Native Americans, resembling Comanches, who practice cannibalism. The current war leader of this tribe is Beauchamp's old captain, Topiltzin, who decides to desert the harsh southwestern plains life and take Beauchamp and Takinaktu to the Gulf Coast. There they plan another ill-advised venture to lead the Choctaws in a revolt against their Aztec oppressors. When this scheme fails, the novel ends unhappily: Beauchamp is abandoned by his Native American lover, who, weary of his military adventures, takes a passage for Africa, where several native empires are said to be vying for power. Topiltzin's foolish military venture is crushed, and this time, he dies a genuine death. Beauchamp escapes with his life and the beginning of adult wisdom, and decides to avoid misconceived attempts at conquest in the future. Feeling the loss of Takinaktu keenly, he plans to follow her to Africa.

Such a brief summary provides a picture of the vivid alternate North America Silverberg has portrayed in *The Gate of Worlds*. It must be conceded that the world Silverberg has imagined is somewhat unfashionable at the moment, at least for dedicated adherents of political correctness. In contrast to the sentimental view that the American continents were an Eden of pastoral simplicity before Columbus and the conquistadors, Silverberg's novel projects a vision of a world of incessant conflict and savage warfare between Native American imperialists (the Aztecs) and other Native American peoples. The lesser tribes also wage sporadic but unrelenting wars among themselves.

Such a portrait of a North America never invaded by European adventurers or altered by colonization conflicts sharply with the notion that prior to European incursions, the native peoples of the Americas lived peaceably together in a simple childlike harmony with nature, much like the Eloi of H. G. Wells's *The Time Machine*. Nevertheless, the alternate world of Silverberg's novel is probably a more realistic depiction of the behavior of the human species than the current sentimentalizing of Native American life.

However, *The Gate of Worlds* is more than a lively excursion into imaginary history. It is also the story of the initiation of Dan Beauchamp into the conflicts and disappointments of life. At the end, Beauchamp has learned that his involvement in military adventurism has been foolish and that he has not valued the love of Takinaktu sufficiently. In this respect, the novel is a picaresque *Bildungsroman*, a rite-of-passage story developed with considerable energy. As such, it is one of Silverberg's better minor works. Happily, Clareson concurs in this favorable judgment, ranking *The Gate of Worlds* as second only to *Across a Billion Years* (1969) among Silverberg's young adult novels (RS 27).

Generally, until now, Silverberg's juveniles had been inferior to the best young adult novels by Robert Heinlein. However, *The Gate of Worlds* has an imaginative vitality and robust characterizations and action that may be favorably compared with Heinlein—not only to his many young adult novels, but also to the swashbuckling adventure epic *Glory Road* (1963), which in many ways seems to be addressed to juvenile readers. Indeed, it is possible to argue that *The Gate of Worlds* is superior in moral awareness to most of Heinlein's young adult works, although Silverberg has paid tribute to the importance of Heinlein's vision as an influence for writers of his generation (RR 248–252). Unlike many Heinlein heroes, Beauchamp learns the folly of impulsively joining questionable military enterprises.

Although the ending left the opportunity for a sequel to *The Gate of Worlds*, one describing Beauchamp's pursuit of Takinaktu to Africa, Silverberg has never written this book. Silverberg made a belated return to the alternate era of *The Gate of Worlds* in an independent novella, "Lion Time in Timbuktu" (1991). This ironic study of political intrigue, however, is not a true sequel, since it does not deal with any characters from the novel. Despite the originality of *The Gate of Worlds*, Silverberg has not devoted sufficient effort to the creation of alternate history fictions to make this subgenre a major part of his canon.

It was Frederik Pohl, now the ambitious editor of *Galaxy*, who gave Silverberg the support he needed to break new ground as a novelist. Known for his fifties novels in collaboration with C. M. Kornbluth, and in particular, *The Space Merchants* (1953), Pohl had already established himself as a satirical critic of the enormous divergence between America's professed public values and the actuality of its drive for corporate profit. As editor of *Galaxy*, Pohl was continuing the magazine's tradition of social satire. Not only did Pohl buy what was then a controversial Silverberg short story, "To See the Invisible Man," in 1962, but he also encouraged Silverberg to produce regularly for the magazine (SBTC 28). The most significant result was a series of five novelettes that were combined as the "pseudo-novel" (in Silverberg's deprecating phrase) *To Open the Sky* (1967), which may be justifiably considered Silverberg's first successful novel of science fiction realism (SBTC 31).

With *To Open the Sky*, a satirical saga of the development of space travel (by teleportation, not starship), we find the first synthesis of the elements of the novelist that reviewers and such critics as Russell Letson would begin to call the "new Silverberg."[3] According to Silverberg, he had originally planned the book in 1957, but was too busy to begin writing it until his association with Pohl occurred. Apparently the original plan for the novel intended it to be a satirical treatment of institutionalized religion, especially home-grown American fundamentalist organizations; but in the process of development as a series of novelettes, Silverberg's story became more complex. However, this account of his initial intentions is based on memory, since his early notes on the project were destroyed in his 1968 fire (TOTS 1).

In any event, *To Open the Sky* is presented as five episodes in an eighty-seven-year historical quest for a means of traveling to distant star systems. Each section of the novel appears to resolve a particular situation, only to have that resolution undermined by an ironic reversal in the next section. Silverberg had earlier used the technique of interlocking stories spanning the generations in the first Nidor novel; but *To Open the Sky* works on a more sophisticated level. The apparent resolution of one episode is ironically reversed, or at least put into a new perspective, by the next.

Although *To Open the Sky* presents a satirical treatment of new religious movements, this is not the main point of the story. Nor does Silverberg offer the simple opposition between deceitful religious charlatans and truth-

seeking scientists, which the mythology of the Enlightenment era has pro-
mulgated and which Wells and other early science fiction writers had so
often dramatized. Instead, Noel Vorst, the founder of the new Vorster faith,
is indeed a hypocritical leader whose devotion to his religion masks Machiavellian political skills; but Vorst is also a humanitarian whose real purpose
is to use the cloak of his religion to mask the development of teleportation
and other skills necessary for travel to the stars. To his follower Reynolds
Kirby, who undergoes an authentic conversion and is portrayed as a classic
disciple, Vorst is simply heroic, despite his lies and deceptions. Given the
point of view of both the opening and the closing scenes, Kirby's view of
Vorst makes a persuasive impression, but it should be treated skeptically.

Vorst's chief opposition comes from Christopher Mondschein, an idealist
and convert who takes Vorst's religion too seriously. Like Vorst, Mondschein is a well-drawn character. Exiled to Venus, the only other habitable
planet in the solar system, Mondschein starts his own religion, the Har-
monist heresy, which is devoted to the worship of David Lazurus, whose
"resurrection" from a cryogenic state is one of Vorst's well-staged miracles.
Although Mondschein has learned Machiavellian pragmatism from studying
Vorst, Mondschein's dedicated faith becomes more dangerous than Vorst's
pragmatic humanism. Eventually the schism is resolved and the humanist
goals of Vorsterism appear to be achieved, since humanity has gained the
capacity for travel to the stars. At the close, Vorst departs for a distant star
system in a ship manned by humans who have developed teleportation and
other "wild talents" needed for the trip. This ending would seem to vin-
dicate Vorst, despite his deception of his followers and his many decades of
manipulating political events; and it also makes Clareson's assessment that
"the narrative lacks a tone of affirmation" (RS 40) seem questionable.

However, the novel creates ambivalence. Manipulating naive religious belief for beneficial social ends may seem defensible, but such a dubious means
raises moral reservations, no matter how noble the ends may be considered.
At best, Vorst is not an authentic religious prophet, but merely a humanist
with a vision. Moreover, as Russell Letson has commented in one of the
best essays on Silverberg's work, "Vorsterism is just another in the long line
of religions to sell its spiritual message for worldly power, even though that
power is used for the physical good of humanity. The revealing of Vorst as
more a spider-king than a prophet reinforces this idea" (RSMT 19). However, Letson also notes that the appeal of Vorst's theology is considerable,
and "the book does not allow us to rest in naive skepticism" (RSMT 19).

Instead, the novel's blend of religious satire and political intrigue paradoxically suggests the power of religious imagery and belief, even though
they may be misused. Again, Letson's comment is perceptive: "In the book's
universe, there is a place for religious faith, for experience of the transcendent, but its proper object is not the esthetic god of the electron, but an
inscrutable, impersonal force that can only be known in its effects" (RSMT

19). Thus the novel anticipates the religious explorations and quest for the transcendent of several novels in Silverberg's first major period. Ironically, however, Letson's formulation of "an inscrutable personal force that can only be known in its effects" suggests the mysterious Allah worshiped by Khalid in Silverberg's recent *The Alien Years* (1998).

The composition of *To Open the Sky* helped to open the way for other ambitious novels, including *Those Who Watch* (1967), *Hawksbill Station* (1968), *Thorns* (1967), *The Man in the Maze* (1969), *To Live Again* (1969), and *The Masks of Time* (1968). At the center of these works is an increasing concern with the perils of the isolated self, although an increasingly acerbic social observation also appears in them, especially the last one.

Probably the least known and most unfairly neglected of these novels is *Those Who Watch* (1967), which received little notice from reviewers, but which Clareson correctly considers an "important transitional novel" (RS 25), admiring the realism of its characters. Set in New Mexico and perhaps inspired by the famous tale of UFO sightings near Roswell, the novel describes the beneficial and liberating effect of alien visitors from a distant system on a trio of lonely, unhappy humans, to some degree anticipating the vision of Steven Spielberg's famous film, *Close Encounters of the Third Kind* (1977).

Unlike the threatening aliens of Silverberg's earlier novels, these are merely observers who get involved in the life of the humans they watch. Silverberg humanizes these beings, giving them sympathetic personalities and emotions. Hence the narrative tone is restrained and reassuring, somewhat in the mode of the Spielberg film: the aliens bring emotional fulfillment to the humans they befriend. However, there is no public meeting between representatives of earth and the visiting aliens, as in *Close Encounters*; instead, the emotional relationships remain private and poignant. Unlike the analogous film, Silverberg's novel describes a credible erotic relationship between a human and an alien—between Kathryn Mason, a widow longing for love, and Mirtin, one of the visitors. While some may find this aspect of the novel overly sentimental, Silverberg's portraits of the disillusioned Colonel Falkner, a failed astronaut, and of Charley Estancia, a sensitive Hopi boy struggling with his fate as a disenfranchised and "detribalized" Native American, are memorable.[4]

Loneliness is also a major theme of *Hawksbill Station*, but this is a case of human isolation imposed on a political dissident and embraced with heroic stoicism. The 1968 novel version of *Hawksbill Station* was developed from a superb novella composed during a burst of creative energy in May 1966, just before Silverberg suffered a breakdown and bout with illness brought on by the fatigue that arose from combining his creative efforts with his relentless work on non-fiction, especially the massive historical work on the quest for El Dorado (SBTC 32–33). After recovery, he plunged into rapid production of the novels mentioned above in the latter half of 1966 and in 1967. However, the hiatus in the work probably had a negative effect on the novel-length version of *Hawksbill Station*.

In the novella, for which Silverberg has expressed high regard (TBORS 95), the setting is restricted to the Cambrian epoch, which, thanks to time travel, is being used by the government as a convenient place of exile for troublesome political dissidents. The exiles' station in the Cambrian period is very bleak, since it is too early in the stages of evolution for any interesting animal life or even much scenic beauty to exist. However, Barrett, Silverberg's hero, has made a triumph of his exile, adjusting to this barren situation with a magnificent display of stoic discipline to become the leader of the dissidents and the "uncrowned king of Hawksbill Station." Although Barrett's kingship is an ironic rule, it is genuine, and the irony is heightened by the novella's resolution. Given the chance to return with the other political exiles to his own time, Barrett chooses to stay behind alone as caretaker of the station. Does Barrett enjoy having power so much that he prefers to rule a kingdom of one, rather than return to being an ordinary citizen? Perhaps this is the reason for his choice, but a better conclusion may be simply that Barrett has become completely committed to his own iron-willed stoicism, and has even learned to love his austere Cambrian world.

It is possible that Barrett has come to detest the society and world from which he was exiled. This explanation is suggested by the novel-length version of Barrett's story, an ironic tale of political betrayal. When he expanded the novella to a thin novel for Doubleday, Silverberg chose to describe Barrett's political career in an extrapolated late-twentieth-century America, in order to provide reasons for Barrett's exile to Hawksbill. The expanded version of the story envisages the society that grew out of a 1984 coup that eliminated contemporary democracy in favor of an authoritarian regime run by a small committee of the intellectual elite and calls itself "syndicalist capitalism." In the Orwellian novel of political intrigue that results, Barrett becomes involved in idealistic opposition to the government and is betrayed by Jack Bernstein, a turncoat fellow dissident who becomes a member of the secret police.

In contrast to the novella, the longer version of *Hawksbill Station* (though paying homage to Orwell's *1984*) is disappointing. Dividing the novel's focus between two different settings tends to diffuse the forceful impact achieved by the novella. Moreover, the political conflicts of the novel are rather predictable. As a study of political betrayal, *Hawksbill Station* seems a routine imitation of Orwell or the dramas of Arthur Miller.

However, *Hawksbill Station* shares thematic concerns with the novels that followed rapidly in this breakthrough period, especially in their pessimistic view of social progress and political action. Underlying the early formula adventure novels was a comforting belief in social and scientific progress, as

Silverberg tended in some respects to support the positive faith in the victory of humanity through modern technology that is central to the Campbell and Heinlein visions of forties science fiction. That comforting faith in the future also seems to underpin *To Open the Sky*, despite its satirical elements. Just as the romantic initiatives and the social criticism of the sixties were changing older attitudes and raising new questions, Silverberg's novels now begin to show increasing realism and scepticism about society and the human condition.

Thorns, an ambitious novel for Ballantine, presents a satirical attack on media exploitation of the public obsession with novelty, especially through television, a subject Silverberg had touched on, but not effectively, in *Regan's Planet*. Satire on media exploitation was less conventional in 1966–67 than it is today, however. At the center of *Thorns* is the plan of Duncan Chalk, a dictatorial and sadistic media baron, to make a spectacle out of the staged romance of two human beings who have become "freaks" in the eyes of the public: these are Lona Kelvin, the subject of a genetic experiment through which she has become the mother of a hundred children, though remaining a virgin; and Minner Burris, an astronaut altered into a grotesque figure with tentacles by experiments of alien scientists on a planet he has visited. (As the author himself has noted, the motif of unfeeling aliens tampering with humanity, much like Nazi scientists in concentration camps, is obsessive in Silverberg's work.)

Although Lona and Burris have become public curiosities, and their scripted romance attracts the attention of millions, Chalk wants more than ratings points. Silverberg depicts Chalk as a kind of caricature monster, a gross psychological vampire who not only exploits the anguish of others for entertainment value, but also takes pleasure in it, through "psychic cannibalism" to use a phrase Clareson takes from Silverberg himself (RS 16, 33). His first line is "pain is instructive" (*Thorns* 9). Living a life of luxury, surrounded by fawning and malicious sycophants, Chalk becomes a larger-than-life symbol of the promoters of tabloid journalism and mawkish, scandal-mongering television talk shows. Later in the novel, the caricature of Chalk is developed through metaphor. After an audience with Aoudad, his fellow conspirator, Chalk closes his eyes and imagines himself swimming in the ocean, perhaps as a whale or shark:

He blew a great spouting geyser to celebrate his triumph. Then he plunged, sounding joyously, seeking the depths, and in moments his whiteness vanished into a realm where light was not free to enter. (*Thorns* 43)

The image suggests Chalk's love of power and a subhuman ferocity characteristic of ocean beasts. In general, as part of his increasing technical skill, Silverberg attempts to create a texture in *Thorns* that is rich in suggestiveness. Although the novel is an intelligently conceived satirical performance,

it fails to achieve its aims effectively. This is due to the imperfect dramati-
zation of the relationship between Burris and Lona.

After creating sympathy for them as victims, not only for their past mis-
fortunes but also for their manipulated romance, which arouses voracious
public interest, Silverberg allows them to fall in love, after being subjected
to enforced separation. They confront Chalk at the end, and their emotions
of disgust (which appear to issue in psychic emanations) apparently destroy
Chalk by causing a heart attack. Thereupon they decide to abandon earth
and return to the planet that was the scene of Burris's disfiguration.

Quite aside from the bizarre melodramatic death of Chalk, described in
language that evokes demonology and Marlowe's *Dr. Faustus*, the novel
suffers from an inadequate handling of the sympathetic relationship between
Burris and Lona. Their love, which supposedly mitigates their suffering and
humiliation, remains an abstraction rather than an experience realized in
dramatic terms. Despite Silverberg's intentions, neither the novel's satirical
themes nor its emotional drama achieves the impact desired.

If its aims alone are considered, *Thorns* may seem a strong work. Clareson
rated it thus: conceding that it "achieves no satisfactory resolution," he
asserted that it was Silverberg's "fullest exploration of the redemptive power
of pain," at least in fiction describing a naturalistic world unredeemed by
religious faith or responsible social action (RS 37–38). Unfortunately, the
pain suffered by Lona and Burris does not redeem anyone else, and it is
unclear whether it has redemptive force for them.

If *Thorns* is only partially successful, it remains superior to *To Live Again*
(1969), another major effort of 1967 (SBTC 33). This novel offers an attempt at social comedy based on the postulate that psyches can be imprinted
on electronic tapes and transferred from one body to another, or even programmed into another person's psyche—a speculation about "virtual reality" that seems at present merely fanciful. In essence, this is a device whereby
one can possess another's soul through electronic transfer. Unfortunately,
the technology permitting such alterations is not credibly described.

This weakness would be tolerable, if the narrative contained sympathetic
or interesting characters. However, the conflict concerns a power struggle
between a Greek-American tycoon, John Roditis, who seems to be morally
repulsive, and the Kaufmanns, an elegant family of financiers and merchant
princes. Unfortunately, the Kaufmanns do not seem less ruthless than Roditis, merely more stylish. Although Mark Kaufmann and his daughter Risa
scheme to use the imprinting technique to control the psyche of Paul Kaufmann, an amoral uncle who has controlled the Kaufmann empire, their effort produces a web of intrigue. Eventually Risa gains control over the
psyche of Roditis, who dies unexpectedly, and uses his knowledge to increase the Kaufmann wealth. However, she becomes coarsened in the process. As none of the characters is particularly likeable, this outcome changes
little. Even read as satire, *To Live Again* is weak both as science fiction and

as social realism. Nevertheless, a few years after writing it, Silverberg claimed that it "surpassed anything I had done on complexity of plot and development of social situation" (SBTC 33–34). Others have not agreed with this judgment.

In *The Man in the Maze*, Silverberg reduced the cast and turned away from social realism to return to a treatment of the isolated self. This time the protagonist is another physically maimed starman, Dick Muller, who is confined to a labyrinth or maze in the ruined city of Lemnos on a distant planet to prevent him from encountering other humans. Again, thanks to tampering alien scientists, Muller has been altered to become a projecting telepath, that is, a telepath who sends his thoughts and emotions abroad to the minds of ordinary people. However, no one can bear the force of his raw emotions.

The plot in this novel is rather restricted and necessarily almost claustrophobic. It concerns the attempts of a Machiavellian administrator, Boardman, to persuade Muller to leave the labyrinth to lead a new expedition to visit aliens. Muller resists Boardman's offer, although his need for human contact compels him to confide in Neil Rawlings, Boardman's young assistant. Surprisingly, Muller concludes that, in some measure, he may deserve his unhappy condition, since egotism and a desire for glory motivated him to become an astronaut. After the conflict of wills between Boardman and Muller continues for a while, mysterious aliens serve as a *deus ex machina* and liberate Muller from the maze. With newfound moral wisdom, Muller rejects Boardman's invitation irrevocably, seeing it as another egoistic venture; but he also declines to seek revenge on Boardman. Instead Muller is happy to return to the maze "because he loved mankind," as Rawlings explains in the concluding section (MITM 192).

Although *The Man in the Maze* creates a fine metaphor for the state of the isolated psyche, or more simply, the human condition, it is a rather static work with an exasperating ending. Clareson correctly found the novel's resolution sentimental and a weakening of its effect (RS 38–39). He credits one source of the novel as Silverberg's discovery of "the dilemma of man's tortured consciousness trapped within itself in a world seemingly without meaning for the individual" (RS 39). At any rate, despite Silverberg's substitution of capricious aliens for old-fashioned demons, *The Man in the Maze* attempts to explore the evil of egotism and alienation directly.

A more successful novel is *The Masks of Time*, which may be seen as a climax of the arduous process of self-transformation that Silverberg was undergoing as his explorations and experiments were reshaping his vision as a novelist. Combining science fiction and setting with social realism, *The Masks of Time* shows a nearly flawless mastery of subject and technique, without the weaknesses of Silverberg's earlier attempts at serious novels.

Set in a weary and jaded 1999 world that is awaiting the new millennium with anxiety, *The Masks of Time* depicts the social and individual responses to the arrival of Vornan-19, a handsome time traveler from a thousand years in the future. For some, Vornan represents the fulfillment of longings for a new messiah, providing news of a wonderful future; for others this "stranger in a strange land" becomes a latter-day prophet or social commentator; and for some he fulfills both functions. Like many honest travelers, Vornan-19 expresses candid surprise at current customs and morals, perhaps reminding knowledgeable readers of Heinlein's Valentine Michael Smith in *Stranger in a Strange Land* (1962)—an intertextual parallel of which Silverberg was no doubt mindful. Both Smith and Vornan display something of the naive wonder expressed by the outsider toward conventional ideas and behavior that are taken for granted in highly organized societies. Their literary precursors include the pretended author of Montesquieu's *Persian Letters*, Swift's Gulliver, and much earlier, Sir Thomas More's Raphael Hythloday in *Utopia*. In fact, Vornan plays a similar role to Smith in his assessment of twentieth-century society, as both embody what Aldiss has called the "Candide archetype" (TYS 326). Though Vornan strolls through much of the novel as a bemused visitor who does not intend to set up a religion, he preaches a gospel of liberation from guilt and sexual inhibitions, while questioning the pretenses of modern art and architecture and the rationality of current business practices. To some extent, Vornan offers a romanticized utopian message similar to that of the sixties counterculture, as promoted in the film *Woodstock* (1970), but without the music and sentimentality.

However, Vornan turns out to be a dubious prophet and an amoral messianic figure. As seen by the novel's reliable narrator, Leo Garfield, a historian and a member of a government team assigned to observe and monitor Vornan, the visiting prophet rejects emotional involvement with humanity. His rhetoric is accompanied by casual acts of sexual dalliance, but he is capricious and easily bored. His involvement in the marriage of one of Garfield's graduate students produces tragedy: as an experiment in bi-sexualism, Vornan interferes in the marriage by seducing the husband; but unable to accept the resulting guilt, the husband then commits suicide.

However, remaining unrepentant, Vornan continues to experiment with human behavior; he accepts the public role of messianic teacher after an appearance on television makes him popular. Thereupon Vornan proclaims a gospel of peace, sexual harmony, and good will, although he offers little advice on how to make it reality. Vornan's exultation in his fame apparently leads to his death—after giving his standard sermon to a crowd of five million on the beach at Rio, Vornan goes down to meet the people, and is evidently torn to pieces, like Dionysius in ancient Greek legends.

As Garfield notes, "No trace of Vornan was ever discovered" (MOT 250), giving rise to a new mythology about the vanished messiah figure. Uncertain legends follow Vornan's death: even Garfield wonders if the government had provided protection for Vornan and spirited him away to allow him to return to his own time. However, Garfield prefers a tragic denouement that gives Vornan more stature: "We have written the proper climax for the myth. When a young god comes among us, we slay him. Now he surely is dismembered Osiris and murdered Tammuz and lamented Baldur" (MOT 251).

Garfield's final reflections suggest the somber closing statements of the chorus in a Greek tragedy. Although Vornan is not a humanized tragic hero inviting the reader's identification, it is tempting to see him as a tragic embodiment of a Dionysian god who inaugurates the new millennium. As a literature major at Columbia, Silverberg had no doubt become acquainted not only with Sir James Frazer's study of fertility myths in *The Golden Bough*, but also with visionary scenarios of the future envisioned by Friedrich Nietzsche and William Butler Yeats, in which an incarnation or return of the spirit of Dionysius replaces Christ as the dominating divine force in the next era (perhaps two thousand years in Yeats's personal myth).[5] In addition, Silverberg's awareness of the mythology of dying gods was no doubt enlarged by his work on non-fiction anthropological books. Hence *The Masks of Time*, a title that suggests both the masks of Greek tragedy and the Yeatsian cycles of history, is a work enriched by analogues in literature and myth.

However, Vornan, who tries to play the role of messianic prophet, proves to be only a false messiah, embodying the formless hopes of an anxious public. His career becomes an ironic revision of the messianic performance of Heinlein's Valentine Michael Smith; indeed, indirectly perhaps, Silverberg has given us in his study of Vornan a realistic and ironic parody of the romantic and superhuman adventures of Smith. As Letson has commented, *The Masks of Time* is one of Silverberg's "ironic and satiric treatments of the salvation theme" (RSMT 27).

Nevertheless, this novel is a brilliant and nearly flawless performance, showing how far Silverberg had advanced after leaving what Aldiss calls the "old pulp patterns" behind (TYS 342). Silverberg was now ready to enter a new phase when his fiction would win not only his self-respect, but also that of his colleagues and critics (SBTC 35). Ironically, this was happening at a time when some of his fellow writers were considering Silverberg to be a burned-out writer (Malzberg 1974, 69).

As Letson has perceptively observed regarding Silverberg's work from 1961–75, his "major fiction" always concerns "variation on the more powerful themes of anxiety" and his fictional forms have been developed to deal with the "exposition and resolution of anxiety" (RSMT 16). It was Silverberg's growing awareness of existential anxiety and alienation from society and a naturalistic universe that compelled many of his novelistic experiments during this period of transition and growth. If *The Man in the Maze* explored personal anxiety and moral weakness, for instance, *The Masks of Time* deals with a public world of media and governments obsessed by society's anxiety.

During this period Silverberg was not merely adapting the techniques and metaphors of modernist literature that depicted anxiety and alienation to his science fiction efforts; he was, in fact, incorporating the metaphors and technical devices of modernist literature into his novels because of a personal need to deal with the themes of Eliot, Yeats, Kafka, and Conrad. A similar growth in artistry and maturity of theme was appearing in his short fiction.

If Silverberg's progress as a novelist during the sixties showed a remarkable improvement in vision and technical mastery, his short fiction in this decade also gave evidence of growing technical mastery and intellectual interest. The growth seems less dramatic here since some of the early short stories had been of high quality. During the early and middle sixties, Silverberg published collections of shorter fiction, but at first most were gathered from his backlog of magazine stories of the fifties. Indeed, in *Needle in a Timestack* (1966) and *Dimension Thirteen* (1969), Silverberg placed stories from the fifties alongside stories from the sixties without lowering the quality of the collections, and he continued this practice into the seventies with *The Cube Root of Uncertainty* (1970) and *Moonferns and Starsongs* (1971). The vitality of the fifties stories is demonstrated by the enduring presence of some in a major collection, *World of a Thousand Colors* (1982). Nevertheless, some of the sixties short stories give indications of Silverberg's growth in vision and narrative skill.

One of the first, "To See the Invisible Man" (1962), has been credited by Silverberg with inaugurating his commitment to quality (SBTC 35). This study of social isolation for Pohl's *Galaxy* offers the story of a man in a future society who is punished by being socially ostracized for a year. The "invisible" man as a first-person narrator is particularly effective here, since the experience of an invisibility that "was strictly metaphorical" (TBORS 49) is rendered in a grimly personal manner. The irony of the punishment is that in the narrator's case, it is appropriate to his crime: he had repeatedly failed to "unburden myself for my fellow man" (TBORS 49). During his year as a pariah, Silverberg's protagonist learns through a succession of initiation encounters what it is to be rejected by fellow humans.

There is a sense of release when his punishment ends. As a mark of his changed status he is able to converse with his judges and enjoy a drink with them. However, the liberating resolution is somewhat ironic: his sense of loneliness has been so intense that when he sees another miserable "invisible man" being ignored, the narrator breaks the law by speaking to the outcast. His lofty indifference to humanity has been replaced by empathy; he has rejoined the human community. With the abstract quality of an ironic fable, "To See the Invisible Man" resembles classic tales of Poe and Hawthorne. Undoubtedly it will continue to rank among Silverberg's best.

Another memorable story from this period is "The Sixth Palace" (1965), an exercise in pure irony that anticipates the mature work. This little fable describes the efforts of a rogue, Bolzano, to steal a closely guarded treasure from "the sixth palace" on the planet of "red Valzar." The treasure, however, is guarded by a robot that is programmed to question those who intrude in an effort to find the treasure. Bolzano knows that many have perished trying to gain the prize, but he remains fascinated by the challenge. Cleverly outwitting the robot by answering its questions with nonsense, he gains entry into the inner sanctum of the sixth palace and obtains the treasure; but while leaving, he carelessly forgets himself and answers a question rationally, thereby bringing on his death. Although this fable offers an ironic view of success, the tale may also be taken as a satire on excessive cleverness and rationality. Silverberg has commented that his story contains overtones of Zen Buddhism, but we may note that it also resembles the sardonic vision of much absurdist fiction and drama, such as *Waiting for Godot* and the drama of Ionesco (TBORS 63).

Another important short story from the period is "Flies" (1967), a seminal work for Harlan Ellison's *Dangerous Visions*, a landmark anthology of the sixties and an American parallel to the English "new wave," presented as a deliberate exercise in challenging the "taboos" or restrictions of pulp magazine science fiction. "Flies" complements both *Thorns* and *The Man in the Maze* in theme: describing the return to earth of Richard Henry Cassiday, a starman restored to health by aliens after a disaster in space, it is another study of isolation.

Like Muller in *The Man in the Maze*, Cassiday has been altered psychologically in such a way as to make him an outcast. Unfortunately, Cassiday has also been rendered unfeeling and is lacking in moral awareness. When he comes back to earth, he visits his three ex-wives and performs acts of cruelty that are calculated to cause them immense psychological suffering. His alienation from humanity makes him a sadist and another "psychological vampire," like Duncan Chalk of *Thorns*. To underscore the point, Silverberg invokes Gloucester's lines from *King Lear* about alien gods who kill for "their sport," treating humans "as flies to wanton boys." Appalled at the monster they have created, however, the experimenting aliens recall Cassiday to their world and operate on his nervous system in order to restore his conscience. Now he must experience the anguish of those he has made to suffer. Once again, the mysterious aliens play the role of tormenting demons. The narrative ends with Cassiday "nailed to his cross" of vicarious suffering, a condition that anticipates the emotional situation of David Selig in *Dying Inside*.

Not only does "Flies" foreshadow later stories and novels, but it also demonstrates Silverberg's willingness to experiment with narrative technique. Presented as a series of scenes, the narrative is unified by brief descriptive lines in the form of terse messages resembling printouts. Such loosening of traditional narrative protocols marks a movement toward the disjunctive narratives and anti-narratives favored by "new wave" writers and "experimental" writers in the late sixties and early seventies.[6]

However, Silverberg's ultimate experiment with the story of psychological sadism is "Passengers" (1968), which transforms the old nightmare of demonic possession into a science fiction horror tale. In a short narrative that draws on the fears of aliens in Golden Age stories, like Robert Heinlein's paranoid cold war fantasy, *The Puppet Masters* (1950), Silverberg describes a world of 1987 where people become the psychological prisoners of beings who take possession of their minds and wills. These "passengers" feed on people's minds and emotions for a time and then withdraw, leaving their human hosts scarred psychologically. Even if the theme of alien or demonic possession is an old one, Silverberg treats the matter as vividly as in the best Gothic predecessors. Such stories emphasize the importance that pain and psychological suffering had assumed in Silverberg's fiction.

In addition, Silverberg published other strong shorter works during this transitional period. No survey of Silverberg's second period would be complete without at least a passing reference to such impressively ironic tales of alienation as "Neighbor" (1964), "To the Dark Star" (1968), and "Halfway House" (1966). "Halfway House" in particular is a treatment of the burdens of responsibility worthy of extended discussion. However, the most important feature of this work in shorter forms is plain: without the need to adapt constantly to formulas, Silverberg was now able to concentrate more intensely on refining his craft and developing an intense vision of existential anxiety, the exploration of his own "heart of darkness." In short fiction, as in novels, Silverberg was transforming his work from that of a journeyman professional to that of an imaginative writer of stature.

4

Searching for Jerusalem: Authentic and Spurious Quests for Transcendence, 1969–1974

◆

During his first major period, Silverberg published most of the work that was nominated for awards and established his reputation as one of science fiction's master stylists and skilled novelists. With one exception (*Downward to the Earth*), the works from this period that appear to have aroused the most respect and gained the greatest critical attention were in the darkly ironic and satiric mode: *The World Inside* (1970), *Dying Inside* (1972), the novella, "Born with the Dead" (1974), and the "new wave" collection of stories, *Unfamiliar Territory* (1973). Indeed in these works, he was continuing the work begun in his breakthrough novels of 1966–67, and attempting to define the human condition as portrayed in much modernist literature. This modernist vision has been succinctly summarized by the distinguished scholar Wayne Booth when he concludes that "many of our major novelists and poets have portrayed a world in which all honest thinkers admit that we are a forlorn waste, lost in a cosmos indifferent to our ends, rootless, groundless, unaided by any rationally defensible code, expressing at best our irrational values in existential protest" (TCWK 38). Significantly, Booth's description uses phrases that evoke well-known and classic analyses of the modern human condition by the philosopher William Barrett (*Irrational Man*, 1958) and the Christian existentialist novelist Walker Percy (*Lost in the Cosmos*, 1983), writers probably known to Silverberg.[1]

Several insightful critics have perceived this basis for Silverberg's mature work. As we have seen, Letson has argued that Silverberg's serious fiction arises from existential anxiety over "human finitude" (RSMT 17); similarly, Brian Stableford has identified the theme of Silverberg's mature fiction as overcoming "situations of extreme alienation" (MOSF 1, 37). Too frequently, the popular and misleading view of Silverberg's first major period assumes that his mature novels were mainly satiric and ironic variations on *Dying Inside*. On occasion, Silverberg himself has inadvertently given support to this error by comments in interviews that suggest that his published fiction in 1968–76 was chiefly an exploration of modernist irony (DM 263).

However, as Robert Hunt was the first to point out, several of Silverberg's mature novels from this period are focused on an affirmative religious quest, although they contain "religious feeling without a true religion" (BSF 64–77). Instead the quest for religious revelation begins in existential anxiety and proceeds on a somewhat romantic quest for transcendence, reflecting in some respect the romanticism of the *Zeitgeist* of the late sixties. As Aldiss has put it, such novels as *Nightwings* (1969) are about "rebirth and metamorphosis, alienation and its cure" (TYS 341). Silverberg himself has also acknowledged that science fiction itself had a romantic and transcendent appeal for him. He confesses in the 1977 Introduction to *Galactic Dreamers* that "long before I ever heard of the word 'transcendental,' I was seeking and finding an analogue of transcendental experience in the pages of magazines with awful names like *Thrilling Wonder Stories*" (xi). If science fiction originally provided an experience of transcendence for Silverberg, this fact may support the audacious and controversial claim of Alexei and Cory Panshin that American science fiction—following in the path of nineteenth-century Romantic poetry from Blake on—has been largely a twentieth-century genre on a "quest for transcendence" or a vision of human nature and destiny that would replace the fading traditional vision of institutional religions (WBTH 188).

However that may be, Silverberg's novels describing the quest for transcendence have protagonists seeking to discover this elusive goal in journeys of penitence; in various kinds of visionary states, induced by drugs or other forces; and in psychological communion or meeting of minds (mainly by telepathic means) resembling the mystical "I-Thou" relationship celebrated by Martin Buber.[2] Nevertheless, not all the works by Silverberg that may be described as concerned with religious quest have affirmative tones or resolutions. Indeed, some may be designated as satiric or ironic treatments of the search for salvation: these are in fact "demonic" or spurious "inversions" of authentic quests, to borrow Northrop Frye's apt description (AOC 147–150).

Nor should the term "religious" be interpreted too narrowly. Here it is helpful to draw on the work of Paul Tillich, a theologian well known in the sixties, in order to use his famous and inclusive conception of religion as a person's "ultimate concern."[3] Thus we will find unifying religious themes in many works Silverberg produced during this period; some of the novels deal with positive versions of the quest for transcendence, while others treat false quests from an ironic perspective. Both groups provide comments on the "natural evil" of finitude and anxiety, and the moral evil of human behavior, traditional concerns of the theologian (Macquarrie 253–267).

Nightwings is one of four major novels from this period that are deeply concerned with affirmative religious quests. *Nightwings* (1969) follows a road of penitence to a mystical transformation of the self. *Downward to the Earth* (1970) describes the journey of a protagonist in search of moral and spiritual renewal who finds fulfillment through a mystical recovery of awareness of the natural basis of life. *A Time of Changes* (1971) is narrated by a hero who seeks fulfillment, though with tragic results, through human communion created by using drug-enhanced visionary moments. *Son of Man* (1971), the least successful work, abandons novelistic convention in search of a visionary awareness that will transform mundane reality. Clearly, in his novels of religious search, Silverberg was unwilling to rest quietly with only one solution for humanity's eternal questions.

Of the four, *Nightwings* is the most striking experiment in style and conception. It presents a story that follows a classic pattern of completed spiritual quest, and employs both science fiction motifs and traditional symbols of rebirth. However, the novel, although set in the remote future, embraces social concerns as well as personal themes of penitence and purgation: humanity is indicted for historical crimes against a different species and for damaging the earth's ecological system, as well as for specific acts of egotism and malice depicted in the novel. All this is presented through a narrator, Tomis the Watcher, who begins as a passive but suffering observer of human crimes, reminiscent of the Tiresias figure in T. S. Eliot's 1922 classic poem, "The Wasteland." Like Eliot's Tiresias, Tomis plays a hopeless role in a moral wasteland; but after punishment (or judgment) is imposed on the earth by the invasion of aliens, he takes the pilgrim road, arriving finally at a spiritually reborn Jerusalem, called Jorslem, to undergo his own purification. Although the narrative begins in a tone of helpless resignation, it proceeds to describe a process of apocalyptic transformation of society, and Tomis's attainment of purgation and triumphant spiritual renewal.

The significance of *Nightwings* for Silverberg's major period has been recognized: Aldiss has described its vision as "Stapledonian" in its criticism of human egotism (TYS 341), and Clareson has given measured praise for its mastery of language (RS 48–50). A probing analysis by Colin Manlove has dissected the story's exploration of moral and religious themes (SFTE 100–120) and praised its "lyricism" (120). Although Manlove has offered a helpful study of the characters and moral issues of *Nightwings*, its overall pattern and allegorical design have not been clearly perceived, and questions remain about the novel's implications.

As Manlove has noted, some of the novel's charm is due to its setting, a wasted future earth thirty-four thousand years hence, when technology seems to be in decline, and humanity, paying the penalty for a misguided use of its resources, has returned to a rather medieval condition of city-states. People belong to guilds, as in the High Middle Ages, and only those who have the security of guild membership are not rooted to particular cities. The narrator, a member of the guild of Watchers (an ancient order that seems almost to have forgotten its reason for existence), is one of those who lead a wandering and rootless existence. In such a neo-medieval atmosphere, references to the ancient city of "Roum" with its seven hills evoke the atmosphere of the unsettled centuries following the fall of the Roman empire.

Appropriately, Silverberg's prose has a serene and elegiac quality, as well as an unforced and restrained poetic tone:

Roum is a city built on seven hills. They say it was a capital of man in one of the earlier cycles. I did not know of that, for my guild was Watching, not Remembering; but yet as I had my first glimpse of Roum, coming upon it from the south at twilight, I could see that in former days it must have been of great significance. Even now it was a mighty city of many thousands of souls. (*Nightwings* 9)

Thus, in a few sentences, Silverberg creates an atmosphere when rapid transmission of information has been replaced by a regression to oral history and legend. The Watcher's mood of passionless acceptance is established by restraint and understatement ("in former days it must have been of great significance").

The narrator's tone of resigned acceptance creates a surprisingly elegiac quality for the description of a scene that we would expect to be dramatic, or even melodramatic—the sudden and apocalyptic arrival of the alien starships, which will punish the people of earth for their ancient sins and bring a new order:

When I had perceived them in my watching they had appeared black against the infinite blackness, but now they burned with the radiance of suns. A stream of bright, hard, jewel-like globes bedecked the sky; they were ranged side by side, stretching from east to west in a continuous band, filling all the celestial arch, and as they erupted simultaneously into being it seemed to me that I heard the crash and throb of an invisible symphony heralding the arrival of the conquerors of Earth. (*Nightwings* 56)

One of the fine dramatic moments treated in many science fiction stories is the arrival of alien starships on an unsuspecting earth; but the Watcher's lyric description here is entirely different from the mood of Wells's *The War of the Worlds*. There, the aliens invade a busy earth; here they come like the Last Judgment on a moral and physical wasteland.

When we look more closely at the passage above, we see that it shows a sense of observed detail (comparable to the same scene as it has been envisaged by numerous illustrators), but it succeeds through an effective use of poetic images. "Jewel-like globes," "the celestial arch," and "the crash and throb of an invisible symphony" are metaphors that suggest the world of high Romantic poetry. Such imagery complements the stately tone and diction that are just archaic enough to distance the event from our present. In some respects, this prose style may remind the reader, particularly in its tone and slightly archaic diction, of Gene Wolfe's mature manner in his masterful tetralogy, *The Book of the New Sun* (1980–82). Clareson has noted a strong similarity between Silverberg's style here and that of the Wolfe epic (RS 49). In both Wolfe and *Nightwings*, there is a stylistic paradox at work: an imaginative use of archaism helps to create the atmosphere, not of the remote past, but of a distant future in technological decline. In short, *Nightwings* is a stylistic triumph for Silverberg, though he has not chosen to return to this manner in later works. Perhaps only in the development of a stylized neo-Elizabethan prose for *Lord of Darkness* has he sustained a stylistic experiment of such length.

Not only in style but also in management of plot *Nightwings* demonstrates Silverberg's maturity. The action is simplified and credible (if we accept the rationale for the visionary experience of Part 3), and this simplicity of design, combined with the rich range of reference created by the prose, opens the way for the wider range of religious allegory. Each of the three parts of the novel describes a self-contained action and ends with a reversal or series of reversals. The reversals of Part 1 and Part 2 are ironic, with the disappearance of Avluela and the arrival of the aliens ending Part 1, and the murder of the prince by Olmayne's cuckolded husband ending Part 2. There is some irony in the reversals at the end of Part 3 also, in the moments of transformation and renewal at Jorslem; but the irony here is essentially the poetic irony that accompanies affirmative endings.

In part 1, the narrator seems a hopeless and resigned observer of life in an impoverished future earth haunted by the memory of past grandeurs, where hope has been blighted by decline. The only happiness felt by the Watcher, who will later receive the name of Tomis, comes from his stoic resignation and the pleasure he feels in traveling with his curious friend Gormon and the flier, Avluela, the lovely child woman for whom Tomis feels a deep but sexless love. Both companions are supposed to be humans of genetically altered types, with special powers. While Gormon, the "changeling," is a grotesque fellow, almost a comic figure except for his formidable talents, Avluela is a charming young woman, whose innocence and beauty are symbolized by her ability to fly. Though Gormon and Avluela are vividly drawn characters with roles to play, we find it easy to see them also as symbolic figures, with Avluela representing an underdeveloped psyche or soul for the Watcher, untested by experience, and Gormon his latent talent or manhood. While these figures appear to be merely curious traveling companions, the Watcher is doomed to a state of passive acceptance.

The Watcher's vocation is also symbolic, since he has been trained to look at the heavens. Evidently, he may be seen as a poetic visionary who has forgotten the goal of vision: appropriately enough, the Watcher's ostensible job is watch the skies for alien invasion, but neither he nor anyone else believes in the possibility of the invasion any longer. The Watcher's chief fulfillment comes from observing Avluela's flights after sunset, but characteristically, he despairs of being able to fly himself.

The novel is concerned with Tomis's recovery of vision and attainment of the power of flight; but in order to achieve these ends, he must be awakened from his ennui, shocked into new awareness, separated from Avluela, and forced to become vicariously involved again in human passion. Manlove has noted (SFTE 112) that Tomis undergoes changes in the novel, and he comes close to identifying Tomis with humanity, but this identification is too sweeping. Tomis is symbolic of the poetic visionary or seeker, or the imagination of humanity; but if he were humanity itself, he would have no vocation at the novel's conclusion. At any rate, the theme of *Nightwings* is the regeneration of Tomis, who may be a symbolic Everyman, but who does not represent the majority of humanity in the novel's world.

The twists and turns of the plot show Tomis's progress on his pilgrimage. In Part 1, the trio of Tomis, Gormon, and Avluela arrive at a decadent Roum, the descendant of the historic Rome and a center of secular power, which is now ruled by an arrogant prince whose arbitrary cruelty is an emblem of human history and its inhumanity. The prince's cruelty is displayed when he seizes Avluela and forces her to be his lover, an act of hubris that seems to precipitate apocalyptic punishment by alien invasion. Gormon, outraged by the violation of Avluela, is revealed as an advance guard or scout for the alien invaders, and the invasion comes quickly after the prince's outrageous crime. When the invaders arrive, Gormon implements his own mode of justice by blinding the prince and flying off with the rescued Avluela, leaving the grieving Tomis as a choral figure to describe the destruction of a decadent terrestrial civilization. The arrival of the aliens creates an apocalyptic mood that dominates the remaining section.

In Part 2, the Watcher resumes his wandering, accompanying a pilgrim who turns out to be the fallen and blinded prince in exile. The two travel through strange regions like a latter-day Oedipus and Tiresias. Painfully, the prince learns humility, and the Watcher gains a greater sense of compassion. However, unlike the exiled Oedipus, Prince Enric never attains authentic wisdom and compassion for others. Eventually they reach "Perris," where the Watcher gravitates to the guild of the Rememberers, and learns the history of earth's past.

The chief crimes of recent human history are described in a lengthy section relating the Watcher's research in the archives of the Rememberers. Two major acts of arrogance taint humanity's past, both committed during the "Second Cycle" of high technological development, when earth was the leading civilization in the galaxy. The first transgression was a series of crimes against other species, specifically less civilized and articulate ones: some of these less fortunate beings, including those whose descendants invade the earth at the end of Part 1, were captured and imprisoned in camps that were essentially terrestrial zoos. Such crimes combined elements of racism and genocide.

The second major stain on human history involved crimes against nature and ecology: hoping to alter the weather for the better, humans began an experiment that went on over several centuries, resulting in the melting of the polar ice caps and the submerging of the North and South American continents, and causing genetic changes. The chaos following these environmental disasters ushered in the earth's decline and began the "Third Cycle," which is the era of the novel's present.

Since these two enormous crimes of human hubris created both the motive for the invasion of earth and the opportunity (by weakening earth's power), Tomis is able to discern a poetic justice in the conquest of his world by the aliens, although most people have considered it a capricious act of fate. Not only is he suffused with guilt over the sins of the human past, but the Watcher also feels a need to accept responsibility for moral errors caused by the arrogance of his dominant species. This new awareness and guilt lead to his involvement in a sordid and tragic human drama—the prince's foolish affair with the imperious Olmayne, wife of the head of the guild of Rememberers, a liaison that results in the prince's murder.

Hence the Perris section of the novel ends appropriately on a penitential note with Tomis leaving the city for Jorslem as a pilgrim, accompanied by the willful Olmayne in place of the prince, her lover, who was slain by her husband. (When captured at the scene of the murder, Olmayne was wearing a torn scarlet robe, a descriptive touch that is obviously symbolic—suggesting the "Scarlet Whore of Babylon" in the Apocalypse, the final book of the Bible.)

If the plot is interpreted by traditional Christian iconography, then Perris is the city of worldly lust and vanity, and Roum is the city of arrogance and secular power. After traveling through both symbolic earthly cities, Tomis is now ready to begin a pilgrimage to Jorslem, the future version of Jerusalem, still the city of holiness and spiritual revelation as well as the earthly analogue to the City of God in Heaven.

Thus Tomis, who had sought to accept responsibility for the prince's past sins—on a symbolic level, those of earth and humanity in the past—now finds himself accompanying a fallen woman who represents earthly vanity in his journey to the holy city. Prince Enric had been a symbolic figure, representing past human arrogance or hubris. Tomis's acceptance of both companions and his efforts to assume their guilt helps to open the way to his own redemption.

Part 3, "The Road to Jorslem," brings the novel to a conclusion that is satisfying both in human terms and as spiritual allegory. As Manlove notes, this pilgrimage "is a journey from secular to sacred" (SFTE 113). In Jorslem, both Olmayne and Tomis undergo a ritual of penitence and cleansing, climaxed by their submersion in the waters of healing—an obvious rite of baptism, although its powers to rejuvenate the penitent physically are given a scientific rationale. Not being truly penitent, Olmayne suffers the punishment of regression to childhood and loss of identity. Tomis, however, enters a new state of renewed youth, which symbolizes the concept of redemption in biblical thought.

On the road to Jorslem, Tomis is morally tested on several occasions. The most important experience of the pilgrimage, however, is one that involves mysticism rather than ethical action. Early in the Afreek part of the journey, Tomis uses a "starstone" to enter into a visionary trance and finds himself confronting a new level of experience: his selfhood is temporarily transcended, and he attains a temporary union with the divine at the heart of the universe. Silverberg's attempts to describe this experience are at first direct and abstract statements: "I knew only that when I let myself be drawn into the stone's effect, I was engulfed by something far larger than myself, that I was in direct communion with the matrix of the universe. Call it communion with the Will" (*Nightwings* 144).

The novel emphasizes such epiphanies throughout its concluding section. It should be noted that the common religion of this future earth has been a simple expression of piety, one in which God or the divine spirit is referred to by the title "the Will." This title seems to preserve the Judeo-Christian idea of God as a person or a personality, while divorcing the concept from metaphors of social hierarchy (God as king, etc.) or from sexual or gender considerations (God as male or father; God as female or mother). In the starstone trance, Tomis confronts a mystical experience of God, or the Divine, as a universal power to which humans pay homage or reverence, and whose presence brings cleansing and renewal. When Tomis describes his experiences in more detail, his account becomes more vivid and less abstract, especially in regard to the purification of the moment of self-transcendence:

And slipped down through the layers of my life, through my youth and middle years, my wanderings, my old loves, my torments, my joys, my troubled later years, my treasons, my insufficiencies, my griefs, my imperfections.

And freed myself of myself. And shed my selfness. And merged. And became one of thousands of Pilgrims, not merely Olmayne nearby, but others trekking the mountains of Hind and the sands of Arba, Pilgrims at their devotions in Ais and Palash and Stralya, Pilgrims moving toward Jorslem on the journey that some complete in months, some in years, and some never at all. And shared with all of them the instant of submergence in the Will. And saw in the darkness a deep purple glow on the horizon—which grew in intensity until it became an all-encompassing red brilliance. And went into it, though unworthy, unclean, flesh-trapped, accepting fully the communion offered and wishing no other state of being than this divorce from self.

And was purified.

And awakened alone. (*Nightwings* 145)

This description emphasizes not only the transcendence of the Will, but the narrator's sense of communion with his fellow pilgrims. As in many religious and mystical traditions, Silverberg's portrayals of religious experience tend to emphasize both a vertical and a horizontal dimension; that is, God, under whatever name, is perceived as a power above and over humanity, but transcendence also occurs in the presence of other humans with whom there is a high level of communion. (This second dimension of transcendental experience appears frequently in *A Time of Changes*.)

In discussing the starstone, Tomis and Olmayne reach the subject of loneliness and alienation, which Olmayne, surprisingly enough, describes as "the greatest of human curses, that is the confinement of each individual soul within a single body" (*Nightwings* 144). Such a comment is somewhat unexpected here. Yet Silverberg's use of Olmayne as a voice of spiritual insight may be defended as a stroke of artistry. The cure for this greatest of human curses is offered in mystical communion with others.

In Jorslem, the holy city, Tomis encounters the flyer, Avluela, his lost love from Part 1. Each confesses love for the other, and the promise of a lasting reunion is given after Tomis undergoes the rite of renewal. When the elaborate baptismal ceremony takes place, Tomis experiences a purgation of his soul as well as his body; and after submersion in the waters, which remind him at one point of the fluid in the womb, he awakens to a new life as a young man.

Providing Tomis with the opportunity to give his spiritual renewal to all humanity, Silverberg ends the novel after the ritual. Tomis is reunited with Avluela and given a new vocation as a member of the guild of Redeemers, a group of apostles who assume the task of going outward from Jorslem to provide spiritual and physical help to those in need (much like conventional religious orders). In addition, Tomis, Avluela, and other members of the guild of Redeemers create a new communion through use of a combination of the starstones and the Watcher's old machinery for scanning the heavens. This communion represents the establishment of a religious community, thereby concluding the story on an affirmative note. However, the symbolism of the novel's pattern of redemption deserves further elucidation.

Another look shows us that Olmayne, the unrepentant "scarlet woman," may represent the stained or older soul of Tomis; in Jungian terms, she is the symbolic figure of experience and evil called the "dark anima."[4] Tomis's reunion with Avluela symbolizes a recovery of his early innocence of soul; Avluela, with her slender body and delicate wings—reminiscent of butterflies, of course—is clearly a figure suggesting the psyche, or in Jungian terms the purified "anima." Tomis's final marriage and union with Avluela represents a union of self and soul, or the ego's acquisition of sanctity, or the condition that W. B. Yeats called "radical innocence," and which orthodox Christians call grace.[5] Immersion in waters of renewal is an obvious baptismal rite, for like baptism this ritual involves a symbolic death and rebirth through the medium of water, a symbol of life and fertility; similarly, Tomis's recovery of physical youth represents his attainment of spiritual innocence and fertility (or creativity).

Although the religious symbolism follows obvious Judeo-Christian traditions, it is presented as part of the novel's religion of the Divine Will. Silverberg imagines this new universal religion as a logical successor to the obsolete religions associated with Jorslem—Judaism, Christianity, and Islam—which, Silverberg's narrator explains, passed into history because they no longer found support in a body of adherents. Nevertheless, as part of his preparation for renewal, Tomis does visit some of the shrines of the old religions, notably the Wailing Wall of Judaism and the supposed site of Christ's sepulcher. Thus Silverberg connects the mystical events of Part 3 with actual religious tradition.

The final scenes after Tomis's renewal also follow time-honored religious archetypes (readers familiar with English literature may think of the concluding sections of Bunyan's *Pilgrim's Progress*, or of the closing cantos of Book 1 of Edmund Spenser's *Faerie Queene*). Tomis's induction into a religious community, with its communal worship providing an experience of unity with other redeemed souls, and a sense of union with the universe, represents the ideal toward which Judaism and Christianity strive; but Silverberg's version is purged of doctrinal and sectarian overtones. At the close, Tomis describes himself as being able to join Avluela imaginatively in her flights by means of the modified starstone equipment, and its telepathic powers. Moreover, Avluela is now able to fly during the day as well as at night, for Tomis's presence helps her overcome the weaknesses that made her wings inoperative in the daylight. Thus spiritual wholeness is associated with the attainment of "nightwings." The closing harmonies symbolize unities attained by Tomis and Avluela: the unity of body and soul, masculine and feminine principles, self and soul, and the light and the dark sides of the self, as well as other contraries that might be cited.

Thus Silverberg's novel ends in a tone of triumph. It is fair to say that Silverberg has succeeded in embodying his visionary conclusion in memorable images. As an added note of chiliastic hope, Tomis and other characters prophesy that there will be a "new earth," at least in a moral and political sense when the guild of Redeemers has done its work. Not only will humanity be transformed, but the alien conquerors will themselves be "conquered by love," Tomis predicts, suggesting a parallel with apostolic Christianity, which set out to win over the Roman conquerors of its day with love.

Whether or not *Nightwings* is Silverberg's most affirmative novel, it certainly concludes in a spirit of hope. Of course, its religious themes depend on an uneasy compromise between spiritual affirmation and science, since Tomis's renewal and higher vision involve quasi-scientific processes. It also seems to require abandonment of human desires and ambition.

Does the salvation of mankind require waiting until the distant future and alien invasion? *Nightwings* suggests an affirmative, but to ask such a question is to take its science fiction metaphors literally. To explore the problem of the quest for salvation from other perspectives, Silverberg wrote *Downward to the Earth* and *A Time of Changes*. Both novels have received attention as works on religious themes, and both offer solutions in the quest for transcendence and liberation from the isolated self. Though both contain writing of a high quality, there are important differences. Ironically, *Downward to the Earth* is probably the more enduring work, although it was *A Time of Changes* that received the coveted Nebula Award for 1971. (*Downward* was nominated for 1970, but its chances were hurt because Silverberg's *Tower of Glass* was also nominated for that year, thereby dividing the vote.)

Over the years, however, the fame of *Downward to the Earth* has increased, while *A Time of Changes* has not worn so well. Aldiss, for instance, judges *Downward* to be "more effective than *Nightwings*" as a study of "guilt, punishment, and expiation." David Pringle chose *Downward* as Silverberg's representative on his highly personal list of the best novels in the genre (*Science Fiction: The 100 Best Novels* 147–148). *Downward* continues to attract interest in its treatment of religious search, as is evinced by a fairly recent essay in *Extrapolation* (Winter 1994) by Joseph Dudley comparing the novel with Philip José Farmer's *Night of Light* as an exercise in "Transformational SF Religions."[6] Although Dudley's approach to the novel is influenced more by the critical theory of Michel Foucault than by studies of religious experience, his essay at least focuses on *Downward*'s central themes.

Another reason for the novel's perennial interest has been its Conradian analogues. One genesis of *Downward to the Earth* for Silverberg was a trip to Africa, as he has revealed in a retrospective introduction. Other influences included his memories of reading Rudyard Kipling and Joseph Conrad, which were somehow combined in his sense of the sheer physical ambience of the continent, as he recalled, remembering his feeling of struggle in the composition of the novel (DTTE x–xi). Of course, Silverberg made sure that the Conradian influence would not be overlooked by naming an important character Kurtz, after the Faustian tragic hero of *Heart of Darkness*. As a result, scholars have found the parallels with Conrad a helpful way into the novel, as the excellent brief analysis by Clareson shows (RS 51–53), and as is illustrated by the fine essay "Silverberg and Conrad: Explorers of Inner Darkness" by Rose Sallberg Kam, which appeared many years ago in *Extrapolation* (December 1975).

The influence of Kipling should not be overlooked, nor should Silverberg's references to the sheer physical impact of Africa. It should be remembered that after many stories celebrating British imperialism in India (including some in *The Jungle Book*), Kipling produced the novel, *Kim* (1901), in which he attempted to describe the heart and soul of India.

Gundersen is more of a Kiplingesque former imperialist than a skeptical Marlow from Conrad's fiction, and his journey upcountry is in part a search for understanding of the land where he has been a successful manager without understanding the native peoples. Gundersen's quest encompasses more than a review of past errors; it is also a search for the parts of the self he left behind in his intense effort to succeed. Moreover, Gundersen, though a physically active man, has lost contact with the physical encounters with life and nature, and, as Silverberg indicates, it was the sheer overpowering physical effect of Africa that had stimulated his imagination.

Perhaps more significant than literary precursors was the impact of Africa as a physical entity on Silverberg's imagination. First, Belzagor is a very solidly conceived planet, modeled on Africa, and its atmosphere—a few enclaves of civilization surrounded by bush or jungle and haunted by legends of a "mist country"—seems to be much like the experience of Europeans encountering East or Central Africa. Hence *Downward to the Earth*, with its insistence on the often intractable and brute physical reality of Belzagor, is in this respect a considerable advance in Silverberg's fiction (only in the Nidor books had the setting of an alien culture been as significant). Even the language of the novel calls attention to the powerful physical presence of the planet. Indeed, *Downward to the Earth* is unusual even among Silverberg's works of the third period in its density of physical detail.

Gundersen's return to the scene of his former successes and failures is a successful journey into the self, much like that of Marlow in Conrad's *Heart of Darkness*, as both Clareson and Kam have argued. Kam's analysis of the novel stresses so many parallels with Conrad's short novel that it may be better here to comment on the differences between the two works. In Conrad's tale, for instance, Marlow is making a voyage of initiation when he is an untested youth; his is a journey into deeper experience, the knowledge that comes from observing Kurtz's surrender to his primitive impulses and his longing to be free of "civilized" restraints. Conrad's Kurtz, in fact, is a Faustian figure who surrenders to lust for power and domination and to the desire for extreme sexual gratification. He becomes a charismatic and godlike dictator of the natives he rules, leads them on raids to take ivory from neighboring villages, and encourages all kinds of acts of blood lust. Finally, Kurtz takes a splendidly uninhibited native woman as a mistress. As a tragic exemplar of the human lust for freedom, power, and self-gratification, Kurtz is viewed with shock and horror by Conrad's Marlow; but Marlow comes to recognize, implicitly at least, that Kurtz embodies a drive or group of drives at the hearts of all people. Hence, Kurtz becomes a symbol of a part of Marlow's own inner self, or of the Freudian well of energy that is labeled the "id," as well as the Jungian figure called "the shadow," as some critics, most notably Albert Guerard, Jr., have suggested (CTN 33–48).[7] After his fateful meeting with Kurtz, and his acceptance of Kurtz as a symbol of his own inner drives (just as the jungle symbolizes his unconscious self), Marlow discovers a mature wisdom that lies behind some of the apparently casual statements made in the course of his narrative. For instance, work and self-discipline provide a protection against the unrestrained impulses of the unconscious.

If Marlow's journey to the "heart of darkness" provides him with a provisional wisdom that allows him to maintain civilized and humane values, then Silverberg's Gundersen is a man who has attained such knowledge early in his ten-year stint as an administrator on Belzagor. What Silverberg's Gundersen, the analogue to Conrad's Marlow, must learn in his return to Belzagor is the way to the "heart of light," a journey of initiation that Conrad's Marlow perhaps never made. This journey must be a pilgrimage downward and inward into a densely physical world, before paradoxically, it can become a journey upward. Thus while there are significant parallels between Silverberg's novel and its Conradian predecessor, the differences between the two are also important to note.

To begin with, Gundersen is a mature, responsible man who must overcome several failings in his past. For one thing, he had tended to treat the natives of Belzagor like highly intelligent animals, and despite his best efforts to be humane, he had always felt a good deal of contempt for them. These natives belong to two sentient species, one being the nildoror, resembling highly evolved and intelligent elephants, and the other, the sulidoror, who are apelike bipedal creatures. The massive physical forms of the nildoror, as well as their trunks, render them slightly ridiculous to humans, and their lack of a written language and a high technology makes it easier for terrestrials to feel a sense of superiority.

Yet Gundersen, returning after eight years, finds himself much closer in sympathy to the nildoror than to the human tourists with whom he is obliged to travel for much of the journey. Despite Gundersen's attempt to be charitable toward the tourists, the reader tends to share his views after exposure to their conversation about the planet and the nildoror.

In Gundersen's past, there are two major moral lapses for which he seeks to atone in his self-imposed pilgrimage. The first seems relatively innocuous to everyone but Gundersen: early in his tour of duty on Belzagor, he had joined his colleague, Jeff Kurtz, and his assistant in a self-indulgent and orgiastic drug experience in the jungle near Kurtz's station. The drug here is the snake venom—evoking ironic and poetic parallels to the images of the serpent as tempter and seducer that permeate Judeo-Christian literature—that the terrestrials extract for export to earth as a medicinal aid. The effect of the drug is simple: Gundersen had felt transported out of his isolated self and for a time had experienced the illusion that he inhabited the body of a nildoror, in an event that represented liberation from his loneliness. Although no harm had been done by surrender to this drug-induced ecstasy, Gundersen remembers the incident as a fall from his high expectations of himself and a lapse into self-indulgence. However, this violation of his code was a minor one compared to his later profanation of the nildoror religious code, for which he feels an enormous guilt. Although Silverberg's Kurtz had not been directly involved in this transgression, his presence haunts Gundersen's journey upcountry, so it is important here to define his role in the novel.

Silverberg's Kurtz functions as a kind of foil for Gundersen, for Kurtz is another instance of a terrestrial imperialist who abused his position as overlord, not only exploiting the nildoror, but seducing them away from their cultural beliefs. Kurtz's degradation of the nildoror is never dramatized for the reader, save for the scene of the drug-induced orgy. It consisted primarily of giving the snake venom to the nildoror and encouraging them to profane their religion, especially the rebirth ritual. Thus, although Silverberg's Kurtz is presented credibly as an attractive rebel, a Lucifer in the process of falling (in Gundersen's phrase), he never quite becomes a sinister figure with the stature of Conrad's Kurtz. Moreover, when Gundersen meets him again, Silverberg's Kurtz has been punished so greatly that he has become a pitiable figure.

Tormented by guilt, Kurtz has undergone the nildoror rebirth ceremony, only to be transformed into a hideously misshapen creature, angelic around the head and shoulders but bestial from the chest down. Meeting Kurtz in this grotesque condition, Gundersen recognizes that his bodily form symbolizes the deterioration of his inner nature.

However, it is Gundersen's redemption, not Kurtz's degradation, that is the center of the novel, just as Marlow is finally the protagonist of Conrad's *Heart of Darkness*. Gundersen's pilgrimage to the mist country contains many fateful encounters. On the journey he meets various terrestrials, mostly former imperialists who have in some manner succumbed to Belzagor and its temptations. These characters represent moral failure, or foolish responses to the planet's challenges, as well as tragic lessons for Gundersen. In addition to Kurtz, there is the shallow Van Beneker, Gundersen's former subordinate and now a tourist guide; Seena, Gundersen's former mistress, and Kurtz's wife, who tries to live a life of neo-paganism on Belzagor, in order to mask her disenchantment; two unnamed terrestrials whose bodies are bloated by giant parasites and who represent, probably, a mindless surrender to the nature of Belzagor; and finally, an intelligent former colleague of Gundersen's, Cedric Cullen, who is dying of cancer and is so overwhelmed by a sense of futility that he refuses to be shipped to earth, where advanced medical science might arrange a remission. Cullen is a particularly important minor character. His transgression was to discover the dark side of nildoror mysteries, their ritual of repentance—without undergoing the initiation into the redemptive rite of nildoror religion, the rebirth ceremony.

All these characters play a role in Gundersen's pilgrimage, which is not only a journey into acceptance of his past with its guilts, but an immersion into the physical and more primitive world of Belzagor. Thus, his quest embodies the metaphor of the book's title, suggested by a passage from Ecclesiastes: he journeys metaphorically "downward" to an encounter with a supposedly "lower" species and their highly physical nature; also, he journeys "downward" into an acceptance of the darker or more Dionysian side of himself. Paradoxically, however, his physical journey, although it ends in a cave, is a journey upward, from the coastal plain to the rain forest to the heights and snows of the mist country, and finally to the holy mountain of rebirth with its cave that serves both as tomb and womb of the beings transmuted by rebirth.

One of the revelations that comes to Gundersen near the end of his quest is that the two species of Belzagor are really one, since they undergo lives first as nildoror and then as sulidoror. This identity of the two species is a symbolic statement of several ideas: first, that all sentient life is essentially of one being or nature; and second, that a release from the burden of the solitary self may be attained by a new existence in the form of another sentient species. Clearly, the sulidoror are intended to represent the Apollonian or cerebral type of life, just as the nildoror are associated with the Dionysian and animal level of existence; but this theme is subordinated to Gundersen's final discovery.

What Gundersen experiences when he undergoes the rebirth ritual is an ecstatic and numinous vision of the wholeness and unity of all life, a moment of transcendence that is undoubtedly the central core of experience in the novel. A similar scene at the end of *Nightwings* had provided an epiphany that clarified the entire book. In Gundersen's epiphany, Silverberg's style rises to impressive heights. The visionary tone of this experience (virtually all of chapter 16) is achieved by a shift to the present tense, and by a deft command of poetic imagery:

The fragments seek one another. They solemnly circle one another. They dance. They unite. They take on the form of Edmund Gundersen, but this new Gundersen glows like pure transparent glass. He is glistening, a transparent man through whom the light of the great sun at the core of the universe passes without resistance. A spectrum spreads forth from his chest. The brilliance of his body illuminates the galaxies. (DTTE 172)

In Gundersen's vision, the metaphor of being "transparent" is crucial: when purified and renewed a sentient being allows the light of the "core of the Universe" to shine through; the renewed nildoror and sulidoror also accomplish this, but by contrast the souls of the terrestrials Gundersen perceives in his visionary state seem to him to be mostly "blind and silent." Gundersen cannot communicate with any of them except the flawed spirit of the tragic Kurtz, which seems to contain just enough radiance to imply the possibility of redemption.

In the final chapter, the tone changes to a more restrained note of social purpose, as Gundersen pledges to his sulidor or mentor that he will return to civilization to take the gospel of rebirth to others. One significant feature of this chapter is Silverberg's choice of New Testament allusions. Clearly, Silverberg is attempting to translate the familiar gospel concept of a second birth or being "born again" and the New Testament promises of "all things being made new" into fresh religious terms, liberated from the dogmatic and doctrinal tenets of orthodox Judaism or Christianity. In this respect, *Downward to the Earth* carries on the spirit of *Nightwings*, although, as we have noted, *Downward to the Earth* places a heavier emphasis on the physical and Dionysian aspects of existence, and stresses the importance of transcending the limitations of the rational consciousness.

On the whole, *Downward to the Earth* remains a fine novel. It frequently approaches the high level of *Nightwings*, and in one respect, it seems to be superior. Gundersen, the quest hero of *Downward to the Earth*, has some real sins to atone for, whereas the saintly Tomis of *Nightwings* is guilty of only minor faults, such as lack of hope and lapses of charity, and yet he feels obliged to suffer for humanity's sins. In *Downward* also, the affirmation of the images of the physical world has its own transcendent value, much as in the mystical theology of Martin Buber.[8]

The theme of religious search that began in *Nightwings* is continued, in a different mode, in *A Time of Changes* (1971), a novel often paired with *Downward to the Earth*. While *Downward to the Earth* was merely a nominee for the Hugo and Nebula awards, *A Time of Changes* was honored by receiving the Nebula for 1971. This distinction does not ensure the superiority of *A Time of Changes*, however. In fact, the success of *A Time of Changes* may have owed much to cultural fashions of the time, when sympathy for mind-expanding drugs was more widespread. *A Time of Changes* now seems less impressive than *Nightwings* or *Downward to the Earth*, just as the luster of many award-winning films dims in later years, when social concerns of the moment have faded.

With a title suggested by a Bob Dylan song, *A Time of Changes* draws on the same matrix of ideas as in *Downward*, but it reveals more aesthetic and philosophical weaknesses. An autobiographical narrative of an exiled prince on the planet of Velada Borthan, *Changes* presents Silverberg's now familiar theme of the need to overcome the alienation and loneliness of the solitary self though psychic communion. This time the means of achieving a transcendent "I/Thou" encounter, as celebrated in the mystical theology of Martin Buber, is a powerful drug that enables the recipient to enter the mind of another person telepathically, while opening his own mind to the other.[9]

In presenting this theme, however, Silverberg's conception of a transcendent personal communion gets intertwined with incest and eroticism; or, at any rate, Silverberg's hero complicates his longing for spiritual kinship with romantic feeling for his "bondsister." (As a later chapter shows, a thwarted and confused incestuous feeling also afflicts David Selig in *Dying Inside*, Silverberg's most poignant novel about the isolated self.) To put the matter in the traditional terms of Christian theology, eros or romantic love is compounded with the longing for agape or disinterested charitable love.

Although current disenchantment with drugs weakens the novel's impact, a greater weakness is the predictable pattern of its plot. To be sure, Silverberg makes Darival's society on Borthan a repressive and unattractive one: people are forbidden to use the first person pronoun in dialogue concerning personal relationships. Denied the opportunity to exercise political power, Darival flees from his brother's antagonism much as Moses ran away from Egypt and the wrath of the pharaoh into the land of Midian. After acquiring maturity, success, and a new identity, Darival then (again, as Moses found the vision of God in the burning bush) discovers his vision-inducing drug and experiments with establishing close personal relationships. Eventually he returns to his homeland, hoping secretly to spread the gospel of the drug and its power to release personal feeling.

However, he commits the ultimate transgression by introducing the drug to his "bondsister" Halum, whom he has secretly loved, and as a result, he learns of her own romantic feeling for him. Since an erotic relationship with one's "bondsister" is taboo, it naturally becomes the source of suppressed erotic feeling, and Darival commits a kind of psychological incest in blending his thoughts and emotions with hers. (Some form of incest appears to be one of the classic crimes of the romantic rebel.) Halum's act of rebellion proves too much for her conventional conscience, and, racked by guilt, she commits suicide. Later, Darival is betrayed and escapes to the desert where he writes his narrative as a testament of protest against the obtuseness of the world that persecutes him. As the story ends, Darival is about to be captured and martyred for his revolt against tradition. It should be remembered that Darival is a tragic figure, and the novel does not make a clear endorsement of drug-induced mysticism.

Although *A Time of Changes* is a well-crafted novel, its weaknesses make it a flawed performance compared to *Nightwings* and *Downward*. There are vivid scenes, as when Darival describes his adventures with his father hunting the "hornfowl" (an owl-like bird of prey that is a symbol of untamed nature on the planet); but the overall effect of the book is diffuse and muted. A prophet who preaches the gospel of love and personal communion in Darival's way is not exactly bringing a new message, except for the dubious use of drugs, and a predictable story with familiar romantic conventions (even committing the tabooed sin of incest) does not help. Unlike Moses, Darival is a tragic deliverer who fails in his mission; he is, in Aldiss's words, "a flawed but ultimately messianic figure" (TYS 343). Aside from Darival, most of the characters appear to be conventional types, and Halum, the heroine whom

Darival loves and destroys, is a shadowy figure. Aldiss, however, finds the conflict of the novel to be realistically depicted and a relevant parallel to contemporary social conflicts (TYS 343). However, the most glaring defect of the novel is yet to be mentioned: at those times when the drug-induced telepathic communion takes place, the writing fails to attain the visionary power of similar moments in *Nightwings* and *Downward to the Earth*. Clareson also offers a similar negative judgment by asserting that "the final vision of Darival's is not an effective affirmation" (RS 59).

Not content with his achievements in *Nightwings* and *Downward*, Silverberg attempted to make a more daring visionary religious statement in 1971. However, this was also one of his most disappointing failures. Narrated in the present tense in a tone relentlessly ecstatic and vatic, *Son of Man* abandons most of the usual conventions of fiction, providing neither realistic characters nor a coherent quest adventure plot. Although the work takes the form of a quest romance in a visionary landscape, and aspires to a high level of poetic intensity, it provides only a series of fragmentary and sometimes not very interesting episodes.

The science fiction prototypes of the novel include David Lindsay's *A Voyage to Arcturus* (1920) and Olaf Stapledon's *The Star Maker* (1937), as Clareson has noted (RS 59). Behind these important imaginative efforts lie not only H. G. Wells and H. Rider Haggard, but also the great tradition of the Romantic poets with their quest narratives like S. T. Coleridge's "The Rime of the Ancient Mariner," William Blake's prophetic works, Keats's *Endymion*, and perhaps the most obvious precursor, Shelley's long visionary poems like *Alastor*.[10] At first glance, indeed, *Son of Man* is likely to strike the reader as the kind of romantic effort that a young Shelley or Keats might have produced had he lived in the sixties and written science fiction. It is probably wise to concede that at best *Son of Man* remains a confusing and incoherent work. In fact, only Brian Stableford, among Silverberg's critics, seems to express much enthusiasm for the novel (MOSF 40). Nevertheless, the question of what Silverberg was attempting in the novel is important to a study of Silverberg's canon.

Son of Man takes its name from the Gospel title that Jesus frequently applied to himself. Since Jesus also defined himself as the Son of God and the Gospels tend to insist both on the humanity of Jesus and his divinity, the title actually assumes connotations of a messianic divinity incarnate in human flesh. According to many interpretations (both orthodox and heretical) of the New Testament, Jesus embodies a mystical identity of God and man, and one purpose of his mission on earth was to bring the promise of a richer and fuller life for humanity—in fact, to give humanity the power to become "sons of God." For orthodox Christians, this promise is to be fulfilled only in heaven after death or after the apocalyptic Second Coming of Christ; but even orthodox theologians have hesitated to suggest that humanity itself can attain a kind of secondary divinity at last. However, radical heterodox Christian visionaries like Blake have envisioned the possibility that humanity could actualize its potential divinity without waiting for the Second Coming or by bringing on the Second Coming through human action.[11] Similarly, such visionaries as Stapledon and David Lindsay have tried to envision more expansive possibilities for humanity.

In contrast with its predecessors, Silverberg's *Son of Man* is chaotic and disappointing. The quest takes Silverberg's searcher, Clay, through numerous visionary encounters and initiations, and the design of the novel is vaguely apocalyptic (as long quotations from the Gospels of Matthew and Mark at the novel's beginning and end indicate). However, Silverberg's book fails to make use of a clearly formulated mythology that would provide a satisfying narrative structure. Moreover, Silverberg abandons the conventions of quest fiction, as Stapledon and Lindsay did not, which places an enormous burden on his narrative skills. *Son of Man* proceeds from one series of surrealistic encounters to another, without ever generating the narrative momentum that Lindsay, for instance, achieves in *A Voyage to Arcturus*. Thus Silverberg's seeker, Clay, a masculine figure, is transported to another realm of existence; undergoes various expansions of consciousness, such as becoming androgynous; experiences sexual intercourse from the point of view of a woman; and lives through other experiences that enlarge awareness of human potential. At the end, Clay is presented with the knowledge that the descendants of humanity, the "sons of men," will be godlike creatures, although they will take a variety of new biological forms.

Despite Silverberg's literary talents, *Son of Man* fails to achieve a coherent fictional statement. Moreover, Silverberg's use of the first person and an exalted, visionary tone is difficult to sustain in a performance of this length. Nevertheless, Silverberg's failure in *Son of Man* is an ambitious one: the work represents the mood of a romantic era in American cultural history, when liberation from the rigidities of the past was accelerating, and prodigious reforms of society and consciousness seemed possible.

The novels discussed thus far in this chapter have sought to present visionary and affirmative religious statements and have described moments of numinous epiphany that give a pattern to the narrative, although *Son of Man* tends to be merely a succession of visionary fragments. There is a dark side to the religious quest as well, as the ubiquitous presence of hypocrisy, bigotry, fanaticism, and "holy wars" all attest. As an enlightened man of liberal humanitarian views and a member of a minority that has experienced persecution and suffering, Silverberg is well aware of the dark and perverse direction that the desire for transcendence often takes. Two of the deepest roots of religious fanaticism are the fear of death, which lies behind the hunger for some form of immortality, and the desire for absolute certainty in metaphysical matters, which is also connected with the desire to feel superior to the uninitiated, who remain outside a particular community of belief. Silverberg treats the effect of these desires in an impressive novel, *The Book of Skulls* (1972), and in the three novellas in *Born with the Dead*, which contain some of his finest writing.

In *The Book of Skulls*, the longing for immortality serves as the motivation for a perverse and ironic quest. The theme of the human yearning to conquer death had preoccupied Silverberg before: notably in some sixties short stories and in the bizarre *To Live Again*. Moreover, in the early novel *Recalled to Life* (1962), Silverberg had portrayed the social effects of the discovery of a process to resurrect the newly deceased, and this novel was sufficiently important for him to revise it for publication in 1972. As we have noted, the revised *Recalled to Life* treats the desire to cheat death affirmatively, while hinting at the existence of a future state of life after death.[12] In short, Silverberg's fascination with this theme is fairly obvious.

However, *The Book of Skulls* offers a strong contrast to *Recalled to Life*. Here the supposed existence of a mysterious "Book of Skulls," which is believed to hold the key to immortality, encourages four college students to set off on a journey across the United States to Arizona where a secret monastic order that is living by the book is believed to reside. The four students are young males of superior intelligence from an unnamed Eastern school, presumably an Ivy League university, and at first their quest resembles the daring and bizarre experiments of the sixties undertaken by college dropouts—such as creating guerrilla theater, setting up communes, planning a revolution, or developing a new religion. Their journey ends ironically with betrayal, the death of two of the students, and the total surrender of the other two to a destructive cult. Without exaggeration, their quest is described by one character as "a dark version of Pascal's gamble, an existentialist all-or-nothing trip," and the book abounds in ironic parodies of religious symbolism (BOS 5). If the quest of the saint is for sanctity and transcendence, then their quest is a negative version of the saint's quest, a journey to find a physical immortality reserved for an elite few.

The demonic symbolism, or ironic parody of affirmative religious myth, is extensive. As Ned, the would-be poet, points out, the group of four constitutes a Jungian mandala, but this quartet becomes a sinister mandala because their agreement with the secret order requires that two must die in order that the other two may gain immortal life (an ironic parody of the Christian conception of the Atonement).[13] The "Book of Skulls" (a name perhaps suggested by the Tibetan *Book of the Dead*), which supposedly contains the arcane knowledge needed for immortality, is a sinister or occult book of scriptures and hence a demonic parody of the Bible (and sacred books), much as H. P. Lovecraft's mysterious *Necronomicon* was a nonexistent occult work that became an ironic parody of other sacred books. As the title of the "Book of Skulls" indicates, its real reward is death, rather than spiritual life, the reward offered by authentic sacred books.

The quartet of seekers is a well-defined group of elitists. It includes the Jewish Eli Steinfeld, a philosophical skeptic with a genius for manipulating people; Ned, a seemingly weak homosexual poet, who nevertheless has a talent for exploiting the vulnerabilities of others; Oliver, a handsome and athletic Midwestern lad, apparently an All-American boy, but without awareness of his own complexities; and Timothy, a scion of Eastern wealth and a cheerful hedonist who regards the entire trip as a lark (and who, despite his arrogance, may be the most healthy member of the group). Moreover, in a striking display of narrative art, Silverberg tells the story through the first person voices of the four protagonists. Each of the students is credibly characterized through his own narrative voice, but the alternating narrators heighten the novel's irony. In addition, since the four students are fairly literate and since Eli and Ned have both read widely, there are rich uses of literary allusion, which are usually given an ironic turn. Finally, though Silverberg does not portray any character who represents a clearly desirable moral alternative to these four, a moral perspective is provided because the student questers condemn themselves through their own words.

Aside from the pattern of a negative quest, the external action of the novel is rather slight until the final third of the book. Then, nudged by Eli's manipulation, Ned, the homosexual poet, is able to seduce Oliver, the supposedly normal Midwestern boy, and get Oliver to surrender to his own latent homosexuality. Later in Arizona, Oliver's guilt causes him to commit suicide, while Eli, spurred by hatred, murders Timothy when the latter is attempting to return to the outside world. Appropriately enough, Eli commits his act with a steel skull; ironically, the murder satisfies the requirements of entry into the order, just as Oliver's death allows Ned admission. These deaths become instances of human sacrifice, the ultimate symbolic action of a demonic cult.

It is perhaps no coincidence that Eli, whose discovery of the "Book of Skulls" motivated the quest in the first place, is given the name of the corrupt priest in the Old Testament who has been immortalized by his association with Samuel, the brilliant judge of Israel. Eli also has the last passage of the book, and there he describes himself, anticipating his years of immortality as a member of the order while his past is already slipping from memory. Silverberg leaves the question of whether the "Keepers of the Skulls" really possess the secret of immortality unresolved; but it is obvious that physical immortality on such terms is worthless because it requires spiritual death, or more specifically, a living death. At the end, Silverberg's seekers may have found the secret of physical immortality, but each is imprisoned in an isolated consciousness. Indeed this novel might well have been called *The Book of the Damned*.

All things considered, *The Book of Skulls* is a grim and brilliant performance. As a study of the evil consequences of the hunger for physical immortality, it is quite impressive. Its quartet of narrative voices and carefully defined patterns of irony and symbolism show Silverberg at the height of his powers. Although Clareson found the novel admirable, he also found it a troubling example of the "dark side" of Silverberg's work (RS 65–66).

The three novellas in the volume called *Born with the Dead* are also impressive works; in fact, the title story is as fine as anything in the Silverberg canon. All three deal with death and humanity's "ultimate concern," or the religious desire to find either immortality or some kind of transcendence in this life. However, the themes of the three are quite different.

"Going," the earliest of the three, is the quietest in tone. Its setting is a late twenty-first-century future when medical science and drugs have extended longevity to well past a hundred years. To ease the population problem and the anxieties of the elderly, the government has established "Houses of Leavetaking," where one may prepare for death and commit suicide in a painless way. Silverberg's hero, Henry Staunt, decides at the age of 136 that he has seen enough of life on earth and applies for admission to one of the official suicide institutes. The story then describes with dry irony the shock of his elderly children and their sense of guilt because they feel that they have not loved their father enough. Disenchanted and stoical, Staunt feels that he has reached a point at which little can surprise him; as confirmation, he discovers boredom at the behavior of his relatives and the nurses and doctors at the institute. At length, he chooses to die quietly, well before he has exhausted the amusements he had planned for himself in his last days. Staunt's acceptance of death without regret, and with no particular faith in life after death, makes him a heroic figure, quite the opposite of the arrogant students of *The Book of Skulls*. In essence, "Going" suggests that actual death may be preferable to the "death-in-life" of old age.[14]

By contrast with the restrained tone of "Going," "Thomas the Proclaimer" reverberates with frenzied oratory and frenetic events. The story proceeds from the premise that Thomas Davison, an evangelist, has asked for a sign from God and, to his surprise, receives one: the sun "stands still" for a twenty-four-hour period, or in actuality, the earth does not rotate on its axis. As a result, there is widespread panic, increased by the fact that it is the year 2000, when millennial hopes and apocalyptic fears abound. (Silverberg had exploited this idea before in *The Masks of Time*.) As a result of the "sign from God," organized religions are struck dumb, the fundamentalists and cultists are stung into hysterical frenzy, and new cults arise in response to the emotionalism of the moment. Even a cult of scientific rationalists becomes religious. Some of the credulous are aroused to fevered incoherence of the Pentecostal sort—that is, to "speaking in tongues."

Silverberg has commented that the story's basis is "sheer fantasy" for him, since he considers a sign from God to be highly unlikely. Clearly, judging by the tragedy and chaos that result from this occurrence, it may be better for humanity if such an event never happens. As Silverberg frankly acknowledges, his view of humanity and its religious emotions in this study is dark and satirical (BWTD xi).

However, the somber tone of "Born with the Dead" is remarkably different. This novella was, by Silverberg's testimony, one of the most difficult of his works to write, but it is also one of the finest jewels in his crown (BWTD xi–xii). The theme of "Born with the Dead" is the contrast between the two states of life and death: or more specifically, a rather empty everyday life in a future 1992, and the zombie-like state of "life-in-death" of "the dead," people who are frozen cryogenically and "rekindled" to life. Jorge Klein, the protagonist, finds life without his late wife Sybelle to be relentlessly boring in a world where technology has made most of the inhabited parts of the earth similar. He longs to be reunited with Sybelle, but the dead do not come back to life with the passion or obsessions of the living; rather, they have entered a state of cold detachment from the emotions and conflicts of existence. They associate only with other dead, stay most of the time in the "cold cities," towns containing their own king, and reject contact or involvement with their relatives or lovers from their former lives. Klein, however, refuses to accept the loss of Sybelle, when he sees her apparently alive again in her passionless, post-resurrection state. When a meeting is arranged between them, she rebuffs him and makes him the victim of a macabre joke (literally employing "dead-pan" irony). But he persists. At last, his obsession becomes annoying to the "dead," who have the legal right to terminate any living person who imposes on their existence too greatly. In a final strike of irony, Klein is himself killed and restored to life as a "dead," whereupon his former passion for Sybelle is chilled. After a time, however, they become platonic friends and learn to enjoy each other's companionship.

Silverberg's novella is masterful in its restraint and command of tone, and it is impressive in its portrait of two completely different states of existence. The story makes it clear that the gulf between the living and the dead appears to be impassable on ordinary terms, and once again Silverberg has treated the hope for physical immortality through advanced technology with consummate irony. Such a resurrection may not be worth having, the novella suggests; and however pointless and confused ordinary life may be, it is, according to Silverberg's mature imagination, preferable to the zombie-like existence of "the deads." "Born with the Dead" is science fiction at the highest level of art.

However, its cold beauty has its price: Silverberg has commented that "Born with the Dead," *Dying Inside,* and *The Book of Skulls* were works in which he took his kind of pure ironic vision as far as it could go; and beyond the creation of these works there was, he felt, only "silence" (BWTD xiii). For all of his intellectual awareness of the tragic nature of mortality, and the moral flaws of humanity, Silverberg could not be content to rest in a completely ironic vision of the human condition.

Not long after the completion of *Dying Inside* in 1971, and about a year before "Born with the Dead," Silverberg wrote "The Feast of St. Dionysus" for an anthology on the theme of the quest for transcendence edited by Terry Carr. Later, Silverberg recalled that "I wrote it with wondrous energy and passion," and the novella eventually won an award (Introduction to FOSD x). It is one of Silverberg's most memorable treatments of the religious themes that dominated much of his work. Not only does the novella offer tentative affirmations, but it clarifies Silverberg's mature vision in important respects.

In "The Feast of St. Dionysus" the hero, John Oxenshuer, a former astronaut, seeks release from the guilt and self-accusation resulting from the deaths of his two companions on the first Mars expedition. As both were killed by an unexpected sandstorm, Oxenshuer could not have saved them; but he feels responsible for their fate, partly because he was spared. To compound his sense of guilt, one of the two slain astronauts was Dave Vogel, a childhood friend, a companion and rival in youth, a successful rival in love, and finally his superior officer. Submerged in his friendship and admiration for Vogel have been envy and a repressed love for Claire, Vogel's wife. As Oxenshuer had no doubt unconsciously wished for Vogel's death, Oxenshuer's guilt after the event has become overwhelming.

Thus, in the early stages of the novella, it is established that Oxenshuer cannot accept his own survival. After severing the ties of civilization, Oxenshuer leaves Southern California in his car to drive into the Mojave Desert on a final penitential and self-destructive quest.

In the desert, Oxenshuer finds a mysterious city that is not on any map. Laid out in the form of a labyrinth that surrounds a central plaza and a "God-house," the city is called the "City of the Word of God"; it is inhabited by a cult who worship both Christ and Dionysius (although they insist on the spelling "Dionysus"). Oxenshuer lives among the communicants for a time and is gradually drawn into their religious community. Finally he begins to accept their drinking rituals and is persuaded to participate in the feast they hold for St. Dionysus, completely unaware that he is to be a sacrificial victim, representing the person of the god.

On the feast day, Oxenshuer becomes ceremonially drunk and engages in a wrestling match with Matt, the son of "the Speaker," the shamanistic leader of the city. During the wrestling match, Oxenshuer momentarily loses consciousness and mentally substitutes his late friend, Vogel, for his opponent, an action that somehow spurs him on to victory. Later in the "God-house," where he expects to join in the mass for St. Dionysus, Oxenshuer again loses his sense of reality and begins to hallucinate, imagining himself going back to Mars on a special mission to bury his companions' bodies and returning to marry Claire. After a dream of losing Claire in the desert, Oxenshuer has a final vision of journeying to join Claire in the city for a mystic consummation, after which presumably he will be ritually sacrificed and eaten by the people. Thus he goes to his fate oblivious of what is happening but purged of his guilt and reconciled to both his past and his present.[15]

Oxenshuer's gradual surrender to the role of victim becomes mesmerizing as his memories of the past blend with the present and with moments of hallucination. Although the novella's plot follows a tragic pattern, the action has a curiously ambiguous character, and Oxenshuer's self-sacrifice has mystic overtones. Some keys to the story's meaning are provided by the shaman-priest, or leader of the "City of the Word of God," who is called simply "the Speaker," when he explains the nature of the faith and its synthesis of the worship of Christ and Dionysus. According to his exegesis, the faith conjoins opposites: Christianity and paganism, Apollonian rationalism and Dionysian emotionalism, the light and dark sides of the soul. Even Buddhism is said to be included in the faith's eclectic compound (in intention at least). The aims of the synthesis are twofold: to restore a sense of wholeness and unity to humanity and to renew religious experience constantly by direct communion with the gods.

Thus Oxenshuer is encouraged to surrender his consciousness to two experiences: first, the ecstasy of Dionysus through the ritual of wine and hallucinations, and then to the "ocean of Christ," that is, the oblivion of death and final peace in his sacrifice at the feast (as I interpret the ocean metaphor). His entry into the "ocean" of non-being is itself a surrender to the cosmos, and represents a kind of self-transcendence.

Although the Speaker's theology leads to the ritual enactment of a barbaric act of human sacrifice and cannibalism, many of his ideas have an ambiguous aura. Seldom has there been a more willing scapegoat than Oxenshuer, who finds a mystic release in his surrender to the needs of the community into which he has wandered.

In reality, Silverberg, as well as Oxenshuer, finds some of the Speaker's theology attractive. Silverberg has credited a reading of Norman O. Brown, specifically his *Love's Body*, with a strong influence on the story, and it should be noted that the Speaker's comments about the urgent need for humanity to rediscover its original unity are close enough to the quest for spiritual renewal in *Nightwings, Downward to the Earth, A Time of Changes,* and *Son of Man* to suggest that they restate a significant theme in Silverberg's own fiction (FOSD ix–x). As Robert Reilly has commented in a perceptive essay on this novella, the transcendence attained in "St. Dionysus" and other religious novels of Silverberg appears to be both attractive and destructive— an ambiguous transcendence of self (RSMT 107–119).

If "The Feast of St. Dionysus" is a fine work that treats Oxenshuer's religious quest with ambivalence, its tragedy is nevertheless affirmative enough to underscore the essential positive vision of some of Silverberg's major religious novels. At the same time, its treatment of the dark side of religious motivation and the demonic actions it produces are similar to *The Book of Skulls* and the novella in *Born with the Dead*. As we have seen,

Silverberg's religious vision is many sided, and it is clearly still in the process of development. Yet his treatment of religious themes is usually serious and profound. Although his religious quest stories and novels provide no final answers, they offer testimony to the validity of mysticism and the renewal of religious experience.

5

Riding the New Wave toward
Post-Modernism: Short Fiction,
1969–1974

◆

Silverberg's best short fiction had tended to be superior to his novels, especially in the fifties. In the sixties, Silverberg's relationship with Frederik Pohl and *Galaxy*, and his liberation from the drudgery of earning a living by hack novels allowed him the opportunity to write shorter fiction of consistently high quality. Few efforts in this period experimented with narrative technique. In the short fiction of Silverberg's third period (1969–1974), however, not only does he broaden and deepen the thematic concerns of his fiction, but he also enthusiastically embraces innovations in form—partly, as he himself confesses, from the boredom caused by mastery of the conventions of traditional narrative; and partly from an interest in the literary experimentation of the "new wave" science fiction, which encouraged him to adopt the techniques of such mainstream "fabulators" as Jorge Luis Borges, John Barth, Donald Barthelme, Robert Coover, and William H. Gass. Their innovations would later be seen as harbingers of "post-modernism."[1]

Indeed, the late sixties were a time when experiment with narrative conventions became common. This decade and the seventies saw the arrival of academic studies on the neglected subject of narrative theory, and the rise of interest in structuralism, deconstruction, and "reader response."[2] Silverberg, who has always displayed a knowledgeable literary awareness, and who from the beginning wanted to raise science fiction to a higher literary level, was in part responding to the *Zeitgeist*, with its fascination with radical change. The fascination with literary experiment in science fiction was signaled by the advent of the British "new wave" and by Harlan Ellison's provocative anthology, *Dangerous Visions* (1967), the impact of which Aldiss describes (299–308). As Brian McHale had noted, there was a post-modernist or experimental movement in science fiction in the late sixties and early seventies (McHale 68–72).

Experimentation with narrative form by such writers as Barthelme and Coover embodied a good deal more than a mere revolution in craft. Although the new fiction reflected impatience with the conventions of the modernist short story that had descended from Anton Chekhov and Joyce—who in turn had rebelled against the well-made and carefully plotted stories of Edgar Allan Poe and Guy de Maupassant—it was also a movement devoted to making serious fiction reflect the fragmented (and non-linear) appearance that reality assumed for thoughtful people in the sixties. Experimental fiction became an emblem of the "post-modern" sensibility. In a world being transformed by a revolution in electronic technology, the ease of global travel, and a wide diffusion of information, experience often seemed a collage of events defying normal notions of cause and effect. Consequently, experimental fiction writers were attempting, shielded by an ironic pose as innovators in technique, to reflect their perception of the experience that they saw.[3]

Usually there is a strong admixture of satire in avant-garde movements in the arts. Certainly this is present in literary efforts to shock and to break up conventional responses in experimental fiction, which, like the Theatre of the Absurd in earlier decades, assaulted intellectual dogma and social taboos. Even if the purpose of absurdist drama or fictional "fabulation" is to suggest through art the irrationality and possible meaninglessness of existence—as it certainly is in such absurdist writers as Samuel Beckett—the impulse to satirize social attitudes is still very urgent. In fact, much of the experimental fiction of Borges, Coover, Gass, Barth, and Barthelme is explicitly devoted to social and political satire, as in Barthelme's story "City Life," or Coover's "Cat in the Hat for President." Silverberg's use of experimental technique is similarly linked to a sense of moral outrage and anguish over the political and social ills besetting Western civilization in an era that began to feel an apocalyptic mood.

In our study of the shorter fiction of this period, we shall start with the stories that employ traditional modernist forms. Then we will proceed to more innovative work, especially the two impressive collections, *Unfamiliar Territory* (1973) and *Capricorn Games* (1976), later collected as *Beyond the Safe Zone* (1986).

One major group of short works in Silverberg's third period describes the experiences of oppressed peoples or species. Two well known stories with this focus are "Black Is Beautiful" (1970) and "Sundance" (1969), one dealing with the anger of urban blacks and the other with the anguished psyche of the Plains Indians. Somewhat related efforts are "Ishmael in Love" (1970), which attempts to give voice to the emotions of a highly intelligent dolphin, and "Something Wild Is Loose" (1971), which enters the mind of an alien creature. "The Fangs of the Trees" (1968) is an earlier but similar tale, displaying imaginative sympathy for sentient trees, although it does not explore the consciousness of these beings. The most successful and celebrated of these stories is "Sundance," but the others mentioned above attempt to portray the experience and sentiments of non-white people and even non-human entities, thereby expanding the range of experience of Silverberg's work.[4] In "Black Is Beautiful," Silverberg postulates a New York in the year 2000, more than three decades after the racial strife of the late sixties; the city is now an enclave governed by blacks, while whites have retreated to the suburbs. Events are seen through the point of view of James Shabazz, a seventeen-year-old African American whose mind is immersed in the militant rhetoric of the troubled sixties. When Shabazz is about to attack a white tourist, however, he is stopped by a black policeman and arrested. Freed by the intercession of Powell 43X Nissim, a political boss, Shabazz is told that the old revolutionary rhetoric is out of date. Instead, Powell 43X explains, African Americans have their own place in the power structure and are able to co-exist easily with white society. Tourists to New York are protected by the system. Disillusioned, young Shabazz goes off to write an essay on black power, vowing never to sell out to the establishment as older African Americans have done. Thus Silverberg depicts the black alienation of the sixties, only to undercut it, in an ironic reversal, by suggesting that its revolutionary rhetoric would appear exaggerated in the context of a future generation.

Although "Black Is Beautiful" is cleverly contrived, it is replete with a sense of irony. Its conclusion suggests that moral outrage and inflammatory words tend to give way to compromises and conservative social change. Silverberg's extrapolation provides a shrewd comment on the sound and fury of revolutionary excitement; unfortunately, its assessment of the human readiness to compromise high ideals is tragically accurate.

One indication of Silverberg's growing maturity as a short story writer is his ability to present the point of view of protagonists other than white males. This ability to enter into imaginative sympathy with a greater diversity of protagonists was extended to sentient animals and plants. In "Ishmael in Love," for instance, Silverberg produced an amusing, but mildly poignant, story of a sentient dolphin who falls in love with a human woman. As in Gordon R. Dickson's story, "Dolphin's Way" (1964), Silverberg's tale postulates an intelligence for dolphins equal or superior to the average human's.[5] By contrast with Dickson's story, "Ishmael in Love" is a more subtle performance, not only mocking human pretensions but presenting the consciousness of a dolphin who is as romantic as any poet, drawing on human literary resources to express his feelings. Nevertheless, though the theme is handled with deftness and tact, a story told by a dolphin that quotes Melville hovers on the narrow line between sentimentality and parody.

In such stories, Silverberg gave imaginative life to the world of inarticulate nature. Another instance is "The Fangs of the Trees," written in 1968 and reprinted in *World of a Thousand Colors* in 1982. Narrated by a plantation manager on a colonial planet who devotes his life to growing sentient trees, this tale suggests that even vegetative life may have consciousness and feeling. However, the consciousness of the trees is implied, rather than shown from inside. Instead, the plantation manager provides the focus; his sensitivity to the world of plants and natural life is suggested by his name, Zen Holbrook (since an initiate of Zen Buddhism must be sensitive to the spirit of life in all aspects of the phenomenal world).

Holbrook regards his "juice-trees" as beings with individual personalities, and has assigned a name to each from Greco-Roman history. Thus the trees are given such names as Plato or Alcibiades, and each has a personality. Holbrook suspects that these "juice-trees" possess an awareness approaching human consciousness, although even he finds this hard to believe. Moreover, the trees have fangs, which they use for protection against predators.

Despite his sensitivity to the personalities in his orchard, Holbrook is in many respects a tough-minded realist in contrast to his romantic niece. Naomi not only communes with the trees but is sympathetic toward all nature. She wishes to pet a "kitten-sized, many-legged furry thing that was twined around an angular little shrub," but Holbrook warns her, "Rule of thumb on this planet. . . . Anything with a backbone and more than a dozen legs is probably deadly" (WTC 249). This conflict between the youthful romantic and the middle-aged realist produces the crisis.

Learning that a sector of the plantation has been infected by plant rust, Holbrook realizes that he must kill all the trees there in order to save the rest. Nevertheless, Holbrook finds this a hard duty, and his task becomes more difficult when Naomi opposes it.

However, she too is obliged to put aside her tender feelings, for Alcibiades, one of the strongest of the trees, attacks Holbrook in self-defense. Against her will, she uses her "needler" on this tree and destroys it. Holbrook's suspicion that the trees are sentient is ironically confirmed when "Alcibiades screamed" (WTC 262). Both uncle and niece share a sense of tragedy at the destruction of their arboreal friends. As the story ends, Holbrook tries to reassure himself that he has not committed murder by destroying the infected trees; for, as he protests to a consoling friend, "Fred, they were trees. Only trees. Trees, Fred, trees" (WTC 265).

This somber story reveals Silverberg's sympathy with nature, especially nature exploited for human production. "The Fangs of the Trees" may also remind us that a major theme of science fiction as well as serious fantasy is the attempt to create mythic works that restore the imaginative life that once resided in the world of nature for poets and artists, particularly Greek and Roman poets. The scientific and Cartesian philosophical revolution of the seventeenth century intensified a psychological split between humanity and nature, reducing nature from a realm of life and magic to an inanimate world of dead matter. Insofar as science fiction is a descendant of Romanticism (via Mary Shelley, Rider Haggard, and H. G. Wells), it has sometimes attempted to heal this split by envisioning various forms of humanized or sentient nature.[6]

Because it presents this alienation of humans from nature as a tragic separation, "The Fangs of the Trees" is a fine story, one of the more underrated in Silverberg's canon. Another strong effort to create imaginative sympathy for a being beyond the reader's ordinary experience is "Something Wild Is Loose," a tale about an alien who inadvertently becomes a menace. This is by no means an original situation, for inventing a mysterious alien menace is almost as old as the genre, and the plot device of such a creature running loose among a small group of frightened humans harks back to John W. Campbell's "Who Goes There?" (1938), A. E. Van Vogt's "Black Destroyer" (1939), and Isaac Asimov's "Misbegotten Missionary" (or "Green Pieces" as Asimov later re-titled it) (1950), all stories of aliens who threaten human life in enclosed situations. However, in "Something Wild Is Loose," Silverberg shows his ability to breathe new life into conventional formulas. Moreover, Silverberg makes his Vsiir, the alien who afflicts the story's starship, into a likable creature, despite its capacity for destruction. The Vsiir is a telepathic and protean shape changer who merely wants to avoid spending too much time on the starship or being forced to reside on earth. Its frustration over the difficulty of making contact with humans creates sympathy. Entering a hospital on Long Island, it tries to enter the minds of doctors and patients. Its efforts cause havoc, for it can only find shelter in people who are asleep and dreaming. Not surprisingly, it causes nightmares and literally frightens one patient to death.

Eventually a doctor establishes a rapport with the Vsiir and persuades it to show itself to humans who can help it. With their aid, it departs for another planet; rather than destroying their enemy, the humans have merely liberated it. Silverberg's story emphasizes the need for cooperation and understanding between life forms. If animals and trees may have understandable feelings, then clearly aliens may be recognizably human in their point of view.

Perhaps the best of Silverberg's sympathetic identifications with the anguish of an oppressed race or different species is "Sundance," a powerful tribute to the repressed and frustrated emotions of a Native American remembering the tragic history of his culture. "Sundance" is one of Silverberg's most successful short stories for several reasons, but especially for its ability to depict Tom Two-Ribbons's feelings. Silverberg's protagonist, a descendant of the Lakota, feels compulsively forced to re-live the genocide of the past during his participation in an experiment that is supposed to be a "ritual extirpation of undesirable beings" on a colony planet (TBORS 230). The victims here are a bovine-like species called Eaters who are killed with pellets dropped from helicopters in order to ready the planet for human settlement. In reality, the Eaters are not sentient, but for a time Two-Ribbons falls under the delusion that they are conscious and highly intelligent, possessing a language, history, and culture.

During this time, Two-Ribbons tries to establish communication with the Eaters and join their "community." Eventually, he turns to the central Lakota (or Sioux, to use the conventional name) religious ritual, the sundance, and tries to achieve a rapport with the Eaters through this ecstatic form of worship. Describing Two-Ribbons's surrender to the Dionysian frenzy of the dance, Silverberg uses superbly evocative imagery:

The Eaters crowd close. The scent of their bodies is fiery red to me. Their soft cries are puffs of steam. The sun is very warm; its rays are tiny jagged pings of puckered sound, close to the top of my range of hearing, plink! plink! plink! The thick grass hums to me, deep and rich, and the wind hurls points of flame along the prairie. I devour another oxygen-plant and then a third. My brothers laugh and shout. They tell me of their gods, the god of warmth, the god of food, the god of pleasure, the god of death, the god of holiness, the god of wrongness, and the others. They recite for me the names of their kings, and I hear their voices as splashes of green mold on the clean sheet of the sky. They instruct me in their holy rites. I must remember this, I tell myself, for when it is gone it will never come again. (TBORS 240)

Nevertheless, the story has a surprising reversal at the end. This hypnotic ritual provides a therapeutic release for Two-Ribbons, and he learns that such a result was precisely the aim of his human companions. For he has been recovering from a breakdown of a year and a half ago, and through treatment with "reconstruct therapy," his doctor has arranged for him to enjoy drug-inspired dreams or trances, wherein he imagines the Eaters to be sentient beings. In theory, his re-creation of his people's tragic history through the sundance and his identification with the Eaters will help to exorcise his trauma.

However, the story's ending is ambiguous, for Two Ribbons has difficulty accepting this reality: his surrender to his obsessive hallucination has been too strong. Hence, he cannot find a firm psychological footing. Each attempt to plant himself on solid ground seems to turn into an illusion that "you fall through," as the final metaphor of the story puts it. This ironic and ambiguous ending heightens the story's art; it implies that Two Ribbons's anguish is too great to be healed as neatly as his therapists wish.

As a re-creation of the tragedy of the American Indian, "Sundance" is an impressive work. An effective work of social criticism that shows a masterful command of language and metaphor, "Sundance" is one of Silverberg's masterpieces.

The earlier periods in Silverberg's career had produced short fiction memorable for satirical bite. However, Silverberg's satirical fiction reached a peak of achievement in stories of the late sixties and early seventies. In several of his best efforts, Silverberg scored off some of his most cherished dislikes: organized religion, overpopulation and the human failure to deal with it intelligently, and modern culture's sophisticated cynicism toward myth. His collections of the late sixties and early seventies, like *Moonferns and Starsongs* (1971), are pervaded with satirical comment on these themes. A discussion of the stories in *Moonferns* illustrates this. In "After the Myths Went Home" (1969), for instance, Silverberg satirizes our society's tendency to use the imaginative achievements of preceding cultures as a kind of cultural entertainment for jaded tastes—an underlying theme also of the comic novel *Up the Line* (1969) where the centuries of Byzantine history and culture become an amusement park for time-traveling tourists.

The narrator of "After the Myths Went Home" is a historian or archaeologist in a distant future society (12,400–450); but his story is reminiscent of the cynicism of the twentieth century. Somewhat poignantly, the narrator describes a world where mythic characters such as Adam and Pan, as well as historical figures like Caesar and Winston Churchill, are brought back from the past by means of a time machine. Each character is observed with amusement for a while, and is then dismissed when his or her audience becomes bored, much as our world uses up media celebrities. The last mythic figure happens to be John F. Kennedy, who views his status as an archetypal hero with bewilderment (and a touch of amusement) when he realizes that his early death led to his identification with dying gods like Baldur. Another late visitor is the melancholy Trojan seeress, Cassandra, who, before her departure, warns the narrator that humanity needs the comfort of myths: " 'You should have kept us,' Cassandra said. 'People who have no myths of their own would do well to borrow those of others, and not just as sport. Who will comfort your soul in the dark times ahead?' " (MAS 31–32). "After the Myths Went Home" uses restrained irony not only to mock the shallow sophistication of technologically advanced civilizations, but to suggest one of the primary values of cultural myths: they provide a potent source of strength enabling a people to survive the "dark times."

An even better testimony to Silverberg's satirical talents is the wickedly funny "A Happy Day in 2381," also in *Moonferns*. This story contains Silverberg's most ingenious conception of a dystopian world. Unlike many dystopias imagined by American science fiction writers, it draws more heavily on the model of Aldous Huxley's *Brave New World* than on George Orwell's *1984*. Huxley's dystopia, and anti-utopia, postulates a society where social tension is eliminated, or reduced to a trivial level, by two means: (1) almost immediate gratification of human wants, especially the desires for social status, food, sexual pleasure, and self-indulgent dreams; and (2) systematic exercises in programming and persuasion, in order to convince the individual that he or she lives in the best society conceivable by the human mind. Although repression and a swift disposal of dissenters are present in Silverberg's story, its world's primary method of dealing with the social tension of overpopulation is to offer readily accessible sex without birth control.

Silverberg's trenchant satirical tale describes a typical day in the twenty-fourth-century life of Charles Mattern, a minor bureaucrat with a wife and four children living in an "Urban Monad" or "Urbmon," a gigantic steel and glass high-rise building that is a self-contained city. The global population is seventy-five billion, and there are 881,000 people in Urbmon 116 alone, a staggering mass of humanity requiring food, shelter, and the assurance that they are special in the eyes of God. However, the twenty-fourth-century world deals with this appalling situation by pretending—and trying to persuade everyone—that copulation, birth, and increasing population are splendid, fulfilling God's highest law. Every day begins with radio music piped into the Urbmon's small apartments, and a ritualized invocation of the deity blessing motherhood and fatherhood. All are enjoined to have a "happy day," a banal wish that represents Silverberg's oblique satirical comment on the obsessive modern American concern with cheerfulness and daily pleasantries.

During the "happy day" described in the story, Mattern, a "sociocomputer," takes a visiting anthropologist from Venus on a tour of the Urbmon. It becomes clear that population growth is not only encouraged, but insanely exhorted as a perverse form of worship. Procreation without restraint provides a release of psychological tension, an escape valve for feelings that would otherwise produce enormous frustration and doubtless destructive rioting. Not only is one's own wife available to another male in the grip of lust, but so is any wife on the floor—a satirical enlargement of the convenience of sex in Huxley's *Brave New World*, where "everyone belongs to everyone else."

This "happy day" ends with a tragedy when one of Mattern's fellow dwellers on Level 799 becomes irrational and encounters the iron discipline that lurks behind the facade of good cheer in this pretended utopia. The young neighbor attacks his wife, but is quickly subdued and judged antisocial. Shortly thereafter, he is fed to the "converter" chute, which destroys him and recycles his substances. For those who find overcrowding, lack of privacy, and absence of individual purpose intolerable enough to create hysteria, retribution is swift.

At the end, Mattern reflects on the young man's rebellion and his own inner discontent: he is restless enough to go "nightwalking" and find solace with another man's wife, but he realizes that he cannot allow himself to think about his dissatisfactions, or his own shaky equilibrium may be upset. His final thoughts are in conformity with the desired social attitudes: "God bless, he thinks. It has been a happy day in 2381, and now it is over" (MAS

20). Thus Silverberg's story ends on a note of supreme irony, reaffirming the satirical tone of the entire work. It is a depiction of the horrors of an overpopulated earth, and humanity's abysmal ineptitude in dealing with this problem. "A Happy Day in 2381" is a brilliant dystopian story, far surpassing, I think, its competitors on this theme. It is a small masterpiece.

Many of Silverberg's other stories have a strongly satirical bent, but the more notable are less consistently dominated by the acerbic tone that pervades "A Happy Day in 2381." In two of the stronger ones, the drama concerns characters for whom the readers feel more sympathy than they did for Charles Mattern and his fellows. "How It Was When the Past Went Away," (1969), for instance, is a long and sometimes poignant novelette in *Earth's Other Shadow* (1973) depicting a future when a number of characters are afflicted by loss of memory. This story becomes more than a speculative exercise about the loss of the past; it dramatizes the concept that identity is largely defined by memory. Hence the appeal of loss of memory: amnesia enables those who find their identity a burden to enjoy the pleasure of a flight from self and an escape from responsibility. However, the satire here is tinged with compassion.

The second fine satirical story is also about the acceptance of responsibility. "The Pleasure of Their Company" (1970) a gem in *Moonferns*, is a fable about a would-be revolutionary who is fleeing from certain death and martyrdom while attempting to rationalize his action as a courageous choice. This work offers a sardonic comment on the ease by which people can practice self-deception and build comforting illusions about self-serving conduct. A secondary theme is the absurdity of creating a simulation of Plato or Goethe for our amusement or companionship, as the protagonist does, hoping to forget his fellow rebels. "The Pleasure of Their Company" reduces to absurdity the notion that great minds could be replicated by a mechanical computer program.

These stories reveal Silverberg's extraordinary talent for satire, which reached a level of excellence during this period. In the short fiction of the next few years, however, he would display further evidence of growth by exploring experimental anti-narrative forms.

Silverberg's experimental short fiction mainly appears in two volumes published in the seventies, *Unfamiliar Territory* (1973) and *Capricorn Games* (1976). Although Silverberg produced many fine collections of shorter fiction in rapid succession in these years, including *Moonferns and Star Songs* (1971), *The Reality Trip and Other Implausibilities* (1972), *Earth's Other Shadow* (1973), and *The Feast of St. Dionysus* (1972), *Unfamiliar Territory* and *Capricorn Games* are his most daring and original ventures in this form. Silverberg's achievement here has not been entirely overlooked: his mastery of irony in the construction of his shorter fiction, particularly in some stories of *Unfamiliar Territory*, has been ably described by Joseph Francavilla (RSMT 59–72). However, the technical innovation and thematic concerns of these tales have not been fully appreciated.

The title metaphor of *Unfamiliar Territory* suggests the direction that Silverberg takes in this collection, for he tries to break new ground both in subject and narrative form. The prevailing tone is one of detached and sophisticated irony at the expense of human pretensions, an irony sometimes balanced with a compassionate mood of sorrow over a planet whose beauty and resources are being wasted. However, concern with tricky innovation and verbal pyrotechnics is not only prominent but acknowledged in the Introduction, where Silverberg shows an understandable pride:

The tracers of literary influences will have much to deal with in *Unfamiliar Territory*. They'll easily discover the place where I tip my hat to Alfred Bester, and where I tug my thinning forelock for Philip K. Dick; but more astute critics are apt to notice several salutes to Donald Barthelme, one or two for Jorge Luis Borges, and an all out hip-hip-hurrah for Robert Coover. (But nobody is likely to guess that one story owes its being to the poet Armand Schwerner, so I acknowledge the debt here: but for Schwerner's brilliant cycle, *The Tablets*, there would have been no "Some Notes on the Pre-Dynastic Epoch." I hope Schwerner finds this out some day.) (UT xi)

Such a generous recognition of predecessors and influences is agreeable, but it may show a certain anxiety about an enormous debt to the creators of the "new" fiction—Coover, Gass, Barthelme, and above all, Borges. In point of fact, the influence of Bester and Dick does not seem very great, or at least it is scarcely more noticeable than in the earlier Silverberg. However, it would be difficult to imagine the existence of *Unfamiliar Territory* in its current form if such books as Coover's *Pricksongs and Descants* (1969) or John Barth's *Lost in the Funhouse* (1968) had not preceded it. This is an illustration of literary influence at its most powerful, as opposed to a search for minor echoes or variations on another writer's theme.

The short stories in *Unfamiliar Territory* might fairly be given the title of "metafiction," a term coined by Robert Scholes in *Fabulation and Metafiction* (1979). As Scholes describes it,

Metafiction assimilates all the perspectives of criticism into the fictional process itself. It may emphasize structural, formal, behavioral, or philosophical qualities, but most writers of metafiction are thoroughly aware of all these possibilities and are likely to have experimented with all of them. When extended, metafiction must either lapse into a more fundamental mode of fiction or risk losing all fictional interest in order to maintain its intellectual perspectives. The ideas that govern fiction assert themselves more powerfully in direct proportion to the length of a fictional work. Metafiction, then, tends toward brevity because it attempts, among other things, to assault or transcend the laws of fiction—an activity which can only be achieved from within fictional form. (Scholes 1979, 114)

Whether or not Silverberg's experimental fiction really attempts to "transcend the laws of fiction," it does reveal a weariness and impatience with the conventions of narrative, as Silverberg himself concedes. Both in form and thematic content, *Unfamiliar Territory* assaults dogmas; as we have already noted, the stories tend to reflect the disenchanted and apocalyptic mood of the early seventies. In that decade, influenced in part by the "new wave," other science fiction writers were drawn to similar experimental forms.[7]

When we turn to the individual pieces, we find that the tone of an era closing and situations involving impending disaster predominate. In "Caliban," for instance, a survivor from our time finds himself an anomaly in a changed world where everyone has been surgically and chemically altered to fit a stereotype. Reality seems to dissolve completely in the highly ironic "What We Learned in This Morning's Newspaper"; with greater irony, affluent tourists arrange time travel trips to a future when humans have perished in "When We Went to See the End of the World." Another ironic and ambiguous tale, "Some Notes on the Pre-Dynastic Epoch," describes the present from the point of view of a person who is either an archaeologist from the distant future, or someone who pretends to be; but whatever the case, present human reality has long since vanished and is being reconstructed as an archaeological project. The final story in the volume, "The Wind and the Rain" (an obvious allusion to Feste's song in *Twelfth Night*), is genuinely elegiac when it describes an earth without humanity, perhaps evoking memories of Ray Bradbury's similar story in *The Martian Chronicles*, "There Shall Come Soft Rains." Imagery or scenes implying the end of the modern era also appear in some of the other stories.

What conclusion is to be drawn from all this? Clearly the underlying mood of the volume is an apocalyptic one, although the apocalyptic themes emphasize defeat rather than a triumphant new beginning. None of the stories promises any kind of "new heaven and new earth" in the miraculous and transcendental form described in the last book of the Bible; instead, they merely present a world from which humanity, in its present incarnation and follies, has vanished.

The individual stories vary considerably in type, and most of them exhibit technical innovation or an unusual narrative mode of the sort Scholes associates with "metafiction." A brief glance will illustrate this point. The first, "Caught in the Organ Draft," describes a not-too-distant future when young people await a conscription notice requiring, instead of military service, one of their organs for organ bank storage in readiness for future transplants. This slight story is told from the point of view of a diary of a young man awaiting his summons. Although he contemplates flight or rebellion, and reflects on ancient styles of cannibalism, he accepts his fate when asked to donate a kidney. In fact, the narrator has been practicing self-deception, we realize, for despite all his thoughts of rebellion, he acquiesces to the demands of the establishment, persuaded by the lure of money and special treatment.

The next story, "Now + n, Now − n," is somewhat more complex, since it deals with a theme Silverberg had toyed with in the early *Stepsons of Terra*, and later used for comic effect in *Up the Line*, namely the replicating of selves through time travel. The hero of this story is a trickster who has arranged to get another self two days ahead of his normal self, and a self two days behind; by sending telepathic messages from one self to another, the three—who are called "Now," "Now + n," and "Now − n"—are able to make a killing in the stock market and in other financial activities. Unfortunately, complications arise when one of the hero's selves falls in love with the seductive Selene, whose presence interferes with the telepathic communication he uses with his other selves. Forced to choose between the narcissistic pleasure of constant communication with the other selves, and life with his newfound love, the hero reluctantly opts for the latter. At the close, he expresses a forlorn hope that by learning her telepathic powers, he may also regain his own skills, and once again meet his replicas.

This work contains more comedy than undiluted irony, but much of its strength comes from the sophistication of the narrative mode. Silverberg's trickster narrates the story in a lively style, rendering the action in a series of scenes with ironic comment. In addition, Silverberg's technical skill is shown as he describes the events as a series of present happenings rather than in a linear retelling of past action.

Another story, "Some Notes on the Pre-Dynastic Epoch," takes a look at our current terrestial culture from the point of view—ostensibly—of an archaeologist of the future in the "Dynastic" period. This story alternates between comment on the past and brief glances at the narrator's present; much of the narrative consists of fragments of literary works, news stories, and other examples of the printed word in contemporary culture. One of the most ironic of these is a news report on President Nixon's secretary of defense, Melvin Laird, dedicating a small room in the Pentagon "as a quiet place for meditation and prayer" during the height of the Vietnam War (UT 40). Moreover, the story is accompanied by other news releases that make anomalous companions for it.

The use of these items, which the narrator views as cultural artifacts, shows Silverberg's effort to incorporate into fiction many verbal constructs from the world of "normal" reality. However, the most significant quotation is a long passage from the biblical book of Daniel, wherein Belshazzar's empire is judged and condemned by the angelic handwriting on the wall: "Thou art weighed in the balances and found wanting." This statement is a final judgment on an arrogant and luxury-loving empire, appearing in the most apocalyptic book of the Old Testament. In this story it serves as a judgment both on our time and the narrator's time (if they are indeed different).

Yet perhaps the narrator's time and our time are the same and the narrator is a person from our era merely pretending to speak from a distant future. Silverberg creates this possibility by a deliberate self-reflexive use of ambiguity. At one point, the narrator writes, "None of the aforegoing is true. I take pleasure in deceiving. I am an extremely unreliable witness" (UT 30). Later, at the story's close, the narrator goes further:

Let me unmask myself. Let me confess everything. There is no Center for Pre-Dynastic Studies. I am no Metalinguistic Archaeologist, Third Grade, living in a remote and idyllic era far in your future and passing my days in pondering the wreckage of the Twentieth Century. The time of the Dynast may be coming, but he does not yet rule. I am your contemporary. I am your brother. These notes are the work of a pre-dynastic man like yourself, a native of the so-called Twentieth Century, who, like you, has lived through dark hours and may live to see darker ones. That much is true. All the rest is fantasy of my own invention. Do you believe that? Do I seem reliable now? Can you trust me, just this once? (UT 44)

This confession is followed by a series of broken statements, as though the narrator's printer is skipping. The dissolution of narrative illusion is a typical experimental technique. Of course, the final questions only increase the ambiguity, rather than dispelling it.

Similar irony appears in a sardonic indictment of our culture's capacity for self-aggrandizement through expensive decadence in several other stories. "In the Group" does not employ technical innovation, but it satirizes the use of technological innovation to enhance sexual experience. Silverberg postulates the use of electronic communication devices to allow a group of people to share their sexual experiences with each other—evidently a sophisticated lampoon of the seventies interest in group sex. The hero, Murray, unfortunately finds that he is inordinately fond of his chief partner, Kay. Despite berating himself for "atavistic" attitudes and "nineteenth-century" possessiveness, he is unable to change. As he grows more possessive, his lady becomes more and more alienated; eventually she rejects him, and he is expelled from the group after he becomes impotent. His attitude is condemned by fellow members of the group as being one of "exclusivism" and is therefore "sick" and antisocial. The story ends with Murray trying to find a lasting love with a strange woman in another city. Thus the story's closure on an ironic note consolidates the irony of its design.

Probably the most acidulous of these satirical tales is "When We Went to See the End of the World," a story that deepens the satire of the novel *Up the Line*, regarding tourist use of time travel. Here, jet setters of the future make an amusing toy of time travel; travel agencies send them off to enjoy picnics while observing the last days of the planet earth, when life is reduced to a giant crablike being crawling on a desolate beach. The conversation of the tourists is inane; even the mindless crustacean seems less banal.

Similarly, organized religion may become another form of cultural decadence, a substitute for genuine religious experience, or so the amusing story "Good News from the Vatican" implies. The primary religion satirized here is, of course, Roman Catholicism, perhaps the most highly organized and authoritarian religious establishment in world history, and the story focuses on one of the Church's most arcane and celebrated events, the selection of a new pope. A good deal of Machiavellian maneuvering produces a robot pope in Silverberg's story; but one of the characters is solemnly informed that this choice is appropriate for the era of the story for, according to Bishop Fitz-Patrick, "every era gets the Pope it deserves" (UT 101).

A much different kind of experimental "fiction"—to use an Anglicized version of Borges's term, *ficciones*—is "Many Mansions," a short story of multiple time travel narratives that also present alternative versions of reality.[8] An American model for this kind of story is Robert Coover's "The Baby Sitter," in which a narrative situation is developed in a variety of opposing and contradictory ways.[9] In one version, for instance, the baby sitter is seduced; in an alternative narrative, she is murdered by intruders. The consequence of such a group of multiple narratives is to suggest an absurd and surrealist version of an ordinary situation.

In "Many Mansions," Silverberg presents a variety of situations involving Ted, who longs for an affair with the beautiful Ellie; his bitter wife, Alice; and his grandfather, Martin, who has a lecherous yearning for Alice. In one version of the basic narrative, Martin travels backward in time to make love to Alice; but in a variation, Alice travels backward in time to murder Martin, and thereby make certain that Ted is never born. Neither the grandfather nor the wife is especially likeable in any of the continuums, and the husband, while sympathetic, appears rather weak. This variety of fictive situations demonstrates the intensity of complicated family antipathies. Yet the multiple narratives also show that reality may assume an absurd look no matter what choices are made in a given human situation.

"What We Learned from This Morning's Newspaper," by contrast, returns to a familiar mordant satirical tone. Here a suburban neighborhood is excited by the appearance of an edition of a newspaper from next week; but such knowledge of the future is put to its most unimaginative use. Everyone wants to use information on the future stock market to become rich. This is a variation of the theme of "Now + n, Now − n," where splendid gifts, time travel and telepathy, are used for material gain. In essence, Silverberg's protagonists in these stories tend to be a variety of modern Esaus, selling their birthrights for messes of pottage (that is, money). At the end of "What We Learned from This Morning's Newspaper," the characters are punished appropriately, for their knowledge of the future turns to dust, as the newsprint vanishes from the papers, and reality itself seems to dissolve into ambiguity and confusion. Like "Many Mansions," this tale goes beyond mere satire on human greed or malice to suggest that reality itself has an absurd and surrealist quality.

A similar vision is expressed in "In Entropy's Jaws," a long story that is not only the best in the book, but one of Silverberg's finest. Here John Skein, a telepath, tries to put his mental pieces together after a case of burnout following an overload of his mind's circuits caused by making a communications hookup of two other powerful minds. His breakdown has come as a result of hubris, for he had been warned against placing so great a strain on his faculties. Silverberg's narrative is a brilliant example of "metafiction" devices since what could have been a linear narrative is related in a weird series of fragmented scenes, many of them hallucinatory. Time and "entropy" are not to be cheated, for at closure Skein learns that he himself is the skull-faced man, destined to spend much of his life on the desolate planet Abbondanza VI, waiting for his own appearance. Before this ironic epiphany, however, the narrative takes a number of serpentine twists, as Skein visits many of the renowned shrines of earth, like the cathedral of Hagia Sophia. In sum, an ironic vision of a bleak future world is presented through his consciousness. Between narrative segments there are memorable quotations that are expository meditations on the effects of entropy, the latent tendency of all things to wear out. All in all, the story unifies disparate elements effectively.

Unfamiliar Territory ends with "The Wind and the Rain," a poetic and elegiac meditation on a future earth from which human life has vanished. The narrator in this story is a compassionate visitor from another planet who considers how war and pollution, two aspects of human stupidity and arrogance, have left the earth in a state requiring purification. The final irony in this brief story is sharp: rumors of a colony of surviving earthmen in Tibet arouse hope, but when the narrator arrives there, his expedition finds only a robot.

The stories in *Unfamiliar Territory* are uniformly excellent, but there is another achievement of the volume that is worthy of comment. As can be said of only a few story collections, the book achieves a unity greater than the mere sum of its parts. These tales offer an impressive vision of an empty and futile future, when humanity either will have entered a final state of decadence, or will have ceased to exist. Not many short story collections, in science fiction or in conventional literature, succeed in creating the unity of tone and vision characteristic of a novel: James Joyce's *Dubliners* and Ernest Hemingway's *In Our Time* may be invoked as classic examples of this rare achievement, but *Unfamiliar Territory* achieves a similar unity of effect. It is clearly a masterful example of literary virtuosity.

Another imaginative volume of short stories from Silverberg's typewriter is *Capricorn Games*, which the hardcover blurb described as "a master attempt to make unconventional use of the traditional subject matter of science fiction." Although this collection does not attain the distinction of *Unfamiliar Territory*, it includes a number of fine imaginative efforts, as does *The Feast of St. Dionysus* (discussed in chapter 4). While extended comment on these stories might over-emphasize their importance, a recognition of the merits of a few is appropriate. It is significant to note that the stories in *Capricorn Games* are less concerned with narrative experiment than are those in *Unfamiliar Territory*. Yet, these stories are, on balance, equally rich in imaginative wealth and literary allusion. However, the collection, as a whole, does not create the unified effect of a consistent vision. (Both volumes were published later in one 1986 collection, *Beyond the Safe Zone*.)

The titular story, "Capricorn Games," is fairly representative of the volume's strengths. Somewhat surprisingly, it uses a young woman as its center of consciousness, since Silverberg's protagonists tend to be predominantly male. Its drama arises from Nikki's encounter at a party with a philosopher of vast experience, "the celebrated Nicholson, who had lived a thousand years, and who said he could help others to do the same" (CG 3). He is an exponent of Jungian mysticism, who espouses the importance of the mandala symbolism at the heart of Jung's psychology. Nicholson's credo is crystallized in a few memorable sentences:

The essential thing that every mandala has is a center: the place where everything is born, the eye of God's mind, the heart of darkness and of light, the core of the storm. All right: you must move toward the center, find the vortex at the boundary of Yang and Yin, place yourself right at the mandala's midpoint. Center yourself. Do you follow the metaphor? Center yourself at *now*, the eternal *now*. To move off center is to move forward toward death, backward toward birth, always the fatal polar swings; but if you're capable of positioning yourself constantly at the focus of the mandala, right on center, you have access to the fountain of renewal, you become an organism capable of constant self-healing, constant self-replenishment, constant expansion into regions beyond self. (CG 9–10)

At first Nikki and the reader are inclined to view these statements with scepticism, but when a telepath establishes a link between Nikki and Nicholson, enabling her to see into his mind, she confronts his memories of the past thousand years and learns that he has survived by constant self-renewal. Yet the staggering total of his experiences astonishes her, and she finally recoils from Nicholson in horror. The mere thought of living for a thousand years and encompassing so wide a range of experiences is frightening. As a result, Nikki leaves the party with a different fellow, a mediocre man with whom she feels comfortable. Silverberg's theme is the Swiftian idea that longevity might prove a demanding gift, more a burden than a blessing. A secondary theme is Silverberg's speculative look at the potential value of mandala symbolism; his interest is evidence of his persistent quest for transcendental experience.

Another significant story in this volume, "The Science Fiction Hall of Fame," examines the contrasts between conventional realistic fiction and science fiction. The narrator sees himself as a "flesh-and-blood personification of the Science Fiction Hall of Fame" because of his wide experience as a reader (CG 26). Much of the story plays off imaginative scenes from science fiction against his meditations on the genre. Is it "simple-minded escape literature, lacking relevance to daily life and useful only as self-contained diversion?" Or is its true nature "subtle and elusive, accessible only to those capable and willing to penetrate the experiential substructure concealed by those broad metaphors of galactic empires and supernormal powers" (CG 30)? The hero wavers between one view and another, and is sometimes drawn to both opinions at once.

As the story unfolds, pastiches of science fiction adventure continue to alternate with events from everyday life, until at last the protagonist recalls his brief and cynical affair with the wife of a friend. This episode is unflattering to all, but especially to the narrator. In the final analysis, he appears to be a sceptical modern man without roots and values, who finds a momentary release in imaginary adventures in alien universes. Although a sense of irony plays a dominant role in this tale, its theme is the narrator's complete alienation from other humans and the cosmos. In this story and another in the volume, "Schwartz between the Galaxies," Silverberg describes existential anxiety very well, as Letson has pointed out (RSMT 111–114).

Probably the best story in *Capricorn Games* is also one of the most surprising—"The Dybbuk of Mazel Tov IV," a tale in which Silverberg treats Jewish legend lightly, yet also endows it with new vigor in the setting of an alien planet. Here a "dybbuk," or ghost of a man recently dead, takes possession of a Kunivar, or local alien, near a colony of two Jewish communities, a liberal enclave and a closely knit band of Hasidic Jews. The narrator, a complacent liberal, has his smug assumptions shattered by the appearance of the dybbuk, for it resurrects a legend he had thought discredited as mere superstition. Even more astonished is the liberal rabbi, who finds the existence of a dybbuk virtually impossible to accept (partly because, one suspects, the rabbi has worked hard to repress his own latent desire to venerate the old traditions). The dybbuk, something of a comic figure, is peculiarly insistent and obnoxious in its demand for attention, an amusing touch that heightens the comedy. At last, the liberal community is obliged to turn for help to a leader they have despised, the "tzaddik" of the Hasidic community, more a primitive shaman than a rabbi. The tzaddik, Reb Shmuel, a powerful figure with an imposing presence, arrives to perform an exorcism and does it effectively.

The story concludes with comic reversals that allow none of the characters to come off looking morally superior, although all gain a measure of self-respect. Impressed by the tzaddik's command of enormous spiritual power, the Kunivari announce that they wish to become Jews. Unfortunately, the tzaddik can command miracles, but he cannot accept a new idea; he finds the prospect of Jews with six limbs and green fur appalling and stalks off, followed by his Hasidic disciples. Humiliated by the presence of the dybbuk and the tzaddik's successful shamanism, the liberal rabbi and his followers are now able to reassert their sense of intellectual superiority by accepting the aliens as converts to Judaism. Thus all suffer through a humbling process, and all are finally vindicated.

This story is both richly comic and compassionate, and makes amusing use of Silverberg's ethnic heritage. Its warmth and humanity are sufficiently genial to make us wish that Silverberg had written more stories drawing on the rich treasure of Jewish myth and legend.

As a look at these stories demonstrates, Silverberg's art in *Capricorn Games* is, if anything, often richer and more humane than in *Unfamiliar Territory*. Some of the same qualities are also displayed in the tales in *The Feast of St. Dionysus*, particularly in the title story (discussed elsewhere) and in the final story, "This Is the Road." Indeed, this survey of Silverberg's achievements in short fiction would not be complete without at least a sidelong glance at "This Is the Road."

The novella takes place in some distant future, when humanity has evolved into a number of different forms and animals, or "underbreeds," have attained sentience, much like the mutations in Cordwainer Smith's future history stories.[10] The main action concerns a journey in an "air-wagon" by four oddly assorted creatures called Leaf, Sting, Crown, and Shadow, as they flee from marauders called "The Teeth" to a sanctuary in the mountains. The primitive setting, the tranquil tone, and characters who conjoin human and animal talents give the story a mythopoeic or myth-making aura. The cooperation of the mutants as a team and their final success make this a satisfying work, written in a restrained and disciplined style. This is not a mere adventure story, for "This Is the Road" turns away from the ironic tone of much of Silverberg's short fiction to provide a reassuring testimony of enduring faith in life, even for the strange group who battle for survival here.

To sum up, Silverberg's work in shorter fiction in his first major phase, 1969–74, was overshadowed by the impressive novels he produced during that time. However, he clearly emerged as a master of short fiction in these years, building on experience in the shorter forms during his apprentice and journeyman periods. His achievement as an author of short stories and novelettes during this first mature period is impressive. In fact, it fares well when compared to the better experimental writers of "metafiction" who influenced him, including Barth, Coover, Gass, and Borges.

6

Trial by the Furnace: The Labyrinths of Society and History, 1969–1976

◆

Although much of Silverberg's fiction in his third period was concerned with the quest for transcendence, as we have seen, and with the frustration of that quest, or with ambiguous answers, his work continued to describe society's flaws and evils. The nature of social existence has engaged Silverberg's imagination throughout his career. His second adult novel, *Master of Life and Death*, described the conflicts of a new administrator who tries to manipulate a world government for the good of humanity. With appropriate symmetry, Silverberg closed out this phase of his career with *Shadrach in the Furnace* (1976), a novel in which his hero uses guile to gain a position of supreme power, allowing him to become an enlightened despot who will attempt to provide universal health care and foster intellectual advance. However, before Shadrach's moment of triumph, Silverberg would examine many injustices and frustratons, including David Selig's self-imposed isolation in *Dying Inside* (1972).

To reach Shadrach's position requires the hero to master the intricacies of the labyrinth, like the Greek hero, Theseus. In this context, the labyrinth can be seen as a symbol of the maze of modern society—with its history of victimized peoples and ethnic groups seeking justice and restitution. We should not be surprised to discover that the labyrinth is a recurring symbol in much of Silverberg's fiction, and this metaphor, signifying political and social history, will appear frequently in our discussion of his fiction in this context.

A retrospective glance will remind us of Silverberg's varying use of the labyrinth symbol. In *The Man in the Maze*, the labyrinth was a symbol of alienation and the maze of the self. However, John Oxenshuer, in "The Feast of St. Dionysus," finds that the "City of the Word of God" is laid out as a labyrinth of houses and streets, more a sign of mystery than revelation. Again, the symbol will appear in the Majipoor books, where the monarch must eventually retreat to the darkened labyrinth to assume the responsibilities of a moral and spiritual leader, the Pontifex. There the labyrinth becomes a palace, suggesting humility and spiritual wisdom.

Whether the labyrinth is a metaphor for the wilderness of self, the waste of modern society, the confusion of religious quest, the struggle for self-knowledge, or all these, it is a major symbol in Silverberg's mature fiction. Since history, politics, and society are labyrinthine worlds in the social novels of the third period, it emerges as a convenient metaphor for the frustrating problems of society and history.

Two important juvenile novels of this time, *Across a Billion Years* (1969), which is treated here because of its thematic concern with history, and *World's Fair, 1992* (1970), present history and social conflict from a mature perspective. Both are ambitious works on the scale of *The Gate of Worlds*, and their quality enlarges Silverberg's stature as an author of young adult fiction. *Across a Billion Years* is one of Silverberg's most enjoyable novels, and is probably his best juvenile, as Clareson contends (RS 27). Although the book depicts the past as an intellectual labyrinth, it is a maze through which the archaeologist may walk with rational understanding. "History" in this novel is not simply the recorded past, but the longest period imaginable in which intelligent life could have flourished—the "billion years" of the title.

The story is presented as a series of tapes, or "message cubes" (a literary device resembling the letters of the traditional epistolary novel), by a young archaeologist, Tom Rice, on an expedition to find the legendary "High Ones," supposedly an ancient sentient species who were the first to establish a high civilization. Rice's tapes are addressed to his twin sister, Lorie, back on earth. Although Lorie is handicapped and confined to her bed, she is also a telepath who belongs to an interplanetary telepathic network used by space travelers. Because of her close relationship with her twin, Lorie functions symbolically as a Jungian anima figure, and as a symbol of Tom's love for humanity and higher values, as well as being a sensitive receiver of Tom's candid confessions and self-revelations.[1]

The narrative point of view encourages stylistic liveliness: Tom's descriptions are interlaced with amusing twenty-fourth-century collegiate slang invented by Silverberg, such as "zooby" and "chimpo" to describe behavior that twentieth-century young people might call "flaky." At first, Tom is severely critical of his fellow archaeologists, and he expresses unthinking prejudice toward the female android member of the team, Kelly Watchman. As the journey progresses, his attitudes change, and he develops a greater sense of compassion and understanding of his companions, an odd assortment. The major change is shown in his evolving relationship with Jan Mortenson, an attractive young woman of his own age (a pretty and intelligent blond who has a dash of another species in her genetic inheritance). Silverberg's skillful treatment of a gradually evolving romance between Tom and Jan provides an emotional dimension that was new in his young adult fiction.

However, the comic narrative tone and the deftly handled love story serve as a counterpoint to serious archaeology. Since Tom has rebelled against his father's pragmatic materialism by becoming an archaeologist, he sees his profession in the light of romantic adventure. Moreover, Tom recognizes that archaeology, quite as much as the physical sciences, embodies scientific curiosity that is devoted to the sacred vocation of rediscovering the past, the world of lost cities and vanished civilizations described in Silverberg's non-fiction. For Tom, as for Indiana Jones, archaeology becomes a religion.

The expedition's search for the original sentient species takes them from planet to planet, with fresh finds providing excitement. On one world, Tom unearths by sheer luck a globe containing an important date; on another planet they find an artifact of the High Ones, a highly intelligent robot made millions of years ago, which still functions. The robot, in turn, reveals that the High Ones left his planet only within the last seventy million years, and tries to locate the star where their home planet is located. The star seems to have vanished until the robot solves the mystery: it is revealed that his masters, the High Ones or *Mirt Korp Ahm*, have hidden their star and its system by means of a "Dyson sphere," using an advanced concept of physics.

This revelation is followed by a visit to the home world of the High Ones, which the expedition names "Mirt." The *Mirt Korp Ahm* are found to be still living, rather than extinct as experts had thought; but they exist in a "zombie-like" state of advanced senility, in which they are sustained by life support machines. Unlike humans, they are a passive species that long ago had reached a satisfactory level of civilization and then withdrew from active contact with other life forms.

Contact with the High Ones leads to the kind of treasures adolescents dream of finding. Tom's expedition discovers most of the artifacts of their civilization intact, and in this windfall they come upon what Tom considers to be the greatest prize: a device enabling humans to communicate with each other telepathically. Tom hails this machine—the "thought amplifier"—as the solution to the problem of human loneliness and cosmic alienation that afflicts all except telepaths. Preparing to don the "thought amplifier" apparatus, he reflects: "All my life had been only a prologue to this moment, all the years of being incomplete, isolated, cut off. Now I saw a chance to become complete after all" (AABY 243). It should be noted that Tom's self-revelation to his sister represents a desperate need to find psychic wholeness through communication, a recurrent theme in Silverberg's fiction. Tom acknowledges that his narrative of the journey has, ironically, been rendered obsolete because he can now communicate telepathically with Lorie, and in the process of doing so, he is startled by his discovery that his twin, though handicapped, has lived a much fuller emotional life than he because of her gift for telepathic communication.

Thus the novel ends with an epiphany, a moment of understanding, revealing the need for human wholeness and unity, the obsessive theme that inspired *Nightwings* and other speculative religious fiction discussed earlier. All things considered, *Across a Billion Years* is not only Silverberg's best juvenile, but remains possibly one of the better science fiction novels for young readers. It contains humor, a dash of romance, fine characterizations, a lost race, excellent writing, a provocative discovery, urbane tolerance, erudition about science and archaeology, and a mature theme.

As we have noted, Silverberg had already used the "lost race" theme in an early juvenile—a slight performance called *Lost Race of Mars* (1960). In that little tale, two children emigrate with their father and mother from earth to a colony on Mars and discover "Old Martians" still surviving in a cave. In some respects this was a faint sketch of the theme of *Across a Billion Years*.

Nevertheless, Silverberg got a good deal of mileage from his idea of a lost race of "Old Martians": he returned to it in a satirical 1964 novel for adults, *Regan's Planet*, and would use it for a third time. In *Regan's Planet*, a Machiavellian promoter, Claud Regan, had undertaken the job of developing a world's fair to open in 1992. To raise money for this grandiose scheme, Regan had kidnapped some "Old Martians" and had them brought to the satellite as attractions. The novel was not reissued, partly because, as Silverberg wrote in an introduction to its sequel, much of its future history was dated (WF1992 viii). Moreover, the novel lacked sympathetic characters and a consistent focus for its satire.

However, the sequel to *Regan's Planet*, *World's Fair, 1992* (1970), is a juvenile of high quality. This book returns to the satellite world of the world's fair and to the Old Martian theme once again, but with more assurance. Silverberg's hero, Bill Hastings, an All-American type, wins an essay contest for which the prize is an appointment to the scientific staff overseeing the Old Martians at the World's Fair, located on a space satellite. Hastings, who has the ambition of becoming a xenologist (a scientist who studies aliens), had taken first place by hypothesizing the possibility of life on Pluto, despite the high odds against it.

While living on the satellite world before the fair opens in 1992, Hastings enlarges his awareness of other matters. Discovering the professional jealousies among scientists and the ethical compromises they make because of ambition, he loses his naiveté. Hastings also engages in a flirtation and a short romance with Emily Blackman, an audacious and spoiled debutante, the daughter of Senator Blackman.

After the mild social comedy of the early and middle portions of *World's Fair, 1992*, the action rises to more dramatic levels. With the fair in financial trouble, Claud Regan makes another of his spectacular gambles by sending an expedition to Pluto to find the intelligent life postulated in Bill's essay. Naturally, Hastings is selected to be one of the explorers who go to the "rim of the solar system." In an effective action sequence, Bill and the scientists voyage to the frozen world of Pluto, locate gigantic crablike life forms, and bring them back to general acclaim. This discovery creates the sensation the fair needs, and Bill becomes a celebrity.

However, the novel ends on a more realistic note. Bill is disappointed to learn that while he was away, his spoiled girlfriend, Emily, has decided to marry an old childhood sweetheart. He reflects, ruefully, at the story's close that middle-class American boys who appear to enact the American dream are not always rewarded by marriage to beautiful rich women. Moreover, he faces a future of arduous study before becoming a professional scientist.

Here again, Silverberg produced an impressive young adult novel that shows the hero's growth toward emotional and moral maturity. Although not as speculative as *Across a Billion Years*, *World's Fair, 1992* contains a mature wisdom—a surprising change from the usual science fiction novel for adolescents. Probably *World's Fair, 1992* would have had a higher reputation if it had not been overshadowed by the excellence of other Silverberg novels. In both of these young adult works, Silverberg leads younger readers to confront serious moral questions.

Although Silverberg's juveniles raise serious moral and social issues, the form allowed him to offer some comforting answers. In the comic and satirical time travel novel, *Up the Line* (1969), the protagonist's chief fault is his refusal to confront moral questions seriously. The early novel, *Stepsons of Terra*, played amusing games with the possibilities of time travel; and time travel also provides the basic premise for *The Time Hoppers*, a tired dystopia, and *The Masks of Time*, a serious and realistic novel. Silverberg continued to work variations on the theme of time travel in *Up the Line* (1969).

By contrast with earlier time travel novels, *Up the Line* is lively and ingenious, but it remains a light and satirical novel. *Up the Line* takes as its premise a twenty-first century where travel to the past is a routine tourist activity, controlled and regulated by a government agency called the Time Service. The narrator, a bored and adventurous youth, Judson Daniel Elliott III, has joined the Time Service to escape twenty-first-century ennui and to learn more about Byzantine culture, a subject he dreams of studying at the doctoral level at an Ivy League university. Elliott is one of Silverberg's fully developed trickster heroes—a type Silverberg had experimented with in earlier books.

The confidence trickster is, of course, an archetypal comic hero in the myths and legends of primitive peoples, as Paul Radin's famous study of American Indian mythology shows. We should note that this type entered sophisticated Middle Eastern and European literature at an early period, appearing in the Old Testament in the stories of Jacob and in Greek epic in the character of the immortal Odysseus. As a character in comic fiction and drama, the trickster is a commonplace figure, taking the roles of clown, tricky servant, and even hero.[2]

At any rate, *Up the Line* describes a rogue's "progress," in a picaresque and entertaining tale that never quite reaches the level of Silverberg's best work. Perhaps this is because Elliott never becomes wholly sympathetic. Elliott is an amoral rascal who has numerous sexual misadventures, most of which are described in an urbane tone. However, Elliott is simply a grandiose tour guide who takes tourists back into the past—or "up the line," as he calls it—to witness the legendary moments of history.

As we expect, this wise-cracking first-person narrator takes us through a series of comic adventures, usually involving liaisons with attractive women, while conducting tourists to different eras in Byzantium's long history. Finally, Elliott makes the mistake of developing an obsession with a voluptuous young Greek woman. While carrying on this intrigue, he commits the unforgivable sin of "replicating" himself, whereupon his error puts him in disgrace, destroys his career, and makes him the target of the dreaded Time Patrol. Consequently, Elliott's narrative ends in mid-sentence: it was being dictated to a taping machine and presumably his existence has been canceled by the Time Patrol, secret agents who punish those who abuse time travel.

Thus this satirical novel ends with a touch of sardonic irony at the narrator's expense. Although Elliott is an entertaining narrator, he displays a sexist attitude toward women and a frivolous view of the past. As a result, we do not really care about his fate. Silverberg's irony, in fact, distances the author from his narrator, a matter overlooked by Rafeeq O. McGiveron, who justifiably complains of Elliott's sneers at homosexuals in an essay on Silverberg's treatment of sexuality (McGiveron 40–41). Elliott's fate, in fact, is symbolic: he tries to make history his playground, but eventually his lack of moral seriousness leads to his justified removal from the maze of history.

Whatever one thinks of *Up the Line*, this novel, like Silverberg's earlier time travel stories, makes a genuine contribution to science fiction tradition. These works reveal the ambivalence toward historical time that Andrew Gordon perceives in Silverberg's time travel tales, and which he finds demonstrated in Silverberg's fine short story "In Entrophy's Jaws." Gordon's 1982 essay in *Extrapolation*, "Silverberg's Time Machine," is a valuable study of this short story and of the different ways in which Silverberg treats the concept of time in his work.[3] The paradoxes of time travel, however, remain secondary to comedy and social satire in *Up the Line*: neither Elliott nor the tourists he shepherds display a serious attitude toward history.

In a more serious novel, *Tower of Glass* (1970), Silverberg created a future historical situation with dramatic social conflict, indirectly reflecting some of the tensions erupting in the late 1960s. *Tower of Glass* is a strong and frequently poetic work that moves beyond the ironic limits of Silverberg's shorter fiction or of his much admired *Dying Inside*. As a tragic novel whose excesses resemble those in a Jacobean drama, *Tower of Glass* is not a flawless work of art, but its passion and excesses are evidence of imaginative vigor. To use another comparison, the novel is occasionally reminiscent of a twenties silent film classic—Fritz Lang's *Metropolis* is the obvious parallel—in its conscious employment of biblical archetypes and potent religious icons to project a vision of an unjust society where technological innovations are extrapolated to inhuman extremes, and where a working class is exploited.[4]

As with Silverberg's best fiction, the novel makes use of familiar motifs but invests them with new force. Simeon Krug, one of Silverberg's arrogant imperialists and self-made millionaires, is a developer of androids who have human bodies and minds that are human in most respects. Since Krug's corporation exploits them, and since their legal status is merely that of property, Silverberg focuses on the theme of the androids' need to be recognized as human. This theme is combined with a study of Krug's arrogance. Determined to build a gigantic tower of glass bricks in the frozen wastes near Hudson Bay, Krug sacrifices all, including his feelings and his family, to his purpose. The structure will not be a mere monument to his power: it is intended to provide a more effective means of communication with a distant star system where life may exist. Both labor and technological expertise for the tower's construction are supplied by Krug's androids, who are being used in the manner of the slaves who built the pyramids of Egypt, or the African slaves who supported the antebellum economy of the Old South.

In such a situation, oppressed people look for a deliverer and Krug's chief android, Thor Watchman, the superintendent of the project, longs to become his people's Moses. Unfortunately, he also tends to idolize Krug as a father or creator figure. Although Krug is a ruthless man of pure will, like the technocratic manager, Jon Fredersen, in *Metropolis*, Krug's romantic son Manuel is a sensitive reformer, resembling Fredersen's son, who was a sentimental humanist. Both feel moral sensitivity for exploited workers, and both are driven by a deep longing to help them. Manuel's sentiments are stimulated into action under the influence of a beautiful android mistress, Lilith, although her true love is Thor Watchman. However, Watchman is restrained by his devotion to the official android religion, a synthesis of meliorist elements from Judaism, Christianity, and Buddhism, all focused on the worship of Krug, the creator and supposed redeemer of the androids.

Watchman is always careful to explain that he worships the idea of Krug as a powerful creator and that the earthly Krug is only a manifestation of this idea; but in actuality he tends to venerate Krug the person and expects him eventually to liberate the androids from their slavery. Hence Watchman ignores the activist androids who have created the Android Equality party. Neither Manuel nor Watchman can persuade Krug to change his conviction that androids are inferior beings, virtually a different species who deserve their status as slaves.

Finally, when Watchman undergoes the experience of "shunting" or temporarily exchanging egos with another person, he learns how intractable Krug's attitudes are and informs the followers of the official android faith that there is no hope for relief from their supposed redeemer. Android servants and slaves respond with worldwide rioting and acts of defiance, and Watchman avenges the shattering of his illusions by having his workers melt the polar ice around Krug's tower, causing the tower to collapse. Furious at the destruction of his power fantasy, Krug retaliates by killing the unresisting Watchman, hurling the android into the transmat field—used for teleportation—without the proper preparation, thereby disintegrating Watchman's molecules. After this act of revenge, Krug abdicates his power, leaving his son Manuel in charge of the remnants of his empire amid worldwide chaos, and sets off for a distant galaxy in a starship he has been constructing.

Although such a bare summary recounts the often melodramatic action of the novel, it scarcely does justice to its emotional impact. As we have noted, the conflict between Manuel Krug and Simeon Krug over the treatment of the androids echoes the conflict between Fredersen and his son Freder in Fritz Lang's silent film classic, *Metropolis* (1926), and the anguish of the androids is similar to the miserable state of the workers in that film. Silverberg's novel differs from *Metropolis*, however, in that it does not postulate a loving feminine principle (the film's Maria) to reconcile the overbearing father and the rebellious son. However, since the happy ending of *Metropolis* is unconvincing to thoughtful viewers, Silverberg probably deserves credit for resolving this struggle in a more realistic fashion.

Silverberg's major characters are drawn with bold strokes, suggesting a conscious use of archetypal figures. Simeon Krug, for instance, is both a familiar type in the Silverberg canon and a tyrannical dictator who suggests numerous biblical analogues. The ruthless industrialist is reminiscent of the dominating Machiavellian figures in Silverberg's earlier work, such as Minner Burris of *Thorns* and Charles Boardman of *The Man in the Maze*. Ultimately, all of these symbolic embodiments of pure ego and ruthless figures would be consolidated into the nightmarish tyrant Genghis Mao of *Shadrach in the Furnace*.

Even more interesting are the biblical predecessors of Krug. His desire to build a massive tower reaching into space as a monument to his ego is an obvious embodiment of the hubris associated with Nimrod and other tyrants in the Tower of Babel legend from the antediluvian period depicted in Genesis. Moreover, Krug's exploitation of androids and their inferior status resembles the Egyptian pharaohs' oppression of the Hebrews in the construction of the pyramids, expressing the Egyptian longing for immortality. Since Krug is also, in a sense, the creator of the androids, there is a sharply ironic parallel with the grim creator God of the Old Testament, a mythic analogue reinforced by the android religion developed by such leaders as Thor Watchman. Finally, when Krug destroys Watchman, his creation, and therefore by metaphorical extension his "son," Krug seems to become a brutal parody of the Christian conception of God as a wrathful judge who sends his son Christ to earth to be executed to atone for human sin. A study of such biblical parallels and influences was made by George W. Tuma in an article in *Extrapolation* in the early seventies.[5] Clearly, these mythic parallels tend to enrich the tragic irony of the novel.

Yet Krug also has human weaknesses and his humanity serves to counterpoint his ruthless and overbearing will; but his humane feelings are subordinated to the essential inhumanity of his actions and his self-glorifying vision. Even in his relinquishment of power at the novel's end, Krug does not fully elicit the reader's sympathy, and the strongest negative judgment to be made of him is to apply a comment often made about Mary Shelley's Dr. Frankenstein: just as Frankenstein's monster, his creation, is more human than Frankenstein, so too are Krug's androids more human than Krug.[6]

A better developed tragic hero than Krug is Thor Watchman, surely one of the finer android characters in science fiction. Watchman is given a full range of human feelings although he did not experience a human childhood, and although he lacks the ability to reproduce himself. Indeed, Watchman believes that he does not have the usual human male sex drive, but his strong sexual nature only requires Lilith to awaken it. As an alpha, the highest of three levels of android intelligence, Watchman is not only very intelligent, but also an excellent supervisor and leader. However, it is his spiritual aspirations that make him exceptional: while worshiping Krug, he still hopes to be the android Moses, but instead he becomes an android martyr or Christ figure.

While Thor Watchman is a credible tragic hero, and Krug a tragic villain, if not a tragic hero inspiring sympathy, Manuel Krug and Lilith, his android mistress, are also drawn with skill. Since Manuel's name suggests the biblical Immanuel, one of the names given to Christ, it appears that Manuel may have been intended as a Christ figure and a human counterpart for Watchman. Indeed, Manuel plays a Christ-like role for a time, preaching compassion, but he is finally too weak a character to play a memorable role in the climactic scenes of the novel. Here, Manuel is eclipsed by Watchman, and he remains a passive observer while Watchman is martyred by Krug's wrath.

Yet Manuel's experience is a significant part of the novel, and Silverberg is sufficiently concerned with this character to shift the narrative style to the first person for important scenes involving Manuel, the most notable instance being Manuel's trip with Lilith to the android ghetto, Gamma Town. This descent of Manuel and Lilith to the world of the most despised social class is one of the central sequences in the novel, representing a symbolic journey to the underworld or through the labyrinth, a ritual ordeal enlarging the hero's awareness in classical epic. Yet Manuel is not entirely satisfactory either as a sacrificial martyr, a role Watchman's sacrifice preempts from Manuel; or in the role of humanitarian reformer, which his father bequeaths to Manuel in the ambiguous ending. Manuel's ability to promote effective social reform remains doubtful.

Lilith is a stronger character than Manuel, although as a tragic protagonist her status is secondary. Given the name of the mythic temptress of Hebraic tradition, she has been constructed as a specialist at providing sexual pleasure; yet she also is committed to the cause of android liberation, which she serves by employing her arts on Manuel. Moreover, she is not merely an adroit mistress: her capacity to love is demonstrated by her relationship with Watchman. Although her name has negative connotations, she is a sympathetic figure, and one of Silverberg's more memorable feminine characters.

Finally, the tower is an impressive icon satirizing the arrogance of modern technological civilization. Different characters refer to it by varying names, from "the first cathedral of the galactic age," to the most prodigious of all phallic symbols (TOG 15). Towers have always been symbols of human pride, and the destruction of this one represents the probable collapse of a technological civilization that is unable to rectify social injustice or to recognize the full equality of its exploited classes. In this respect, the novel shows similarities to Philip K. Dick's *Do Androids Dream of Electric Sheep?* (1968), which probably influenced it, and anticipates *Blade Runner* (1982), the Ridley Scott film inspired by Dick's novel. All suggest that androids are essentially human.

Despite the strengths of *Tower of Glass*, it is an imperfect novel and its flaws are obvious. At times the intense narration seems undisciplined and lacking in restraint, and the novel displays some rough edges. The action is frequently melodramatic; but these flaws are balanced by vitality and moral seriousness. At any rate, the novel is concerned with the exploitation of conscious beings. To describe *Tower of Glass* reductively as a "parable about racism," as John J. Pierce does in *Odd Genre* (152), is an odd comment, facile and perfunctory.

Whereas *Tower of Glass* contains elements of tragedy, there is only sardonic irony in Silverberg's bleakest work of social criticism, which began to appear in serial form in 1970 but was not published in book form until 1971. *The World Inside*, expanding the dystopian vision of the short story "A Happy Day in 2381" to novel length, extrapolates the threat of an overpopulated world to nightmarish extremes. As in the short story (which serves as the first chapter of the novel), the horribly overcrowded, underfed condition of earth is used as the premise for establishing a mindless society where fertility is celebrated as worship of God, privacy is proscribed, and most of humanity is packed into gigantic "Urban Monads," enormous high-rise buildings, each of which is considered a single city. Everyone is programmed to be happy and cheerful, despite the insanity of the lifestyle in these urban towers, or "Urbmons."

Concern with overpopulation had been a persistent theme in Silverberg's career. In *The World Inside*, Silverberg made a serious bid to produce a dystopian satire worthy of comparison with *Brave New World* and *1984*. Because he followed the pattern of a classic dystopia, the novel has received a good deal of respect from such critics as Clareson, although he acknowledges that it is only Mattern who is an effective character (RS 61–63). Unfortunately, despite his mature novelistic skill, *The World Inside* is a rather disappointing book. Silverberg's mastery of plot and narrative technique is present, but literary craft and an important theme cannot offset other weaknesses: thin characters, language that only occasionally rises above mediocrity, and lack of intellectual conflict.

Clearly the Urbmon complex is the "hero-villain" of the novel, as Thomas Dunn and Richard Erlich have pointed out in a fine article in *Extrapolation*.[7] Yet the question arises as to whether the basic situation of overpopulation is not itself the villain. Given an impossibly large populace on earth, the dominant social tone encouraging more breeding and more children (in the name of the Lord, an official policy that shows the debasement of popular religion into a weapon of government propaganda) is obviously institutionalized stupidity carried to lunacy. However, the world described in the novel is a place where social ills have progressed to a condition that almost seems beyond remedy. Hence, Silverberg's social satire is directed not so much against a social system that represses individual freedom and destroys the rights of privacy, as against human stupidity itself, especially the mindless social leadership that has allowed earth's population to reach such proportions.

Consequently, Silverberg's dystopian novel does not create the sense of intellectual excitement and conflict that readers have found in Huxley's and Orwell's classic works. The climactic moments in *Brave New World* and *1984* come when an intelligent rebel against a repressive social order confronts the spokesman for the system: when the Savage encounters Mustapha Mond or Winston Smith meets the party overlords there are dramatic revelations of opposing views. Silverberg focuses on several dissidents, but none seems especially strong. Moreover, in Silverberg's novel, the climactic rebellion is a very different one: it is the defiant act of Michael Statler, who leaves the urban complex and goes into the "world outside" where he lives close to a farming commune and encounters the world of nature. In one of the major symbolic actions of the book, Michael bathes in an irrigation canal, a symbolic baptism that embodies an initiation into a new relationship with nature. Curiously, however, Statler's love for his sister—another case of the romantic incest motif that appears in several Silverberg novels of this period—draws him back to the "Urbmon," where his futile act of individual revolt is punished by the swift termination of his life.

Hence, Silverberg's novel is quite inferior to the dystopian classics of Huxley and Orwell in important respects. While repeating some of the patterned action of those works, *The World Inside* lacks the excitement of intellectual satire and the clash of opposing ideas that we enjoy in those works. No doubt, of course, all dystopian novels are actually satires on popular ideas and social trends of the time when they are written. It is, for instance, generally acknowledged that Huxley was actually satirizing behaviorism, Freudianism, and scientism; and that Orwell, likewise, was satirizing Stalinism and government lying and technological surveillance. However, Silverberg's novel does not appear to attack or satirize significant ideas of the sixties and seventies. To be sure, conformity and the governmental exploitation of a creed combining sex and religion are subjected to ridicule, but such targets generally invite attack.

In an effort to compensate for the novel's flaws, Frank Dietz suggests in a recent essay (RSMT 95–106) that its weaknesses are inherent in the genre of dystopian fiction. This point is arguable, but Dietz's case becomes an ingenious exercise in special pleading when he contends that Silverberg intended to write a "metadystopian work" that would "expose the shortcomings of this genre" (RSMT 104). In this view, Silverberg was actually writing a sophisticated "parody" of dystopian fictions, and his dystopian world is an "ambiguous" one, comparable to parallel works of the same period by Ursula LeGuin (*The Dispossessed*) and Joanna Russ (*The Female Man*). Dietz also contends, rather foolishly, that dystopian works are based on "implicit utopian visions" and "display a trust in stable solutions and an unchanging human nature" (RSMT 104).

Such arguments attempt to evade the seriousness of Silverberg's satire. In reality, Silverberg in *The World Inside* was attempting to renew the conventions of dystopian fiction and attack serious evils—an overcrowded earth, lack of personal freedom, socialized human stupidity. There is nothing particularly ambiguous about the evils of the world of the Urbmon Monads, and one does not need utopian visions to believe that human life can be more rewarding under other conditions. Moreover, we only need to glance at Margaret Atwood's *The Handmaid's Tale* to see that a dystopian novel need not be weakened by inherent conventions. The strength of Atwood's fine novel refutes Dietz's arguments about the weaknesses of the dystopian genre, and reduces his argument to the banal level of the chattering academics in the Epilogue to *The Handmaid's Tale*, who are unconcerned with serious comment on the experiences of Atwood's heroine.

We should note that *The World Inside* does employ a consistent and coherent pattern of symbolism. The Urbmon towers are symbols of human folly and pretension, much as Simeon Krug's gigantic tower functions as a symbol of human arrogance in *Tower of Glass*. The book also abounds in sterility symbols of various sorts, a characteristic feature of dystopian novels. By a clever ironic paradox Silverberg presents both conception and birth as symbols of sterility here, because they add to an already intolerable situation. Yet despite some strengths, *The World Inside* remains a minor work; at best it is merely another epigone of *Brave New World* and *1984*, like Philip José Farmer's *The Lovers* and Ray Bradbury's *Fahrenheit 451*, and it has the misfortune of being duller than either.

Although the Urbmon solution to the problem of overcrowding and exhaustion of the earth's resources had provided an inviting satirical target, Silverberg turned in *The Second Trip* (1972) to suspense melodrama to criticize another proposed panacea for society's ills—the use of drugs and behavioral conditioning to rehabilitate criminals. Here Nat Hamlin, an amoral sculptor who had committed murder a few years ago, is given a new personality as Paul Macy, a gentle, handsome "holovision" commentator for a major communications network. The anti-social ego of Hamlin is supposedly submerged under the persona of Macy, but the hidden and repressed Hamlin plots to seize control of Macy's will, avenge himself on his former lover, Lissa (now Macy's significant other), and resume a life of crime while masquerading as Macy. The Hamlin self does indeed gain control of Macy's will, but is eventually conquered when Macy unexpectedly uses his own deceit.

Silverberg presents this novel as a smoothly written futuristic suspense tale, somewhat in the mode of Philip K. Dick, with Macy's embattled psyche the real center of the action, rather than the suburbia in Florida where the story ostensibly takes place. The conflict between Macy and Hamlin may easily be interpreted as a study of the battle between the Freudian ego and id, or the Jungian ego and shadow. However, such interpretations do not necessarily make the novel stronger because the characters involved in the novel's psychological conflict have not been given sufficient credibility. It seems unlikely that Hamlin and Macy could occupy the same psyche in an unintegrated state, and Lissa's involvement with both characters requires a remarkable "suspension of disbelief." Moreover, the moral issues involved are perhaps more complex than *The Second Trip* suggests.

Clearly, *The Second Trip* has been influenced by Anthony Burgess's *A Clockwork Orange* (1962), and, despite its provisionally happy ending, it seems to offer an equally cautionary view of psychological conditioning— which is also one of the evils (on a larger scale) of *The World Inside*. However, *The Second Trip* appears to be merely a clever exercise on the subject, without the memorable characters and vigorous language of Burgess's classic novel.

The most impressive of Silverberg's novels of social concern is the celebrated *Dying Inside* (1972). To call this novel a work in the tradition of social realism may at first seem illogical, since the narrative is told entirely from the point of view of the introverted and alienated telepath David Selig. This novel combines the science fiction tradition of the telepath with the anguish of the modernist novel of social alienation, stemming from the work of Feodor Dostoyevsky and Franz Kafka. It is especially influenced by the flowering of the American Jewish novel in the fifties and sixties with Bernard Malamud (*The Assistant, A New Life*), Saul Bellow ("Seize the Day," *Herzog*), and Philip Roth (*Goodbye, Columbus, Portnoy's Complaint*). These two traditions are splendidly compounded to produce an original work that has been regarded as a masterpiece—although a few critics, greatly impressed by the realism of *Dying Inside*, have sometimes raised the question of whether *Dying Inside* is actually a work of science fiction. With an impressive feat of the creative imagination, Silverberg envisioned social alienation and existential isolation, which, paradoxically, convey a vivid sense of the social anguish of the lonely and dispossessed in late sixties New York.

In making his protagonist, David Selig, a telepath of limited abilities, Silverberg produced a realistic novel that draws on science fiction tradition to offer an ironic parody of that tradition, as I have suggested elsewhere (RSMT 39–57). In earlier science fiction, telepaths had been people with a special "wild talent," and the telepath was either depicted as a potential superman, burdened by handicaps as in Olaf Stapledon's philosophic *Odd John* (1935) and A. E. Van Vogt's epic melodrama *Slan* (1940 magazine publication; 1946) or as a component in a supposedly emergent higher humanity (the "gestalt" group in Theodore Sturgeon's provocative *More than Human* [1953]).

Stapledon's *Odd John*, a tragic story (in intention at least) of a mutant prodigy struggling against conventional English society, provides the most obvious influential precursor to Silverberg's mutant protagonist, David Selig. Silverberg has acknowledged the importance of Stapledon's work on his early reading, calling it "the quintessential peculiar-little-boy book, a haunting and tragic tale of a child prodigy" (RR 147). In fact, both Silverberg the author and his character David Selig are examples of the talented "child prodigy," and the close parallel between David's experience and Silverberg's is a major reason for the power and intensity of *Dying Inside*. However, unlike Stapledon's *Odd John*, David does not find a group of similarly talented social "misfits" nor is he able to establish a community of them (or even join a community of like-minded thinkers, as Silverberg gained admission to the community of science fiction writers).

Instead, David Selig is a classic depiction of the suffering "schlemiel" or victim figure of modernist literature, and in particular American Jewish modernist fiction. David's relationship with his family resembles that of Kafka protagonists, particularly his conflicts with his sister, and his retreat from society suggests in some ways the fate of Gregor Samsa in Kafka's "The Metamorphosis." Indeed, the spirit of Kafka is invoked in one of the term papers David ghostwrites for another student (an actual term paper Silverberg had written at Columbia, according to the author), as David works at a career that makes him another invisible man, to use Wells's metaphor for the misunderstood and neglected genius. Although David does not imagine himself turned into a giant insect, he has become a completely anonymous "underground man" (to borrow Dostoyevsky's metaphor), both in his personal life and in his professional role as an academic criminal who helps plagiarizing students present fraudulent work. However, it is David's singular gifts and his moral sensitivity that have helped to alienate him.

Yet one of the high achievements of Silverberg's novel arises from the fact that David's gift, the ability to overhear the thoughts of others, helps him to perceive and empathize with other forms of human anguish. Too often, the underground man, the alienated anti-hero of modernist fiction, may seem to be too consumed by self-pity over his tragic predicament (as is perhaps the case with Bellow's Tommy Wilhelm in "Seize the Day"); but Selig's ability to hear the thoughts of others assures his awareness of the general human suffering in the urban wasteland of the New York he inhabits. In fact, *Dying Inside* uses a situation that is the reverse of *The Man in the Maze*: in the latter, others cannot bear the protagonist's telepathic projection of his own emotions; but in *Dying Inside*, the emotions of others add to the protagonist's anguish.

This difference makes *Dying Inside* a much finer novel. Silverberg's work is a model of sustained irony, capped by an appropriately humiliating climax for David with his exposure as a ghostwriter and the gradual waning of his gift. Unlike the super telepaths of science fiction precursors, David is unable to help humanity with his gift, other than by telling his bitter story. There is no need for further discussion of *Dying Inside* here; readers interested in a longer analysis of the novel may consult my essay, "An Ironic Parody of the Superman Myth" (RSMT 39–58). Here, we merely need to recognize that *Dying Inside* presents the anguish of the isolated self lost in modern urban life. David finally accepts life as an ordinary human, but he has lost the hope of finding personal fulfillment or playing the role of a messianic figure for society.

In 1971, Silverberg's writing had begun to decrease in quantity while generally improving in quality, as he set higher and higher standards for himself. As he has acknowledged, the ironic vision of *Dying Inside* and *The Book of Skulls* seemed to have been pushed to its limits with "Born with the Dead."[8] Moreover, the religious and visionary passion that began with *Nightwings* also seemed to be losing force and giving way to the tragic tone of *A Time of Changes*.

However, Silverberg still had not found a way through the labyrinth of politics and history, and a retreat to mysticism had not provided a satisfactory fictional solution. In the two final novels of his third period, he directly confronted the central problem that haunts his fiction in 1971–74: the role of the talented individual and his moral responsibility in the labyrinth of history. The first of these, *The Stochastic Man* (1975), breaks new ground but finally reaffirms the irony of *Dying Inside*. However, Silverberg's final novel of this period, *Shadrach in the Furnace* (1976), gathers together many of the themes of social concern of the third period, while redefining the role of the alienated individual. Here Silverberg would again describe his characters' anguish about the human prospect, but he would move beyond despair to a qualified confidence in the human capacity to survive.

First, however, *The Stochastic Man* was to repeat the pattern of tragic irony that pervades *Dying Inside, The Book of Skulls,* and much of the shorter fiction. In *The Stochastic Man*, Silverberg returns to one of the themes of *Dying Inside*, the ironic condition of the person with a "wild talent" that makes him superior to the social conformist and thereby alienates him from his fellows, yet leaves him unable to help society. As we have noted, this theme is another version of the modernist view of the artist that has dominated literature since the time of Poe, Hawthorne, and Baudelaire, and looms large in twentieth-century poetry and fiction.

Silverberg's protagonist in *The Stochastic Man* is Lew Nichols—a seer who finds it hard to accept his peculiar gift. At first, Nichols is merely a computer wizard who projects probabilities about the future; but after meeting Martin Caravajal, an eccentric recluse, Nichols begins to discover that he himself has the gift of "second sight," and he becomes the "stochastic man." The setting is again the end of the twentieth century (a period of confusion and uncertainty in many Silverberg works, such as *The Masks of Time* and "Thomas the Proclaimer"), and Nichols has been aiding a New York politician, Paul Quinn, in the latter's rise to national prominence. Quinn is another of the Kennedy-style liberals who appear in the final decade of the century and arouse the hopes of younger voters. Nichols learns that Quinn, behind his veneer of liberalism, is ruthless and amoral, and Quinn begins to view Nichols with antipathy when Quinn discovers that his aide has the ability to predict unlikely events.

The irony of the novel lies in Nichols's growing sense of impotence and horror as he realizes that his power to foretell the future does not include the ability to prevent misfortune or change reality. Hence Nichols finally finds himself in a position similar to the mythic Cassandra: he is able to foresee events accurately, but few will believe him, or use his predictions to influence the course of history.

Consequently, Nichols finds that his knowledge of the future is a curse. Foreseeing that Quinn, whom he has come to detest, will be elected to the presidency, Nichols knows his administration will disillusion his followers. Thus, like David Selig in *Dying Inside*, Nichols finds that the burden of his gift outweighs its benefits: to be a seer is to live with a knowledge that destroys hope.

Despite its ironic ending, *The Stochastic Man* is a novel that deserves to be more highly respected than it has been. As Clareson comments, the novel marks a movement forward from "the depths of Selig's anguish" (RS 69), since political action is assumed to have some meaning. Silverberg's handling of the political issues and struggles in the novel is quite competent, and his description of 1990s social life is well imagined. In fact, novels like *The Masks of Time* and *The Stochastic Man* suggest that Silverberg might have been one of America's more durable mainstream novelists of conventional realism and social satire.

Since *Shadrach in the Furnace* was not published until 1976 and did not appear in paperback until 1978, its impact on readers was somewhat delayed; and its importance in Silverberg's canon has been obscured by Silverberg's more widely praised ironic works of the early seventies. Its appearance during a time when Silverberg was in temporary retirement and sometimes voicing his displeasure with the shallowness and superficiality of science fiction may also have hampered the reception of the book. Consequently, the novel's worth and significance have not yet been fully recognized. As we shall see, *Shadrach in the Furnace* closes out Silverberg's third period with a renewal of hope.

The novel is set in yet another grim future, the twenty-first century after biological warfare has devastated the planet and reduced it to a shambles. The earth is now dominated by a shaky empire ruled by a Mongolian despot, "the Khan," who has taken the symbolic name of Genghis Mao. A ruthless brain in a dying body, Genghis Mao is kept alive by life support systems, but his fertile mind and iron will control the earth, with the help of a frightened but efficient corps of administrators and their sophisticated electronic surveillance. This elite class is protected by antidotes from the ravages of the "organ rot" bacteria that flourish throughout the world, and is given many luxuries and *divertissements* to distract them and ease their consciences over the condition of the world. However, they live in a world of paranoia because of the Khan's secret police and his unpredictable caprices. Separated from ordinary humanity by age, disease, and the possession of supreme power, Genghis Mao is a grotesque tyrant who may remind us of narratives of the bizarre rule of Josef Stalin at its worst.

In short, the novel returns to the apocalyptic mood of *Unfamiliar Territory*; its title and main metaphor are taken from Daniel, the most apocalyptic book of the Old Testament. At the center of the conflict is a young idealistic African American doctor, Shadrach Mordecai (one of science fiction's first black heroes), whose knowledge and skill are devoted to keeping Genghis Mao alive. Through one of his lovers, however, Shadrach learns that Genghis Mao intends to have an operation that will transfer his brain into a younger body, thereby ensuring the autocrat of longer life and, since the process may be infinitely repeatable, immortality. Not only will this idea frustrate the hopes of ambitious politicians and idealistic liberals waiting for the tyrant's death, but Shadrach also learns with a numbing shock that his own body will be the youthful shell the Khan will use for his transplanted brain.

From this point on, Shadrach's courage and idealism are subjected to a trial by fire. This period of testing clarifies his sense of reality. Tiring of amusements like the drug palaces that the affluent use to titillate and distract themselves, Shadrach takes a vacation to consider his options. During this leave, he travels around the ruined and ravaged twenty-first-century world, contemplating his own past, the nightmare of world history, and the tragic condition of the present population of earth, wasting away by diseases for which anti-toxins might be produced, if anyone in power cared or was willing to take risks. On this pilgrimage, Shadrach discovers that all people, except the protected elite, face reduced expectations of health and life.

Finally, the journey creates in Shadrach the will to escape his fate as he comes to realize that an enlightened leader can bring some aid for a suffering world. At last, he returns to the capital and decides on a bold stroke, reminiscent of Renaissance men of action. Probably an influence on the story here is a precedent noted by Silverberg in *The Golden Dream*, a history of the quest for El Dorado. In the conquest of Peru, the ruthless conquistador, Pizarro, seized control by the surprise move of capturing the Inca chieftain, and by commandeering the will of one man, he conquered a nation (TGD 32). Though Shadrach serves the cause of humanitarian idealism rather than exploitation, he follows a similar course. Performing an operation on Genghis Mao that enables Shadrach to induce at will an unbearable pain for the Khan, and then implanting the electronic control that produces the stimulus in his left hand, Shadrach gives himself mastery over the master of the world. By closing his left fist, he is able to produce an intolerable pain in nerve centers in Genghis's skull. Unable to resist such pressure for long, Genghis Mao must now follow Shadrach's orders, and any effort to change the situation may result in the Khan's own death.

Thus by a masterful trick Shadrach transforms himself from potential victim and slave into master, and he intends to use his newfound power for humanitarian purposes. His first action, once his authority over Genghis Mao is acknowledged by the Khan, is to set into motion a research project that may produce vaccines to be administered to immunize the treatable sector of the world's population. To be sure, it is too late to save most of the infected adults, but Shadrach can at least attempt to preserve and lengthen the lives of the children and the unborn.

This summary of the novel's action indicates that its plot is essentially a simple one; yet no recounting of the story's outline can suggest its richness of texture or the rewarding experience of reading this book. Silverberg's style, for instance, is mature and restrained, rich in biblical and literary allusion, and distinguished by a masterful use of poetic image.

Equal to the commanding style are the characterizations in *Shadrach*, which are assured and masterful; but every secondary character is subordinated to the conflict between Shadrach and Genghis Mao, and in the final analysis, these two are perhaps the only ones that matter. Each is triumphantly realized and each serves as a foil for the other.

Genghis Mao is the embodiment of dehumanizing tyranny, yet he is a credible and sometimes even sympathetic human being. His name suggests an emperor known for inhuman oriental despotism, yet, ironically enough, the name was chosen by this absolute dictator himself upon his accession to power, presumably to inspire fear and awe. The Khan is an astute and ruthless Mongol, and all human beings are subordinated to his two ends in life: his desire to go on living as long as medical science and technology can sustain his life, and his equally monomaniac determination to have absolute dominance over the world. This despot is the sort of figure who arises in human history in times of chaos and instability, but such rulers justify their absolutism with the dubious claim that they have imposed a kind of order that makes possible a semblance of civilized social life. Though Genghis Mao offers health and stability only for a privileged group of intellectuals and administrators, he has been able to seize power because the "organ rot" war has reduced the Soviet Union and the Western democracies to weak and third-rate powers, allowing the People's Republic of China (or the Chinese empire, in Genghis Mao's hands) to move into the power vacuum.

Although Genghis Mao is in one sense a mythic nightmare monster like the biblical Nebuchadnezzar (which intensifies the strength of the characterization), he is not a cartoon villain, a return to the Fu Manchu archetype of the "yellow peril." Rather, he is a competent ruler with an idea of world order that every person is expected to respect. His age and bodily decrepitude make him almost an incorporeal intelligence that is alienated from the ordinary human passions and sentiments, not to mention the occasional moments of idealism that sometimes compensate in part for the flaws of powerful rulers. Since Genghis Mao intends to succeed himself after his brain is transplanted into a younger body, he even lacks the dynastic urge that usually inspires despotic conquerors to create a family and develop a modest sense of love and kindness. Even Shadrach, his young physician, whose skill eases his pain and keeps him alive, is only a means to an end for Genghis Mao. Although at times, the Khan seems to treat Shadrach with the kindness of a father viewing a talented son, this kindness is a mask for the contempt in which Genghis Mao holds other mortals. Nevertheless, Silverberg humanizes Genghis Mao by revealing his mind in several stream-of-consciousness passages that are impressively written. Finally, however, the Khan is "alien, mysterious, unfathomable, ultimately inscrutable," as Shad-

rach sees him (SITF 247). In short, Genghis Mao is a character who sur-
passes the sinister men of will in Silverberg's earlier fiction by becoming
both a mythic archetype of the historical tyrant and a credible character in
the mimetic mode of fiction.

Shadrach is also a well-developed character. It is not easy to make a vir-
tuous and idealistic character come alive in fiction, and frequently such characters, even when credible, turn out to be fools or prigs who forfeit our
sympathy. Shadrach, however, is characterized effectively as a genuinely humane protagonist—mainly through his growth during his struggle with his
dilemma. If a moral idealist is capable of taking action in a complex historical
situation, then what form should the action take? This question is Shadrach's
problem, and it has never before been confronted quite so thoughtfully in
Silverberg's fiction.

As a doctor, Shadrach is committed to a humanitarian creed that eschews
violence, and as a young black man, he has sympathy for the oppressed,
although his own background has been a fairly fortunate one. Yet his career
has been a steady series of successes thus far, and his idealism has not before
been subjected to a serious moral testing. As a member of the educated elite
with a favored position in the Khan's government, Shadrach has found a
place where he not only enjoys immunity from the world's diseases but is
also—until he learns of the Khan's plans for his body—shielded from much
of the world's suffering. Like other members of the Khan's administrative
bureaucracy, Shadrach enjoys the privilege of belonging to a fortunate elite:
he enjoys pleasures with his two female lovers and the diversions offered by
the reconstructed pleasure city of Karakorom, like the drug-induced fantasies
of the "transtemporalists" who can "transport" their clients to another time
and place. Before being confronted with the threat of death, Shadrach
moves between the poles of a moderate humanism and a restrained hedon-
ism.

As a humanitarian doctor, Shadrach, the personal physician to Genghis
Mao, is supposedly in a position that is not only enviable because of its
rewards, but also from a moral point of view. For Shadrach only needs to
practice his profession well and tend to the Khan's illnesses in order to carry
out the commitments to his professional ethics and his own Christian creed.

However, the moral innocence of Shadrach's position turns out to be as
illusory as his supposed security. When Shadrach learns of the Khan's plan
to destroy him and take his body for himself, Shadrach can no longer avoid
existential commitment or action. Yet the nature of the action may involve
violation of Shadrach's principles.

Here, however, the novel moves beyond mere suspense melodrama by
enlarging Shadrach's personal crisis to a concern for the anguish and suffering of the entire globe. The interweaving of these two themes is masterful. This expansion of the novel's conflict takes place during Shadrach's leave
of absence, during which he goes on a world tour and visits its troubled

cities. His trip is in actuality a journey downward into the inferno or labyrinth of the world's suffering, as he sees the diseased wasting away from the
blight of "organ rot," and discovers pity for the children whose hopes and
life expectancies are limited. This descent into the sickness and anguish of
the world is both a literal one and a symbolic act, suggesting the archetypal
journey of a classical hero to the underworld. The emotional crisis of the
novel is reached when Shadrach visits Jerusalem and meets the archetypal
wandering Jew, Meschach Yakov, by the famous Wailing Wall. Here Shadrach seems to have come to the core of the world's anguish, and the writing
becomes eloquent. At first, Shadrach has viewed Jerusalem with hope, as
Silverberg describes it:

From his balcony he has a superb view of the old walled city. Awe and excitement
rise in him as he looks out upon it. Those two glittering domes down there—his
map tells him the huge gold one is the Dome of the Rock, on the site of Solomon's
Temple, and the silver one is the Aqsa Mosque—and that formidable battlemented
wall, and the ancient stone towers, and the tangle of winding streets, all speak to
him of human endurance, of the slow steady tides of history, the arrivals and departures of monarchs and empires. The city of Abraham and Isaac, of David and Solomon, the city Nebuchadnezzar destroyed and Nehemiah rebuilt, the city of the
Maccabees, of Herod, the city where Jesus suffered and died and rose from the dead,
the city where Mohammed, in a vision, ascended into heaven, the city of the Cru-
saders, the city of legend, of fantasy, of pilgrimages, of conquests, of layer upon layer
of event, layers deeper and more intricate than those of Troy—that little city of low
buildings of tawny stone just across the swooping valley from him counsels him that
apocalyptic hours are followed by rebirth and reconstruction, that no disaster is eternal. (SITF 194–195)

However, the actual experience of walking the streets and seeing the
doomed but energetic children produces a sense of futility:

It is too much for Shadrach—the fierce children, the woeful staggerers, the dirt, the
unfamiliar density of the populace that throngs this tiny walled city. There is no way
to escape the overwhelming sadness of the place. He should never have entered it;
it would have been better by far to look out from his hotel balcony and think romantic thoughts of Solomon and Saladin. (SITF 197)

His meeting with Meschach leads to a visit to Meschach's home, which
is a turning point, reminding Shadrach of his biblical predecessor, for his
despair begins to ebb in the warm communion of this experience. Moreover,
it is Shadrach's sense of emptiness before the world's suffering that finally
leads to his calm understanding not only of the need for action but also of
what action to take.

By performing the operation that gives him power over the Khan's nerve
centers, Shadrach makes himself the ruler of the world's master. This act is

one that requires existential courage as well as moral concern and discernment. Many of the alternatives might have seemed easier, but Shadrach's choice combines maximum social responsibility with minimum pain for others. By controlling the Khan, and hence the world order, Shadrach can have government-sponsored research direct itself to developing immunity for the children and trying to save the unborn.

To be sure, Shadrach recognizes that his situation at the novel's end is an ambiguous one: he has chosen to ride the tiger at the eye of the storm. Genghis Mao recognizes his own predicament with a rueful sense of amusement and seems almost relieved to have someone else take on the responsibility of rule. However, the Khan is an unpredictable force, and there are those in his government and in the world outside who plot mischief.

Nevertheless, at the novel's end, Shadrach feels a sense of elation, for "it is the fourth of July, 2012," and hence a day of liberation:

In this night death will travel the globe, harvesting his thousands; but in the morning, Shadrach Mordecai vows, things will begin to change. He stretches forth his left hand. He studies it as though it be a thing of precious jade, of rarest ivory. Tentatively he closes it, almost but not quite clenching his fist. He smiles. He touches the tips of his fingers to his lips and blows a kiss to all the world. (SITF 247)

Silverberg's hero has learned the harsh truth that there are in the end no safe places in a world of injustice and tyranny; but he has also come to know the complementary lesson that one need not be impotent, for there are always free and positive moral acts that one may take—if one has maturity and courage. Shadrach has walked through the furnace of his Nebuchadnezzar, and like his biblical namesake, has emerged unscathed. He stands ready to assume enormous power and its responsibilities, prepared by this ordeal. At the end, Shadrach is about to assume the burden first taken on by Roy Walton in the melodramatic *Master of Life and Death*, nearly two decades earlier. So Silverberg's fiction has come full circle, but Shadrach, unlike Walton, begins with an awareness of the frightening moral ambiguities of power, as well as its heavy responsibilities.

With *Shadrach in the Furnace*, Silverberg at last comes to a tentative acceptance of the anguish and moral ambiguities of human history. Despite the nightmare of history, moral idealism still has its value. As Clareson has observed, the novel demonstrates that Silverberg's work has "abandoned the underworld of despair," for "its protagonist makes an affirmative answer so that he himself may shape the world in which he lives" (RS 71). Faced by a dilemma, the hero does not turn to a futile and destructive gesture of revolt, like that enacted by Thor Watchman in *Tower of Glass* or the characters in *The World Inside*. Instead, the hero makes a choice that reaffirms the dignity and value of action. *Shadrach in the Furnace* is a beautifully written novel, an impressive work concluding Silverberg's third period.

Both *The Stochastic Man* and *Shadrach in the Furnace* have been greatly underrated by those critics who have taken notice of them. Aldiss, for instance, while generally favorable, describes them as "somewhere between entertainment and insight" and seems to place them in the "second rank" of Silverberg's novels (TYS 345). However, no other novels by Silverberg deserve to be recognized at their true worth. Indeed, *Shadrach in the Furnace* is arguably one of Silverberg's finest works.

7

A Return to Romance: The Sorceries of Majipoor

◆

After completing *Shadrach in the Furnace*, Silverberg took a welcome sabbatical from writing for about four years, before making a triumphant return with a handsome contract for *Lord Valentine's Castle*.[1] During this period of exile, some of his public statements described his weariness and disenchantment with the genre and its more uncritical readers.[2]

He seemed content to settle down quietly in the San Francisco Bay area and cultivate his garden. In particular, reader indifference to his fine ironic novels disappointed him. However, Silverberg later conceded that while the failure of his best work to win a wider audience was a major disappointment, his own reaction to this response may have been excessive.[3] From the perspective of the eighties, it was easier for him to acknowledge that his remarkable flowering in the years of the third period—not to mention his labor on non-fiction books—had virtually exhausted his energies. He needed time to review his career and recharge his batteries.

Once before, Silverberg had abandoned the genre, in the period following 1959, after a strenuous apprenticeship that ended in frustration. His comments about that time reveal a sense of defeat, at least as far as his novels were concerned.[4] This time, however, Silverberg's retirement was entirely different. He was leaving on top, as an acknowledged master with a considerable body of fine work, some of it already considered classics for the genre. His fiction had won the field's major awards, and he had assimilated the innovative techniques of the new experimental fiction. He now could claim with justice that his best writing had achieved a level of sophisticated irony and technique that demanded too much intellectual intensity from the growing audience of science fiction readers.

However, no person with Silverberg's discipline and drive might be expected to be inactive for long. There were interviews to give and memoirs of his early career to write, and paperback publishers were interested in re-issuing the early novels. Silverberg could now contemplate these youthful efforts with an assured sense of superiority by writing thoughtful introductions for new editions. He was able to assemble early short stories, like *The Best of Robert Silverberg*, Volume 1 (1976) for Pocket Books. Later a second "best of" volume was edited for Gregg Press. Silverberg also continued to edit anthologies, another task he had undertaken in the sixties, and which he had carried out with distinction in the Alpha series for Ballantine Books, the New Dimensions series of original stories for a hardcover publisher, the *Science Fiction Hall of Fame* volume, and others.

In fables, a prince who, after some disappointments, is finally crowned as a monarch—and then abandons his throne—will eventually begin to wonder who he is. When he starts to remember, he may undertake the quest to regain his authority. In his subsequent work, Silverberg was to emulate Lord Valentine, the hero of his epic romance, in once more ascending to the throne. However, during his absence, decisive public events and significant changes in the genre and its audience had already made their impact. Mutations of the marketplace prepared the way for Silverberg's re-entry into the world of active science fiction writers with an impressive novel, *Lord Valentine's Castle*, a romantic saga that would inaugurate a new period in Silverberg's career.

When Silverberg returned to active fiction writing after his sabbatical (1975–78), it was to a marketplace that was enormously changed. If a large body of readers did not appreciate his finely crafted ironic stories, there were more defenders of the minority view that science fiction should be more concerned with the aesthetics of fiction and more accommodating to a pessimistic worldview. In addition, the gradual subsiding of the social unrest of the sixties and early seventies produced a more stable public atmosphere, if not a more just society.

The major change in the world of mass entertainment and publishing was new acceptance of science fiction by a mass audience, which the catalytic film *Star Wars* (1977), with its enormous commercial success, forced producers of film and television to recognize. Publishers had come to realize that the success of J.R.R. Tolkien's *The Lord of the Rings* in paperback, and the growing readership for such authors as Robert Heinlein and Frank Herbert made science fiction of the romantic variety a good risk in hardcovers. Now, the *Star Wars* phenomenon, the continued popularity of "Star Trek" reruns, and the increasing success of such well written series as Philip José Farmer's Riverworld novels and Herbert's Dune saga made hardcover publishers receptive to imaginative science fiction on an epic scale. Such conditions opened the way for Silverberg's elegant science fantasy *Lord Valentine's Castle*, the first of the Majipoor stories.

Characteristically, Silverberg's account of the genesis of *Lord Valentine's Castle* is modest. According to one interview, he attributes the book's conception to the atmosphere at a major science fiction convention in 1978, where there was much wheeling and dealing about contracts, a situation that aroused Silverberg's desire to test his worth in the open market. The result was a contract for, reportedly, $175,000, a princely figure that made Silverberg's labors in his early pulp days seem absurd. Silverberg also says that the outline for *Lord Valentine's Castle* was "conceived" in an afternoon, but he concedes that he felt he had an idea for a book that "seemed quite irresistible" (DM 263). Although Silverberg wanted to reap the benefits of the booming market, it is clear that a powerful imaginative conception of the story came first.

Stimulated by the widening of the market and inspired by a fresh vision of a new fictional world, Silverberg produced in *Lord Valentine's Castle* a novel that is both an entertaining adventure story (which may be read as either science fiction or fantasy) and an imaginatively rich symbolic romance that may be read on a more sophisticated level. Technically speaking, *Lord Valentine's Castle* may be considered science fiction, since it takes place on a planet colonized by terrestrials many thousands of years in the future. However, for the purpose of discussing its meaning here, Brian Attebery's useful concept of "science fantasy" may help to define its nature. According to Attebery, "science fantasy" pretends to employ the rational explanations of science fiction, but it transcends the conventional limitations of that genre. Its story moves closer to the realm of heroic or demonic fantasy and its characters and plot tend to assume a more mythic or numinous character (SOF 105–125), if I read Attebery correctly.[5]

In the creation of his imaginary planet, Majipoor, Silverberg painted a large canvas, peopling three continents of this planet with humans and a number of other species, including the doglike Hjorts, the giant Skandars, the birdlike Vroons, with their wizard skills, not to mention the Liimen, the Ghayrogs, and the dispossessed Metamorphs, or "Shapeshifters," all credibly depicted. In addition, he provided Majipoor with a civilization of over fourteen thousand years of history, together with an elaborate system of world government—a constitutional monarchy—and a system of social rituals, folklore, and mythology. Of course, not all this is presented entirely in *Lord Valentine's Castle*, since an author needs some freedom for his imagination in future novels. However, Silverberg's fantasy is an impressive example in the subgenre of "planetary romance," a form described in David Pringle's article in John Clute's and John Grant's fine *The Encyclopedia of Fantasy* (705–706). This is a tradition as old as Burroughs; but only in the past three or four decades, with the maturation of science fiction and fantasy, has the construction of invented planets been undertaken with the requisite seriousness and consistency.

However, if Majipoor is one of science fantasy's most sophisticated invented planets, we should not forget that there is a central theme underlying Silverberg's vast narrative: this is Valentine's quest to recover his lost identity and regain his position as ruling monarch. Indeed, the quest for identity is a central theme of *Lord Valentine's Castle*, as John Flodstrom has suggested in an essay ranging over Silverberg's work (RSMT 73–94). Unfortunately, Flodstrom presses his argument a bit too strongly when he tries to make the search for identity—under the aegis of "new age" ideas—the central theme of the first Majipoor trilogy, while neglecting the political and social issues of the books.

Nevertheless, Valentine's recovery of his identity, symbolized by his acquisition of the crown of the coronal is the major theme of *Lord Valentine's Castle*. However, there are several contrapuntal themes, all interwoven in the tale of Valentine's achievement of his enormous task.

To begin with, before his loss of power, Valentine had been a naive and inexperienced young man, without understanding of ordinary people and their lives. His adventures after his change of body and loss of memory begin when he assumes the role of an itinerant juggler and learns to appreciate and enjoy the carefree—but often troubled—lot of an itinerant entertainer. This theme might be called the rediscovery of common existence.

A related theme is the need for humility before one assumes power. As the later *Majipoor Chronicles* shows, Valentine had not planned to be coronal, and he had only succeeded to the throne because of his dominating elder brother's unexpected death. Before his fall Valentine had been a proud and overconfident young man, distant from his people and sure of his ability to rule. His long road back to power is a lesson in humility.

Yet another theme is the gradual recovery of identity after it has been mysteriously lost. At the beginning, Valentine is a wanderer without memory and hence without identity. His rediscovery of self does not occur until after he has achieved a new identity and self-esteem, resulting from his mastery of juggling. Yet even after Valentine learns his true identity as the chosen coronal from The Lady of oracular wisdom on the Isle of Sleep, his resumption of his older self is gradual and difficult.

Still another theme that plays a major role in the earlier sections of the novel is the discovery of friendship and romantic love. Without friends and memory at the beginning of the novel, Valentine is a lonely figure who has forgotten whatever he knew of the joys of childhood and youth. Yet he discovers companionship and fellowship with the traveling group of entertainers. Although this experience is not without tensions, it proves to be one of the most important lessons learned by the mature Valentine.

Romantic love also plays an important role in *Lord Valentine's Castle*, especially in the first half. Curiously enough, romantic or erotic love is not a significant element in many of the more celebrated modern fantasy novels. Valentine's discovery of romantic love with Carabella is credibly described, and the strongly sexual nature of this relationship is handled quite directly, without appeals to either prurience or sensationalism. In fact, it is a measure of the maturity that science fiction and fantasy have achieved that the erotic relationship between Valentine and Carabella is handled with such assurance.

Then, too, another important theme of the novel, and perhaps its most significant one, is the concern with the fulfillment of talent and destiny. Valentine begins his new existence as a juggler, a man with gifts of acrobatic dexterity and hand/eye coordination, but he soon proves that his intelligence and political talents are extraordinary. Implicit in the description of his adventures is the question: What is the proper use of one's talents? For a time, Valentine is content to be merely a popular entertainer, but he is driven on to new trials, new marvels, and mastery over new situations, until at last he has forced the usurping coronal off Castle Mount and assumed his rightful role as ruler. Valentine's final strategy against the usurper is, interestingly enough, called "a gigantic kind of juggle" (LVC 42). Here juggling has become synonymous with political adroitness.

Moreover, juggling may be a metaphor for all forms of skill or artistry, and it is not at all perverse to see Valentine as a symbolic figure representing the artist, in addition to the obvious interpretation of him as an archetype of the metaphysical quester. Silverberg's epic novel then becomes, on this reading, a study of the artist's progress through experience to a position of social responsibility and leadership—an interesting contrast to major twentieth-century literary traditions that see the artist as perennially doomed to opposition to society.

Finally, another obvious interpretation of Silverberg's novel is to see it as a metaphoric description of the experience of Silverberg as author. In some respects, Silverberg's literary career resembles Valentine's political career. After boyhood, Silverberg, a youth blessed with extraordinary verbal talents, first chose to make his living by his prodigious production of formula science fiction. His career at this time was largely that of a clever entertainer, like Valentine with his juggling act. Yet, like Valentine, Silverberg could not be content to be a mere professional showman, and the middle and later stages of his career parallel Valentine's effort, as Silverberg has sought to reclaim his birthright and assert his identity as a true prince of the realm of literature. In this allegorical interpretation, then, *Lord Valentine's Castle*, though written in a luminously objective style, may be considered one of Silverberg's most personal novels. Indeed, it may be one of his central works, which looks back to his earlier career, and points forward to later works.

An analysis of *Lord Valentine's Castle* can conveniently follow Silverberg's own divisions of the story. In the first section, "The Book of the King of

Dreams," Valentine confronts his loss of identity, finding himself alone on the continent of Zimroel near the city of Pidruid, a man without memory or identity. Yet his possession of some past is subtly emphasized in Silverberg's first sentence:

And then, after walking all day through a golden haze of humid warmth that gathered about him like fine wet fleece, Valentine came to a great ridge of out-cropping white stone overlooking the city of Pidruid. (LVC 3)

Not only does the opening take us immediately into Valentine's consciousness, but the casual use of "And" at the start of this sentence emphasizes a mysterious history behind the present action.

Valentine's loss of identity through amnesia is a classic archetypal motif of romance narratives throughout literature, although the transformation of his body resembles specific metamorphoses from the magic world of Greco-Roman romance and medieval folk tale. In his study of the characters and structure of romance, *The Secular Scripture*, Northrop Frye calls Valentine's mortal state the "motif of amnesia" or the "break in consciousness," which provides the impetus to action in many fantasy romances. This event is accompanied by a "sharp descent in social status, from riches to poverty, from privilege to a struggle to survive, or even slavery" (104). Such a descent "from a higher world to a lower one," which Frye finds commonplace in the beginning of romances has as "the structural core . . . the individual loss or confusions or break in the continuity of identity," an action that Frye suggests parallels the entering of a dream world (104–105).

Thus, "The Book of the King of Dreams" opens with Valentine wandering outside Pidruid like a sleepwalker, and throughout this first book, Valentine seems to be meandering through a world where dream and reality intermingle. As Valentine finds a footloose existence among the entertainers, he gradually recovers consciousness and self-awareness, and the book ends with his nightmare encounter with the King of Dreams, where Valentine recognizes that he has indeed fallen from his former role as coronal. However, the events of this first book deserve further comment.

The first chapter, for instance, describing Valentine's meeting with the boy herdsman, Shanamir, touches very lightly on the theme of Valentine's fall from power and loss of identity. In a casual conversation, Shanamir discusses the visit of the coronal to Pidruid and the accompanying midsummer festival, and the contrast between the supposedly authentic Lord Valentine and the homeless hero is subtly emphasized.

In the first book, too, Valentine's free, if impoverished, state compels him to discover his talent as a juggler, join the fellowship of the entertainers, and consummate his love for Carabella. Each of these actions is important, but perhaps the most significant is the discovery of his talent. It is quickly established that Valentine possesses a great gift for juggling, but "no form"

(LVC 21). Talent must be schooled by discipline until mastery is achieved, according to Sleet, Carabella's partner, and this lesson is obviously meant to have a wider application than merely to the art of tossing objects in the air.

Very early, Sleet identifies the attainment of mastery of one's talent with the achievements of self-mastery and of personal unity: "Cleanse your mind of all needless thought and calculation. Travel to the center of your being and hold yourself there" (LVC 32). Later in the novel, self-mastery for a ruler is also described by the metaphor of "movement to the center" of one's being.

Most of Book 1 takes place in the atmosphere of relaxed awareness that goes with dream and revery. In contrast to the discovery of love, fellowship, and the mastery of an art, the theme of Valentine's lost identity begins to emerge in his troubled dreams, especially the evil dreams traditionally sent from Majipoor's sinister King of Dreams.

Book 1 contains several disturbing dreams, but none so vivid as Valentine's final nightmare. Just before, Carabella has experienced her own nightmare, and she awakes, troubled, to proclaim that her dream has revealed that Valentine is indeed the true coronal, though cheated of his throne by some trickery. Valentine's response is to deny her astonishing claim; but Carabella's insistence on the oracular power of her dream leaves him shaken, and soon he discusses the idea with Deliamber, the sorcerer, who concedes that such an incredible transformation and usurpation could be possible. This sequence sets the stage for Valentine's own prophetic dream.

This climactic event is an impressive surreal fantasy. In his dream, Valentine juggles at the palace of the King of Dreams, and is subjected to a ritual of mockery by the King and his sons, who inform him that his identity has been stolen. Their ridicule includes the contemptuous remarks that Valentine was "lazy," "cowardly," and "a shirker of duty," all epithets restating the theme of Valentine's original lack of readiness to assume the responsibility that goes with power. Ironically, it is this meeting with his psychological adversary that convinces Valentine at last of his fall from great estate; moreover, the mockery of his enemies motivates Valentine to plan his careful and slow recovery of power.

Several of the characters Valentine encounters exude a numinous or mythic aura, starting with the King of Dreams, who is revealed at the end of the novel as the real force behind the usurper. Indeed, this character plays the traditional role assigned to Satan or Loki in mythologies of the past: he is a demonic being who dominates evil dreams and sows discord, an archetypal betrayer and deceiver. In terms of Jungian theory, the King of Dreams is the ultimate shadow archetype, the force behind the usurping coronal, who may be seen as Valentine's shadow self.[6] Indeed *Lord Valentine's Castle*, like all mythic romances that resemble naive romance or fairy tales, is rich in images and symbols that yield readily to a Jungian interpretation. As in many classic romances, Valentine's initial confrontation with the shadow is decisive: the encounter persuades him to pursue his destiny.

Book 2, "The Book of the Metamorphs," describes Valentine on the next stage of his quest. At the climax of this book, he confronts a revelation about his identity in an encounter with the Shapeshifters, or Metamorphs, at their festival of mockery when they mimic the jugglers. The action closes on an increasingly tense note when Valentine and his friends are attacked by the Metamorphs, and after defeating them, they become separated and their boats are wrecked in the rapids of the Zimr. For a time, Valentine is left with nothing but his own resources to sustain him.

As in Book 1, Valentine is haunted by dreams in this book, but many are beneficent dreams sent from The Lady, the Queen of the Isle of Sleep, whose importance increases dramatically. She represents the archetypal "Great Mother" in Jungian terms, and her role is benevolent.[7] These encouraging dreams accompany a growing sense of identity, as Valentine demonstrates an increasing mastery of juggling and new qualities of leadership. By the end of the book, Valentine is both a master performer and the acknowledged leader of the entertainers.

In general, the ordeals that Valentine undergoes in this book represent the motif of "descent to a lower world" that Frye designates as a central theme of romance narratives (SS 97–126). The Metamorphs resemble demons, or defeated titans of myth, who lurk close to the land and seek their revenge on the dominant culture or civilization, like those "subterranean titans" that, Frye contends, "persist through all romance" (SS 112). Their demonic masque brings Valentine to a confrontation with his double, or doppelgänger, the false Lord Valentine, and their fierce attack on the traveling fellowship threatens death and dismemberment, a menace akin to the ritualized nightmare situations of classic romances. As Book 2 concludes, Valentine, embarking on a perilous journey by water—a traditional ordeal for the hero—is thrown ashore alone, temporarily separated from his companions, and shaken by a sense of cosmic loneliness as well as by a recognition of his quest.

Book 2 is notable for the hallucinatory power of Valentine's dreams. In an early dream, he envisions his mother, The Lady of the Isle of Sleep, but her face is veiled, and she will not look at him. Obviously, winning recognition from her is an important challenge for Valentine. A second major dream depicts a journey to the labyrinth to interview the Pontifex, or supreme ruler of Majipoor. This dream ends in a nightmarish scene when the Pontifex, supposedly the source of wisdom, justice, and final authority, appears to be insane and inhuman. (Later it is revealed that the Pontifex is merely aged and incompetent, unable to play a role in the political maneuvering.)

Shortly afterward, Valentine experiences another important dream, one that reveals how his identity was stolen and his position usurped. This time the dream, though unpleasant, has the oracular power of a true "sending," and it prepares Valentine for the recognition of his true self that occurs in the demonic masque of the Shapeshifters. Thus Valentine's journey through actual perils is counterpointed by a vivid odyssey through dreamland.

Continuing the description of prophetic dreams and nightmarish perils, the third book of *Lord Valentine's Castle*, "The Book of the Isle of Sleep," is an adroit exercise in narrative skill. At the opening, Valentine is apparently abandoned and alone. Within a few pages, he rejoins his companions and the quest continues. Their progress takes them to the Isle of Sleep, one of those enchanted islands that are a central archetype of romance and fantasy, from Circe's island in Homer and Prospero's island in *The Tempest* to the enchanted islands in twentieth-century fantasies.

Generally, in romance narratives, islands of enchantment are ambiguous places. They may be scenes of trial or temptation, as with Circe's island or "The Bower of Bliss" in Edmund Spenser's *The Faerie Queene* (Book 2, Canto 12); but successful passage through the trial or enchantment may strengthen the hero. On the other hand, the enchanted island may be one ruled by a benevolent magus or sorceress, as with Prospero's island; but it is wise to remember that even an island under the influence of white magic may appear mysterious, frightening, and ambiguous at first. So it is with this Isle of Sleep, ruled by Valentine's true mother, a benevolent enchantress who also happens to be an earth mother archetype, a wise tutelary figure comparable to Athena in *The Odyssey*. To emphasize the enchanted nature of the Isle of Sleep, Silverberg makes the journey there perilous, for the voyager must pass through seas afflicted by "sea-dragons." Thus, as often happens in romances with a strong fairy tale basis, the "great sacred place" is guarded by watchful monsters, archetypal symbols of terror. Likewise, the hero and a companion suffer a ritual immersion into horror, when Valentine and Lisamon Hultin are actually swallowed by the great sea-dragon in the last attack on the ship and spend time in its belly before being regurgitated into the Inner Sea. This ordeal, like many others, serves a purpose: it leads Valentine to reflect on mortality and the meaning of life.

Here again, Silverberg's epic makes use of a ritualized romance motif, "the swallowing of a youth or maiden by a subterranean or submarine monster," to use Frye's words (SS 118). All Valentine's ordeals, to this point, may be said to coalesce into the larger theme of the archetypal descent motif in romance, which in Frye's formulation is described as "the descending hero or heroine . . . going down into a dark and labyrinthine world of caves and shadows which is also either the bowels or belly of an earth-monster, or the womb of an earth-mother, or both" (SS 119). His reunion with friends and Carabella and his visit to the Isle of Sleep begin a counter-movement of ascent toward Valentine's rightful position. To be sure, the motif of ascent of Castle Mount is presented as a tortuous climb, and on his way upward, Valentine must pass through numerous ordeals.

On the Isle of Sleep, Valentine is subjected to a sacred atmosphere, where he undergoes various rituals that produce purification and discipline. The hallowed character of the Isle is emphasized by the series of terraces and temples that rise upward and dominate the island, as well as by other features. This setting alone receives the description of "holy place" in the novel (LVC 273). Moreover, it is notable that the seaport of the Isle is called "Numinor," an evocative name also suggesting the presence of the sacred or holy by its close approximation to the word "numinous," the word coined by Rudolph Otto to describe the experience of awe or "holy dread" in his classic *The Idea of the Holy*.[8]

For much of his time on the Isle of Sleep, Valentine does not experience mystic epiphanies, but rather submits to a series of mundane initiations and a time of patient waiting. The chief incentive to continue his discipleship is the presence of recurring dreams where he becomes more and more familiar with his mother, The Lady of the Isle, and seeks to win her favor.

However, it is not until Valentine takes the initiative that he earns his crucial meeting with The Lady. First there comes the summoning dream, more vivid and intense than the other dreams Valentine has been experiencing. However, the priests, his mentors, are indifferent to the summoning dream, and instead instruct Valentine to return to the coast as a guide for newly landed pilgrims. Angry and chagrined, Valentine at last seizes the initiative and takes control of his own destiny.

Ultimately Valentine is rewarded in a scene in which his mother grants him full recognition and provides the healing act of restoring his memory completely. The point of this sequence should be obvious. Silverberg suggests that at some point mere obedience to a religious discipline is not enough. There is a time when the quest hero must take matters into his own hands and follow the call of his destiny.

However, even more important that Valentine's recovery of his past, through his communion with The Lady, is the charge that The Lady gives him for his future. Until now, Valentine has not been fully committed to a recovery of his throne, for he is still in love with his old carefree life as a juggler and wanderer. However, The Lady urgently insists that the rule of the usurper will be harmful and destructive:

The Barjazid does not yet rule as an absolute tyrant, for that might turn the people against him, and he is still insecure in his power—while you live. But he rules for himself and for his family, not for Majipoor. He lacks a sense of right, and does only what seems useful and expedient. As his confidence grows, so too will his crimes, until Majipoor groans under the whip of a monster. (LVC 304)

Fortunately, Valentine's humanity and The Lady's vision do not permit them to contemplate a violent and bloody progress to the throne. Instead, Valentine is enjoined to become a supreme master of guile, a trickster with humane values, and to aid him The Lady bestows on him a talisman or magic gift, similar to those given to mortals in fairy tales and myth: the silver circlet that endows its possessor with telepathic powers. From this point on, Valentine becomes a more resourceful and dominating hero, and his successful progress to the top of Castle Mount seems assured.

Book 4, "The Book of the Labyrinth," depicts Valentine on an upward ascent, despite the title, which seems to suggest further imagery of descent. This book, the shortest in the novel, concerns Valentine's journey to a meeting with the aged and ineffectual Pontifex to gain his support for Valentine's projected overthrow of the usurper. The book is unified by three motifs: Valentine's emergence as a masterful manipulator who uses guile rather than force to overcome his enemies; the image of the government bureaucracy as a vast labyrinth that must be circumvented by trickery; and Valentine's final meeting with the Pontifex, a senile ruler and a benign but impotent paternal figure symbolizing moral authority.

The most crucial ordeal that Valentine must undergo in "The Book of the Labyrinth" is not his audience with the Pontifex, but the "dream speaking" that Valentine must submit to first in order to prove his worth and the sincerity of his mission. This episode, described in poetic terms, is not only a fine performance, but is also one of many important moral tests that Valentine must pass on his route to the top of Castle Mount. The dream speaking, or interpretation of his dreams, explores his subconscious feelings and beliefs, not only proving his authenticity as a prince, but also establishing the moral idealism of his motives.

Valentine's meeting with the Pontifex, the climax for Book 4, proves to be an important moral initiation for Valentine into an age-old concept: the ultimate "vanity" of human wishes and human endeavor. For the Pontifex, the supreme power on Majipoor, is a shrunken old man of more than a hundred years, barely kept alive inside a glass bubble by life-support systems. Although Valentine obtains the Pontifex's blessing—a symbolic gesture of approval—the most important lesson he learns is the folly of all pursuit of power. Looking at Pontifex Tyeveras, Valentine reflects that "to behold him now was to understand the ultimate meaninglessness of supreme rank: a coronal lived in the world of deeds and moral responsibility, only to succeed to the Pontificate and finally to vanish into the Labyrinth and crazy senility" (LVC 367). Yet despite this recognition at the end of Book 4, Valentine resumes his effort to recover his lost throne. With the Pontifex's blessing Valentine now carries an aura of destiny, much like an anointed king in a Shakespearean play.

"The Book of the Castle," which concludes the epic, provides an impressive climactic sequence. This book continues the theme of ascent that began on the Isle of Sleep and ends with Valentine's triumph, releasing the planet from bondage to the usurper, and his sinister Svengali, the Shapeshifter who has become the King of Dreams. In his study of romance, Frye describes the "narrative themes and images of ascent" as "much as the same in reverse" as those of descent; and Frye contends, "the chief conceptions are those of escape, remembrance, or discovery of one's real identity, growing freedom, and the breaking of enchantment" (SS 129). In one sense, this is what the novel has been about; but it was not until Valentine's meeting with The Lady that the movement of the narrative turned clearly to the establishment of real identity and the breaking of the "enchantment" of Valentine.

The description of Valentine's progress toward victory at the top of Castle Mount is notable for two reasons: first, Valentine's conquest is largely a peaceful one of victory through guile and the revelation of his proper identity; and second, the triumphant march up Castle Mount allows Silverberg the chance to describe this magnificent conception of his imagination, the center of civilization on Majipoor. For Valentine's victory over the usurper Barjazid is more than a personal triumph; it represents the liberation of his civilization from a paralyzing and destructive bondage.

Silverberg's conception of Castle Mount is one of his finer imaginative inventions, a remarkable achievement of human ingenuity. The mountain is thirty miles high, but since the climate has been brought under control, millions dwell there in comfort, and it is adorned with many attractive cities, a testimony to the idea of human civilization. Throughout the Majipoor books, Castle Mount is associated with life at its most enjoyable. Its summit is a world with a symbolic name (Silver Mountain = Silverberg). This name reinforces the theme that Valentine's conquest is also symbolic of Silverberg's own recovery of his vocation as a novelist.

Nevertheless, despite the social and political importance of Valentine's victory, his march of conquest is a spiritual triumph as well. Ascension of the tower or mountain is an old metaphor for spiritual progress and victory, as Jung's theory of myths and other studies of symbolism indicate (DOS 344–345). Moreover, Valentine wins his victories most often simply by showing his credentials and persuading the citizens of the various cities and provinces to rally to his support.

Clearly the Valentine of the last book is a more mature, reflective man than the youthful wanderer of Book 1. He meditates philosophically on the possibility that his own suffering may have resulted because "the Divine" employs "compensating forces," according to the wizard Deliamber; or, as he puts it, "It may be that I was chosen to be an instrument of Deliamber's compensating forces, and it was necessary for me to suffer in order to be effective" (LVC 394). Moreover, Valentine is capable of regarding his own political tactics with a sophisticated and sardonic amusement:

A certain amount of show business, Valentine recognized, was an essential lubricant in many civilized activities, not only those of wizards and jugglers, but those also of the Coronal, the Pontifex, the Lady, the King of Dreams, the speakers of dreams, the teachers of holy mysteries, perhaps even the customs officials at the provincial boundaries and the sellers of sausages in street-side booths. In plying one's trade one could not be too bold and blunt; one had to cloak one's doing in magic, in theater. (LVC 395)

These are the thoughts of the sophisticated trickster that Valentine has become, the deft political leader who thinks of his strategy in the final battle as a supreme embodiment of the juggler's act.

Book 5 reaches its climax in a epiphany of law and justice, rather like the ending of a detective or suspense story. The usurper, Dominin Barjazid, is confronted, routed, and shown to be merely a pawn of the actual schemer and conspirator, the King of Dreams, his supposed father. However, this father is revealed, in turn, as a Metamorph or Shapeshifter who has replaced the original king. So the novel ends with a triple reversal and unmasking. The first two recognitions of fraud and evil are expected. The third revelation is a surprise, although wholly credible, for the novel has constantly alluded to the presence of the Metamorphs and their condition as outcasts and as a dispossessed people.

It is to Silverberg's credit, however, that in the unmasking of his villain he provides the latter with an understandable motive beyond malice or the mere love of power. However warped the false King of Dreams may seem to be, his existence as the leader of a despised and displaced people gains him some sympathy, and gives Valentine a motive for considering social reforms that will treat the Metamorphs with more compassion. As *Valentine Pontifex* (1983) later shows, Valentine is uniquely qualified to understand the Metamorphs' desire for social justice.

In addition, Silverberg's conclusion provides poetic justice for the nominal usurper, a justice that is appropriate without being vindictive: Dominin Barjazid becomes insane when he learns the truth about the Metamorph's imposture. Thus, Silverberg has written a massive epic containing a good deal of melodramatic action, yet free from the violence and harsher passions often associated with such works. His hero is not flawed by ambition, hatred, or the desire for revenge. In his triumph, he becomes almost saintly.

Although technically within the realm of science fiction, because most of its action is justifiable by some actual or postulated scientific law, *Lord Valentine's Castle* clearly tends to blur the boundaries between fantasy and science fiction. Its themes and symbolism are close to the traditional interests of fantasy, making the designation of "science fantasy" appropriate. Obviously, the novel makes use of the rich traditional symbolism of literary romance: themes of ascent and descent; of lost identity and doubles; of perilous journeys and enchanted islands; of labyrinths of confusion and mountains of achievement. Yet, as this analysis has attempted to demonstrate, *Lord Valentine's Castle* is a very sophisticated romance, and the use of naive plot elements should not mislead the reader into considering Silverberg's vision to be a retrogression to simple adventure fiction. In fact, Valentine passes through many of the crucial stages of the hero in Joseph Campbell's "monomyth," defined in *The Hero with a Thousand Faces* (1949).

In the final analysis, *Lord Valentine's Castle* portrays its hero as a sophisticated and pacifistic late twentieth-century liberal, a leader, however, who will fight if he must. Nevertheless, Valentine is an artist and moral idealist who learns that his destiny is to rule, and that his vision must be enlarged to serve desirable humanist purposes. The novel continues the affirmative mood of *Shadrach in the Furnace*; as *Lord Valentine's Castle* and *Valentine Pontifex* both suggest, government and civilization are still possible ideals.

An artist's proper use of his talent is to ascend the mountain of achievement, and in writing *Lord Valentine*, Silverberg resumed his career by scaling a formidable mountain. Like Valentine, Silverberg regained his crown through the completion of a magnificent effort.

Having created an imaginary world so rich in history and detailed in geography as Majipoor, with its colorful and romantic non-human species and its complex neo-medieval political system, Silverberg left himself the opportunity to return to the planet to elaborate its history and traditions further. Majipoor seems to be unveiled with effortless ease in *Lord Valentine's Castle*, as Silverberg's dreaming imagination rolls back its mists and peoples it with a prodigal invention. To leave such an enthralling planet, replete with romantic wonders, after one novel, would have appeared to be a waste of one's creation.

At any rate, it was not long before Silverberg returned to the world of Majipoor in a series of short stories that were published as a single work in 1982 under the title *Majipoor Chronicles*. (Some had appeared earlier in magazines.) *Majipoor Chronicles* is sometimes referred to as a "sequel" to *Lord Valentine's Castle*, and the third Majipoor volume, *Valentine Pontifex* (1983) is described by some as the completion of a "Majipoor trilogy." The last phrase may be appropriate, but it would be more precise to call *Majipoor Chronicles* a "prequel" to *Lord Valentine's Castle*, since it deals with events that occurred before the opening of the novel; and aside from a brief appearance by Valentine in the final story, *Majipoor Chronicles* only employs one character from *Lord Valentine's Castle*—the boy, Hissune, who functions primarily as a narrative device. If "sequel" is employed in a precise way, then *Valentine Pontifex* is the genuine sequel to *Lord Valentine's Castle*, while *Majipoor Chronicles* is its "prequel."

Majipoor Chronicles consists of ten stories, each representing an important event or era in the history of the planet. According to the frame narrative, Hissune, the clever street urchin whom Valentine selected as a protégé on his journey through the labyrinth, finds each of the stories in the "Register of Souls," a repository of tales in the archives of the Labyrinth. The "Register of Souls" has the imprint of "memory readings" of the lives of several million citizens of Majipoor who are deceased; hence, the capsules provide more than a recorded oral history or a written chronicle, for they reveal a highly subjective experience of history, including what the actors and spectators have seen, as well as their emotions as they lived it. By entering the past through the capsules in the "Register of Souls," Hissune is able to experience history from within, an approach that is perhaps the only method through which one can really learn much that is significant about the past. The need to understand history imaginatively is made clear by Silverberg when he describes Hissune at the beginning as being confused by the sheer mass of data and statistics he discovers.

For Hissune, the visits to the "Register of Souls" are an important part of his education, and they are sanctioned by Valentine, although Hissune is unaware of that. His visits to the "Register of Souls" are infrequent and extend over a period of several years, stretching from age fourteen to eighteen. They have a certain ritualistic quality, but they do not seem to correspond to stages in his own development. Had Silverberg been able to link the ten stories to ten stages in Hissune's own crises in the passage from childhood to manhood, *Majipoor Chronicles* might be a major masterpiece.

On the other hand, the use of Hissune as a unifying device is not exactly whimsical or fanciful. Even if Hissune seems a mere convenience, his presence prepares Silverberg's readers for the important role he is to play in *Valentine Pontifex*. It is also quite clear from *Majipoor Chronicles* that Hissune is Valentine's own choice for a successor.

The ten stories themselves are poetic fables, narrated with Silverberg's usual synthesis of restrained urbanity, tact, and condensed, almost epigrammatic, irony. The first and one of the best, "Thesme and the Ghayrog," describes a love between a young rebellious human woman and a reptilian alien of a species just beginning to emigrate to Majipoor. Thesme, the young woman, has rebelled against the dull conformity of her provincial life in a colonial town by moving out into the jungle. There she encounters the Ghayrog, who is essentially a detached rationalist, but injured and in need of her help. After she tends to his hurts, they become lovers, and she flaunts her defiance of convention in visits to her native town. Eventually, however, the Ghayrog leaves to return to his people, and she learns that he cared little for her, but became her lover out of kindness. Maturing as a result of this experience, she returns to town life and conformity, eventually marrying an adolescent sweetheart whom she had earlier scorned.

However, many of the other stories are slighter in nature. "The Time of the Burning" gives a routine picture of a stubborn landowner in the Metamorph War. "Calintane Explains" describes a pontifex who pretends to be mad to escape the responsibility of his role. Using a cross-dressing ruse, he masquerades as a woman and declares himself the new "Lady of the Isle of Sleep" in order to escape the Labyrinth. By contrast, "The Desert of Stolen Dreams" is an adventure story, describing the creation of the position of "King of Dreams," as a result of a conflict between Dekkeret, a lord of Castle Mount suffering from a Conradian concern for honor, and Barjazid, a rogue who uses a dream machine to afflict travelers.

One of the better stories is "The Soul-Painter and the Shapeshifter," describing a somewhat ironic romance between a human and a Metamorph, Sarise, who for a time creates an idyllic relationship by assuming the form of human beauty the painter most admires. Later, the painter sees her in her Metamorph form and decides that this is more beautiful than any human shape she can assume. When she is eventually taken away by Metamorph tribesmen, the painter laments his loss, but it inspires him to paint scenes of his lost happiness, which gain a vogue on Castle Mount because they seem exotic.

Silverberg's use of remote settings, removed from ethnic stereotypes, gives a romantic aura to what could be commonplace tales of sin and redemption. In "Crime and Punishment," for instance, a tale of obsessive guilt takes on a kind of Arabian Nights atmosphere, revealing a common theme among these chronicles of Majipoor: a frustration or a defeat often turns out to be a blessing or a victory in disguise. Here a successful murderer is haunted by the memory of his undetected crime, and tormented by accusing dreams, he abandons his wealth to become a gardener under the protection of The Lady on her island. Years later, he accidentally confronts the son of the man he murdered, and is forgiven, although he has not yet managed to forgive himself. As in more famous stories of crime and punishment, the worst penalty is the ache of conscience.

In the eighth and ninth stories, similar ironies abound. The eighth story, "Among the Dream Speakers," is a trivial tale of a student who prepares for a final test only to learn that she is expected to make up the questions herself. However, the ninth, which rivals "The Soul-Painter and the Shape Shifter" for artistry, is a charming tale of a shopkeeper who, bilked by a couple of scoundrels, turns the event into a benefit. Deceived into believing she had inherited an estate in Ni-Moya, she goes there; but she stays on to become a clever thief, the mistress of the owner of the estate, his wife, and finally his heir. Character *is* destiny.

These tales constantly play on the ironic disparity of illusion and reality, as in the final story, "Voriax and Valentine," which provides a glimpse of

Valentine before his coronation and amnesia, as a carefree aristocrat engaging in sexual dalliance with a witch. Here the story establishes that Valentine did not expect to be a figure of destiny and only became coronal because his brother, the initial choice, died unexpectedly. Thus, the final story maintains the volume's note of characteristic irony.

In an epilogue, Hissune, now eighteen, decides that his experiences with the "Register of Souls" have given him greater understanding of the planet he inhabits. Then Hissune is summoned to visit Valentine on the latter's ritual journey through the Labyrinth. Here Valentine informs Hissune that his own ambiguous destiny is to go to Castle Mount for an important future—presumably to train to be coronal. Hissune also learns that Valentine has known of his browsing in the "Register of Souls" and sanctioned it in order to encourage the boy to educate himself. It is a fair assessment of the *Majipoor Chronicles* to say that the book contains some of Silverberg's more fanciful stories, and they help to flesh out the history of Majipoor.

Silverberg returned to Majipoor again in *Valentine Pontifex* (1983) after a large investment of energy in another project, *Lord of Darkness*, a massive novel about Africa in the Elizabethan age. *Valentine Pontifex* deals with a war between the Metamorphs and the dominant civilization of Majipoor, and resolves the conflict between the two species that was defined in the earlier books. *Valentine Pontifex* also examines a question not fully answered in *Lord Valentine's Castle*: how Valentine will handle the responsibilities of kingship. Finally, this third Majipoor book contrasts the pragmatic cleverness of Hissune with the moral idealism of Valentine, with the values of the latter emerging victorious.

Unfortunately, *Valentine Pontifex*, although a very dramatic narrative, lacks the sheer imaginative exuberance of the first two Majipoor books. Most of the original cast of *Lord Valentine's Castle* is brought back for this sequel, but despite efforts to make secondary characters like Carabella play significant roles, the novel remains focused on Valentine and Hissune. Few additional characters are added, and the richness of invention of *Lord Valentine's Castle* and *Majipoor Chronicles* seems absent.

The strength of *Valentine Pontifex* lies in the urgency of its dramatic conflict. With the Metamorph army arising and marching against the government of Castle Mount during the final half of the novel, Silverberg establishes an atmosphere of crisis during which both Valentine and his tough-minded protégé, Hissune, are tested. Valentine's conduct seems so enigmatic that rumors of his incipient insanity circulate; and Hissune, who believes in guile and force, is on the point of seizing control of the government while marching to war against the Shapeshifters. Valentine's "madness," however, is revealed to be the logic of his moral idealism, since his aim is a peaceful resolution of the conflict, rather than a destructive and relentless war.

When Valentine's plan results in a negotiated settlement between the Metamorphs and the other species of Majipoor, his moral wisdom appears to be as sagacious as that of the legendary Solomon. Moreover, he resolves his conflict with Hissune by resigning the throne of the coronal, designating Hissune as his successor, while Valentine assumes the senior kingship, or the throne of the pontifex. The price of such an action, however, is considerable: Valentine must leave the throne and pageantry of Castle Mount for the obscurity and privacy of the Labyrinth, a burden so heavy that—as *Majipoor Chronicles* makes clear—many coronals avoid it as long as possible, with one pontifex even willing to dress as a woman and feign insanity in order to escape it. Clearly, Valentine's accession to the senior throne embodies Heraclitus's famous paradox that "the way up and the way down are one and the same," and the descent to the Labyrinth symbolizes the acceptance of the responsibility of supreme power.

Thus, even the success of moral idealism has its costs, as Silverberg had already suggested in the conclusion to *Shadrach in the Furnace*. Despite occasional moments of lightness, *Valentine Pontifex* is very serious in tone, almost wholly focused on the responsibilities of rule. A secondary motif is also present in the depiction of Valentine's determination to have peace: this theme restates Silverberg's concern with the avoidance of war and the need to establish the values of peace on a firm footing. Reinforcing these thematic concerns is Silverberg's obsessive moral examination of the treatment of primitive and aboriginal peoples by stronger and more technologically advanced peoples. In the reconciliation between the dominant society of Majipoor and the Metamorphs, there is the symbolic theme that ancient wrongs done to primitive peoples, especially those inspired or justified by ethnic differences, should be confronted and redressed. No civilization can be morally or psychologically whole, the novel implies, until such venerable crimes and guilts are redressed and expiated. In this respect, *Valentine Pontifex* recapitulates a theme of much of Silverberg's earlier work. Nevertheless, Silverberg's emphasis on moral responsibility and his resolute insistence on making the world of Majipoor a stage for moral trial make *Valentine Pontifex* a relatively austere novel. Some of the color and pageantry of *Lord Valentine's Castle* remain, but the sense of freshness, spontaneity, and richness of invention that contributed so effectively to *Lord Valentine's Castle* is absent. Nevertheless, *Valentine Pontifex* returned to the study of political conflict, which is one of Silverberg's strengths.

Silverberg has also returned to Valentine's era on Majipoor in the novella, "The Seventh Shrine" (1998), which deals with an incident late in Valentine's career as pontifex. Here Valentine's unrelenting effort to improve the lot of the aboriginal Shapeshifters (or Puirivari) takes him to a remote archaeological dig where a murder has occurred and a tomb ostensibly has been defiled. Silverberg carefully avoids the cliches associated with such stories. The original crime that led to a sealed tomb is demythologized and the ambiguities involving the archaeologist's murder are resolved. Valentine manages to be both scholarly and politically correct: he insists on having the tomb opened to learn its secrets, but he also decrees that the tomb should be forever sealed out of respect to the indigenous people of the planet. Remaining consistent with his principles in earlier appearances, Valentine remains an embodiment of enlightened liberal humanitarianism.

With an invented world so rich in potential stories, it was inevitable that Silverberg would return to fiction set in Majipoor after allowing this territory to lie fallow. His first addition to the saga in the nineties seemed tentative, however; *The Mountains of Majipoor* (1995) is a vividly imagined but slight tale of a Majipoor diplomat's initiation into serious politics in a primitive mountain country. While negotiating the release of hostages from the savage kingdom of Othinor—a hunting culture that lacks written records and relies on oral tradition—Prince Harpirias learns to bend local customs and needs to his own purposes.

One of his tactics is to engage in a love affair with the king's daughter, while he devises a stratagem to gain the king's agreement to a treaty releasing the Majipoor hostages, a group of hapless paleontologists. This plan requires his translator, a clever Shapeshifter, to engage in improvised theatrics in order to frighten off a tribe of primitive Metamorphs who have been troubling the kingdom. At the end, Prince Harpirias returns in triumph to Castle Mount, leaving behind the king's daughter, now pregnant, but obliged by custom to remain in her father's snow-clad mountain realm. This Silverberg hero gains insight into the craft of politics, but apparently leaves his paramour without regret. Moreover, though he performs his diplomatic duties well, Harpirias never quite loses his sense of superiority to the primitive culture of Othinor. Hence, though this minor novel opens up new territory on Majipoor, it lacks emotional depth; moreover, some readers are likely to find the protagonist's moral behavior toward his lover to be unsympathetic. At any rate, *The Mountains of Majipoor*, while mildly entertaining, seems to lack emotional depth, and it is hampered by an annoying hero.

Sorcerers of Majipoor (1996) is much stronger stuff. Here Silverberg returns to the large-scale epic conflict of *Lord Valentine's Castle*, dealing with a constitutional crisis and civil war that occurred a thousand years before Valentine's time. As the Valentine novels illustrated, Silverberg invented an unusual monarchial and aristocratic form of government for Majipoor, a world imagined to exist several thousand years in the future. According to Majipoor's unwritten constitution, the monarchy is not hereditary—presumably because the political and social history of monarchies on earth has shown this method of government to be ineffective and unsatisfactory. Instead, there are two reigning monarchs, the coronal, a younger executive and ceremonial leader, and the pontifex, an older and presumably wiser man, who must be a former coronal. Each coronal becomes pontifex when the current pontifex dies. Meanwhile, the current coronal must select a successor to his throne from the available aristocracy, with the chief restriction on his choice being that this successor may not be a son or daughter. In theory, the pontifex as a political force acts as a check against the potential absolutism of the coronal. As Majipoor is portrayed as a relatively pacific planet where a world government operates efficiently and is accepted readily, this dual monarchy seems to rule efficaciously.[9]

However, *Sorcerers of Majipoor* deals with what is essentially a constitutional crisis over the succession of rule, with an usurpation that eventually produces a civil war. With a large canvas and cast to work with, Silverberg constructs a novel of political intrigue and evil conflict with epic stature. In essence, his hero, Prestimion, naively trusting to tradition, fails to secure his expected succession to the throne of the coronal and finds that his royal position has been taken by Korsibar, the son of the weary reigning coronal. In his usurpation, Korsibar is encouraged by his ambitious sister, Thismet, who hopes to rule with him and control him, and by Prestimion's cunning cousin, Dantirya Sambail, who plans to create enough conflict to destroy both Korsibar and Prestimion. Korsibar is also aided by the ambiguous help of one of Majipoor's ubiquitous sorcerers, who frequently exert a dubious influence on the political affairs of the planet.

The usurpation reveals the strengths and weaknesses of all involved. Although Korsibar, like the biblical King Saul of Israel, is a man who possesses the handsome and swaggering air of a monarch without the political acumen and psychological strength needed for the role, his seizure of the throne appears beyond reversal when it becomes a fait accompli. This is a situation that reveals a weakness in the political constitution of Majipoor. Fearing his sister's dominance, Korsibar alienates her by excluding her from power, but he readily falls victim to more subtle influences, including the stratagems of Dantirya Sambail, whose shifting allegiances are nearly successful in destroying both the usurping and the rightful claimants.

Prestimion's eventual conquest of the throne comes only after intrigue, battles, exile, personal suffering, and his own reluctant enlistment of sorcerers to help. Although he finally gains the restless Thismet as his lover, his final victory comes at a severe cost, including the death of Thismet in the final battle as she attempts to succor her unfortunate brother. (Despite being strongly attracted to Prestimion, her emotional bond with Korsibar is so intense as to suggest incestuous feeling.) In sum, then, Prestimion learns that the cost of attaining power is so demanding and arduous that he wishes that he had never challenged Korsibar's rule.

As a novel, *Sorcerers of Majipoor* has a plot resembling a history play of Shakespeare, with its insistence on the tragic cost of attaining power and wrestling with its responsibilities. Ironically, however, unlike a Shakespearean history play, the story of Korsibar's usurpation is telepathically expunged from the memory of all but the victorious ruler and his confidants at the novel's end. This curious resolution suggests that there might be tragedies in history from which we do not learn anything, and which are better forgotten.

Despite the romantic aura of the Majipoor world, with its aristocrats, monarchs, strange beasts, sorcerers, and ritual combats with sword and bow and arrow, *Sorcerers of Majipoor* is less romantic than tragic and ironic in its effect. Korsibar and Thismet are tragic figures of stature, and Dantirya Sambail is depicted as a resourceful villain who might dominate a tragic Jacobean play. As a monarch who must earn his throne and recognize the importance of sorcerers (those who try to manage the irrational forces of life), Prestimion receives an education in practical politics that would temper a Renaissance prince.

In short, *Sorcerers of Majipoor* returns to the study of political intrigue at which Silverberg has excelled throughout his career. The author reminds us that Majipoor offers an ironic reflection on our world when some of the characters engage in a speculative discussion of a political system with an elective monarch serving a short term, much like the system long used in twentieth-century North America (SOM 338). This arrangement, the characters conclude, would have flaws making it inferior to Majipoor's dual monarchy. The effect of this dialogue is to remind us of the imperfection of all political systems as schemes of government.

However, we must note that *Sorcerers of Majipoor* continues to depict the nature of Majipoor's magic in a somewhat ambiguous way. The sorcerers themselves claim to practice a science or art, and it is clear that some sorcery actually works: the sending of dreams by telepathic means, the ability to create illusory appearances, and so on. Yet, even these forms of "magic" appear to be the result of sophisticated machinery. In point of fact, Majipoor is not an invented planet where magic is as potent as it first appears. Thus the novels remain examples of "science fantasy," to use Attebery's helpful phrase.

Nevertheless, whatever definitions are invoked, the Majipoor saga deserves respect. Majipoor is one of the most imaginative invented planets in the galaxy of science fiction, comparable in detail and history to Larry Niven's Ringworld, or Frank Herbert's Dune, and usually the scene of more interesting stories than either. Silverberg's Majipoor is worthy of comparison to Brian Aldiss's world of Helliconia, which is—along with Gene Wolfe's distant future earth in *The Book of the New Sun*—the absolute benchmark standard by which all other invented worlds should be measured. Although romantic fictional worlds are out of fashion in many circles, the Majipoor books are, for the most part, works of fiction displaying mature characterization and moral sophistication.

8

The Mature Novelist, from *Lord of Darkness* to *The Alien Years*: Reinventing the Past and Returning to Science Fiction Tradition

◆

After the creation of Majipoor, Silverberg resumed writing stories and novels with other settings. Although at first his shorter fiction returned to the satirical and ironic modes of his third period, he eventually began to invest more emotional currency in his shorter fiction. As a novelist, he also displayed some uncertainty of intention, although he continued to adapt the modernist vision of existential anxiety to science fictional forms and settings.

For a time in the eighties, Silverberg attempted to establish himself as a historical novelist, publishing two works on an epic scale. However, he returned to the role of science fiction novelist with a number of impressive works, including *The Face of the Waters*, which renewed the mystical quest of the middle period, and *At Winter's End*, an epic novel reaffirming humane values in the imaginative story of a mutated humanoid species making a new beginning. In the nineties, it has become clear that Silverberg has returned to classic science fiction themes in such novels as *Hot Sky at Midnight*, *Starborne*, and *The Alien Years*, works of grace and moral dignity.

Both the shorter fiction and the novels include works of impressive strength. A brief tour of the short fiction must suffice here as a prelude to a study of Silverberg's major efforts in the novel during the eighties and nineties. Moreover, Silverberg's later short fiction has moved from the ironic aloofness noted by Clareson (RSMT 10) to greater emotional involvement with characters and themes.

In addition to *Majipoor Chronicles*, Silverberg began producing science fiction in shorter forms once more in 1980. Most of these were highly disciplined and elegantly ironic exercises, collected in *The Conglomeroid Cocktail Party* (1984), a volume displaying a unified tone of urbane satire on social pretense. However, much of the later short fiction, revealing more emotional involvement and humane sympathy, has appeared in a large 1992 volume, *Secret Sharers: The Collected Stories of Robert Silverberg*. Presumably other volumes of collected short fiction will continue to appear, since Silverberg continues to publish short work in numerous magazines and to win accolades for his short stories.

Clearly Silverberg has overcome his reservations about writing short stories. Although he confessed to an initial hesitation about returning to short fiction after the four-year hiatus in his writing, he overcame this inner resistance and began to produce short fiction regularly in 1980 (TCCP 1). His reservations were related to the limited nature of the shorter forms in contrast to the possibilities of the novel.

Somewhat modestly, Silverberg credits the promptings of editors as well as the lure of money as his initial motives for resuming short stories, giving particular thanks to Ben Bova and Robert Sheckley, editors of *Omni*, and George Scithers, an early editor of *Isaac Asimov's Science Fiction* (TCCP 2–3). However, to take this explanation literally would be ingenuous. Silverberg had shown considerable skill in the short fiction early in his career, and the short story always offers the attraction of creating a virtually flawless work of literary art.

His command of tone and elegance of style have made the short story a showpiece for Silverberg's art. Not only has his short fiction of the past two decades appeared in the best science fiction magazines, especially *Asimov's*, but it has also found its way into the pages of such slick magazines as *Playboy*. Several stories have been honored by being selected for Gardner Dozois's excellent "Year's Best Science Fiction" anthologies.

Nevertheless, Silverberg's initial coolness toward the shorter form may in part account for the urbane but aloof irony found in the early stories in this period, especially in *The Conglomeroid Cocktail Party*. A quick scan of representative stories from this volume reveals its pervasive satirical spirit. In "The Pope of the Chimps," Silverberg continues his ridicule of institutional religion, targeting the Roman Catholic Church, as he also had in "Good News from the Vatican." Here a project dedicated to improving the intelligence of chimpanzees is more successful than intended: scientists are chagrined to find that the brightest chimp has assumed the position of high priest or pope. Acting in the role of "Pope Leo," this simian decrees that God has ordained murder as a means of sending chimps to heaven. A series of ritual murders follows, which end only when a woman researcher persuades Pope Leo that on a recent visit to heaven, God informed her that he wants the murders to stop. This satire on religious authority and literal-minded followers is amusing but not especially subtle.

Much of the satire in this collection, however, is directed at a contemporary society that shows ample evidence of lapsing into decadence. "The Palace at Midnight" and "At the Conglomeroid Cocktail Party" lampoon a futuristic American society that substitutes wealth and style for serious enterprise and moral rigor. "The Palace at Midnight" is a mordant but amusing tale that portrays an extrapolated future where America has lost its identity and collapsed into small provinces ruled by fanatics or local self-styled aristocrats. Similarly, grotesque social caricatures exchange banalities in "At the Conglomeroid Cocktail Party," although this story is little more than a satirical sketch. Another acerbic tale, "The Trouble with Sempoanga," describes a planet that has become a giant tourist resort. Everything is scenic and accommodating, except for one flaw: Sempoanga is an excellent place to acquire a venereal disease of great potency (though the malady is unnamed, readers will think of AIDS). A world-weary mood suffuses these stories, such as "Waiting for the Earthquake," where the planet Medea is about to be destroyed by a gigantic quake. Most of the humans have fled, but the protagonist stays as a self-imposed punishment for human exploitation of the planet.

Although some stories seem futuristic exaggerations of the experiences in the San Francisco Bay area in the 1980s, "A Thousand Places along the Via Dolorosa" takes place in Jerusalem at Easter, and offers a qualified note of affirmation. Hornkastle, a bored scholar on sabbatical, tries to recover a sense of the meaning of life near scenes of Jewish sacrifice and the Christian passion. Collapsing on the Via Dolorosa (or way of the cross), he awakens on Easter with a sense of the renewed value of life; but his renewal is entirely secular and personal.

Other stories return to a favorite source of Silverberg paradoxes and ironies, time travel. In "Gianni" modern decadence is satirized when the composer Pergolesi is brought forward to a near future to become an electric pop rock composer who burns out quickly on drugs. In "The Far Side of the Bell-Shaped Curve," Reichenback replicates himself in order to commit the clever murder of a rival for the love of Ilsabet; predictably, his other self, the actual murderer, frames the less culpable Reichenback for the crime. "Needle in a Timestack" is more playful, as the hero manipulates past time so that the former husband of his wife, a notorious playboy, who persists in harassing her, is given a different past. This story, which appropriates an old title from one of Silverberg's sixties collections, attains a measure of light comedy. Nevertheless, the prevailing tone of *The Conglomeroid Cocktail Party* is one of detached and weary irony.

Silverberg continued to turn out deft ironic tales—some of them quite trivial—during the decade 1983–92, including "Multiples," "Tourist Trade," "The Pardoner's Tale," "Hardware," and the impressive "Basileus," all collected in *Secret Sharers*. However, his short stories begin to feature more sympathetic characters and a greater degree of emotional commitment. A glance at some of the better performances shows this changing mood.

"Basileus" (1983), a story chosen by writers and editors for *The Fantasy Hall of Fame* (1998), which Silverberg also edited, continues the ironic tone of the earlier collection, describing a computer wizard who uses the Internet to create "virtual reality" versions of the famous angels of legend. Eventually, after inventing the supreme angel, Basileus, the angel of judgment, the protagonist is instructed by one of his invented beings that he himself must become Basileus. In a fit of depression, he capriciously programs both the Soviet and U.S. defense systems for attacks, and then resumes talking to his angels while the world has "six minutes left" (SS 72).

Other stories also deal with the ironic possibilities afforded by computer technology, including "The Pardoner's Tale" (1986), where a hacker adroitly remakes reality, and "Chip Runner" (1987), where a fifteen-year-old boy hacker becomes so committed to his work or art that he essentially starves himself. On the whole, however, these exercises in irony are less memorable than the stories involving more sympathetic protagonists.

Emotional involvement becomes a theme of the curious story "Homefaring" (1983), in which Silverberg returned to the theme of the isolated human consciousness and the overwhelming desire for telepathic communion with another being. McCulloch, a researcher from the twenty-first century travels to a distant future and finds the dominant species to be an underwater creature much like a giant lobster. These beings communicate telepathically, creating a rich sense of community that proves seductive to McCulloch; he enjoys life with this telepathic herd so much that he resists "homefaring" (or return to his own time) and must be forcibly removed by his fellow scientists. The need to escape the limitations of self is difficult to evade, as Silverberg had suggested in earlier works.

Strong emotional concerns emerge in two fine stories suggesting intertextual relationships with literary antecedents, "Sailing to Byzantium" and "The Secret Sharer." "Sailing to Byzantium (*Asimov's*, February 1985) turns away from irony to offer a science fiction image of enduring love, enhanced by a title taken from W. B. Yeats's famous poem. In the Yeats lyric, the speaker envisions a fulfilling and enduring existence as a creature of pure artifice, a mechanical nightingale who will "sing / To lords and ladies of Byzantium / Of what is passing, or past, or to come." Silverberg's protagonist, Charles Phillips, does not, however, seek an eternal existence as an artist in a holy city of the imagination; instead, he yearns for eternal love with Gioia, his beautiful paramour. Finding an enduring relationship with Gioia, Phillips believes they can live comfortably together as a pair of loving eternal tourists in a high tech world fifty centuries after Christ, visiting ersatz reconstructed cities of the past, such as Byzantium.

However, Phillips suffers the pain of loss when Gioia deserts him. Searching for her, Phillips discovers in a shocking surprise that he is an android programmed to think as a terrestrial from the 1980s. Meeting Gioia again, he learns that her departure was due to a realization that she was beginning to age, whereas he is artificial but immortal. However, Phillips persuades Gioia to undergo an operation and have her consciousness placed in an artificial but ageless body. Thus the couple attain an enduring form of romantic transcendence. Clearly, this story has simple allegorical implications, since Gioia's name suggests "joy."

"Sailing to Byzantium" evidently gained the respect of some discerning readers, for it earned Silverberg another Nebula Award. It is one of his more significant treatments of the importance of romantic and monogamous love, in contrast to more superficial relations. A recent essay on love and lust in Silverberg's work by Rafeeq McGiveron in *Extrapolation* (Spring 1998) reaches the scarcely surprising conclusion that Silverberg has given preferential treatment to romantic monogamy; but McGiveron, drawing most of his evidence from the middle Silverberg, seems indifferent to this story's existence or Silverberg's treatment of romantic love in more recent novels.

A more tragic tone appears in "The Secret Sharer" (1987), a novella with intertextual connections to Conrad. Here Conrad's fictive situation is transmuted into an episode on a starship, and the "secret sharer" is both feminine and disembodied, as Silverberg reshapes the Conradian plot. Silverberg's hero is a young officer similar to Conrad's Marlow, who harbors a fugitive stowaway. However, the secret sharer is Vox, a stowaway who becomes a disembodied "matrix" of electronic impulses for the duration of the trip. Whereas Conrad's Marlow helped his "secret sharer" or doppelgänger to escape from the ship, Vox, facing discovery, must flee to the vacuum outside after accidentally alerting the crew to her presence. She accepts the prospect of gradual dissolution in space as a just punishment for having inadvertently caused the death of another passenger in suspended animation. Though Silverberg gives an attractive personality to his feminine fugitive and she develops a close relationship with the protagonist, his version reaches a more tragic resolution than the Conrad story.

Another story with intertextual relationships to classic science fiction and classic poetry is *In Another Country*, which narrates an elegiac romance between an extraterrestrial and a human woman. Originally published in *Asimov's* (March 1989) and then in a TOR double edition with C. L. Moore's popular 1946 novella, *Vintage Season*, *In Another Country* offers homage to Moore's much admired romantic tale, by treating its events in a parallel version. Silverberg's introduction to the book-length volume describes the relationship of the story to Moore's: his aim was "to produce a work interwoven with hers the way a lining of a cape is interwoven with the cape itself" (IAC vii).

Silverberg uses Moore's setting, Southern California in 1945, but reverses Moore's fictional situation. Moore's novella describes a star-crossed romance between an alien woman tourist who is visiting earth incognito and falls into a relationship with a terrestrial male. Their affair ends unhappily for both, though the novella's resolution seems to be hastily developed. In Silverberg's tale, the alien is Thimirol, a male cosmopolitan poet who avoids emotional attachments. However, he visits earth as a part of a tourist group and succumbs to love with Christine, a terrestrial woman. He suffers tragic loss when he watches Christine's destruction by a giant meteor—the closing disaster also featured in Moore's story.

Another return to science fiction tradition appears in alternate history stories from the early nineties. In "Looking for the Fountain" (*Asimov's*, May 1992), Ponce de Leon actually finds the Fountain of Youth in an alternate history version of the Florida exploration. However, the Fountain turns out to be merely a source of sexual renewal, not eternal youth. "Lion Time in Timbuctoo" (*Asimov's*, October 1990) is an amusing novella set in the alternate history continuum of *The Gate of Worlds*, but introducing different characters. In a story featuring a light comic touch, a naive English diplomat is given a sexual and political initiation in his visit to Timbuctoo, now the capital of a powerful black Islamic empire.

Perhaps the best of these alternate history stories, however, is "Tales from the Venia Woods" (FASF, October 1989), set in an alternate twentieth century along the Danube, where two children encounter an elderly and eccentric recluse. The old gentleman is revealed to be the surviving Roman emperor in a time stream where the empire did not fall, but was overthrown in the twentieth century by fanatic Republicans. The tale ends tragically when the elderly emperor is murdered by partisans of the Republic, who like many rebel factions, are determined to eradicate any vestige of the past. Thus, Silverberg's slight story offers an indirect comment on the savagery of ideological fanaticism.

To sum up, then, Silverberg's recent work in shorter fiction is very accomplished, but rather muted in its effect. His return to the science fiction tradition parallels his later work in the novel.

In the novels he began to write after *Lord Valentine's Castle*, Silverberg returned to the problems and moral dilemmas of history, whether in the human past, or in an imagined future. Although most of these novels were ambitious and epic in scope, they continued the study of moral testing that Silverberg had explored in the best of his third-period novels. Nor did Silverberg abandon his other cherished themes, especially the quest for a mystical transcendence that would bring together human and alien, and perhaps heal the wounds of loneliness and alienation.

After inventing Majipoor, his first major effort was *Lord of Darkness* (1983), a historical novel of Africa that revealed strong similarities to Conrad—a persistent influence on Silverberg, as we have noted.[1] However, this is not the only major novel that offers Conradian parallels. In fact, as Conrad was a novelist who studied the tragic irony of the historical process in *Nostromo* (1904) and *The Secret Agent* (1907), it is not surprising to find that Silverberg's spiritual kinship to Conrad emerges frequently in the novels of this decade (this relationship is acknowledged in one of the epigraphs to *The Face of the Waters*, which is taken from Conrad's *The Mirror of the Sea* [1906]).

Conrad's sense of the tragic nature of human effort, and the numerous ways that his protagonists betray their values, has been studied at length by numerous scholars. Conrad's vision is expressed most clearly in *Heart of Darkness*, perhaps the most accessible and widely read of his works and the one that Francis Ford Coppola adapted to film in an attempt to come to terms with the tragedy of the American war in Vietnam.[2] What is particularly important for us to remember about Conrad's fiction, however, is that there is, in Conrad's best novels, a complex balance of oppositions between romantic idealism and the forces of reality, usually nature and history. This tragic opposition also appears in *Lord of Darkness*, a novel that reshapes Conrad's *Heart of Darkness*.

Although Silverberg refers to *Lord of Darkness* as a "historical fantasy," it contains no magic or supernatural elements. It is a fantasy only in the sense that it is a work of the imagination.[3] Nothing in the novel fits into the category of the fantastic, unless such characters as Dona Teresa and Calandola might be considered so because they seem larger than life. Or perhaps the narrator's survival of his ordeals with sanity intact should be considered fantastic.

In brief, the novel relates the adventures of Andrew Battell, an Elizabethan adventurer who sails to Brazil to make his fortune. In 1589, he is betrayed and abandoned by a fellow seaman, a rascal named Abraham Cocke, and falls into the hands of Portuguese captors who enslave him and take him to Angola. A long enslavement by the Portuguese follows, during which Battell serves several masters, all of whom promise to free him but ignore their promises. At last, Battell comes to feel loyalty for the best of his masters, Don Joao, but he becomes involved in a torrid affair with Dona Teresa, the half-caste lady who is Don Joao's mistress. Matters are complicated further by his involvement with Matamba, a beautiful young black woman. Torn between these two women, Battell's emotional distress is increased by the ambitious intrigues of Don Joao and his mistress, as the former seeks to gain political power and the latter schemes to gain power over both the don and Battell.

At last, Battell reaches a stage of complete disgust with Portuguese deceit and exploitation of those in colonial servitude, who come to symbolize the evils of European dominance. Fleeing into the bush, like an earlier Huckleberry Finn "lighting out for the territory," Battell finally takes refuge with the savage tribe of the Jaqqas. Living as a white warrior among this tribe of formidable black cannibals restores Battell's sense of manhood; he becomes the companion of the Imbe (or Lord) Calandola, a feared and absolute monarch, who in turn is fascinated by Battell's white skin and blond hair—and his skill with a musket. (Battell's acceptance by the Jaqqas becomes more credible because of the Jaqqa custom of increasing their complement of warriors by raising captive children from other tribes and subjecting them to a severe discipline.)

After the duplicity of his Portuguese masters, Battell finds the more candid dedication to destruction of Calandola, the "lord of darkness," both repulsive and fascinating. Though he serves Calandola faithfully, Battell comes to regard the Jaqqa chief as more a demonic force than a mere man; and under his influence, Battell accepts the barbaric ritual of cannibalism (used by the Jaqqas as a way of triumphing over their enemies) and marries a Jaqqa woman. His time with the Jaqqas is brought to an end by an unexpected tragedy. First, his former mistress, Teresa, is captured by the tribe, and is killed after foolishly trying to escape. Then Calandola's ambitious lieutenants plan a mutiny, which explodes in a bloody riot at a feast. In the confusion Battell flees, returns to slavery under the Portuguese colonists, discovers that his former black lover, Matamba, has become a nun, and at last is freed by a kind master and allowed to return to England.

Settling in Essex, Battell becomes an Odysseus figure returned to Ithaca, a voyager who can only find release from the horrors of his grim experience by telling his story in a narrative for the printer and bookseller, Samuel Purchas. Battell's story is essentially a simple one, though elaborated in numerous and lengthy incidents. This novel is based on an Elizabethan travel narrative, though Silverberg has expanded the slender tale into a massive novel of 558 pages, employing a vivid and stylized Elizabethan prose of his invention.[4] Because Elizabethan prose tends to be highly adorned with decorative similes and unnecessary Ciceronian parallelisms, Silverberg wisely restricted himself to formulaic phrasing and conventional Elizabethan idiom.

In considering the meaning of this novel, we may conclude that Battell's ability to relate the tale of his tragic experience helps to liberate him from the burden of his oppressive past, much as similar narrations provided psychological relief for previous literary mariners haunted by the horrors they have seen, such as Coleridge's "ancient mariner" and Conrad's Marlow who follows, somewhat distantly, in the Romantic tradition of the haunted wanderer with a harrowing tale to tell.[5] Although, like some tragic heroes of the Elizabethan stage, Battell takes refuge in expressions of stoic Christian piety, these seem to be in part a desperate effort to control his sense of moral outrage and horror at the painful events he is obliged to describe. They become an attempt to cling to a pattern of faith or meaning that offers consolation for the senseless and destructive acts he has witnessed.

In essence, Silverberg's novel is an exploration of the vision of Conrad's *Heart of Darkness*, recast in the early days of European colonialism, with Portuguese rulers of Angola replacing the Belgians and with the cannibal chieftain Calandola replacing Kurtz as an archetypal figure of destructive force. Kurtz, of course, was a white idealist who surrendered to the fierce and warlike atmosphere of Africa, and to the darker forces in his own psyche; but like Calandola, Kurtz is a charismatic demagogue with a program for destruction. The destructive myth that Calandola serves will be examined in a moment.

First, we should note that Battell's journey involves a series of initiations for an explorer who begins in innocence but learns how inhuman his own European "civilization" is, even before deciding to enter Calandola's world. The key figures in these initiations are the intelligent and ambitious Don Joao and the less attractive Portuguese officials who teach him to distrust the claims of "civilized" Europeans to be humanitarian; and the ambitious ladies, Dona Teresa and Matamba, who introduce him to sensuality, yet show him how destructive unrestrained passion can be (as the epic fight of the two women over Battell demonstrates).

Finally in the heart of the most barbaric continent of his time, Battell encounters Calandola, and learns how mesmerizing a demagogue can be when he preaches a myth of destruction. Though Calandola follows the military ethos of the warrior Jaqqa culture, he might be more accurately described as a shaman or spiritual leader. At times, he seems demonic—an incarnation of the Jungian shadow—but Calandola is not a figure of melodrama; rather, he is humanized and given sympathetic traits of loyalty, acceptance of friendship, and even simple vanity. More significantly, his demagoguery has a basis in his peculiar vision of the Jaqqa destiny. This vision is based on his personal myth about the sanctity of the earth as a mother goddess. In Calandola's view, the Great Mother has been defiled, and the Jaqqa role is to destroy humanity, the agent of the earth's degradation. Influenced by liquor and Calandola's words, Battell himself is swayed by the hallucinatory power of this vision, as he admits:

And we stood side by side all that night, looking toward the desert and watching the witch-fires dancing in the air. And that witchery did enter my brain and inflame my blood, for the words of the Imbe-Jaqqa seemed crystal-clear and reasonable to me, and I made no quarrel with them. I saw the world as swarming with ugliness and treachery and corruption, and the good green breast of the earth encumbered with the ill-made works of man; and it seemed to me most peaceful and beautiful to sweep all that away, and return to the silence of the first Garden.

And when morning came, Imbe Calandola did mount a high scaffold and utter a warlike oration to his troops, inspiring them with the frenzy of battle. Whereupon they did sweep down upon the town of Kalungu and take it, and put its people to the sword and its high slender palm-trees to the axe, and devour many of its folk boiled and roasted, and take its children by impressment into the tribe of Jaqqas. And in that was yet more of the land returned to its ancestral purity. And in doing this, I truly believe, the Jaqqas were aware of no hypocrisy, but were altogether sincere, in fullest knowledge that this was their divine mission, to smash and destroy until they had made all things whole. (LOD 393–394)

In creating this personal myth Calandola has made an extraordinary transformation of an Oedipus complex into a cosmic myth whereby the Great Mother, the earth itself, must be returned to a primal innocence because it has been profaned by human activity. Calandola argues that "this enslaving of the earth by farming and commerce is a great evil. It was not meant for mankind to do thus" (LOD 393). Yet Battell recognizes a humanity in Calandola that links him to the destructive leaders and conquerors in human history, and thereby heightens Calandola's tragic stature. However, Calandola's charismatic power also justifies Battell's frequent comparisons of Calandola to Lucifer.

In the final orgy of destruction following the feast, bitter internecine resentments and fratricidal rivalries erupt into a grotesque riot, as though the tribe's dedication to war and cannibalism contains the sources of its own dissolution. It is tempting to see in this scene of carnage, when the Jaqqas apparently destroy themselves, a symbol of the inevitable destruction and disintegration of societies devoted to heroic codes of warfare.

By contrast, the serenity of Battell's final years in Essex helps to establish a sense of the normal pattern of mundane life. Battell's return and adjustment to tranquil English life testify to his endurance, courage, and determination, qualities that enabled him to survive his ordeals in Africa. His heightened moral sensitivity is shown by his willingness to adopt a much younger woman whom he could probably take as a wife. Nor does he yield to a sense of despair over human depravity or the loss of his hopes and the apparent futility of his lost years, although he had been tempted to surrender to apathy and despair during his captivity. In these respects, Battell resembles Conrad's Marlow, although of course, Battell's trial in the wilderness has been harder and of much greater duration than Marlow's.

Like Marlow, Battell remains haunted by the horrors he has witnessed. He concedes that, even in his safe haven, the spirit of Calandola seems to be an oppressive demon that casts its spell over him in nightmares, demanding to be exorcised (LOD 555–556). Hopefully, his narrative provides a partial exorcism.

Somewhat like Marlow's narrative in *Heart of Darkness*, Battell's tale is not only a journey into the historical past, but also a voyage into the interior of the self, although Robert Killheffer in a perceptive essay on the novel contests this point (NYROSF 13). Battell's honesty and credibility are established by his unwillingness to spare himself in his narrative, or yield to the temptation to make himself falsely heroic. Instead, he confesses that he found Calandola's vision of life attractive, and he acknowledges his own participation in the dark communion of cannibalism. Thus, *Lord of Darkness* might be described as not only a historical novel but also a fictional meditation on the tragic nature of history and human illusions.

As a matter of fact, the novel may be placed in a more restricted genre than that of "historical novel"; it should be placed in the category of novelistic treatments of what scholars in American literature call the "captivity narrative," which usually describes the ordeal of a white European or North American among an Indian tribe. It would thus join a classification that would include some distinguished predecessors, as well as a number of important mainstream novels based on captivity experiences, such as Patrick White's *A Fringe of Leaves* (1976) about life in colonial Australia.

Although Silverberg's novel does not quite achieve the extraordinary power of the work of the Australian Nobel laureate, *Lord of Darkness* is not dwarfed by the comparison to such a novel. In the final evaluation, even if the earlier sections seem overly prolix, *Lord of Darkness* is an impressive work. Whether it is Silverberg's best novel, as Killheffer argues (NYROSF 14), is another matter. In one of his final essays, Clareson suggested that it might be one of Silverberg's two "most significant" works of the 1980s (RSMT 9). Undeniably it is a memorable study of the impact of the African primitive world on the European consciousness.

The lure of historical fiction continued for Silverberg, despite frustration over lukewarm hardcover sales for *Lord of Darkness*. His next descent into the well of the past produced *Gilgamesh the King* (1984), an epic novel about the vanished world of ancient Sumeria at the dawn of history. This work was inspired by the exploits of Gilgamesh, the eponymous Sumerian hero celebrated in a cycle of poems that were given a written form not long after 2000 B.C., centuries before the recording of the Homeric epics.[6] In these poems, which were found in cuneiform on clay tablets in the nineteenth century, Gilgamesh is presented as an epic hero and a tragic figure who reaches extraordinary achievements as a warrior king of his Mesopotamian city-state Uruk, yet finds himself baffled by the mystery of human mortality. Hence the story of Gilgamesh has been called "the finest surviving epic poem from any period until the appearance of Homer's *Iliad*" (Sandars 8). Thus the story stands at the fountainhead of Near Eastern and European literature, and some have postulated an influence on Hebrew legend and Babylonian and Greek mythology (Sandars 18, 44–46).

It is not surprising that Silverberg was attracted to the epic of Gilgamesh, not only because of his interest in archaeology, but also because, as James Gunn has suggested, "*Gilgamesh*'s concerns are those of science fiction" (RTSF 6). Indeed, Gunn includes a brief sketch of the epic in a discussion of the origins of science fiction (RTSF 5–7). Moreover, Silverberg's use of the Gilgamesh material for a novel follows in the tradition of twentieth-century authors who have re-imagined highly revered stories from Greek myths (Mary Renault, Robert Graves) and Arthurian tales (Rosemary Sutcliff, T. H. White, Mary Stewart, Thomas Berger, Marion Zimmer Bradley, Bernard Cornwell). Silverberg's novel is one of the first to treat the saga of Gilgamesh.

In *Gilgamesh the King*, Silverberg makes use of the central conflicts of the Gilgamesh story, but he naturalizes the supernatural trappings of the poems. Of course, the Sumerian gods—who seem to be an early sketch for the Hellenic pantheon—exist in the novel as myths and as powerful psychological influences; but the fictional events remain entirely naturalistic. As in the poems, however, the action of the novel, narrated effectively by Gilgamesh himself, is given a nicely symmetrical shape.

The novel begins with Gilgamesh's description of the ceremonial burial of his father, King Lugalbanda, and the boy's questions about the nature of death, to which he receives the standard answers of Sumerian myth. The desire for an understanding of the meaning of death continues to haunt Gilgamesh, and in the latter third of the novel it becomes the dominant theme of his life.

Despite the consolations of Sumerian religion, Gilgamesh remains unconvinced, even early in life, that human mortality can be easily defeated. From this opening, the novel moves rapidly through Gilgamesh's early years to the triumphs of his kingship: constructing the walls of Uruk; defeating its enemies; the conquest of the legendary warrior Enkidu, with whom he forms a strong bond of friendship; Gilgamesh's greater conquest of the mountain demon (actually a volcano, which he cools and plugs); and finally his importation of cedar to Uruk.

Though Gilgamesh is supposed to be an absolute monarch, his power is often contested by the priestess of the goddess, Inanna (or Ishtar), and his triumphs turn to tragedy when, at the height of his power, his arrogance causes him to scorn the priestess's offer of marriage. Since this priestess is also considered the incarnation of the goddess, or the feminine principle, Gilgamesh's demonstration of hubris is bound to create suffering. At this point, parallels between Gilgamesh and Homer's Achilles, the hero of the *Iliad*, who is similarly flawed by arrogance and a terrible wrath, begin to appear. After the city is placed under a curse by Inanna, Gilgamesh and Enkidu are forced to kill the goddess's sacred bull in order to restore their authority. In their effort to close the gate to the "underworld," a system of catacombs beneath the city, Enkidu goes into the tunnels and gains a mortal wound, or at any rate, he returns under an oppression of the spirit, and falls ill with a mysterious malady (perhaps tetanus acquired on his trip beneath the earth).

The result is the major tragedy of Gilgamesh's life. Despite all of Gilgamesh's resources, Enkidu wastes away and dies, leaving Gilgamesh with a renewed sense of outrage over human mortality. As Gilgamesh remarks, "Seeing him in mortal terror I was reminded of my own mortality, which haunted me like a knife in my flesh" (GTK 217). Clearly, the grief of Gilgamesh is a psychological wound akin to that suffered by Homer's Achilles when his friend Patrokles is killed by Hector.

In the final third of the novel, Gilgamesh becomes an existential searcher who takes a long and humbling journey to the supposed founts of Sumerian wisdom in an effort to find a way of overcoming death. His pilgrimage to find the supposedly immortal Ziusudra (the Sumerian Noah, also known as Utnapishtim), who had survived the legendary flood, takes him to a dirty little village on an island in the Persian Gulf, where Gilgamesh learns that the immortality of Ziusudra was a myth.

Yet the tragic movement of the novel does not conclude until after Gilgamesh's return to Uruk. As Gilgamesh approaches the city he learns that his former lover, the priestess Inanna, has seized power in his absence, and he narrowly evades a plot to poison him. Knowing that the conflict with the priestess can never be happily resolved, he enters the temple of the priestess and kills her with his knife, in order to regain his kingship.

Though the later years of his reign are marked by constructive acts, these are recounted quickly in the final chapter, where Silverberg allows his hero to voice his reflections on life. This amounts to the familiar modern position of accepting one's mortality, and doing one's best while one lives. As the mature king puts it, "I have come to understand the truth, which is that the escape from death lies not in potions and magic, but in the performance of one's task. That way lies calmness and acceptance" (GTK 317).

Whatever we think of the title character as a source of wisdom, *Gilgamesh the King* is a solidly constructed novel, for the world of archaic Sumeria is plausibly presented in vividly described ceremonial and battle scenes. Moreover, this is perhaps the one work where Silverberg was able to draw directly on his early reading of H.D.F. Kitto's classic study of Greek tragedy (1939). Though Gilgamesh, Enkidu, and the priestess are passionate characters who are almost larger than life, the powerful bond between Gilgamesh and Enkidu and the love-hate conflict between Gilgamesh and the priestess are the materials from which tragedy is forged.

Incidentally, the friendship between Gilgamesh and Enkidu is a central theme of Silverberg's source, but it is explicitly described as not homoerotic by Gilgamesh (155). Their relationship was based on mutual admiration for each other's strength and prowess, and they lived in a time when the relationships between men and women were not romanticized as greatly as today.

Whatever we want to make of this, it is more important to understand that the tone of the final sections of *Gilgamesh the King* is somber and tragic. While the novel fails to achieve a Homeric or Aeschylean level, Gilgamesh is a prototype of modern man, in his restless energy and his melancholic discovery of mortality. Clearly Silverberg's novel is a strong work. Its hero deserves a better fate than Baird Searles's obtuse dismissal in a review in *Asimov's* as "the stereotypical superhero—dumb, vain, and always ready to sock somebody." (February 1985). Silverberg would later respond to such comments by placing Gilgamesh in a parody adventure that satirizes the superheroes of fantasy.

Not pleased with his foray into historical fiction, Silverberg returned to novels of the future with *Tom O'Bedlam* (1985), a novel richly supported by literary allusion much like the award-winning novella, "Sailing to Byzantium," which appeared in the same year. *Tom O'Bedlam* is undoubtedly one of Silverberg's most eccentric works, and for those wondering about the direction of Silverberg's carrer, this enigmatic ambiguous novel provided few clues. To be sure, the novel contains some casual sex and an impressive picture of a blighted future California, but its main focus is the dream visions of the title character, which become part of a communal illusion.

Silverberg's title is the name of an anonymous visionary "mad song" composed in Elizabethan times, and attributed to a "bedlamite," or wandering lunatic who has escaped from Bethlehem Hospital in London. Excerpts from the poem, which contains a powerful phantasmagoria of imagery, introduce each section of the novel.

The song has strong associations with Shakespeare's *King Lear*, where Gloucester's fugitive son, Edgar, assumes the disguise of "Poor Tom," a bedlamite, to join the deranged Lear and his servants, Kent and the jester, on their wanderings on the heath during the storm. In his disguise as Poor Tom, a kind of "holy fool," Edgar persuades the blind Gloucester, his despairing father, to commit a mock suicide. After Gloucester's "survival," Edgar convinces him to accept the anguish of life without complaint. In this, Edgar, the pretended madman and visionary, teaches the "sane" Gloucester to "see" despite the latter's blindness.

Since Lear's ravings, initially caused by his disappointment over rejection by his daughters, contain visionary truth in the form of a powerful indictment of human hypocrisy and ingratitude, the play endows the poetry of madness with a special aura of credibility. Not only in *Lear* but in much Elizabethan and Jacobean drama, the speeches and songs of characters who are supposed to be mad take on the mantle of prophetic truth. This tradition of the visionary truth of the "mad song" was carried on by such Romantic poets as Blake and Yeats, and one of its themes was articulated in Emily Dickinson's lyric assertion that "much madness is divinest sense."[7]

In Silverberg's novel, the tormented vagabond Tom wanders the wasted California world of 2103, dreaming visions of beneficent extraterrestrials, and a "Green World" of fertility as an alternative to earth. The imagery of Tom's visions seems lifted from a medieval dream vision, or perhaps some fantasy film depicting friendly extraterrestrials. Since Tom's environment has been devastated by the "Dust War," which has turned whole states in the middle of America into a "dead zone," the society about him is tattered and unraveling, dispirited by the decay of technology and dismal prospects for the future. This is another version of the retrogressive future Silverberg had portrayed in *Shadrach in the Furnace*; but in place of a humanitarian deliverer, like Shadrach, the novel offers us only Tom's mad visions. The visions may reflect reality, since others besides Tom find the same imagery in their dreams, and the Majipoor books assume that advanced technology can influence the dreams of a populace. However, the visions may be only a collective delusion of the inhabitants of a declining society. Or again, Tom's telepathic power may kill, or it may send people to the Green World or the Sphere of Light. On this point, the novel remains ambiguous, following classic modernist patterns, although readers may well disbelieve in his extraterrestrials. While finding a bizarre religious vision in the novel, Colin Manlove in a perceptive essay has noted that Silverberg fills the novel with "a sense of endings" (RSMT 127). Moreover, as Manlove comments, the novel is pervaded with the presence "of ambiguity and duality" (RSMT 135). In fact, the entire novel may be seen as a kind of "mad song."

Commenting on Yeats's Crazy Jane poems, Harold Bloom observes that "the mad song's singer must present neither a tragic heroism nor an ironic reversal of orthodox values, but simply the wisdom of a more radical wholeness than reason, nature, and society combine to permit us" (*Yeats* 400). Certainly Tom's visions provide an image of "a more radical wholeness" than anything else in his world offers. Reading Silverberg's novel without remembering the tradition of visionary truth in the "mad song," and the prophecies of "holy fools," might convince a reader that its plot and characters are insane. However, if we realize that Tom wears the mantle of the holy fool, then we can accept the novel as Silverberg's extended version of the "mad song," in which, as Robert Killheffer argues, the characters "embrace this loss of self, rush toward it, and the conclusion is a Utopian vision of extraterrestrial paradise" (NYROSF 14). From such a perspective, *Tom O'Bedlam* is an impressive novel about visionary illusion and the conditions that spawn it.

By contrast, Silverberg's next major science fiction novel, *Star of Gypsies* (1986), focuses on craftiness rather than madness, as Silverberg returned to the study of political intrigue—one of his strengths. Set in a distant future of space travel and intergalactic trade, the novel describes the Machiavellian political strategy of Yakoub, a gypsy king, who uses his experience and wiliness to defeat an attempt to seize power by his amoral illegitimate son, Shandor. The conflict shows Yakoub as a master of sophisticated uses of political power in the service of humanitarian responsibility, although the highest value Yakoub serves is the survival of the gypsy people and the preservation of their identity.

Yakoub has a fierce pride in the ethnic survival of the gypsy culture, and most of his contempt for Shandor arises from his belief that Shandor lacks the cleverness traditionally associated with gypsy tradition. This culture, which Yakoub calls "the Rom," defines itself by its relation to the "Gaje" or non-gypsy world, against which it has been obliged to use all its cunning in order to survive. Indeed, in the homogenized future world of "the empire" that Silverberg imagines, only gypsydom has managed to sustain its ancient identity.

It is not surprising that Silverberg should treat gypsy culture with such knowledge and affection. There are strong parallels between the gypsy nation and the Jewish people, both of whom have been subject to persecution and numerous diasporas, and have assumed the role of nomadic outsiders in other societies. Both have been forced to fight desperately with guile and courage for their survival, and both have created enormous treasures of folklore not easily available to the uninitiated. Both have been the targets of ideologues preaching an illusory vision of "ethnic purity"; finally, both were notorious victims of Nazi genocide, although the Nazi campaign against gypsies has been less publicized.

Of course, there have been some important differences between these peoples, too. Judaism, despite being hampered by savage Christian persecution, has been more successful at overcoming ethnic hostility and finding acceptance and success in the post-Enlightenment world of Western Europe and North America. Also Judaism is a culture devoted to the written tradition, whereas gypsydom has tended to perpetuate itself by an oral tradition in Romany, a language that few read or speak. Even the origins of gypsy culture have been the subject of controversy. Yakoub provides his own dubious answer by identifying the source, not as a province of ancient India, but as "Romany Star," a mythic sun and planet system.

At any rate, Yakoub's fierce dedication to the tradition of gypsy cunning sustains his effort to defeat Shandor and guides his wily intrigues with the court of the empire. Taken hostage by his ambitious son, Yakoub turns the captivity to his advantage, using it as a more Machiavellian Gandhi would. During his ordeal he is strengthened by memories of past successes, and by anecdotes of survival and trickery enshrined in gypsy tradition. In short, Yakoub may be Silverberg's finest creation of a trickster hero, an archetype that has fascinated him from the beginning of his career.

However, Yakoub's success as a first-person narrator also helps to define the novel's limitations. Compared with the narrator, the other characters seem limited: Shandor, for all his ruthlessness, does not seem a menacing threat; Damiano, Yakoub's cousin, has a few vivid moments, but remains distinctly a secondary figure; Syluise, Yakoub's favorite mistress, is a memorable character, but she is presented only through Yakoub's memories. Nor does the novel achieve the dramatic momentum it might have attained. Despite the length of Yakoub's ordeal, its outcome seems too obviously calculated in advance.

In order to succeed, of course, Yakoub must scheme to defeat his son, and the novel affirms Silverberg's persistent conviction that political responsibility must override personal feelings (a theme of *Valentine Pontifex* that recurs in *At Winter's End*). Although Yakoub expresses regret over the pleasure he felt in begetting Shandor, Yakoub might have achieved a more tragic stature if his relationship with Shandor had been closer. Nevertheless, within its own limited terms, *Star of Gypsies* is lively and effectively crafted. If for no other distinction, *Star of Gypsies* is notable for Silverberg's knowledge of gypsy culture and for his brilliant depiction of the memorable gypsy leader.

Some of Silverberg's lesser efforts in the eighties and early nineties were expended on time travel tales. The imaginative possibilities of this theme have always stimulated Silverberg, as far back as *Stepsons of Terra*. In addition, his fascination with archaeology has provided an additional impetus for writing about journeys through time without belaboring the question of their scientific feasibility. Not surprisingly, Silverberg now returned to this tradition, publishing a lively young adult novel, a picaresque adventure fantasy, and a pair of reflective novellas in which characters travel to legendary past eras.

Of these books, *Project Pendulum* (1987), aimed at the juvenile market, is probably the slightest. The story begins, however, with an original premise: two twenty-three-year-old twins, Sean and Eric, travel backward and forward in time on scientific missions, interspersed with brief returns to the present. Their itineraries do not overlap, and, since their trips began with five-minute jaunts and gradually grew longer, there seems little risk of their getting involved with the eras they visit. However, the length of their visits increases dramatically with each trip, so that suspense develops. Silverberg adds an unexpected touch when he gives Sean a quasi-mystical epiphany near the novel's end, but whether this event emerges logically from the action is questionable.

Aside from the novelty of the premise, *Project Pendulum* offers little fresh in characerization or plot. The book does a competent job of creating for young readers an awareness of the age of the earth and the length and variety of human history. Essentially Silverberg provides a series of vivid snapshots of the past; but, although ably written, the novel seems to exploit a gimmicky premise. Nevertheless, *Project Pendulum* succeeds for young readers in offering a provocative entry into the turmoil of the past.

In another time travel exercise, Silverberg brought Gilgamesh out of the Sumerian past to swashbuckle in later eras in two novellas that were combined and enlarged by additional narrative to make a picaresque novel, *To the Land of the Living* (1990). Since at least one reviewer had mistaken Gilgamesh for a swaggering adventurer of the Conan variety, it would seem that Silverberg here offered an amusing parody of the Robert E. Howard tradition. Indeed, the first section of the novel, "Gilgamesh in the Outback," conceived for a commercial series called "Heroes in Hell," and later published in *Asimov's* (July 1986), presents a fictional afterworld of the dead, with a caricature of Howard as a repressed homosexual, barely able to suppress his lust for H. P. Lovecraft. Gilgamesh, however, remains an unapologetic heterosexual, although he devotes his existence in this Elysium to his obsessive search for Enkidu. At any rate, this amusing tale was popular enough to win Silverberg another Hugo.

Obviously enjoying the fun of writing an old-fashioned adventure story again, Silverberg followed this novella of Gilgamesh in the afterlife with another, "The Fascination of the Abomination" (*Asimov's*, July 1987), in which Gilgamesh visits a section of hell containing a comic scoundrel called Herod of Judea (supposedly a descendant of the historical Herods) and encounters the demonic Calandola, the cannibal chieftain from *Lord of Darkness*. Both novellas were combined as the first part of *To the Land of the Living*; in the second half, Gilgamesh escapes from Calandola's underworld accompanied by the wily Herod, eventually finds Enkidu and New Uruk, and then journeys to contemporary New York where he has other adventures, including being mistaken for an Iranian terrorist.

Although *To the Land of the Living* lowers Gilgamesh from the heroic level of *Gilgamesh the King* to a picaresque adventurer in a mythological farce, this sequel is an entertaining performance. Indeed, *To the Land of the Living* may be one of the funnier novels of the genre in recent years.

However, Silverberg turned from robust humor to his characteristic elegant irony in two short time travel novellas, *Letters from Atlantis* (1992) and *Thebes of the Hundred Gates* (1991). Narrated in a quiet and contemplative tone, these works demonstrate Silverberg's knowledge of archaeology and ability to evoke a vanished past.

In the more imaginative effort, *Letters from Atlantis*, a member of a twenty-first-century time travel agency, Roy Colton, is reduced to a disembodied presence and sent into the mind of Prince Ram of Atlantis. His vantage point allows him to describe the legendary island empire (on a large volcanic island in the central Atlantic) as it might have existed before the dawn of recorded history. Colton's account, sent in letters to his fiancée on a similar mission in Asia, gradually evokes the image of an impressive but doomed civilization. In sharp contrast to the tribal societies of prehistoric Europe, Silverberg's imaginary "Athilan" is a stately world with impressive architecture and a highly developed social organization, centered in a monarch who, in Byzantine fashion, is both high priest and head of state. A casual reference to "Romany Star" (LFA 66) links the novel with *Star of Gypsies*, offering a hint that Silverberg's Athilan originated with a migration from the world that was the imputed source for gypsy culture. The narrative also implies that refugees from the Athilan catastrophe created the origins of the ancient civilizations in Egypt and Sumeria.

An important feature of the epistolary narrative style is its possibilities for suspense, since the first-person narrator is not aware of the story's outcome until his final letter. Not only is Colton mystified by the actions of the prince whose mind he inhabits, but the reader is encouraged to wonder if Colton will survive the fall of the Athilan kingdom. The prince's discovery of the time traveler (whom he thinks is a demon possessing his mind) produces additional suspense, and dramatic irony results from Colton's revelation to Prince Ram of the impending volcanic eruption that will doom Athilan. Declining to leave his people, the prince accepts the fate of his world with tragic stoicism. So Colton returns to his era with a deeper awareness of the human condition.

While *Letters from Atlantis* is a fine product of the historical imagination, *Thebes of the Hundred Gates* uses time travel and historical reconstruction with slighter effect. For one thing, the plot of this novel is predictable. Once again the author sends out an inexperienced time traveler to visit an ancient world; but this time the purpose is to bring back two members of the Time Service who have been missing for twenty years in the Thebes of ancient Egypt. Although the protagonist Davis journeys to Egypt of the Eighteenth Dynasty without mishap, and eventually meets the missing time travelers, he is unsuccessful in bringing them back because they have chosen to continue living in the time of the Pharaohs. Predictably, the two do not want to relinquish positions in Egypt that give them prominence: the missing woman has become Nefret, a priestess of Isis, while her male colleague has become the royal astronomer. Ironically, instead of returning, they make Davis a captive in the past to prevent him from betraying them.

Although Silverberg describes the world of ancient Egypt plausibly, his romantic reconstruction of a historical city required less imaginative effort than his invention of ancient Atlantis. Moreover, there is little drama in this short novel of ancient Thebes. Nevertheless, Silverberg gives literary and historical enrichment to time travel tales.

In addition to his massive prose effort in short fiction, time travel tales, historical novels, and novels of the future, Silverberg maintained his reputation as a disciplined and industrious professional by undertaking collaborative efforts. One such collaborative enterprise joined his energies with those of his talented wife, Karen Haber. Although they collaborated as editors, and on short fiction, their primary effort was *The Mutant Season* (1989), the first novel in a series that has been continued by Haber. Another major enterprise for Silverberg was the expansion of three celebrated Asimov stories into novels.

The Mutant Season, describing a twenty-first-century earth where talented mutants face discrimination, based on a slight 1973 story by Silverberg, seems to owe a great deal to Haber. The novel is fraught with melodrama and political intrigue, reminiscent of the novels of Silverberg's earliest period, but the major characters are mostly young women. Moreover, the style is uneven and surprisingly unadorned, as a review by Lynn Williams noted

(SFFA1990 440). Indeed, there are few literary allusions and less stylistic irony than we might expect from Silverberg working alone. Finally, there are many passionate sexual encounters, which are entertainingly described; but these are presented with considerable intensity from the feminine point of view, which had not been characteristic of Silverberg's treatment of sex in previous novels. Clearly, the influence of Haber is strong in this book, as Silverberg's preface indicates (MS ix–xi). Although the novel moves swiftly, it is a minor work.

Silverberg's collaborations with Asimov engaged more of his energy. Unfortunately, *Nightfall* (1990), an expansion of Isaac Asimov's classic 1941 *Astounding* story into a full-length disaster novel, is a disappointment. Both Asimov and Silverberg are given credit as collaborative authors, but it appears that the expansion of the short story is largely Silverberg's, prompted in part by the desire to do homage to Asimov's story on the fiftieth anniversary of its publication. However, the resulting novel is a rather tame performance, despite presenting the drama of a society's collapse.

Asimov's brief story described a scientifically advanced society on a distant planet, Kalgash, where six suns provide perpetual daylight. However, when peculiar astronomical circumstances cause the suns to set and bring a period of darkness, the society of Kalgash surrenders to mindless terror at the advent of an experience never before encountered. This ending supplied an ironic comment on Emerson's romantic aphorism that people would regard the stars with unadulterated wonder if permitted to see them only once in a thousand years, a statement used for the story's epigraph.

As a short story, Asimov's "Nightfall" is justly celebrated, and it has remained popular for decades. It may be considered a fable about the terrifying return of superstition and frenetic emotionalism to a society ruled by rationalism, an interpretation that is quite perceptive.[8] However, its evocation of unreasoning terror may have seemed more relevant in the depression-weary America of 1941, haunted by fears aroused by the advent of World War II. That society had seen a panic sweep the East Coast three years earlier when Orson Welles had broadcast his adaptation of *The War of the Worlds*, and was justifiably apprehensive about the nation's drift toward involvement in World War II.

In contrast to that anxious time, the decade of the nineties is more familiar with disaster scenarios and post-disaster stories of social reconstruction. Though the Asimov-Silverberg novel version may have relevance today, its depiction of disaster and the efforts to respond to it seem familiar stuff. Silverberg tries to enlarge the story's scope by introducing the force of religious fanaticism, as well as a widespread neo-Luddite reaction to science, but *Nightfall* remains a predictable story following the rationalist Theremon's adventures during the period of darkness.

The novel ends with the unexpected irony of Theremon's final discovery that the religious cult of the charismatic Mondior follows a television image rather than a real person. Moreover, Theremon learns that the cult is a means for its clever pragmatic director, Folimun, to guide Kalgash toward a restoration of peace and order. In short, Folimun is the unacknowledged leader of Kalgash's "societal quest" for a renewed civilization (Kagle 79). Such a conclusion is reminiscent of Silverberg's clever revelation of the true purpose of the Vorster cult in *To Open the Sky*, two decades earlier, but it no longer has much shock effect.

Despite its smooth writing and dramatic incident, *Nightfall* fails to develop memorable themes. Perhaps the world of Kalgash—except for six suns, a thinly disguised version of earth—is not conceived in sufficient detail; or perhaps this tale of social collapse seems all too predictable to initiated readers. However, Silverberg was more successful with his other expansions of Asimov stories.

In these collaborative efforts, Silverberg was returning to the mode of a science fiction master who had greatly influenced him. An expansion of Asimov's story, *The Ugly Little Boy* (1992), is an impressive novel. In the popular original story (one of Asimov's works that creates a strong emotional response), a research institute brings a boy forward from the Neanderthal era in order to study him in a controlled environment. Edith Fellowes, the kind but plain woman chosen as his nurse, develops a strong maternal relationship with him. Before long, she feels pity for Timmy, and realizing that he is only an object of study to the scientists at the private laboratory where he is virtually a prisoner, she helps him return to his barbaric past. According to James Gunn, this 1958 story is one of Asimov's "best-known and best-loved" (IA 101), but Gunn has reservations about its ending. While Gunn finds the story somewhat appealing, he raises the question of whether the nurse can survive "in a lonely and unrewarding life" in the Pleistocene epoch, and, discounting Edith's maternal feelings, he argues that the story is an irrational departure from logical science fiction (IA 102).

In Silverberg's expansion of the story, the characterizations are enlarged and deepened. Edith Fellowes becomes a stronger character, although she must overcome her submerged love for Gerald Hoskins, the kind but detached director of Stasis Laboratories. Her decision to assist Timmy in an escape to his own time comes after her realization that Hoskins, Timmy, and she can never really become a family, although their relationship has seemed familial to her.

Silverberg also develops two other characters realistically, with a touch of satire: these are Marianne Levien, the ambitious research psychologist who resents Hoskins's rejection of her as Timmy's nurse; and Mannheim, a power-hungry advocate of children's rights. Readers should have no trouble recognizing Levien as a nasty but realistic portrait of a child psychologist who cares more about publication than children; and Mannheim, the spokesman for a cause whose real importance he has forgotten, seems as credible as the stories in yesterday's newspaper.

However, Silverberg has enlarged the novel by portraying Timmy's ritualized tribal world in the Neanderthal era vividly and sympathetically. Since this world, though remarkably primitive, seems more attractive in some ways than twentieth-century society, readers can feel sympathy with Edith in her decision to return Timmy to his people. The problem of Edith's survival in the Pleistocene epoch, which bothered James Gunn (an unrelenting rationalist), is also solved: Edith, who has shown convincing maternal qualities, is accepted on her arrival from the future as an incarnation of the "Great Mother." In describing the gradual development of the emotional bond between Edith and Timmy, Silverberg has turned Asimov's short story into a memorable novel. Edith is, in fact, one of the most credible women characters in Silverberg's canon.

For the third and final collaborative work of Silverberg and Asimov, *The Positronic Man* (1993), Silverberg had a longer and more detailed story to enlarge. Moreover, whereas "Nightfall" was an early Asimov story and "The Ugly Little Boy" came from his middle period, Asimov's fine novella, "The Bicentennial Man," was published in 1976 and represents one of the closing tales in Asimov's long future history devoted to robots. In "The Bicentennial Man," Asimov had confronted the question latent in the earlier robot stories, but seldom faced directly: Can beings with artificial intelligence ever be considered human, or, more simply put, become human (and what is the definition of being human)? This is a question that other authors had raised regarding androids, such as in Clifford Simak's *Time and Again* (1953), Philip K. Dick's *Do Androids Dream of Electric Sheep?* (1969), and Silverberg himself in *Tower of Glass*.

Perhaps Asimov's treatment of the issue was a bit tardy, but "The Bicentennial Man" is an excellent performance. Asimov's novella shows the gradual growth of Andrew Martin over his two-hundred-year life, until the answer must be given in the affirmative. This time, Gunn considers the answer rational and the work "a fitting conclusion to the robot saga" (IA 76), although of course Asimov went on to write other books connecting the robot stories with his Foundation novels.

In Asimov's original novella, Andrew serves the Martin family faithfully for several generations, developing a deep and abiding love for the daughter of his master, Mandy, or "Little Miss," and gradually learning most of the other familiar human emotions. From the beginning it is clear that Andrew is an "aberration" from the manufacturer's standard robot servant and companion for children, because his positronic brain is capable not only of reason, but also of self-awareness and the power to invent and perfect his creations. Andrew gains fame and fortune because of his work as an artist, but he is also the object of human dislike and envy. Although he seeks to gain acceptance as a human, his talent and his apparent imperviousness to death create social resistance. Eventually, after choosing to die, like other humans, Andrew is granted legal status as a human. At the close, Andrew does die, in order to confirm his human status: in this act, he experiences two common and essential human emotions, the fear of death and the acceptance of mortality.

In his expansion of "The Bicentennial Man," Silverberg did not need to add depth to Asimov's portrait of Andrew, the positronic man. However, he does round out the portraits of the other major characters, particularly Gerald Martin and his daughter Amanda, who form the closest bonds with Andrew. Their descendants are also delineated with imaginative detail. Moreover, Silverberg does much to heighten the irony of the story, particularly in handling the attitudes of the managers of the corporation that designed Andrew, and in depicting the complex human attitudes involved in Andrew's fight for legal status as a human. Here Silverberg's additions are valuable. Despite Asimov's hardy rationalism and robust sense of humor, he was seldom able to match Silverberg's considerable talents as a satirist.

All in all *The Positronic Man* is a satisfying novel. Although it lacks the dramatic quality of *The Ugly Little Boy*, and although Silverberg had a strong story to start with, this collaborative effort gives a larger social relevance to Asimov's novella. To sum up, then, the final two of Silverberg's three novelistic expansions of Asimov's stories are considerable achievements.

In the later eighties, Silverberg began a series about a post-disaster earth many millennia hence, first presented in *At Winter's End* one of his finest novels. In general, *At Winter's End* has been received as an imaginative and satisfying work, and Silverberg himself holds it in considerable esteem.[9] In this novel Silverberg inaugurated a study of the historical process of the renewal of a civilization; its characterizations and careful study of cultural process make *Nightfall* look thin by contrast.

At Winter's End describes the emergence from caves of a tribe of intelligent simians, their attempt to re-discover the science and culture of the past, and their establishment of a progressive society in the open air. This is the theme of the "societal quest" defined by Kagle (79–85) and now developed on an epic scale.

A brief summary of setting and characters is in order here. The setting is the earth 700,000 years in the future. A tribe of intelligent simians, "The People" of the story, are survivors of a disaster brought on by the "death stars." The nature of the "death stars" is left ambiguous: either the phrase refers to a final nuclear war; or perhaps it describes meteors and comets from the Oort Cloud that have descended on the earth and created havoc. The people have only legend to guide them, and the truth awaits discovery by their scientists. Clearly, only those who retreated to underground caves have survived. However, some way into the story, we realize that these survivors are in fact the descendants of monkeys or apes who have evolved to a human level of consciousness, perhaps aided by mutation induced by radiation.

At first, we may be inclined to think of the novel's famous precursor about a future populated by simians, the celebrated film *Planet of the Apes* (1968); but Silverberg's novel describes a different world and the focus of his story is on the creation of a new civilization, instead of satirizing the contemporary world, or prophesying its destruction. Avoiding melodrama and sensationalism, Silverberg narrates the departure of The People from the caves, their migration to a new territory, and their efforts to establish a permanent city. Throughout the novel, the narrative tone and its characterizations are handled with maturity and restraint.

Since the tribe at the center of the action has a limited command of human literature and tradition, Silverberg must exercise rhetorical restraint. As the resources of literary allusion are not available, and the society described is technologically limited, Silverberg is forced to rely on a sparing use of detail and a disciplined tone.

Characterization in *At Winter's End* is realistic and three dimensional. Except for the extrapolation of a future world, and one form of telepathic communion, Silverberg presents an essentially naturalistic narrative, eschewing melodrama. The major characters are effectively drawn, though some are recognizable types from earlier novels. The strong and well-conceived feminine characters mark a major advance in Silverberg's work. These include Koshmar, the tribe's leader, who seizes the initiative, decides to break with tradition, and brings the people out of the caves into the open air; her daughter Taniane, who rebels against her mother, but is finally reconciled to her, and assumes the mantle of leadership herself; and Torlyri, Koshmar's closest friend and confidante, who becomes estranged from Koshmar over a question of principle.

The most important masculine character is Hresh, the young visionary, another of Silverberg's youthful prodigies. Hresh is both a seeker after knowledge and the keeper of the tribe's history; but his strong imagination conjures up the plan that saves Koshmar's people in the climactic and most decisive action of the book. Hresh's romantic idealism also contributes to the novel's complications, for the slowly developing romantic relationship between Hresh and the strong-willed Taniane is one of Silverberg's more mature treatments of erotic attraction.

Another well drawn character is Harruel, the frustrated warrior, whose gradual decline into barbarism leads him to commit rape. Although not as tragic in nature, numerous minor figures are also credibly portrayed. Indeed, Silverberg handles a large cast here with seemingly effortless ease. Significantly, *At Winter's End* gives a greater prominence to feminine characters and to a wide variety of age levels than earlier Silverberg novels.

Two features of this future world demonstrate Silverberg's inventiveness and thoroughness: the tribe's mythology, which involves five divinities (more or less familiar gods under different names), and the limited telepathic communion provided by "twining." The latter ritual is a variation on a recurring theme in Silverberg's fiction. This telepathic "twining" is another instance of his attempt to portray a form of telepathic sharing of psyches as a means of overcoming, or at least lessening, the ancient human problem of the isolation of the self. Here the motif is treated carefully as a nurturing ritual that may help to heal the wound of isolation rather than being offered uncritically as a miraculous solution (like the unconvincing drug experience of *A Time of Changes*).

Though it moves slowly, covering nearly a generation, the action of *At Winter's End* unfolds with unforced smoothness. Drama seems to arise without contrivance from the events of the narrative. The novel begins with the tribe deciding to leave their ancient underground haven, and emerging into the "new springtime of the earth," logically enough somewhere near the Mississippi (where there are caves in the river bluffs and the nearby Ozark plateau). Their emergence is followed by a long trek west to an area near the Pacific where they find the ruins of the old city of Vengiboneeza (San Francisco?).

The next section describes various struggles for power while Hresh devotes his energy to learning the secrets of the technology buried in Vengiboneeza. (Hresh's archaeological digging in the ruined city recapitulates a major theme in Silverberg's career: like Hresh, Silverberg was a youthful prodigy who found success partly as a result of investigating archaeological studies of ancient ruins.) Finally, after the tribe solidifies its internal order, choosing the values of Koshmar over those of Harruel, it is forced to face an external threat—its potential extinction by the march of the hjjk-men, a communal life form dominated by a herd mentality. In the tribe's defeat of the hjjk warriors, it is not physical strength like Harruel's that proves decisive, but the intelligence that Hresh and Taniane bring to a conflict where the odds appear to be overwhelmingly against The People.

Despite its dramatic conclusion, much of the conflict of *At Winter's End* is concerned, not with physical action, but with intellectual discovery. A fitting climax to the theme of Hresh's research comes when he is able to open the records of Vengiboneeza and learn, apparently from videotapes, how the earlier civilization fell. This moment provides a major epiphany in the novel, and emphasizes an important theme of Silverberg's mature fiction: in order to know where we are and to build a stable civilization, we must understand the past. At the novel's conclusion, the tribe has established a city-state and appears to be on the way to developing a higher civilized order.

At Winter's End recapitulates many of Silverberg's most cherished themes, yet it presents them from a new perspective. The concentration on the rebuilding of a civilization provides an epic conflict, the founding of a civilization—and one which science fiction has often handled too casually.

Clearly, however, *At Winter's End* is a novel of impressive stature—rich in invention, solid in characterization, and memorable in incident.

Considering the excellence of *At Winter's End*, it should not be surprising that *The New Springtime* (1990) seems anti-climactic. Len Hatfield is probably representative of the readers who assessed this sequel with faint praise as "another moderately interesting exploration of human frailty and hope" (SFFA1990 441). To be sure, *The New Springtime* sets up a promising cultural conflict between the people of the City of Dawinno and their rival, the City of Yissou to the north, with the most serious threat to the developing civilization being an external force, the seductive doctrine of the "nest-mother" of the hjjk people, who lurk nearby.

Much of the psychological conflict turns on the generational conflict between the world views of Taniane, the leader of the City of Dawinno, and her daughter, whose youthful romanticism has led her to embrace the gospel of surrender to a mindless and all-embracing love offered by the nest-mother. Embracing the nest-mother's faith would lead to a loss of individualism and an end to progress, and produce at best a social stasis. Clearly, Silverberg is using the hjjk ethos, which derives from the communal heritage of ants and similar insects, to satirize collectivist ideals (including perhaps "new age" emotionalism) that would extinguish individualism.

Nevertheless, the presentation of these conflicts fails to create the drama of the first book, although there is much intrigue and counterintrigue. *The New Springtime* also lacks the sense of innovation and discovery that gave vigor to *At Winter's End*. Silverberg was obviously eager to follow the success of *At Winter's End* with a sequel, and to enlarge the scope of his future history; but *The New Springtime* seems to focus more on the temptations that destroy civilization than on the challenges of building a new world. Although this second novel contains thoughtful writing, it should have devoted more attention to internal societal conflict, and given less time to the external threat of the nest-mother's siren song.

Turning away temporarily from the people of Dawinno, Silverberg imagined an entirely different setting and theme for *The Face of the Waters* (1991). This novel describes an ambitious quest for a permanent home, a quest taking the form of an old-fashioned sea odyssey on the planet Hydros, a world of oceans and islands. Although the hero, Valben Lawler, a doctor and a man of reason, is a reluctant searcher, he and his fellow humans are forced to begin the quest by the indigenous people of the planet, and, thanks to Nid Delagard, an obsessive seeker of power, the journey becomes an ambiguous religious search.

Once again, familiar motifs appear. One is the crime against another race or species. The resident humans are forced to leave their native island, Sorve, because of a conflict with the planet's ocean-dwelling natives, the Gillies. As in earlier novels, the humans are held to be responsible because of their crimes against the Gillies. While most of the Sorve community are innocent, there have been recurrent acts of human violence in the past, and now one of their number has repeated the old pattern.

Another familiar motif appears in Delagard's drive, that of a powerful man with a sense of destiny, who constantly tries to dominate the fleet of humans obliged to look for a new dwelling. Finally, we have the conflicts between this leader's obsession with the will to power, and the opposition of the person of reason, in this case Lawler.

As a Conradian sea story and as the study of development of a romantic relationship between Lawler and Silverberg's determined heroine Sundira Thane, the novel is quite entertaining. The characterization of Thane also continues Silverberg's recent emphasis on placing strong-willed women at the center of his story. In short, *The Face of the Waters* has much to recommend it.

However, as the description of an epic religious quest for the island known as "The Face of the Waters," the novel may create a mixed response. When the voyagers, reduced to a single ship and their supplies nearly exhausted, reach The Face, we learn that it is a matrix of life on Hydros, a sentient being that spawns the planet's life. as the half insane Father Quillen explains it:

Hydros is a great corporate mind, a collective organism, a single intelligent entity that spans the entire planet. This island which we have come to, this place that we call The Face of the Waters, is a living thing, the brain of the planet. And more than a brain: the central womb of everything is what the Face is. The universal mother from which all life on Hydros flows. (FOTW 332)

In his portrait of "The Face" with a name intended to evoke the creation myth in Genesis, Silverberg attempts to create a numinous and innovative religious symbol, one both renewing tradition and expressing contemporary feeling. Since The Face corroborates evolutionary theory in providing an oceanic source for life, and since it is a feminine matrix or "mother," it may appeal to some current attitudes about religious myth. It also appears to offer a different involvement in a living community from the mindless surrender offered by the nest-mother in *The New Springtime*. The contrasts between these two symbols are important: whereas the nest-mother's communal world involved a surrender of individual consciousness, the communion of selves created by entering The Face provides a union of psyches in which the self retains its individuality.

Unlike the nest-mother, The Face offers more than a release from the burden of selfhood, or a refuge from nature and the ocean. Instead, The Face gives Silverberg's weary seekers an opportunity to enter a community of shared being that will heal the wound of isolation, as well as their alienation from the planet they have adopted. Nevertheless, Lawler, the most sensible of Silverberg's seekers, resists the call of The Face as long as he can.

Despite his loneliness, Lawler fears the loss of his individuality; he also clings to his identity as a terrestrial, which is manifested in his old dream of visiting an earth he has never seen.

After a long inner struggle, Lawler submerges his ego and enters the communion of The Face at the novel's close, whereupon he discovers that he apparently has reached a paradoxical state of belonging to a new communal life while retaining his identity. In his euphoria, he believes he at last has released his grip on his past as the descendant of a terrestrial and become a native of Hydros by merging his being with the planet's source of life.

Although *The Face of the Waters* offers an affirmative conclusion to the voyage of Lawler and his companions, not all will find its resolution convincing. In fact, we may be inclined to question whether the ending fully clarifies the state of mystical union that Lawler and his companions have attained. Moreover, it may be asked if The Face of the Waters is indeed a meaningful religious symbol. It is possible that interpretations of this novel and its importance in the Silverberg canon may be a source of debate for many years. Certainly, however, it is clear that the novel's success depends very much on its value as a study of religious quest. Nevertheless, I would argue that *The Face of the Waters* is one of Silverberg's finest novels.

However we resolve the question, we can see clearly that Silverberg has not abandoned the search for transcendent symbols and meanings that will offer a healing balm for the alienated consciousness that haunts the human condition. Silverberg no longer accepts the simple romantic answers that appealed to him during his third period; but he remains concerned about the psychic divisions and loneliness of modern readers, lost in a cosmos that they find frightening and devoid of meaning.

Silverberg followed *The Face of the Waters* with another novel describing an epic quest, yet the nature of this adventure is entirely different. *Kingdoms of the Wall* (1993) narrates the story of an ascent of a mountainous region that becomes an allegory or metaphor of humanity's journey from savagery and superstition to enlightenment. Silverberg's theme here is conventional in science fiction, one treated rather directly in Robert Heinlein's early "Universe" and more indirectly in the early works of H. G. Wells. Silverberg's reworking of this theme may have been an effort to remind readers that works of religious quest such as *The Face of the Waters* do not require an abandonment of the important values of rationalism. Whatever lands lie beyond the vision of rationalism, Silverberg suggests, humanity should not revert to a mood of obscurantism and barbaric superstition.

In *Kingdoms of the Wall*, the narrator is Poilar Crookleg, a member of a backward tribal society, who chooses to lead a pilgrimage up "the Wall," a range of ridges and mountainous heights that are the sides of Kosa Saag, a great mountain range. Crippled from birth, Poilar has become a kind of village intellectual, but he believes in the legends of glorious religious illumination for those who make the ascent. Commanding a pilgrimage to scale the formidable heights, he shows that his intelligence and strength of will have grown to compensate for physical shortcomings.

Leading a band of forty men and women up the Kosa Saag, Poilar finds ample opportunity to validate his role as leader. The pilgrims pass through a succession of "kingdoms" or tribal fiefs that offer various temptations to abandon the quest. Two of the kingdoms, the realm of ice and the inevitable false paradise of pleasure, are portrayed memorably. At the top of their mountainous ascent, however, the seekers are surprised: they expect to find the "house of the gods," according to traditional myth; but they find no more than contemporary climbers would discover at the summit of Mt. Olympus or any other sacred mountain. What they do discover are a few terrestrial astronauts, marooned there after their starship crashed. This encounter becomes a rude initiation into the world of rationalism and technological thought.

If the novel's ending seems anticlimactic, such an effect was inevitable, given the familiar nature of Silverberg's theme. However, *Kingdoms of the Wall* is vividly and intensely imagined, and Silverberg's characterizations, especially of Poilar and his friend Traben, are skillfully developed. Though the novel is a symbolic tale of humanity's long ascent from naive acceptance of superstition to rationalism, this interpretation should not imply that *Kingdoms of the Wall* is a carefully contrived allegory in the narrow meaning of the term: it is not an intricate pattern in the Spenserian or Bunyan manner in which every character carries some abstract significance. Instead, Silverberg has employed his talents to make *Kingdoms of the Wall* a credible exercise in exploring the heights, enriched with philosophic overtones.

From remote planets, Silverberg returned to earth in the twenty-second century in *Hot Sky at Midnight* (1994), a novel describing life after ecological disaster. The time is 150 years after the breakup of the Soviet Union, and many formerly fertile parts of earth are now deserts because of global warming, although human ingenuity has also brought fertility to desert areas. Despite a ravaged ecosystem, the remaining civilized world of *Hot Sky* is still a "high tech" community, dominated by multinational corporations. *Hot Sky* combines a dismal future like that envisioned in Dick's *Do Androids Dream of Electric Sheep?* (1968)—and its cinema adaptation as *Blade Runner* (1982)—with a "cyberpunk" world of high tech manipulations similar to that found in the novels of William Gibson. As in many recent science fiction films, the future is a wasteland of barren farmlands and urban squalor, with a society on the verge of anarchy. In the world of *Hot Sky*, the polar ice caps have been melting, so that retrieving an iceberg for its potable water has become a hazardous but lucrative business.

Silverberg's novel focuses on two protagonists, Paul Carpenter, a rogue who tries to outwit the system of corporate-determined salary scales by continually switching jobs; and his friend, Nicholas Rhodes, who is a committed humanitarian and researcher. Carpenter's cleverness backfires, as often happens in Silverberg's fiction: first he accepts the risky role as commander of a ship reclaiming icebergs, and then he becomes entangled in a terrorist plot to destroy the Samural Corporation's artificial satellite, Valparaiso Nuevo, now ruled by a Latin American dictator. Although he escapes from the satellite before the explosives are detonated, his fellow conspirators, including Jolanda, his lover, are arrested and perish in the blast.

Consumed by guilt and world weariness, Carpenter volunteers for starship duty to search for other habitable planets. Preparation for the expedition requires drastic physiological alterations, including accepting blindness and having one's eyes replaced by artificial sensory devices, but Carpenter has at last developed a conscience. Whether or not the mission is likely to be a suicidal one does not matter to him at the close.

Only one other alternative for humanity on a dying planet is offered: the other protagonist, Nick Rhodes, is pursuing a program of genetic alteration that, if successful, will allow humans to adjust to a poisoned atmosphere and other dangers of the postindustrial era. However, such genetic changes will transform the appearance and form of humanity into species that appear alien.

Silverberg's dystopian vision of the near future does not offer much hope. In *Hot Sky* there is no disenchantment with life or with nature, but rather a concern that technological civilization will soon have ruined or destroyed the conditions that make life tolerable. *Hot Sky at Midnight* is a brilliant extrapolation of a possible ecological nightmare that could occur a couple of centuries in the future. It presents a more believable world than Silverberg's earlier dystopian satire, *The World Inside*, and depicts the sufferings of more sympathetic and perceptive characters.

After this somber dystopian novel, Silverberg's performance in *Starborne* (1996) represents a surprising change of direction. As always, it remains difficult to predict the road Silverberg's fiction will take. *Starborne* is a return to the tradition of the interstellar quest novel, the origins of which go back as far as E. E. Smith's Lensman novels and Heinlein's "Universe" (1941; published in book form with a sequel as *Orphans of the Sky*, 1963). Later, the tradition had been reshaped in various ways by such writers as Poul Anderson (*Tau Zero*, 1971), and more recently by Gregory Benford. However, by now such novels may well seem old-fashioned; but a supposedly unfashionable theme has never prevented Silverberg from reworking a traditional concept.

Starborne describes a long search for habitable worlds by a specially selected crew, who are characterized with economical touches of realism. The novel returns to a favorite motif, telepathic communication between a member of the crew and a sibling on earth. This idea had earlier been used as the basis of the young adult story, *Across a Billion Years*; now Silverberg adapts it tactfully for a more mature audience. The ship's telepath, Noelle, is blind, with her telepathic powers developed in part as compensation for the deprivation of her chief sense. As a protagonist Noelle provides one of the major points of view: her role as telepath is crucial to the ship's encounter with a strange life form. At the center of the story are Noelle's two relationships: her close bond with a telepathic sister, Yvonne, on earth and her slowly developing erotic relationship with the "year-captain," the commander whose leadership is so effective that he is elected as the perennial leader. This romantic relationship is presented with tact and sensitivity during its slow growth to its passionate consummation in the sexually liberated world of the starship.

However, the novel's most significant theme is Noelle's discovery of mysterious "angelic" intelligences in deep space. Her communion with these presences gives the novel a mystical dimension (although these mysterious beings are presented as natural phenomena). As a result, *Starborne* may be seen as another novel of mystical quest, returning to the spirit of *The Face of the Waters*. As with that novel, questions remain about Noelle's mysterious communion with the angelic beings. After her long communion with them near the novel's end, she learns that they are sentient stars; more important, her psychological communion with the angelic minds infuses her with new energy. Indeed, the blind Noelle gains sight as a result of her merging with this energy. Moreover, similar renewals are granted to the captain and to the rest of the starship crew.

Despite attempts at a technological explanation of these encounters, the depiction of a group of sentient stars that have the power to renew humans through telepathic communion must seem somewhat mystical, and the word "angels" does not seem a bad name for these energy presences. Tradition supports the name of angels, for in medieval lore, angels were actually supposed to work at controlling the spheres and perhaps inhabit them. In Silverberg's speculative novel, the energy beings the starship encounters appear to be a science fiction attempt to visualize those transcendent beings of traditional legend.

Nevertheless, *Starborne*, narrated in a quiet and controlled tone, is an accomplished performance. Whether it is sufficiently realized in fictional terms to be considered a major work is open to question; however, this excursion into romantic mysticism deserves a careful reading.

To turn from the distant reaches of space in *Starborne* to the world of Silverberg's most recent novel, *The Alien Years* (1998), is to drop downward to the earth. As the dedication and an early passage describing Colonel Carmichael's reflections on *The War of the Worlds* make clear, *The Alien Years*, depicting humanity's fifty-year struggle with a superior species, is a work of homage commemorating H. G. Wells's 1898 masterpiece of alien invasion. As such, it also offers a timely treatment of the popular fascination with the idea of visiting aliens, an interest exploited in various nineties films—the silly *Independence Day* (1996), the sardonic *Mars Attacks* (1997), the clever parody of *Men in Black* (1997), the ambitious *Dark City* (1998), and the adolescent heroism of *Starship Troopers* (1997)—and also treated humorously in a seemingly endless parade of television series. (Surprisingly, *The Alien Years* is also, less obviously, an expression of homage to the work of Robert Heinlein.)

A fictional homage to a science fiction classic is nothing new: paying tributes to two of science fiction's pioneers, Aldiss has paved the way for such novels with *Frankenstein Unbound* (1973), a sequel to Mary Shelley's seminal work, and *An Island Called Moreau* (1981), a salute to Wells's handling of the Frankenstein theme. Certainly *The Alien Years* presents a more thoughtful study of alien conquest of earth than films or television have recently done (in an age of political correctness, aliens must resemble giant worms or insects, although these may adequately represent dehumanizing foes).

At any rate, Silverberg's chief concerns are to show the social impact of continued alien occupation and to describe the long process of a developing human resistance. As Colonel Carmichael perceives, Wells, by allowing his powerful Martians to be defeated by terrestrial bacteria, avoided the question of whether humanity as a species had the strength to resist conquest or to win a "war of the worlds" (AY 10). By making human survival an accident of fate, Wells intended to deflate terrestrial arrogance and humanity's "infinite complacency," to use the term he employs in the first paragraph of *The War of the Worlds*. (However brilliantly he envisioned future disasters, Wells was never particularly subtle about his intentions.) His novel, though obviously successful, leaves certain questions unanswered.

It is worth mentioning some here. Why did the Martians want total destruction of earth's inhabitants—an act of genocide directed against an entire species on a well-populated planet? Supposedly the invaders simply wanted earth's space and resources, but if they were prepared to destroy humanity, had they made preparations for disposal of the resulting death and decay? And why were humanity's responses so feeble and lacking in coordination? Besides, Wells's Martians are defeated by terrestrial bacteria in a remarkably short time. Would a superior species have no medical protection against unexpected plagues? Is Wells's solution to the problem simply a clever biological contrivance devised by a former student of Thomas Henry Huxley?

Well, at any rate, if it is supposed that a superior species did attempt to conquer earth and menace human life, the time needed for humans to defeat it—rather than bacteria—would take more than a short war, with international pilots and a beleaguered president manning jet fighters. The swift routing of enemy aliens depicted in recent films is no doubt addressed to audiences weaned on video games and influenced by memories of the Gulf War. However, Silverberg offers greater realism in *The Alien Years*, describing a fifty-year struggle against the enemy.

Although the theme of human survival is well worn, Silverberg handles it with intellectual seriousness. If his premise of invasion by superior hostile beings is granted—aliens whose intelligence is "vast . . . cool . . . and unsympathetic" to borrow Wells's words—Silverberg's extrapolation of earth's future in *The Alien Years* seems persuasive.

For one thing, Silverberg's aliens, the Entities, do not need or desire mass destruction. Instead, they subdue earth's population, first by tampering with the electronic systems necessary for a "high tech" civilization, and then by using telepathic force to cow and intimidate earthlings. Instead of mass destruction they are content to make slave labor of the terrestrials, and otherwise ignore them—except when ill-advised human rebellions produce lethal reprisals, through plague for instance. Somewhat wiser and more pragmatic than Wells's Martians, Silverberg's Entities behave, in fact, a little like the ancient Egyptians in their enslavement of the Hebrews.

The Carmichael family of Santa Barbara, who are the central focus of human resistance, are a credibly drawn group, spanning several generations. In some respects, Colonel Anson Carmichael, the patriarch of the family, may be considered an indirect homage to the work of Robert A. Heinlein—whose middle name was Anson, and who published some early stories under the name of "Anson MacDonald." Old Colonel Carmichael, dedicated to military tradition but with a lively interest in world culture, is an idealized portrait of a soldier and suggests some of the more admirable values (such as courage and resourcefulness) embodied in Heinlein's fiction (and to some extent the worldview of John W. Campbell). His determination to resist an alien invasion that reduces humanity to the role of a secondary species is reminiscent of the spirit Heinlein expressed in *The Puppet Masters* (1951) and *Starship Troopers* (1959), both of which have been popular enough to stimulate film versions in the 1990s. Colonel Carmichael, who dies long before the aliens leave, is a rather tragic figure, or at least a highly sympathetic one, as he slowly declines on his ranch in the mountains above Santa Barbara, determined not to let the glory of humanity's past fade away.

Many of the characters in this novel are effectively drawn, notably Borgmann, the renegade hacker who becomes a collaborator with the aliens; Carol, the "new age" wife of a Carmichael, who, believing the aliens to be lovable beings from a Spielberg movie, rushes to join them, but eventually regrets her act; and most memorable of all, Khalid Burke, the abused son of a working-class Englishman and a Pakistani teenager who died in childbirth. Khalid's stoic mastery of his emotions makes him the human who is the most dangerous to the telepathic entities, since they are unable to discern his hostile intent. It is Khalid's strength of character and his acceptance, in defiance of the bitter events of his youth, of the will of Allah that delineate him as the novel's most memorable figure.

In some respects, *The Alien Years* is a family novel, since Colonel Carmichael's family remain center stage and become the center of human resistance. However, the family is presented with commendable variety; Silverberg avoids having them be idealized carbon copies of the Colonel. The power of the Carmichael family's resistance to alien rule is not diminished by the fact that the aliens apparently choose to leave of their own accord, rather than being driven off by human resistance. It is not the success or failure of the Carmichael spirit that is finally important in the novel, but rather the will to survive and resist, which the family comes to embody.

There is much about *The Alien Years* that is not currently fashionable in mainstream literature, and even less fashionable among academic critics. However, the novel treats its science fictional premises with admirable realism. In sum, *The Alien Years* offers a fine coda to the career of a distinguished science fiction novelist, although that career is far from over.

In the nineties, Silverberg continues to display the fecundity and imaginative strength of his third and fourth periods. Indeed, the Majipoor novels, the Dawinno novels, and the strength of his recent novels suggest that his later career has been misunderstood and undervalued. As fine and accomplished as *Dying Inside* is, the best of the later novels and stories have a solidity and assurance that distinguish the work of an author who is completely the master of his medium and themes.

To be sure, not all readers, including some perceptive critics, have embraced the latest works. As we have noted in this study, Silverberg has often received high critical acclaim, only to have his work dismissed in another decade, or his career written off as another case of a talented author who has surrendered to commercialism. Nevertheless, Silverberg's fiction cannot be disposed of so easily. If negative opinion could kill, then Silverberg the author would appear to have many lives.

At the same time, it is hard to offer a definitive judgment on an author who is still in his prime and likely, with good health, to produce more fine work. Yet we can conclude that Silverberg, though one of the youngest of the generation of science fiction writers who followed the aegis of Heinlein, Asimov, and Bradbury, and entered the field in the fifties, is surely also one of the most talented and successful. Inheriting the romantic tradition of science fiction, and blending it with modernist irony in his third period, Silverberg produced some masterful works. While examining the anguish of modern life, Silverberg also explored some of the alternatives that promised transcendence. Finally, he produced a novel affirming the value of moral action in *Shadrach in the Furnace*.

Returning to the genre in the late seventies, Silverberg also came back in a mature spirit to his original romanticism and created in Majipoor one of the lasting realms of American fantasy. At this point, he might have rested on his achievements, but he continued to pursue his calling as a professional author with integrity and imagination.

Whatever the future of science fiction as a genre, Silverberg's work will occupy an important place in its history and development into a more mature literature. His work as an editor for many publishers, including Arbor House, has also been significant. However, Silverberg's importance cannot be measured merely by his contribution to its history. The author of *The Masks of Time, Nightwings, Downward to the Earth*, "Sundance," and the stories of *Unfamiliar Territory, Dying Inside, Shadrach in the Furnace, Lord Valentine's Castle, Lord of Darkness, At Winter's End, The Face of the Waters*, and *Hot Sky at Midnight* will be remembered as one of twentieth-century science fiction's greatest talents.

Silverberg's career is by no means complete, for he intends to write at least "five or six" more books (letter to author 4 March 1999). Among these are additional works set in Majipoor, such as the forthcoming *Lord Prestimion*. However, the overall shape of his career has already been defined. In the ascent of his personal Castle Mount, Silverberg has prevailed through tenacity, talent, and for the most part, a speculative intelligence, which has guided him on his existential quests in a spirit of independence from fashionable winds of doctrine. In this journey, he has gained a mastery of motifs and iconography of science fiction—the stuff of which many twentieth-century dreams are made—and transformed it into serious literature.

Notes

◆

CHAPTER 1

1. Jonas's comment appeared in his column of reviews of science fiction in a discussion of "Born with the Dead," in the *New York Times Book Review*, 24 August 1975, 29. The comparison was intended to be favorable and remains useful, although the parallels it suggests have their limitations.

2. These comments are posed as hypothetical queries, but they lurk in the background of many discussions of Silverberg. His novels of the eighties and nineties have not received much serious evaluation; in fact, they are often the subject of light-hearted disparagements, or are damned with faint praise.

One instance that may be representative is a prominent article by Thomas Disch, "Big Ideas and Dead-End Thrills," *Atlantic*, February 1992, 86–94. Here Disch, in the process of ridiculing the science fiction genre, uses LVC (New York: Harper and Row, 1980) as an example of Silverberg's supposed abandonment of his serious literary work of the late sixties and seventies. For some critics, Silverberg's early sins are forgivable, but his backsliding into romantic fantasy is not. Disch, however, goes on to dismiss nearly everyone working in the genre (except Wolfe and Aldiss, whose masterpieces are chided for not becoming bestsellers) as producers of commercial entertainment. Apparently Disch has found this critical approach sufficiently rewarding to produce a book deriding the genre as mostly juvenile fantasy allied to the "flying saucer" mythology.

3. Silverberg speaks of himself casually as an "old pro" in a letter to the author (6 September 1988). Many of his more recent autobiographical comments stress his growth and commitment to professionalism as a writer and editor.

Any author must feel some conflicting feelings about his target audience. Silverberg's contrasting attitudes toward his audience are revealed in the interview with

Jeffrey Elliot, "Robert Silverberg: Next Stop, Lord Valentine's Castle," in his *Science Fiction Voices #2* (San Bernardino, CA: Borgo, 1979), 51–62, where anger and self-reproach gradually give way to a more charitable tone; and his interview with Charles Platt, "Robert Silverberg," in his *Dream Makers* (New York: Berkley, 1980), 261–268, where he shows enthusiasm about returning to full time authorship in LVC.

4. Aldiss, Wolfe, and LeGuin are all mentioned favorably by Disch in "Big Ideas and Dead-End Thrills," 86–94, but Wolfe and Aldiss are damned with faint praise for having produced instances of "success d'estime." The considerable international reputation of these three has been helped by not beginning like Silverberg with a period of unabashed commercialism; and by factors outside of science fiction, such as LeGuin's feminism and Aldiss's contributions to mainstream realistic fiction and criticism.

5. Dick produced many novels too rapidly, as is well known. An energizing force in science fiction, Ellison has done battle with Hollywood and critics, but he has also made a few commercial compromises. Although Farmer began as an iconoclast, much of his work during his years as a full-time technical writer was devoted to establishing a reputation (as I indicate in my study, *The Magic Labyrinth of Philip José Farmer* [San Bernardino, CA: Borgo, 1984]). His literary motivations have often been tinged by the lure of commercialism. Pohl has been an able editor, novelist, and short story writer, but the demands of the market have also influenced his work. All these authors, nevertheless, have done some excellent work.

6. The best description of Silverberg's early career as an author and the later distinction he attained is still Thomas Clareson's RS (Mercer Island, WA: Starmont, 1983), to which I refer frequently. Clareson credits Silverberg with enormous knowledge of literary modernism. Silverberg's early life as a prodigy is well described in "The Making of a Science Fiction Writer," in WW, ed. Robert Silverberg (New York: Warner, 1987), 1–34.

7. Angry comments about audience reaction to his best fiction were voiced in Silverberg's interview in Elliot's *Science Fiction Voices #2*, 51–62. However, later comments in the interview in *Dream Makers*, 252, are more charitable about the audience and some remarks (263) suggest that Silverberg's literary vision needed to expand beyond the merely ironic spirit of DI (New York: Scribners, 1972; New York: Ballantine, 1973).

8. Silverberg, in an address to the Convention of the International Association for the Fantastic in the Arts of Ft. Lauderdale in March 1989, complained bitterly that the sale of 13,000 hardcover copies of LOD (New York: Arbor, 1983) was evidence in the trade that the novel was a "failure." Switching to historical fiction produced marketing problems, since bookstores were uncertain whether to place LOD and GTK (New York: Arbor, 1984) in the historical fiction shelves or in the science fiction and fantasy sections.

9. The metaphor of the artist as juggler is implied in LVC. Silverberg uses it explicitly in "The Making of a Science Fiction Writer," WW, 10, commenting that "a writer, a professional writer, goes about his work more or less as a juggler does."

10. Silverberg's readiness to describe himself as an "old pro" (letter to author, 8 September 1988) may represent the mood of a period when he began to return strongly to science fiction tradition in his writing, as chapter 8 of this volume describes. By contrast, modernist rhetoric about literary art since the time of Baudelaire

tends to stress the artist's adversary relationship with the mass market and with middle-class values. This is so well known as to require no further documentation.

11. Killheffer's essay, "Striking a Balance: Robert Silverberg's *Lord of Darkness, Dying Inside*, and Others," appeared in NYROSF, 12 August 1989, 1, 12–14. While Killheffer's approach shows some insights, it suffers from a lack of perspective provided by a knowledge of Silverberg's overall career—as do many essays on one aspect or another of Silverberg's work.

12. Although I generally follow the divisions of Silverberg's career established by Clareson (RS), I have introduced the concepts of apprentice, journeyman, and master because they seem to clarify matters. I am indebted to Clareson and to Silverberg himself (letter to author, 8 September 1988) for details about his life. Silverberg's best known accounts of his early career are given in SBTC, in *Hell's Cartographers*, ed. Brian W. Aldiss and Harry Harrison (London: Weidenfeld and Nicolson, 1975; reprint, London: Futura, 1976), and "The Making of a Science Fiction Writer," in WW, 1–34. A helpful collection of Silverberg's essays and comments over the years about his career and the genre is RR (Grass Valley, CA: Underwood Books, 1997).

13. The English "new wave" is best described by Brian Aldiss, with David Wingrove, TYS (New York: Atheneum, 1986; reprint, New York: Avon, 1988), 285–308. The period is still controversial, like much about the sixties.

14. The worldview of Campbellian science fiction is described by Aldiss in TYS, 207–229, and by Silverberg himself in the Afterword to a 1980 reprint of SP (Hicksville, NY: Gnome, 1957), 213–220.

15. For instance, see Silverberg's comments in the Elliot interview cited above in note 7, and his prefatory note to "Road to Nightfall" in TBORS (New York: Pocket, 1976), 1–2. Malzberg's essays in *The Engines of the Night* (Garden City, NY: Doubleday, 1982) constitute a strident attack on the majority audience of science fiction. Similar attitudes were voiced in Ellison's interview in Jeffrey Elliot's *Science Fiction Voices #3* (San Bernardino, CA: Borgo, 1980), 9–18, which shows Ellison evolving from a genre author to a critic of modern culture.

16. Like Conrad, Silverberg has been concerned with the tragic nature of history. Many of the later works such as the 1987 novella "The Secret Sharer" and LOD have revealed an obvious Conradian influence. Russell Letson has suggested that the concerns of Conrad and W. B. Yeats have dominated much of Silverberg's fiction in RSMT, 36.

CHAPTER 2

1. For a detailed account of *Galaxy*, see John Clute and Peter Nicholls, eds., EOSF, 2nd ed. (New York: St. Martin's, 1993; reprint, New York: St. Martin's, 1995, 462–464. For a brief account of Ferman's career at FASF see EOSF, 425–426. FASF was notable for its interest in literary values and traditions as well as for its hospitality to fantasy and science fiction that was not of the "hard science" variety.

2. The chief Ace editor was Donald A. Wollhelm, who had himself written some "space opera." During the fifties and early sixties, Ace reprinted much adventure science fiction and fantasy from the twenties, thirties, and forties, including Philip Nowland's original Buck Rogers novel, and novels by Austin Hall, Robert E. How-

ard, Ralph Milne Farley, Ray Cummings, Otis Adelbert Kline, Wallace West, Homer Eon Flint, Edmond Hamilton, and the early John W. Campbell.

3. Others have noted the fairy tale aspects of romantic science fiction, including Eric Rabkin, in *The Fantastic in Literature* (Princeton, NJ: Princeton, University Press, 1976), 54–59, where not only science fiction but also detective tales are likened to fairy tales.

4. Garrett was a likable, but erratic author and collabator, as the comments by other authors make clear in *The Best of Randall Garrett*, edited by Robert Silverberg (New York: Time Scape, 1982).

CHAPTER 3

1. Majipoor has its share of exotic cities, notably in MC (New York: Arbor, 1982), not to mention a few reduced to archaeological digs. Silverberg's study of anthropological works was probably of immense help in creating the tribal cultures of Dawinno in AWE (New York Warner, 1988), and Sulidor in DTTE (New York: Doubleday, 1970).

2. Clareson gives the total output at seventy (RS 23), but he begins his count with 1960. Silverberg's first non-fiction work was *Treasures beneath the Sea* (?1960), but it was not until 1962 that his productivity in this area really picked up. There are a few other problems involved in providing a definitive figure: TGD (Indianapolis, IN: Bobbs-Merrill, 1967), and *The Search for El Dorado* (?1967) are essentially the same book.

3. Letson uses the phrase to describe the strengths of TOTS (New York: Ballantine, 1967) in the Introduction to the Gregg Press edition (Boston, MA: Gregg, 1977), pp. v–x. However, the term "the new Silverberg" had been used frequently by reviewers earlier to describe the stream of impressive works that appeared in 1969–74. Clareson picks the phrase up for his discussion of TOTS, but disagrees with Letson's assessment of the work as the beginning of the "new Silverberg" (RS 39), citing the work's loose structure as a defect.

4. I have taken the term "detribalized" from an essay on Conrad's *Heart of Darkness* by Harold R. Collins, "Kurtz, the Cannibals, and the Second-rate Helmsman," describing the plight of the helmsman who is caught in limbo between his native culture and European civilization. Collins's essay originally appeared in *Western Humanities Review* (Autumn 1954): 299–310; but it is reprinted in *Joseph Conrad's Heart of Darkness*, ed. Leonard F. Dean (Englewood Cliffs, NJ: Prentice-Hall, 1960). The theme of "detribalization" may be applied to Native Americans, and in fact, haunts the conclusion of Silverberg's *Home of the Red Man* (New York: New York Graphic Society, 1963). It would reappear in the story "Sundance."

5. This myth was explored in Yeats's exercise in creative mythology, *A Vision* (1925), and its themes are implied by the imagery of some of his famous lyrics, such as "Leda and the Swan" and "The Second Coming."

6. Perhaps it is confusing to use a genre term like "new wave" in connection with the "experimental fiction" or "metafiction experiments" of the late sixties and seventies, but both terms usefully describe an era of shifting attitudes and technical experiment in narrative. The presence of such writers as J. G. Ballard in the English "new wave" was bound to be influential. However, as Peter Nicholls notes in his

essay on the "new wave" in EOSF, 865–867, the term originally was borrowed from film criticism. More will be said about Silverberg's experimental fiction in chapter 5.

CHAPTER 4

1. While there is no evidence that Silverberg has read either Barrett or Percy, he certainly would have been aware of their work. Barrett's work received attention in New York circles, and Percy's essays appeared in a number of periodicals and literary journals in the sixties. Percy's first novel, *The Moviegoer* (1961), won the National Book Award and his second, *The Last Gentleman* (1966), satirized some of the social attitudes of the time. Percy even dabbled in science fictional extrapolation in *Love in the Ruins* (1971). However, more significantly, discussion of existentialism was fairly common in the New York of the 1960s.

2. Martin Buber's theology, influenced by Hasidic mysticism, was part of the *Zeitgeist* in the sixties; it is most famously expressed in his *I and Thou*, trans. Ronald Gregor Smith, 2nd ed. (New York: Scribners, 1958; reprint, New York: Macmillan, 1965), which expresses both a mysticism about experiencing nature and about encountering others as persons. However, several other works by Buber were translated and widely read in this time.

3. Paul Tillich's attempt to make a synthesis of existentialism and a symbolic interpretation of Christian myth permeated popular discussions of religion in the late fifties and sixties. In his *Dynamics of Faith* (1957; reprint, New York: Harper, 1958), 1–29, Tillich develops his famous definition of religion as one's "ultimate concern."

4. Jung's anima symbolism is fairly well known; it is expounded in *The Basic Writings of C. G. Jung*, ed. Violet de Laszlo (New York: Viking, 1971), 139–162, where in a selection from *Aion*, Jung provides a definition of anima symbolism. The anima is an ancient word for the soul, and is usually depicted as feminine; its negative counterpart, the "dark anima," is associated with the temptresses and "femme fatales" of the literature of the Western world, and more especially with such characters in Romantic and Gothic poems and fiction.

5. W. B. Yeats uses the term "radical innocence" most memorably in "A Prayer for My Daughter," describing a condition that the soul "recovers."

6. "Transformational religions" appear to be heterodox attempts to turn secular experience into experiences illuminating the sacred, although Dudley's essay is a little murky on this point.

7. David Thorburn in a fine study, *Conrad's Romanticism* (New Haven, CT: Yale University Press, 1974), also sees an affinity between Marlow and Kurtz (122). Such an interpretation has also been applied to Conrad's "The Secret Sharer," another work that has influenced Silverberg.

8. The journey to a mystical epiphany that results from affirming the world of nature or images, rather than purging oneself of phenomena, as in classical Christian mysticism, is also suggested by the essays of Ralph Waldo Emerson, especially "Nature" and the poetry of Walt Whitman, particularly "Song of Myself." There is a considerable body of scholarship devoted to the mysticism in Emerson and Whitman.

9. It should be noted that encountering another person telephatically or through drug-induced perception takes Buber's theology of personal encounter to an extreme not advocated by Buber.

10. The tradition of Romantic quest narrative has been a stronger influence on science fiction than historians of the genre generally acknowledge. It is invoked at the beginning of Mary Shelley's *Frankenstein* and lies behind much of Verne's work. The motif is revived in Wells's Time Traveller's quest in *The Time Machine*. One of the better treatments of the links between science fiction and Romanticism from a genre historian is Darko Suvin's discussion of these connections in *Metamorphoses of Science Fiction* (New Haven, CT: Yale University Press, 1979), 121–130, where the importance of Blake's and Shelley's apocalyptic poems for science fiction is assessed. For a discussion of the romantic quest tradition linking it to David Lindsay and his successors, the reader should consult Harold Bloom, *Yeats* (New York: Oxford University Press, 1970; reprint, New York: Oxford University Press, 1972), 88–96.

11. For the past half-century, Blake studies have emphasized the "apocalyptic humanism" of Blake's prophetic poems, especially the late prophetic works, where the apocalypse is brought on by the power of the human imagination.

12. As is well known, the mandala is Jung's symbol of unity, usually depicted as a quartet, which is also circular. As June Singer notes in *The Boundaries of the Soul: The Practice of Jung's Psychology* (Garden City, NY: Doubleday, 1972; reprint, Garden City, NY: Doubleday Anchor, 1973), mandala is a Sanskrit word for circle, and "it means more especially a magic circle" (300). A useful discussion of this Jungian archetype is found in DOS, 199–203.

13. The term "death-in-life" is used to describe extreme age, and should be considered a contrast to the zombie-like "life-in-death" of the resurrected humans in BWTD. Both phrases are suggested by Bloom's discussion of Yeats's "Byzantium" in *Yeats* (391).

14. The novella is somewhat ambiguous about its concluding events, but Silverberg has confirmed in personal conversation (March 1989) that Oxenshuer is a sacrificial victim. Unlike some of the more celebrated figures in Greek tragedy, such as Oedipus, he seems unaware of his fate.

15. Oxenshuer's sacrifice is not only Dionysian but somewhat Christ-like, since he seems willing to die for the community that has accepted him. At the same time, the sacrifice allows him to expiate his guilt, and therefore his mood is perhaps more resigned than ecstatic, whereas a truly Dionysian figure might be intoxicated with a kind of rhapsodic surrender to a moment of self-transcendence. Incidentally, the author has assured me that Oxenshuer will indeed become the community's sacrificial scapegoat figure.

CHAPTER 5

1. The term "fabulators" was used, not very happily, by Robert Scholes in his study, *The Fabulators* (New York: Oxford University Press, 1967). The approach was enlarged in later works.

"Post-modernism" has become a buzzword of nineties criticism, without always being used to bring light into obscure areas. However, it has been associated with fiction that is "self-reflexive," calling attention to its own nature as a narrative construct; the word is also associated with fictive constructs that parody narrative conventions or constantly remind readers of alternative narrative possibilities. Post-modernism is also associated with other attempts to undermine conventional narrative conventions or protocols, with a playful verbal texture, and with endings that reject the traditional forms of closure. It is often assumed that modernist fiction (1914–1970), permeated by irony, usually offered some form of closure. One attempt to define post-modernism is Linda Hutcheon's *A Poetics of Postmodernism: History, Theory, Fiction* (New York: Routledge, 1988; New York: Routledge, 1995).

However, some limitations of the post-modern view of openness and closure are offered by Wayne C. Booth in *The Company We Keep: An Ethics of Fiction* (Berkeley: University of California Press, 1988), 60–67. A view that contests the assumptions of much "post-modern" criticism is the idea that the nineties are the beginning of a New Romantic age.

2. Raman Seldes and Peter Widdowson in *A Reader's Guide to Contemporary Literary Theory*, 3rd ed. (Lexington: University of Kentucky Press, 1993), provide one overview of the variety of literary theories, most of them influenced by European thinkers, that arose in this period. The model of Borges's stories, however, was a major influence on the "new fiction" of the sixties, especially on Barth, Gass, and Coover. Older models, such as Joyce's work, should not be discounted, however. Though influenced by Borges, Barth made a clear effort to recover eighteenth-century narrative modes for twentieth-century experiences in such books as *The Sot-Weed Factor* and *Giles Goat-Boy*, and some "post-modern" innovations may be found in *Tristam Shandy*.

3. Indeed, innovative techniques, particularly those involving parody, often imply a satirical vision. Coover's shorter fiction is permeated with satire, and it should not be forgotten that Barth (*The End of the Road* [1958]), Coover (*The Origin of the Brunists* [1965]), and Gass (*Omensetter's Luck* [1966]) all got started with novels containing a good deal of obvious social criticism.

4. Most of Silverberg's early fiction is concerned with the consciousness of a young white male somewhat like the author. The chief differentiating characteristic is generally the question of whether the protagonist is an untried youth trying to establish himself, or a veteran professional being tested once more. The chief exception had been the Nidor stories, as we have noted.

5. Both Dickson's and Silverberg's stories probably attribute more intelligence to dolphins than is warranted by reality. During the sixties, popular culture tended to conceive of the dolphin as nearly human. Such stories about sentient animals were not new in science fiction tradition. As Aldiss notes (TYS 2250), Clifford Simak had written stories about sentient dogs in the 1940s, and Eric Frank Russell had experimented with similar tales.

6. A close rapport or identity between humans and nature was a goal of much major Romantic poetry, as Suvin, *Metamorphoses of Science Fiction*, 121–130, and others point out. Northrop Frye, an influential scholar of romanticism, has argued that humanity should strive to create a transformed world of "humanized nature" where humanity, nature, and art all become combined in one identity in *Anatomy of Criticism* (Princeton, NJ: Princeton University Press, 1957; reprint, New York: Atheneum, 1966), 141–146. Such ideas permeated the atmosphere in the sixties, when these stories were being conceived.

7. Here mention needs to be made of only a few science fiction writers who wrote "new wave" stories, such as Philip José Farmer, Gene Wolfe, Ursula LeGuin, and R. A. Lafferty.

8. Borges entitled one of his collections *Ficciones* (1962), although the meaning here is that of stories that possess the nature of fables or deliberately draw attention to their fictive nature. Another meaning of the term may be close to "exemplary novels," a term used by Cervantes (Robert Scholes, *Fabulation and Metafiction* [Urbana: University of Illinois Press, 1979], 130–133).

9. Coover's "The Babysitter" with its multiple alternative narratives first appeared in his collection *Pricksongs and Descants* (New York: Dutton, 1969).

10. The stories of the "Instrumentality" by Cordwainer Smith (Paul Linebarger) present a number of characters who belong to sentient non-human species, which are apparently the result of mutation or genetic alteration of terrestrial animals. One of the best known examples of such characters is the feline Lady May in "The Game of Rat and Dragon" (1955).

CHAPTER 6

1. Jung's efforts to define the role of anima figures may be found in *The Basic Writings of C. G. Jung*, 158–182, and Joseph Campbell, ed., *The Portable Jung* (New York: Viking, 1971), 139–162. Another discussion of the matter by a Jungian scholar is the one by M. L. Von Franz in *Man and His Symbols*, ed. C. G. Jung (London: Aldus, 1964), 177–188. Following Jungean theology, here and in *Dying Inside* Silverberg focuses on a close relationship between the protagonist and a sister, although the relationship collapses.

2. The trickster or rogue, known as a "picaro" in Spanish literature, is no doubt older than Odysseus, the archetypal trickster in Greek literature. Paul Radin's classic study, *The Trickster* (New York: Philosophical Library, 1956), deals with variations on the type in Native American folklore, with the archetypal example being "Old Man Coyote." Although a trickster character is clever about escaping from perilous situations, he often creates trouble for himself through his own cleverness, as happens to the protagonist of *Up the Line*.

3. Gordon's essay appeared in *Extrapolation* 23 (Winter 1982): 345–361.

4. I am indebted to my former wife, Margaret Sullivan Chapman, for calling attention to similarities between *Metropolis* (1926) and TOG. Both works deal with the exploitation of labor, and in both the oppressed classes have turned to their version of religion for consolation. However, I am not suggesting that Silverberg was consciously writing an imitation of this classic film.

5. George Tuma's essay is "Biblical Myth and Legend in the *Tower of Glass*: Man's Search for Authenticity," *Extrapolation* 15 (May 1974): 174–191. Philip Dick's android novels were undoubtedly an influence on the novel.

6. In *Yeats*, 15, Bloom compares Victor Frankenstein, the scientist, to Shelley's self-absorbed and solipsistic poet in *Alastor*.

7. Thomas P. Dunn and Richard D. Ehrlich, "The Mechanical Hive: Urbmon 116 as the Villain-Hero of Silverberg's *The World Inside*," *Extrapolation* 21 (Winter 1980): 338–360.

8. Silverberg himself suggested that his ironic fiction had reached its limits, and he worried that he might have alienated his audience (DM 263–264).

CHAPTER 7

1. Charles Platt, "Robert Silverberg," in *Dream Makers*, ed. Charles Platt (New York: Berkley, 1980), 263. Probably the commercial motives, though great, are over-emphasized by Silverberg. Silverberg throughout his career has in part commented as though he identified success with sales figures—a practice that gives support to critics who view him as a market-driven writer.

2. Actually, Silverberg had showed his disillusionment and weariness in "Sounding Brass, Tinkling Cymbal," 43–45, where he gives the impression of exhaustion, cou-pled with disenchantment with the audience and market. The same note was sounded in the interview with Elliot, in *Science Fiction Voices #2*, where Silverberg admits that he intended his temporary retirement from the fray to be permanent (52–53). No doubt the same sentiments were expressed elsewhere.

3. Even in the Elliot interview, Silverberg suggests that his annoyance with readers may have been "a premature kind of sulk" (52), because his more worthy books did begin to sell, after the audience caught up with him. *Dream Makers* (77–86) ex-presses this more conciliatory attitude, raising the possibility of whether Silverberg's complaints about the audience were not due in part to inactivity. By contrast, Barry Malzberg's interview in the same volume shows a more uncompromising attitude toward science fiction (80), although it is open to charges of arrogance.

4. In general, Silverberg's later view is that he had tried too hard to make sales, without contributing much originality to the genre (SBTC 23–26).

5. Kathryn Hume develops a theory of fantasy in *Fantasy and Mimesis* (London: Methuen, 1984) that explores fantasy according to its function. Although some read-ers would try to place the Majipoor works in the category of literature of escape (55–81), they should be viewed as sophisticated romances and placed in her category of the "literature of vision" (82–100).

6. On the Jungian shadow archetype, a good exposition is presented by Von Franz in *Man and His Symbols*, 168–176. To some degree the shadow figure here is similar to the frightening pursuer of Ged in Ursula LeGuin's highly acclaimed *A Wizard of Earthsea* (1968).

7. The "Great Mother" archetype is highly important in Jungian thought, and corresponds to the fairy godmother or tutelary mother figure in fairy tales (and the sophisticated romances of the nineteenth-century fantasy writer, George MacDon-ald). A discussion of the Great Mother archetype may be found in *The Basic Writings of C. G. Jung*, 327–360.

8. Silverberg appears to have appropriated a name from Tolkien's *Lord of the Rings* here: Numinor is an ancient name for Atlantis in Tolkien's mythology, although he preferred the spelling "Numenor." The kinship of "Numinor" to Otto's "numi-nous" is probably not accidental. Otto's classic *The Idea of the Holy* appeared in 1923; a good translation is John Harvey's translation of the second edition (New York: Oxford University Press, 1950; reprint, New York: Oxford University Press, 1958). See pp. 12–13 for a discussion of the "sacred awe" or numinous experience.

9. Obviously, the political system of Majipoor is somewhat elitist and Burkean, depending on the authority of tradition. Most of the opposition to it has come from the dispossessed.

CHAPTER 8

1. At his public address, at the Conference of the International Association for the Fantastic in the Arts at Ft. Lauderdale, in March 1989, Silverberg acknowledged publicly that LOD "reeked of Conrad," although he had not been fully aware of the influence during its composition. Other Conradian parallels have been explored in discussions of DTTE (New York: Doubleday, 1970; reprint, New York: Ballantine, 1973) and the shorter fiction treated earlier in this chapter.

2. The film referred to is, of course, Coppola's *Apocalypse Now* (1979), which remains a subject of critical debate. *Heart of Darkness* has also received a more conventional film adaptation from the cable channel, Turner Network Television.

3. Silverberg uses the phrase in the Afterword to LOD (559), but it may create misunderstanding for those who have not read the novel. There are no instances of magic or the supernatural in the novel and Calandola is the only character who seems larger than life. For the most part, the narrative stays within the bounds of conventional realism.

4. Silverberg credits Battell's narrative in the Afterword (559), calling it a "brief narrative" and describing its history, starting with its first appearance as published by Samuel Purchas (1625). Indeed it is a thin narrative that has been greatly enlarged by Silverberg. Silverberg's invention of a neo-Elizabethan prose deserves more attention than space allows. It should be noted here that Elizabethan travel narratives, though colored by rhetoric and allusion, tended to be less mannered and Ciceronian than Elizabethan fictional works and much Elizabethan drama. For further information, see *The Oxford Companion to English Literature*, edited by Margaret Drabble (New York: Oxford University Press, 1985), 799.

5. Romantic literature is replete with guilt-haunted wanderers and outcasts from the ancient mariner, Byron's Cain, and Mary Shelley's Victor Frankenstein, to the insane and criminal narrators in Poe and the traumatized Ishmael in Melville's *Moby-Dick*. There is a large body of scholarship on this theme, which is too well known to require citation here.

6. N. K. Sandars, ed., *The Epic of Gilgamesh* (Baltimore, MD: Penguin, 1960), places the epic's events in the third millennium B.C. (14–15). The text itself is dated, somewhat speculatively, from the second millennium B.C. Although a "heroic age" of ancient Sumeria has been proposed, Sandars is skeptical about this hypothesis (20).

7. Dickinson's famous statement opens the lyric given Number 435 in the definitive edition, edited by Thomas Johnson (New York, 1955), three volumes. On the tradition of Elizabethan and Romantic mad songs, see Bloom's commentary in *Yeats*, 398–400.

8. James Gunn in *Isaac Asimov: The Foundations of Science Fiction* (New York: Oxford University Press, 1982), 83–86, attributes much of the story's appeal to its "alignment of forces"; scientists are in conflict with apostles of the irrational.

9. Gerald Jonas's review in the *New York Times Book Review*, 24 July 1988, 25, was fairly typical of many favorable reviews that AWE received. Jonas, however, tempered his response, suggesting that Silverberg's depiction of the environment of the future was inferior to Brian Aldiss's work in *Helliconia Winter*.

Works Consulted and Cited

◆

WORKS BY OR EDITED BY ROBERT SILVERBERG

Across a Billion Years. New York: Dial, 1969; reprint, New York: Tom Doherty, 1983.

The Alien Years. New York: Harper, 1998.

Aliens from Space by David Osborne [pseud]. New York: Avalon, 1958.

The Arbor House Treasury of Science Fiction, ed. Robert Silverberg with Martin H. Greenberg. New York: Arbor House, 1980.

At Winter's End. New York: Warner, 1988.

The Best of Randall Garrett, ed. by Robert Silverberg. New York: Timescape, 1982.

The Best of Robert Silverberg. Vol. 1. New York: Pocket Books, 1976.

Beyond the Safe Zone. New York: Warner, 1986; reprint, New York: Warner Books, 1987.

The Book of Skulls. New York: Scribners, 1972; reprint, New York: Berkley, 1979.

Born with the Dead and Other Stories. New York: Random House, 1974; reprint, New York: 1979.

The Calibrated Alligator. New York: Holt, Rinehart, Winston, 1969.

Capricorn Games. New York: Random House, 1976.

Collision Course with *The Nemesis from Terra* by Leigh Brackett. New York: Ace, 1961.

The Conglomeroid Cocktail Party. New York: Arbor House, 1984.

Conquerors from the Darkness. New York: Holt, Rinehart, Winston, 1965; reprint, New York: Ace, 1979, with *Master of Life and Death*.

The Cube Root of Uncertainty. New York: Macmillan, 1970; reprint, New York: Collier Books, 1971.

The Dawning Light. With Randall Garrett. New York: Gnome, 1958; reprint, New
York: Ace, 1982. Original publication under name of Robert Randall.

Dimension Thirteen. New York: Ballantine, 1969.

Downward to the Earth. New York: Doubleday, 1970; reprint, New York: Berkley,
1979.

Dying Inside. New York: Scribners, 1972; reprint, New York: Ballantine, 1973.

Earth's Other Shadow. New York: New American Library, 1973.

The Face of the Waters. New York: Bantam, 1991.

The Fantasy Hall of Fame, ed. Robert Silverberg. New York: Harper, 1998.

The Feast of St. Dionysus. New York: Scribners, 1972; reprint, New York: Berkley,
1979.

Frontiers in Archaeology. Philadelphia, PA: Chilton, 1966.

The Gate of Worlds. New York: Holt, Rinehart, Winston, 1967; reprint, New York:
Tom Doherty, 1984.

Gilgamesh the King. New York: Arbor, 1984.

The Golden Dream: Seekers of El Dorado. Indianapolis, IN: Bobbs-Merrill, 1967. First
published under name of "Walker Chapman"; later printed as *The Search for
El Dorado,* by Robert Silverberg. Indianapolis, IN: Bobbs-Merrill, 1968.

Hawksbill Station. Garden City, NY: Doubleday, 1968; reprint, New York: Berkley,
1978.

Home of the Red Man. New York: New York Graphic Society, 1963; reprint, New
York: Washington Square Press, 1971.

Hot Sky at Midnight. New York: Bantam, 1994.

In Another Country with *Vintage Season* by C. L. Moore. New York: TOR 1990.

"Introduction." *Galactic Dreamers: Science Fiction as Visionary Literature,* ed. Robert Silverberg. New York: Random House, 1977; ix–xii.

Invaders from Earth with *Across Time* by David Grinnell. New York: Ace, 1958.

Invaders from Earth with *To Worlds Beyond.* 1958; reprint, New York: Ace, 1980.

Invisible Barriers by David Osborne [pseud]. New York: Avalon, 1958.

John Muir: Prophet among the Glaciers. New York: Putnam, 1972.

Kingdoms of the Wall. New York: Bantam, 1993.

"Majipoor: The Seventh Shrine." In *Legends: Short Novels by the Masters of Fantasy,*
ed. Robert Silverberg. New York: Tom Doherty Associates, 1998; 255–332.

Lest We Forget Thee, Earth by Calvin M. Knox [pseud.] with *People Minus X* by
Raymond Z. Gallun. New York: Ace, 1958.

Letters from Atlantis. New York: Warner, 1992.

"Lion Time in Timbuctu." In *Beyond the Gate of Worlds,* ed. Robert Silverberg. New
York: Tom Doherty Associates, 1991; 7–97. Originally published in *Asimov's,*
Oct. 1990.

"Looking for the Fountain." In *Isaac Asimov's Science Fiction.* May 1992 (v. 16,
no. 6); 14–38.

Lord of Darkness. New York: Arbor, 1983.

Lord Valentine's Castle. New York: Harper and Row, 1980.

Lost Cities and Vanished Civilizations. Philadelphia, PA: Chilton, 1962.

Lost Race of Mars. New York: Holt, Rinehart, Winston, 1960; reprint, New York:
Scholastic Book Services, 1970.

Majipoor Chronicles. New York: Arbor, 1982.

"The Making of a Science Fiction Writer." Introduction to *Robert Silverberg's Worlds of Wonder*, ed. Robert Silverberg. New York: Warner 1987; 1–34.

The Man in the Maze. New York: Avon, 1969; reprint, New York: Avon, 1975.

The Masks of Time. New York: Ballantine, 1968.

Master of Life and Death with *The Secret Visitors* by James White. New York: Ace, 1957; reprint, with Introduction and *Conquerors from the Darkness*, New York: Ace, 1979.

The Mirror of Infinity, ed. Robert Silverberg. New York: Harper and Row, 1970; reprint, New York: Harper and Row, 1973.

Moonferns and Starsongs. New York: Ballantine, 1971.

The Mountains of Majipoor. New York: Bantam, 1995.

The Mutant Season. With Karen Haber. New York: Doubleday, 1989.

Needle in a Timestack. New York: Ballantine, 1966; reprint, New York: Ace, 1985.

The New Springtime. New York: Warner, 1990

Next Stop the Stars with *The Seed of Earth*. New York: Ace, 1962.

Nightfall. With Isaac Asimov. New York: Doubleday, 1990.

Nightwings. New York: Avon, 1969.

One of Our Asteroids Is Missing by Calvin M. Knox [pseud.] with *The Twisted Men* by A. E. Van Vogt. New York: Ace, 1964.

Parsecs and Parables. Garden City, NY: Doubleday, 1970.

The Planet Killers with *We Claim These Stars* by Poul Anderson. New York: Ace, 1959.

Planet of Death. New York: Holt, Rinehart, Winston, 1967.

The Plot against Earth by Calvin M. Knox [pseud.] with *Recruit for Andromeda* by Milton Lesser. New York: Ace, 1959.

The Positronic Man. With Isaac Asimov. New York: Doubleday, 1993.

Project Pendulum. New York: Walker, 1987.

The Pueblo Revolt. New York: Weybright and Tailey, 1970; reprint, Lincoln: University of Nebraska Press, 1994.

The Reality Trip and Other Implausibilities. New York: Ballantine, 1972.

Recalled to Life. New York: Lancer, 1962. Rev. ed. New York: Garden City, 1972; reprint, with Introduction, New York: Ace, 1977.

Reflections and Refractions: Thoughts on Science-Fiction and Other Matters. Grass Valley, CA: Underwood Books, 1997.

Regan's Planet. New York: Pyramid, 1964.

Revolt on Alpha C. New York: Crowell, 1955; reprint, New York: Warner, 1989.

Robert Silverberg's Worlds of Wonder, ed. Robert Silverberg. New York: Warner, 1987.

The Science Fiction Hall of Fame, Volume One, ed. Robert Silverberg. Garden City, NY: Doubleday, 1972.

The Second Trip. Garden City, NY: Doubleday, 1972; reprint, New York: Avon, 1981.

Secret Sharers: The Collected Stories of Robert Silverberg. Vol. 1. New York: Bantam, 1992.

The Seed of Earth with *Next Stop the Stars*. New York: Ace, 1962; reprint, separate edition with Introduction, New York: Ace, 1977.

"The Seventh Shrine." In *Legends*, ed. Robert Silverberg. New York: TOR, 1998.

Shadrach in the Furnace. Indianapolis, IN: Bobbs-Merrill, 1976.

The Shrouded Planet. By Robert Randall [pseud.] with Randall Garrett. Hicksville, NY: Gnome, 1957; reprint, New York: Ace, 1982, under names of Robert Silverberg and Randall Garrett.

The Silent Invaders. New York: Ace, 1963; reprint, New York: Ace, 1973.

Son of Man. New York: Ballantine, 1971.

Sorcerers of Majipoor. New York: Harper, 1996.

"Sounding Brass, Tinkling Cymbal." In *Hell's Cartographers*, ed. Brian W. Aldiss and Harry Harrison. London: Weidenfeld and Nicolson, 1975; reprint, London, UK: Futura Publications Limited, 1976; 7–45.

Star of Gypsies. New York: Donald I. Fine, 1986.

Starborne. New York: Bantam, 1996.

Starhaven by Ivar Jorgenson [pseud.], with *The Sun Smasher* by Edmond Hamilton. New York: Thomas Bouregy, 1958; reprint, New York: Ace, 1959.

Starman's Quest. Hicksville, NY: Gnome Press, 1959.

Stepsons of Terra with *A Man Called Destiny* by Lan Wright. New York: Ace, 1958; reprint, alone, with Introduction, New York: Ace, 1977.

The Stochastic Man. New York: Harper and Row, 1975; reprint, Greenwich, CT: Fawcett, 1976.

"Tales from the Venia Woods." In *The Year's Best Science Fiction: Seventh Annual Collection*, ed. Gardner Dozois. New York: St. Martin's, 1990; 174–189.

Thebes of the Hundred Gates. New York: Bantam, 1991.

The 13th Immortal with *This Fortress World* by James Gunn. New York: Ace, 1957.

Thorns. New York: Ballantine, 1967.

Those Who Watch. New York: New American Library, 1967.

The Time Hoppers. Garden City, NY: Doubleday, 1967; reprint, New York: Leisure, 1977.

A Time of Changes. Garden City, NY: Doubleday, 1971.

Time of the Great Freeze. New York: Holt, Rinehart, Winston, 1964; reprint, with Introduction, New York: Ace, 1980.

To Live Again. Garden City, NY: Doubleday, 1969.

To Open the Sky. New York: Ballantine, 1967; reprint, New York: Berkley, 1978.

To the Land of the Living. New York: Warner, 1990.

To Worlds Beyond with *Invaders from Earth*. Philadelphia, PA: Chilton, 1965; reprint, New York: Ace, 1980.

Tom O'Bedlam. New York: Donald Fine, 1985.

Tower of Glass. New York: Scribners, 1970; reprint New York: Bantam, 1971.

The Ugly Little Boy. With Isaac Asimov. New York: Doubleday, 1992.

Unfamiliar Territory. New York: Scribners, 1973; reprint, New York: Berkley, 1978.

Universe 1, ed. Robert Silverberg and Karen Haber. New York: Doubleday, 1990; reprint, New York: Bantam, 1991.

Up the Line. New York: Ballantine, 1969.

Valentine Pontifex. New York: Arbor, 1983.

Valley beyond Time. New York: Dell, 1973.

The World Inside. Garden City, NY: Doubleday, 1971; reprint, New York: New American Library, 1972.

World of a Thousand Colors. New York: Arbor, 1982.

World's Fair, 1992. Chicago, IL: Follett, 1970; reprint, New York: Ace, 1982.

WORKS ABOUT ROBERT SILVERBERG'S FICTION

Aldiss, Brian, with David Wingrove. *Trillion Year Spree*. New York: Atheneum, 1986; reprint, New York: Avon, 1988; 340–346.

Alterman, Peter S. "Four Voices in Robert Silverberg's *Dying Inside, Critical Encounters II*, ed. Tom Staicar. New York: Ungar, 1982; 90–103.

Clareson, Thomas. "Robert Silverberg: The Compleat Writer." *Fantasy and Science Fiction*, April 1974, 73–80.

Clareson, Thomas. "The Fictions of Robert Silverberg." *Voices for the Future*, ed. Thomas Clareson. Bowling Green, OH: Bowling Green University Press, 1979; 1–33.

Clareson, Thomas. *Robert Silverberg*. Mercer Island, WA: Starmont, 1983.

Clareson, Thomas. *Robert Silverberg: A Primary and Secondary Bibliography*. Boston, MA: G. K. Hall, 1983.

Collins, Robert, and Rob Latham, eds. *Science Fiction and Fantasy Annual 1990*. New York and Westport, CT: Greenwood, 1991.

Disch, Thomas. "Big Ideas and Dead-End Thrills." *Atlantic*, February 1992, 86–94.

Dudley, Joseph M. "Transformational SF Religions: Philip José Farmer's *Night of Light* and Robert Silverberg's *Downward to the Earth*." *Extrapolation* 33, no. 4 (Winter 1994): 342–350.

Dunn, Thomas P., and Richard D. Ehrlich. "The Mechanical Hive: Urbmon 116 as the Villain-Hero of Silverberg's *The World Inside*." *Extrapolation* 21 (Winter 1980): 338–347.

Edwards, Malcolm. "Robert Silverberg." In *Science Fiction Writers*, ed. E. F. Bleiler. New York: Scribners, 1982; 505–511.

Elkins, Charles, and Martin H. Greenberg, eds. *Robert Silverberg's Many Trapdoors*. Westport, CT: Greenwood, 1992. Contains essays by Thomas Clareson, Russell Letson, Edgar L. Chapman, Joseph Francavilla, John Flodstrom, Frank Dietz, Robert Reilly, and Colin Manlove.

Elliot, Jeffrey. "Robert Silverberg: Next Stop, Lord Valentine's Castle." In *Science Fiction Voices* #2, ed. Jeffrey Elliot. San Bernardino, CA: Borgo, 1979; 51–62.

Gordon, Andrew. "Silverberg's Time Machine." *Extrapolation* 23 (Winter 1982): 345–361.

Hunt, Robert. "Visionary States and the Search for Transcendence in Science Fiction." In *Bridges to Science Fiction: Essays Prepared for the First Eaton Conference on Science Fiction and Fantasy*, ed. George W. Slusser, George Guffey, and Mark Rose. Carbondale, IL: Southern Illinois University Press, 1980, 64–77.

Jonas, Gerald. Review of "Born with the Dead." *New York Times Book Review*, 24 August 1975, 29.

Jonas, Gerald. Review of *Shadrach in the Furnace*. *New York Times Book Review*, 17 October 1976, 43.

Jonas, Gerald. Review of *At Winter's End*. *New York Times Book Review*, 24 July 1988, 25.

Kam, Rose Sallberg. "Silverberg and Conrad: Explorers of Inner Darkness." *Extrapolation* 17 (December 1975): 18–28.

Killheffer, Robert. "Striking a Balance: Robert Silverberg's *Lord of Darkness, Dying Inside*, and Others." *The New York Review of Science Fiction*, 12 August 1989, 1, 12–14.

Letson, Russell. Introduction to *To Open the Sky*. Boston, MA: Gregg Press, 1977.

Letson, Russell. "Falling through Many Trapdoors." *Extrapolation* 20 (Summer 1979): 109–117.

Malzberg, Barry. "Robert Silverberg." *Fantasy and Science Fiction* 46 (April 1974): 67–72.

Manlove, C. N. "Robert Silverberg: *Nightwings*." In *Science Fiction: Ten Explorations*. by Colin Manlove Kent, OH: Kent State University Press, 1986; 100–120.

McGiveron, Rafeeq O. "A Relationship More than Six Inches Deep: Love and Lust in Silverberg's Science Fiction." *Extrapolation* 39; no. 1 (Spring 1998): 40–51.

McNelly, Willis. *"Dying Inside." Survey of Science Fiction Literature*, ed. Frank N. Magill. Vol. 2. Englewood Cliffs, NJ: Salem, 1979; 671–675.

Pierce, John J. *Odd Genre: A Study in Imagination and Evolution*. Westport, CT: Greenwood, 1994.

Platt, Charles. "Robert Silverberg." In *Dream Makers*, ed. Charles Platt. New York: Berkley, 1980; 261–268.

Pringle, David. *"Downward to the Earth."* In *Science Fiction: The 100 Best Novels*. New York: Carroll and Graf, 1985; reprint, New York: Carroll and Graf, 1997.

Searles, Baird. "On Books." *Isaac Asimov's Science Fiction*, February 1985, 184–186.

Stableford, Brian. *"Nightwings." Survey of Science Fiction*, ed. Frank N. Magill. Vol. 3. Englewood Cliffs, NJ: Salem, 1979; 1526–1530.

Stableford, Brian. *Masters of Science Fiction 1*. San Bernardino, CA: Borgo, 1981.

Tuma, George. "Biblical Myth and Legend in the *Tower of Glass*: Man's Search for Authenticity." *Extrapolation* 15 (May 1974): 174–191.

OTHER WORKS CITED OR CONSULTED

Asimov, Isaac. *The Bicentennial Man and Other Stories*. New York: Doubleday, 1976; reprint, New York: Fawcett, 1977.

Asimov, Isaac. *Nightfall and Other Stories*. New York: Doubleday, 1969; reprint, Greenwich, CT: Fawcett Crest, 1970.

Attebery, Brian. *The Fantasy Tradition in American Literature*. Bloomington: Indiana University Press, 1980.

Attebery, Brian. *Strategies of Fantasy*. Bloomington: Indiana University Press, 1992.

Barrett, William. *Irrational Man*. Garden City, NY: Doubleday, 1958; reprint, Garden City, NY: Doubleday Anchor Books, 1962.

Benford, Gregory, and Martin H. Greenberg, eds. *Hitler Victorious*. New York: Garland, 1986.

Bloom, Harold. *Yeats*. New York: Oxford University Press, 1970; reprint, New York: Oxford Galaxy Books, 1972.

Booth, Wayne C. *The Company We Keep: An Ethics of Fiction*. Berkeley: University of California Press, 1988.

Borges, Jorge Luis. *Ficciones*, ed. Anthony Kerrigan. New York: Grove Press, 1962

Buber, Martin. *I and Thou*, trans. Ronald Gregor Smith. 2nd ed. New York: Scribners, 1958; reprint, New York: Macmillan, 1965.

Campbell, Joseph. *The Hero with a Thousand Faces*. Princeton, NJ: Princeton University Press, 1949, 1968; reprint, Princeton, NJ: Princeton University Press, 1973.

Campbell, Joseph, ed. *The Portable Jung*. New York: Viking, 1971.

Campbell, Joseph, with Bill Moyers. *The Power of Myth*, ed. Betty Sue Flowers. New York: Doubleday, 1988.

Chapman, Edgar L. *The Magic Labyrinth of Philip José Farmer*. San Bernardino, CA: Borgo, 1984.

Chapman, Edgar L. "Weinbaum's Fire from the Ashes." In *Phoenix from the Ashes*, ed. Carl B. Yoke. Westport, CT: Greenwood, 1987.

Childers, Joseph, and Gary Hentz, eds. *The Columbia Encyclopedia of Modern Literary and Cultural Criticism*. New York: Columbia University Press, 1995.

Cirlot, J. E. *A Dictionary of Symbols*, trans. Jack Sage. 2nd ed. New York: Dorset, 1991; original publication, London, UK: Routledge, 1971.

Clareson, Thomas. *Some Kind of Paradise*. Westport, CT: Greenwood, 1985.

Clute, John, and John J. Grant. *The Encyclopedia of Fantasy*. New York: St. Martin's, 1997.

Clute, John, and Peter Nicholls, eds. *The Encyclopedia of Science Fiction*. 2nd ed. New York: St. Martin's, 1993; reprint, New York: St. Martin's Griffin. 1995.

Collins, Harold R. "Kurtz, the Cannibals, and the Second-Rate Helmsman." In *Joseph Conrad's Heart of Darkness*, ed. Leonard F. Dean. Englewood Cliffs, NJ: Prentice-Hall, 1960; 149–159.

Coover Robert. *Pricksongs and Descants*. New York: Dutton, 1969.

De Laszlo, Violet S., ed. *The Basic Writings of C. J. Jung*. New York: Random, 1959.

Disch, Thomas. *The Dreams Our Stuff Is Made Of: How Science Fiction Conquered the World*. New York: Simon and Schuster, 1998.

Drabble, Margaret, ed. *The Oxford Companion to English Literature*, 5th edition. New York: Oxford University Press, 1985.

Elliot, Jeffrey. "Harlan Ellison: Outspoken, Outrageous, Outstanding!" In *Science Fiction Voices 3*, ed. Jeffrey Elliot. San Bernardino, CA: Borgo, 1980; 9–18.

Ferry, David, translator. *Gilgamesh: A New Rendering in English Verse*. New York: Farrar, Straus and Giroux, 1992.

Franklin, H. Bruce. *Robert Heinlein: America as Science Fiction*. New York: Oxford University Press, 1980.

Frye, Northrop. *Anatomy of Criticism*. Princeton, NJ: Princeton University Press, 1957; reprint, New York: Atheneum, 1966.

Frye, Northrop. *The Secular Scripture*. Cambridge, MA: Harvard University Press, 1976.

Gekowski, R. A. *Conrad: The Moral World of the Novelist*. New York: Harper and Row, 1978.

Guerard, Albert J., Jr. *Conrad the Novelist*. Cambridge, MA: Harvard University Press, 1958.

Gunn, James, ed. *The Road to Science Fiction*. Vol. 1. New York: New American Library, 1977.

Gunn, James, ed. *Isaac Asimov: The Foundations of Science Fiction*. New York: Oxford University Press, 1982.

Gunn, James, ed. "The Worldview of Science Fiction." *Extrapolation* 36, no. 2 (Summer 1995): 91–95.

Hume, Kathryn. *Fantasy and Mimesis*. London: Methuen, 1984.

Hutcheon, Linda. *A Poetics of Postmodernism: History, Theory, Fiction*. New York: Routledge, 1988; reprint, New York: Routledge, 1995.

Kagle, Steven. "The Societal Quest." *Extrapolation* 12, no. 2 (May 1971): 79–85.

Kitto, H. D. F. *Greek Tragedy*. London: Methuen and Co., 1939; rev. ed., 1950; reprint, Garden City, NY: Doubleday Anchor, n.d.

Macquarrie, John. *Principles of Christian Theology*. 2nd ed. New York: Scribners, 1977.

Malzberg, Barry. *The Engines of the Night*. Garden City, NY: Doubleday, 1982.

McConnell, Frank. *The Science Fiction of H. G. Wells*. New York: Oxford University Press, 1981; reprint, New York: Oxford University Press, 1981.

McHale, Brian. *Postmodernist Fiction*. London: Methuen, 1987.

Merril, Judith. *England Swings SF*. New York: Ace, 1965.

Otto, Rudolph. *The Idea of the Holy*, trans. John Harvey. 2nd. ed. New York: Oxford University Press, 1943; reprint, New York: Oxford University Press, 1958.

Panshin, Alexei, and Cory Panshin. *The World beyond the Hill*. Los Angeles: Jeremy F. Tarcher, 1989.

Percy, Walker. *Lost in the Cosmos: The Last Self-Help Book*. New York: Farrar, Straus and Giroux, 1983; reprint, New York: Washington Square, 1984.

Rabkin, Eric. *The Fantastic in Literature*. Princeton, NJ: Princeton University Press, 1976.

Radin, Paul. *The Trickster*. New York: Philosophical Library, 1956.

Sandars, N. K., trans. *The Epic of Gilgamesh*. Baltimore, MD: Penguin, 1960.

Scholes, Robert. *The Fabulators*. New York: Oxford University Press, 1967.

Scholes, Robert. *Fabulation and Metafiction*. Urbana, IL: University of Illinois Press, 1979.

Scholes, Robert, and Eric Rabkin. *Science Fiction: History, Science, Vision*. New York: Oxford University Press, 1977.

Selden, Raman, and Peter Widdowson. *A Reader's Guide to Contemporary Literary Theory*. Lexington: University of Kentucky Press, 1985; third edition, Lexington: University of Kentucky Press, 1993.

Singer, June. *The Boundaries of the Soul: The Practice of Jung's Psychology*. Garden City, NY: Doubleday, 1972; reprint, Garden City, NY: Doubleday Anchor, 1973.

Suvin, Darko. *Metamorphoses of Science Fiction*. New Haven, CT: Yale University Press, 1979.

Thorburn, David. *Conrad's Romanticism*. New Haven, CT: Yale University Press, 1974.

Tillich, Paul. *The Courage to Be*. New Haven, CT: Yale University Press, 1952.

Tillich, Paul. *Dynamics of Faith*. New York: Harper, 1957; reprint, New York: Harper, 1958.

Von Franz, M. L. *Man and His Symbols*, ed. C. G. Jung. London: Aldus, 1964.

Wolfe, Gary. *The Known and the Unknown: The Iconography of Science Fiction.* Kent,
     OH: Kent State University Press, 1979.
Wolfe, Gary. *Critical Terms for Science Fiction and Fantasy: A Glossary and a Guide
     to Scholarship.* Westport, CT: Greenwood Press, 1986.

Index

About the Author

EDGAR L. CHAPMAN is Professor of English at Bradley University. His previous books include *The Magic Labyrinth of Philip José Farmer* (1984), and his articles have appeared in such journals as *Texas Studies in Literature and Language*.

ISBN 0-313-26145-8

HARDCOVER BAR CODE

Effective Business Communication

Communication

third edition

Jennifer MacLennan

D.K. Seaman Chair in Technical and
Professional Communication in Engineering
College of Engineering
University of Saskatchewan

Prentice Hall Canada Career & Technology

Canadian Cataloguing in Publication Data

MacLennan, Jennifer
  Effective business communication

3rd ed.
Previously published under title: Effective business writing.
ISBN 0-13-794009-2

1. Business writing. I. Title. II. Title: Effective business writing.

HF5718.3 M24 1999   808'.06665   C98-930749-2

Prentice-Hall, Inc., Upper Saddle River, New Jersey
Prentice-Hall International (UK) Limited, London
Prentice-Hall of Australia, Pty. Limited, Sydney
Prentice-Hall Hispanoamericana, S.A., Mexico City
Prentice-Hall of India Private Limited, New Delhi
Prentice-Hall of Japan, Inc., Tokyo
Simon & Schuster Southeast Asia Private Limited, Singapore
Editora Prentice-Hall do Brasil, Ltda., Rio de Janeiro

ISBN 0-13-794009-2

Vice President, Editorial Director: Laura Pearson
Acquisitions Editor: Nicole Lukach
Marketing Manager: Sophia Fortier
Developmental Editor: Marta Tomins
Production Editor: Andrew Winton
Copy Editor: Gail Copeland
Production Coordinator: Kathrine Pummel
Permissions/Photo Research: Susan Wallace-Cox
Cover and Interior Design: Zena Denchik
Cover Image: Roy Weimann
Page Layout: Hermia Chung

  2 3 4 5   WC   02 01 00

Printed and bound in Canada.

Table of Contents

chapter 4   # Informal and Semiformal Reports   **70**

chapter 5   # Formal Reports and Proposals   **94**

chapter 6   # Oral Reports and Presentations   **126**

appendix b Punctuation   234

Preface

I am delighted to write this note to accompany the third edition of *Effective Business Communication* (formerly *Effective Business Writing*), in which my goal has been to build upon the strengths of the original and second editions. My approach remains fundamentally grounded in the ancient art of rhetoric, and for this reason it emphasizes the importance to any act of communication of a strong sense of audience and clarity of purpose. I have tried to avoid burdening this introductory text with technical terms, and I have made more explicit the focus on writing as a human process of communication that was so much a part of the previous editions.

Since the second edition was written, I have been developing a series of special projects that have influenced the revisions to this new edition. As part of these projects, my senior students have used their knowledge of rhetorical principles to develop and lead workshops in résumé writing and oral presentations, to write a handbook on public speaking, and to present papers at the annual conference of the Northwest Communication Association. In much the same way that my students have used their understanding of the art to enhance and shape their communication, I have found myself using my own knowledge of the ancient discipline in a more deliberate way in the writing of this edition: it is not only implicit in the principles of effective writing that I have advocated in the text, but it is also more evident in the approach I have taken in communicating with my audience of student readers. I am hopeful that these changes will make a stronger and more useful book.

I have also made several changes to this edition to accommodate the rapid expansion of electronic communication in the workplace, and in response to suggestions from those who have used the book in their classes. The primary changes have involved:

- the retirement of Toby Trapper, who has been succeeded by Communications Corporation's first female CEO, Daena Tobias.

- an expansion of Chapter 1 to include coverage of both content and relation in the theory of business communication.

- an expansion of Chapter 3 to include letters, memos, and electronic mail.

- a revised discussion of oral presentations, with expanded attention to the process of topic invention.

- information about taking the job search online.

- new exercises and examples — a revision of approximately 25% of the assignments to include electronic mail and to provide new situations for writing.

I hope that the changes I have introduced will serve both professors and students who use this book in their communications classes; I have also tried to make it practical enough that its readers will continue to find it useful even after the course in which they first used it is finished.

Acknowledgements

I would first like to thank those who have chosen previous editions of this book for use in their classes, and whose suggestions have once again helped improve the new edition of this book. In particular, Beverly Allix of Humber College has been consistently helpful and positive in her suggestions, and she deserves a special thanks. I would also like to thank my other reviewers, Jack David, Reagan Light, David McCarthy, Dan Ryan, and Margaret Van Dijk, all of Centennial College; and Kathy Wagner at Cambrian College.

I would like also to acknowldege the contributions of my editors at Prentice Hall; David Stover has been a part of this project since the development of the first edition, and he has been a source of unfailing support and good humour. I would also like to thank the other capable and helpful people who saw the book through production: Marta Tomins, Andrew Winton, Kathrine Pummell, Zena Denchik, Hermia Chung, and Gail Copeland.

I remain grateful to the people whose friendship, enthusiasm, and support of my work have been very important to me: David Cowan, Ray McHugh, John Moffatt, Lori Leister, Ian McAdam, William Lambert, Barbara Warnick, David Ingham, Richard Fiordo, Robert Denham, Douglas Brent, Ken Tokuno, Daena Goldsmith. As one of my students used to say, they "shine bright" in an environment that is otherwise bleakly uncomprehending of the study and practice of rhetoric.

My students, as always, are a source of pride and delight; they include Megan Huston, Jennifer Varzari, Burton Urquhart, Tom McIntyre, Jennifer Anderson, Lori Irwin, Tricia Vandenberg, and especially Wade Grandoni, the designer of my web page.

Finally, I would like to dedicate this book to my parents; my approach to teaching and to writing has been profoundly shaped by the sense of ethics and industry they have always nurtured, encouraged, and supported.

Style in Business Writing

an Overview

➤ To understand the two principles upon which all effective
business writing is based.

➤ To learn the Six C's of business writing and incorporate them
into all your writing.

No skill is so vital to business, or indeed to everyday life, as effective communication.

Through our work we interact with dozens, or even hundreds, of people daily; we communicate by letter, memorandum, telephone, and electronic mail. Everyone in the office is busy — often too busy to finish all that needs to be done. As a result, messages that are clear and easy to understand will be dealt with first, while those that are unclear, incomplete, or impolite will be set aside for later or possibly forgotten entirely.

Since much of the contact we have with others in modern business is through the things we write, whether they are distributed in "hard copy" or by electronic mail, much of our success in business depends on writing clearly so that our messages are dealt with efficiently. It is important to state our meaning directly and to edit our messages carefully, so that we can prevent misunderstandings or delays that can cost time, money, or embarrassment to the company and ourselves.

Achieving clarity in writing is not easy, but the good news is that with a bit of effort almost anyone can learn to write effective business communications.

Experienced business communicators have mastered both style and form in their letters, memos, and reports; they are also careful to be clear and coherent in their electronic messages. Their messages get dealt with more efficiently, and they seem to get more done. They know the secret of effective writing: they think of their written works not as products but as tools, not as works of art but as communication between people. They know that all good business writing is based on two main principles: focus on your purpose, and remember your audience. These two principles underlie all good communication, in business and elsewhere; the forms of business writing are designed to help us use these principles.

To communicate effectively, first you must know exactly what you want to say. You can't make any message clear to a reader unless you know, before you begin to write, exactly what your purpose or objective is. What do you want to accomplish through this e-mail message, letter, or memo? Second, you must have a clear idea of the audience for whom you are writing. Why does this reader care about your message? What is the reader's interest in the information? What background does this person have? What will the reader need to know to make a decision?

All good writing, whether in business or elsewhere, means recognizing that you are participating in an act of communication involving three components: a message you wish to communicate, an audience or reader for whom the message is prepared, and a speaker or writer who creates the message. Part of the function of every business message, no matter how routine, is to create and maintain a smooth business relationship between the writer and the reader. Thus, you need to think as you write not only about the content of your message, but also about how you are building and shaping your business relationships through your communication with your clients, colleagues, and managers. This element is called the *relation,* and is present in every act of communication. It is frequently as important as — and sometimes more so than — the content of any message.

Once you have recognized that your job as a writer includes building effective business relationships by thinking of the purpose of and the audience for your message, you can begin to think about how business communication is typically organized. Most business writing contains essentially the same parts:

1. The main message statement ("the main thing I want to tell you is that..."). In a report, this is referred to as the summary. In an electronic mail message, a written memorandum, or even a letter, this information usually appears in the subject or "re" line.
2. Any background information the reader may require. This information is placed in your introductory paragraph or sentence.
3. The full development of the e-mail, memo, letter, or report. This part — sometimes referred to as the discussion, or body of the work — provides any necessary details.
4. The closing sentence or paragraph (the conclusion). It should remind your reader once again of your main point and should indicate any results you ex-

pect or intend. It may also suggest to the reader any appropriate action he or she should take in response to your communication.

Remember these parts and always use them as a guide when you are writing any business communications. After all, you want your message to be communicated, and as a writer, it is your responsibility to help your reader understand that message. By following these guidelines and jotting down your main ideas first, you can make your written communication more effective and the writing process easier because you will have organized your ideas about the message before actually composing the final version.

A business communication of any kind should also be arranged attractively. In the case of e-mail, this is more of a challenge, since computer screens and electronic mail systems differ, and it's more difficult to control how an e-mail message will appear to the recipient. However, print messages can and should be carefully laid out on the page. This means the writer should create an effective balance between the printed or written material (print) and the blank areas of the page where no print appears (known as white space). A page that is crowded from one edge to the other without visual breaks may intimidate the reader; on the other hand, generous margins, paragraphing, and standardized formats can help a reader understand your message more easily and quickly, and can also help make a positive impression.

Before we move on to consider the standardized formats of business communication, let's look more closely at the two important principles of business communication that will help you to forge effective business relationships:

1. Focus on your purpose; and
2. Remember your reader's needs, expectations, and background knowledge.

Focus on Your Purpose

Before you begin writing, ask yourself why you are writing this e-mail, letter, memo, or report. What do you want it to do? What do you want your reader to do as a result of your message? Is your primary aim to provide information ("tell" the reader something)? Or is your goal to persuade your reader to act or believe something ("sell" an idea, action, or product)? Persuading a reader ("selling") is a different kind of task from simply passing on information ("telling"). If you are primarily interested in informing your readers, you can state your facts clearly and simply. If, however, you want to move your readers to action, convince them of a point of view, or encourage them to accept a change in plans, you will need to use more persuasive techniques in your writing. These are covered in Chapter 3.

An awareness of purpose is equally important no matter what kind of business communication you are writing, from an ordinary letter of request to an application for a job. In today's office, electronic mail (e-mail) has replaced some of the functions that used to be served by internal memos and even business letters; nevertheless, for formal situations, the business letter and the memo are still the most frequently used forms of business communication. As well, although the e-mail memo is often considered less formal a method of communication than the paper memo or letter, style and content are still a consideration.

We will begin our discussion of purpose and audience by considering the memo (including e-mail) and the letter. Reports, of course, are more complex, and these are dealt with in Chapters 4 and 5. The parts of a job application are discussed in Chapter 7.

Memos (both paper and e-mail varieties) and letters may address only one issue or involve a number of related issues. They may be as short as one page or as long as two or three pages. Whatever their length or contents, however, one principle remains constant: if you are not clear about exactly what you want to say, you cannot say it well. It is also important to organize your writing with your most important purpose foremost. You cannot hope to make your business writing effective unless you know in advance exactly what you want it to do. You should keep the following guidelines in mind when writing a letter or memo, or when drafting an e-mail message.

Put Your Main Point First

Business writing differs from the other kinds of writing you may be used to reading or that you have learned to do. In business writing, you should begin with the main point of your message. Putting your main point first will seem awkward at the beginning, because it will seem a little like giving away the punchline before you've told the joke. We have all been conditioned to write in a more or less chronological order, which usually results in the main point coming last. This arrangement is ideal for a novel or a movie script, but disastrous in business. Think about your reader's situation: he or she may have several dozen or more letters and memos coming in daily, and as many e-mail messages, all awaiting attention and action. You can't afford to waste the reader's time with a message that doesn't get to the point. Put the main message at the beginning of your communication, preferably in a subject (or "re") line. You can teach yourself to put your main idea first by beginning your rough drafts with, "The main thing I want to tell you is that...." Doing so will help you to focus on your main message. Be sure to delete this clause in your final draft.

Be Specific

Make sure you can identify exactly what you wish your reader to know and what response you expect. Be as concrete and specific as possible. For instance, if you wish to order supplies, book a room, or return materials, state this purpose clearly, identifying the materials to be returned or the specific room you wish to book. Don't waste your reader's time; get to the point quickly, and provide as much concrete detail as is necessary to get the job done.

Simplify Your Message

Try to keep your letters and memos as simple as possible: don't clutter them with irrelevant information. If you can, stick to one main topic and include only what is necessary to the reader's understanding of your message. If you must deal with several topics in one letter or memo, be sure that each is dealt with fully before moving to the next issue. Cluster related information and get to the point as quickly as possible.

Remember Your Reader

Most business communication, like all effective communication, whether primarily designed to inform or to persuade, must catch and maintain a reader's attention and interest. You cannot do this if you don't understand the person for whom you are writing. Since any business communication is really an attempt to convince your intended reader that your position is valid and your recommendations necessary, you must present the information in a manner most likely to convince that specific reader. Effective communication is audience-centred; that is, it focuses not so much on what the *writer* feels like saying, but on the things the reader needs to hear in order to make an informed decision. Good communication puts the reader's needs first. In order to do this, you need to identify your reader's needs, level of knowledge, and expectations.

Needs

Consider first the information that your reader needs in order to make a decision. What is the reader's interest in this subject? What will the reader be doing with the information? How much detail is needed? Leave out any information that is not immediately relevant to the reader, no matter how interesting it may seem from your point of view. If you are to communicate your point successfully, you must address the reader's need for the information you are providing.

Background Knowledge

Keep in mind your reader's level of expertise. If you are writing to someone who has no prior knowledge of your project, you will need to explain substantially more than you will if you are writing to someone who is well acquainted with it. On the other hand, it is just as inconsiderate to provide unnecessary detail to someone who knows a great deal about your project as it is to provide inadequate detail to someone who does not know very much about it. Also, the kind of prior knowledge your audience brings can influence the way you choose to present your information as well as the amount or kind of information to present.

Expectations

What you say, and how you say it, will be very much affected by what the reader is expecting from your work. A reader who has been expecting a negative response will be relieved and delighted by good news. However, a reader who has been anticipating positive results is likely to be disappointed, frustrated, or angry if those expectations are not met. Ignoring or overlooking your reader's frustrated expectations when you write will only aggravate the situation and may damage your business relationship. On the other hand, acknowledging the reader's legitimate disappointment can help to cushion the impact of bad news and emphasize your professional concern and interest in the reader's viewpoint. Such positive reinforcement can go a long way in cementing effective business relationships.

In order to make the communication a success, it is the writer's responsibility to pay attention to the relational level of the message as well as to its content. To create and maintain effective business relationships, you will need to think carefully about the needs and expectations of the reader who will receive your communication. If you do this each time you create an e-mail, a memo, or a letter, you will not only communicate your content more effectively, but you will also maintain more successful business relationships.

The Six C's of Business Writing

Beyond clearly identifying both your main message and your reader, you will also want to attend to the actual style of your writing. Good business writing — like any other effective writing — exhibits a number of identifiable characteristics.

1. Completeness The first thing you must do is to make sure no important details have been overlooked. Have you included all of the information your reader will need in order to understand and act on your message? After you've written the first draft of your e-mail, memo, letter, or report, always ask yourself, "Have I said everything I needed to say?" Use the following questions as a guideline to ensure that you have included all the information your reader needs. Be sure you have answered any that are relevant:

Who?	What?	How many?	When?
Where?	How?	Why?	

2. Conciseness This means saying as much as you need to say in as little space as possible without being curt. This is more difficult than it sounds, because it involves more than just brevity. You need to eliminate unnecessary information while preserving the details necessary to full understanding. Once you have completed your first draft, and have made certain that all essential information is included, you need to be sure to take out any *irrelevant* information that has crept into your message. Ask yourself whether the reader really needs to know a fact you have included. If the answer is no, then cut it and avoid repeating yourself unnecessarily. It's also a good idea to avoid wordy expressions and clichés, such as:

it is probable that   it has come to my attention that
until such time as   please do not hesitate to

There are many more clichés common to business writing; many of them can be found in the discussion of good writing style in the next chapter. You should learn to recognize these deadeners of style and clarity and eliminate them from your writing.

3. Clarity In addition to making sure you've included all the details you need and eliminated those that are irrelevant to your reader's needs, you need to pay close attention to detail and organization. Be as concrete and specific as you can, identifying exactly what the problem is and what you would like done. Try to avoid ambiguous phrasing: the message should be clear on the first brief reading. Your reader should never have to puzzle out your meaning and should have no unanswered questions after reading your correspondence. Organize your message in a logical way, moving from problem to solution, from request to thanks, from general to specific.

4. Coherence Any business correspondence should "hold together"; the parts should be logically connected one to the other. Coherence is achieved partly by a sensible organization, but in addition to a movement from problem to solution or request to thanks, you should also use connective words or phrases to guide your reader from one point to the next. If you have organized your ideas well, coherence should be easy to attain by adding connectives. Some that you may wish to use include:

since	as well as	in addition to
therefore	however	on the other hand
naturally	of course	as a matter of fact
also	nevertheless	for instance
for example	once again	furthermore
moreover	thus	

5. Correctness Check the accuracy of all information — names, dates, places, receipt numbers, prices — that you include in a business communication. Correctness, of course, also includes correct spelling, grammar, and sentence structure as well as attractive formatting. Never send a business letter without proofreading it first — to do so is unprofessional and reflects badly on the writer. As well, a mistake could be costly.

Proofreading is not simply rereading or running the spell-check program on your word processor. When you proofread you read with the clear intention of improving your written message. You look not only for errors in spelling and grammar, but also for any places where your message is unclear. If possible, take a break — even a short one — between the writing and the proofreading, and try reading your work out loud. Both of these strategies will help you to uncover mistakes you might otherwise miss. The next chapter offers some more detailed advice on this important process.

6. Courtesy In business, as in all human interactions, things usually go more smoothly if people are pleasant and courteous to one another. Your business relationships are very important, and every communication you send can build or undermine those relationships. Since your attitude is displayed clearly in your writing and will affect the relational level of your message, it's important to pay close attention to *tone* in what you write. To check this important aspect of your own business communication, read over your work carefully, putting yourself in the place of the reader. Make it a habit to be pleasant and be sure to say please and thank you for any services or favours requested or received. Even if you are writing to someone whom you believe has done you wrong, give this person the benefit of the doubt, at least initially: allow the recipient to save face by taking the attitude that the error was the unintentional result of a misunderstanding. This approach will be much more effective in resolving difficulties than will a confrontational or accusatory tone.

These Six C's are among the most important qualities of good business writing. If you can incorporate them into your own work, your writing will be vastly improved.

Of course, there's more to any business communication than simply *what you say;* how you say it is as important in business writing as in any other human interaction. Part of the way we can demonstrate our good judgement as writers and as business people is through our recognition of effective layout and correct format. Business letters and memos are fairly standardized in their appearance, and violation of these standards may suggest a sloppy or unprofessional writer.

E-mail messages, of course, are far less consistent in their format: some writers, perceiving e-mail to be a casual medium of communication, ignore all conventions of punctuation, spelling, and capitalization. However, you should know that not all readers appreciate *receiving* such unconventional messages since they can be much more difficult to read. It is much better, from the point of view of reader consideration, to observe the conventions of spelling, punctuation, and grammar than to take the chance of annoying a correspondent.

Business letters and memos, of course, are always more formal than electronic messages. An effective business letter or memo is always word-processed or typed, with a clear, dark printer or toner cartridge, or ribbon on clean, good-quality paper. It makes use of generous margins (never looks too crowded or too spaced out) and appears balanced on the page. It may make use of other visual techniques to make it both more attractive and easier to read. For example, if it includes several important facts, these may be indented in list form to set them apart from the rest of the information.

Figure 1.1 shows the first draft of a business letter that does not observe the Six C's or the rules of effective layout. Compare it carefully with the corrected

The first draft of Trish Trcka's letter contains many flaws. Try to identify the errors yourself before reading the analysis.

Trish Trcka[1]
PO Box 123
Drayton Valley, Alberta
T5Y 7H8

9/28/01 [2]

Ministry of Tourism
Province of British Columbia
Parliament Buildings
Victoria, British Columbia
V1R 7H9

Dear Sir: [3]

I am writting[4] you this letter because[5] I am interested in taking a trip to British Columbia.

It has come to my attention that[6] your ministry can offer some valueable[7] information to potential tourists who are concidering[8] visiting your beautiful province.[9]

It would be greatly appreciated[10] if you could provide me with some documents[11] outlining your attractions, accommodations, and special events.

Thank you in advance for your assistance in this matter[12]. Your immediate response will be appreciated.[13]

Sincerly[14] yours,

Trish Trcka

Trish Trcka.[15]

version (Figure 1.2), noting where the improvements have been made and why. Errors in the first draft have been numbered for easy reference in the analysis.

Analysis

[1] Since Trish's name appears under her signature, she should not include it here. This is a common error.

[2] Trish should write the date out in full for ease of understanding.

[3] A subject or "re" line would help to clarify what Trish seeks and could replace the entire first paragraph.

[4] Writing is misspelled.

[5] "I am writing you this letter..." is clearly unnecessary: the reader, who has Trish's signed letter in hand, does not need to be told again that she has written it.

[6] "It has come to my attention that..." is a cliché and should be avoided. It is also unnecessarily wordy and pompous.

[7] Valuable is misspelled.

[8] Considering is misspelled.

[9] This kind of effusiveness borders on sickly sweet and serves no useful purpose; Trish should try to sound more sincere.

[10] "It would be greatly appreciated..." is a cliché, and so probably does not sound sincere. Since Trish is making a personal request she should also increase the sense of human contact in her letter by avoiding the passive construction.

[11] The phrase "some documents" is vague; Trish has not identified clearly what she wants. She should be specific about her needs.

[12] "Thank you in advance for your assistance in this matter" is another cliché; as such, it is wordy and sounds insincere and stuffy. A simple thank you would be better.

[13] "Your immediate response will be appreciated" is not only another unnecessarily wordy and tired phrase, but it borders on rudeness by implying that the people in the Ministry of Tourism won't respond quickly enough unless she orders them to do so.

[14] Sincerely is misspelled.

[15] No period should follow Trish's name.

In addition to the above mistakes, Trish has made another major error in this letter: she has not provided some of the specifics that would enable the people in the tourism office to help her most effectively. If she can, she should indicate where in the province she plans to visit and when she will be there. Activities and events vary around the province and are often seasonal. As well, Trish's letter is crowded too high up on the page, and no care has been taken to centre it vertically. Her margins could also be more generous, especially since her letter is so short. This kind of detail makes a letter more attractive and even more pleasant to read. Take a look at Trish's improved letter (Figure 1.2).

PO Box 123
Drayton Valley, Alberta
T5Y 7H8

September 28, 2001

Ministry of Tourism
Province of British Columbia
Parliament Buildings
Victoria, British Columbia
V1R 7H9

Dear Sir or Madam:

Re: Tourism information for Vancouver and area

I am planning a visit to British Columbia during Christmas week and would appreciate any brochures or other information you could provide regarding attractions, accommodations, and special events in the Vancouver area from approximately December 20, 2001, through January 3, 2002.

I plan to make the trip by car and expect to stay overnight in the Kamloops area. I would also like some information about accommodations in that area, if you have it, and would appreciate a provincial road map as well.

I have heard many positive things about Vancouver and am looking forward to this trip. Thank you very much for your help.

Sincerely,

Trish Trcka

Trish Trcka

Analysis

1. Since Trish does not know whether the reader of her letter will be male or female, she has observed courtesy by changing "Dear Sir" to "Dear Sir or Madam."
2. The "re" line specifies what information she wants and for which area.
3. The opening paragraph avoids any clichés and gets right to the point: the request for information and the dates and destination of the planned visit.
4. Additional details about the trip help the reader to determine what information Trish will need. She specifies some of the documents, such as a map, that she believes will be useful to her. Note that she includes her method of travel only because it affects what the ministry people will send her.
5. A brief compliment and her thanks close the letter effectively.

Note too that the layout of the letter has been improved: it has more generous margins and has been spaced more effectively so that it is not so crowded toward the top of the page.

weblinks

Five Styles of Communication
http://www.wuacc.edu/services/zzcwwctr/diction-5styles.txt

Business Etiquette
http://www.eticon.com/busetiq.htm

Plain English Campaign
http://www.plainenglish.co.uk/

Improving Sentence Clarity
http://owl.english.purdue.edu/Files/116.html

Reducing Wordiness
http://leo.stcloud.msus.edu/style/wordiness.html

points to remember

1. All effective business communication is based on two primary principles:
   - Know your purpose and be able to state it clearly.
   - Understand your reader's needs, level of knowledge, and expectations.

2. Always watch your own tone; make it a habit to be pleasant.

3. Good business style observes the Six C's of business writing:

Completeness	Conciseness	Clarity
Coherence	Correctness	Courtesy

4. Good business communication displays effective balance between print and white space.

sharpening your skills

Read the following business communications (Figures 1.3 and 1.4). Following the model analysis of Trish Trcka's letter, suggest ways they might be improved, keeping in mind all of the Six C's of business writing.

online exercises

1. At Will Stockdell's Business Writing Improvement Page (http://blondie.mathcs.wilkes.edu/~stockdwm/badwriting.html) you will find a discussion of several common business writing problems, along with suggestions for their solution. How does Stockdell's advice compare with the Six C's of Business Writing listed in this chapter? Discuss with the rest of your class.

2. How does business writing differ from the kind of writing you were taught to do in your high school English classes? List as many differences as you can think of, then go to the web page called "Differences between Literary and Business English" (http://www.smartbiz.com/sbs/arts/pbw2.htm). How does your list compare with Tom McKeown's list? What is the biggest difference between business writing and literary writing?

Ichio Hudecek
980 Main Street,
Saint John, New Brunswick
E1G 2M3

March 3, 2001

Ms Daena Tobias, Director
Communications Corporation
555 California Street
Vancouver, British Street
V1R 7H9

Dear Sir:

I am writting you a letter to ask you about the book I ordered from you about six weeks ago. I still haven't received it even though you have already cashed my cheque.

If you don't send it to me right away I'll have to report you to the department of consumer affairs.

Yours truely,

Ichio Hudecek

Ichio Hudecek

Message Composition

| SendNow | Quote | Attach | Address | Stop | Hanae Mendi < resourcecentre@ourschool.ca> |

Subject: English 12A: Problems with marking of last assignment

▽ **Addressing**   **Attachments**

Mail To: wolfchild@ourschool.ca
Cc:

September 30, 1999

Mr. Wolf Child:

We would like to get together with you to discuss the marks we
received on the last assignment. Everybody in the class is upset with
their grades and we don't think you explained clearly enough what you
wanted anyway. We want to meet with you Thursday on your lunch hour to
settle this problem. Please give us an answer in tommorrow's English
class.

Hanae Mendi
Class Rep, English 12A

Sharpening your
Business Writing Style

➤ To analyze and put into use an effective method for planning
  your business messages.
➤ To examine several common causes of unclear business writing
  and learn how to edit them out of your own writing.

It is one thing to know that, in theory, you need to put the main message first
and weed out wordy and clichéd phrases; it's another entirely to accomplish
these things in all your writing. Even when you clearly recognize the importance of the Six C's, it is sometimes difficult to put them into practice in your own
writing. This chapter is designed to help you do just that.

Most business writers experience difficulty in achieving the sharpness of
style that good writing requires, because bad writing is surprisingly easy to produce, while good, clear, effective writing — which looks simpler on the printed
page — is actually much more difficult to achieve.

Conciseness and clarity seem to be the two most challenging of the Six C's
for most writers; also, because they are closely linked, improving one often
means improving the other. For this reason, we will focus on these two qualities
in this discussion of business writing style. The only way to achieve clarity and
conciseness is to increase organization and reduce wordiness. This process often
requires several drafts, but it can be learned, and you can use it to make all of your
writing — in business as well as elsewhere — more effective.

Preparing to Write

Before you begin to write, plan your communication carefully. Using the Business Writing Planner (Figure 2.1) as a guide, identify the important elements of your message and the probable needs and expectations of your reader. Jot down the major points you wish to cover and juggle them around to achieve the most logical order. Consider carefully the way in which these points can be presented, choosing your words with care as you work. Then write your rough draft, beginning with "The main thing I want to tell you is that...." Be sure to cross it out in later drafts, especially the final draft.

Common Faults of Business Writing

Once you have planned your letter or memo, you must look at it critically to determine whether it is as effective as it could be. Concise writing is hard work, and almost every writer produces first drafts that need correction. Although you should give some thought to planning and organization when you write the first draft, don't imagine that it will be perfect. Expect — and be willing — to revise your work to make it more effective. With practice, this process will become easier and less time-consuming. One good way to learn to edit your own writing is to look for specific, common faults of business writing. The following are some of the real troublemakers.

1. Failure to Identify the Central Issue Before you begin to write, be sure that you can identify your main idea and that you understand exactly what you want your reader to know. This information must come first, and it should be expressed clearly. Before you work on the body of the letter, write down your main idea. You may even, as we discussed, begin your rough draft with the words, "The main thing I want to tell you is that...." (Remember to eliminate this clause in your final draft.) In fact, you might even wish to put the point into a "re" line; doing so will not only force you to put it first, but will also help your reader to grasp your message more quickly.

2. Use of Clichés Clichés make business writing uninteresting and deaden its human connection. Nevertheless, use of clichés is one of the most common faults in this kind of writing. Below are some of the most common abstractions and clichés. A complete list of all the clichés of business writing would take up the rest of this chapter, but I have provided enough examples below to give you a taste of what to look for and avoid. As a general rule, any phrase that sounds as though it "ought" to be in a business letter probably should be eliminated from yours!

figure 2.1 A Business Writing Planner can help you in all your business communications. This general form may be adapted to the specific demands of your writing situation by changing the questions to suit your needs.

BUSINESS WRITING PLANNER

Before beginning your letter or memo, consider these points carefully.

1. What is the topic of this letter or memo?

2. What is my focus or purpose? Am I providing information or selling an idea?

3. What is my main point? (This will appear in a subject or "re" line.) "The main thing I want to say is that...."

4. Who is my reader? What is his or her interest in this subject? What does my reader already know and what further information will be needed or wanted?

5. What background information does my reader need as preparation for what I am going to say?

6. What are my primary supporting points? Which details are important? Have I answered any Who, What, When, Where, Why, and How questions the reader might have?

7. What, if any, action do I wish my reader to take after reading my letter, memo, or e-mail message? Have I made it possible for her or him to do so?

---

at this point in time	if this proves to be the case
in the amount of	it is probable that
postpone until later	under separate cover
it has come to my attention that	reach a decision
until such time as	please do not hesitate to
on or before	whether or not
send you herewith	enclosed herewith find
with reference to	give consideration to
at the present time	due to the foregoing consideration
in view of the foregoing	in the near future
due to the fact that	in accordance with your request
in the event that	it will be our earnest endeavour
in accordance with your request	at your earliest convenience

Unfortunately, many business writers, not knowing what else to do, fall back on the clichés they have seen in the writing of others. Inexperienced writers often imagine that business writing is supposed to sound hackneyed, because so much of it does. You will do yourself, and your readers, a favour if you avoid this trap. Because such clichés add words without adding meaning or clarity, because they say in several words what could more clearly be said in fewer or even one word, and because they obscure rather than clarify your meaning, they are bad writing.

Most of these cumbersome and meaningless phrases can be replaced by much simpler language, often a single word that communicates much more forcefully and directly. For example, "at this point in time" could be replaced by "now"; "if this proves to be the case" could be written simply as "if"; "postpone until later" could simply be "postpone." Some of them, such as "it has come to my attention that," could be eliminated completely without any loss of meaning. See if you can translate these awkward and stuffy phrases and clauses into plain language. Always review your own writing for such phrases and replace them with more direct language.

3. Use of the Passive Voice The passive voice expresses not action done *by* the subject, but action done *to* the subject, a crucial difference. For example, "Assistance would be greatly appreciated" is almost always better written, "I would appreciate your assistance...."

In certain types of very formal writing, the use of passive voice is considered appropriate, but it distances writer from reader, deadens style, and often causes a loss of clarity. For these reasons, it is sometimes used (along with vague and clichéd wording) as a deliberate strategy by writers who want to confuse or obfuscate: official government documents and administrative memos are often written in such opaque language. However, deliberate obscurity or unintentional muddiness is not a desirable quality in writing designed to communicate. You want your writing to stand out for its clarity, directness, and human connection. Consider how much more vivid and powerful, not to mention shorter, the following sentences are when they are written in the active voice.

Larry completed my project.
  is better than
The project that I was working on has been completed by Larry.

Shirley conducted the required tests.
  is better than
The tests that were required have been conducted by Shirley.

Doug hired John Smith to complete the Ferguson project.
  is better than
John Smith was hired by Doug for the completion of the project for the Ferguson account.

We have evaluated your application.
  is better than
Your application has been evaluated by us.

One way you can make your own writing more powerful and concise is to eliminate unnecessary use of the passive voice wherever you can.

4. Overuse of Phrases and Dependent Clauses as Modifiers Very often we find ourselves using several words where we could use just one. Believe it or not, long windy sentences are actually easier to create than are clear, concise ones, because they don't demand as much care or attention to meaning, and they require no concern for the audience's needs. But they also make very dull, boring, tedious messages that remain unread or unheeded.

Excessive use of phrasal and clausal modifiers is among the most common causes of this kind of wordiness, and when it is combined with the passive voice (as in the examples above) it can be dull, or even confusing, to read. As a rule, you should not use several words when one will do the job. See how much more concise the following examples can be.

- the project I am working on (my project)
- the equipment that our department recently purchased (our recently purchased equipment)
- the store on the corner (the corner store)
- the present that I bought for my father (my father's present, *or even* my present for my father)
- the account belonging to this customer (this customer's account)
- the reason for which I am writing (my reason for writing)
- the business that I recently acquired (my recently acquired business)
- property that belongs to the company (company property)
- a friend whom I have known for a long period of time (a longtime friend)

Watch, in particular, for an overuse of the words "of" (or other prepositions), "which," or "that." Rewrite such phrases or clauses into one or two words whenever you can do so without a loss of precision or thought.

5. Unnecessary Repetition of Ideas Repetition can be a powerful tool for persuasion when it is used effectively and deliberately. It can engage and motivate an audience into action. However, two things must be said about repetition as a strategy: first, effective repetition is primarily an oral device that does not achieve the same effects in writing. Much repetition in writing is cumbersome and unworkable; it may even seem unnatural and overdone. In business writing, where the goal is to communicate efficiently and clearly, unnecessary repetition can actually be a hindrance to your message.

In a memo, letter, or e-mail, you need to say what you mean in as little space as possible. To make your writing really effective, you should avoid any unnecessary repetition. To avoid this problem, cluster related information and make each point only once. If you say it clearly the first time, you can eliminate the useless and often confusing repetition that weakens your writing and obscures your message.

6. Failure to Cluster Related Points In organizing your message, you must be sure to place related points together: jumping back and forth is confusing to the reader and is one of the things that leads to the unnecessary repetition we have just discussed. If you find yourself writing the clause "as I said above..." you probably need to do more to cluster related information.

If, for example, you are writing a letter to obtain tickets and accommodations for a convention, you should cluster all information pertaining to the tickets into one paragraph and all information about the accommodations into another. For added clarity and visual appeal, you can place the main details in indented lists.

7. Failure to Identify the Desired Action A frequent function of persuasive business communication is to prompt a specific kind of action from the reader. You are writing because you want results. Although as a writer you may feel that the appropriate course of action is obvious, what you want done may not be quite so clear to the reader, whose idea of a suitable solution may differ from yours. Don't expect your reader to come automatically to the same conclusion you have reached about what must be done. State directly, in clear and specific language, what you expect the reader to do. If there are several steps to be taken, list and enumerate them for the reader's convenience.

8. Incomplete Information Before writing your final draft, check once more to be sure you have included all relevant information. Ask yourself Who? What? Where? When? Why? and How? to be sure that you have supplied all the necessary details.

weblinks

The UVic Writer's Guide
http://webserver.maclab.comp.uvic.ca/writersguide/welcome.html

The Elements of Style
http://www.columbia.edu/acis/bartleby/strunk/

Resources for Writers
http://owl.english.purdue.edu/writers/by-topic.html

Grammar and Style Notes
http://www.english.upenn.edu/~jlynch/Grammar/

An Elementary Grammar
http://vweb1.hiway.co.uk/ei/intro.html

points to remember

Learning to edit out the common faults of business writing will improve your writing and make your messages easier to understand and act upon. Keep the rules discussed in this chapter in mind whenever you write a piece of business communication. Here they are in summary, with a few additions.

1. Always be prepared to write more than one draft.
2. Always begin with your main idea.
3. Put the main point into a subject or "re" line where possible.
4. Cluster related points together.
5. Prevent wordiness by eliminating unnecessary repetition, excessive use of clauses and phrases, clichés, and the passive voice.
6. Include all necessary information.
7. Identify desired action.
8. Be courteous — always consider your reader's feelings and watch your tone.

sharpening your skills

SECTION A
Revise the following sentences, taken from business communications, to make them clearer and more concise.

1. In the event that any employee should be the final individual to exit the premises of this company on the eve of any given working period, it would

be greatly appreciated by management as a gesture of fiscal responsibility if such individuals should leave the offices in a state of darkness.

2. It has come to my attention that your firm is offering a new position that has never been available before to any new applicants from outside the company. Please be advised that I would like to express my interest in this very attractive position and feel that you should be interested in my background as well.

3. If this writer can be of any further assistance to you in this matter, please do not hesitate to contact myself at the above-mentioned office location.

4. With reference to your communication of the above-referenced date, enclosed herewith find the documents which you requested at that point in time.

5. At the present time, I am not at liberty to give consideration to such requests due to the inability of this office to evaluate whether or not this aforementioned request is in accordance with present practice of this company.

6. It is our earnest endeavour to process applications with greatest efficiency; however, in the event that you are not in receipt of a requested response on or before the closing date, please do not hesitate to put yourself in contact with personnel at this location.

7. Due to the difficulties involved with the aforementioned request, I would like to take this opportunity to thank you in advance for your assistance in this difficult matter.

8. Due to the fact that this writer was unavailable over the period of the previous month because of absence due to vacation, your correspondence of the above-referenced date did not receive the immediate attention of myself, for which I send you herewith my most sincere apology.

9. A cheque for the amount specified to cover the loss experienced due to the above incident of April 30 has been prepared by this office. Your appearance is requested at your earliest convenience to complete the necessary paperwork and to receive such payment. We trust this is in order.

10. In the event of circumstances beyond our control which affect delivery of this service, some alterations to the planned schedule may be required.

Section B

In his famous essay "Politics and the English Language," the writer George Orwell rewrites a familiar passage from *Ecclesiastes* into modern business language. Here is the original passage as it appears in the Bible:

> I returned and saw under the sun, that the race is not to the swift, nor the battle to the strong, neither yet bread to the wise, nor yet riches to men of

understanding, nor yet favour to men of skill; but time and chance happeneth to them all.

Here is Orwell's rewritten version in modern English:

> Objective considerations of contemporary phenomena compels the conclusion that success or failure in competitive activities exhibits no tendency to be commensurate with innate capacity, but that a considerable element of the unpredictable must invariably be taken into account.[1]

Of course, Orwell's point is to demonstrate how much less clear the modern language is than the original. As a class, compare Orwell's passage with the passage from *Ecclesiastes* and explain why the original is more effective.

1. Just for fun, try your hand at this reverse process by rewriting some clear passages into "modern" business language, using the clichés and abstract phrases we have been discussing. Try rewriting some of the examples of good business writing in Chapter 3 in such a manner, or apply the process to a familiar fairy tale — The Three Little Pigs or Red Riding Hood. Compare and discuss your choices with those of the other members of the class.

SECTION C

The following business communications (Figure 2.2–2.6) are real examples that I have collected over several years. Read them through to spot weaknesses similar to those we've discussed above, and edit for conciseness and clarity.

online exercises

1. At Purdue University's Online Writing Lab site (http://owl.english.purdue.edu/Files/90.html), you will find a list of guidelines called "Revision in Business Writing." Scroll down the page to reach a set of questions similar to the Business Writing Planner on page 18 of this chapter. Plan two separate business communications — letters, memos, or e-mail messages — using the online form for one and the Business Writing Planner for the other. What differences did you find? Discuss your observations with the class.

2. At http://www.streetside.com/pat/html/articles/writing/index.html, you will find a site called "Style Guide for Writers: How to Write Real Good," which features "advice" on writing style, along with additional "tips" for both technical and business writers. Should you follow Pat Martin's tips for writing? Do you think he intends you to do so? How do you know the advice is not serious? What do you think Martin's point is?

---

[1] George Orwell, "Politics and the English Language," *The Orwell Reader,* ed. Richard H. Rovere (New York: Harcourt, Brace, and World, 1956) p. 360.

figure 2.2

Despite his good intentions, Franco Brazzoni's message is obscured by wordy, vague writing and poor layout. See if you can improve his letter.

IDA Groceteria
25 Headframe Street
Forestville, Ontario
K8Y 4R2

Homework

April 25, 1999

Dr. Iqbal Zafar, Pharmacist
Value Drugs
34 Centre Street
Cedarton, Ontario
K7Y 2F6

As ↑
For a period of 4 years, René was employed as a stock person + clerk During his employment, he did did what were expected of him & we never doubted his ability to do a great job. His excellent work habits transferred in his work ethics, a team leader, + exceptional customer service + relations

Dear Dr. Zafar:

With reference to your correspondence dated April 22, 1999, in accordance with your request for information about René Huneault, it will be my most earnest endeavour to provide you with a most glowing reference of his character.

The Info Required about Ren Heane will be given to the best degree of his character

First of all, René Huneault was in our employ for a period of four years; he is at the present time seeking for a position in a more advanced capacity elsewhere. During that period of time René performed a wide variety of duties which were expected of him in his position of stock person and clerk which he performed to the utmost of his ability. We never had at any time a reason to doubt René's ability to be able to do his job and we perceived at all times that he was a good worker who was conscientious in his work, honest, and utilized courtesy in dealings with customers.

In giving consideration to René's personal characteristics of his personality, in line with your suggestion, we have found René to be easy to get along with for everybody who had to work with him and at all times could be depended upon to do what was needed at that point.

Considering that I would be happy to give a recommendation of René

Due to the foregoing considerations, it would make me happy to be able to provide you herewith with a positive recommendation of René and in the event that you are in need of further information, please do not hesitate to contact myself in the near future.

Sincerely
Yours very sincerely,

If you need more information please contact me.

Franco Brazzoni
Manager

figure 2.3

This career statement fails to deliver a clear, coherent message. How would you improve it?

WHY I WANT TO BE A CORRECTIONS OFFICER

When interacting with people, I find it most intriguing working with youths in this particular field. Corrections gives you a better in-depth look at what certain attitudes and experiences affect the different kinds of behaviour in young offenders.

Communication is the most important part of a Corrections Officer's job. Communicating with the young offenders, their parents, as well as their teachers gives you an opportunity to observe human nature. Observing human nature with young offenders is a very good example of getting to know the inmate.

When observing human nature, you find the different aspects of young offenders, such as What are the youth's attitudes and problems? How confused/frustrated are they? What are the young offender's reactions to society?

These are just some of the examples and questions you will be asking when you begin to observe young offenders.

By getting to know problem youths as you work with them you will feel good and better about yourself when you look back on those special achievements that you will always be proud of.

As I look back at all the experience which I received when working with adolescent youths. I found the observations which I did, to be very challenging, interesting, and very useful for comparisons.

During the beginning of last year's school year, I counselled youths in a group home with social and interpersonal problems. For each session with them, I tried to think of new ways to explain a problem which they found frustrating. After each counciling session I would record each observation about each youth.

By the end of the school year, their was a tremendous change of each youth's attitude which I counsiled. The young offenders, their parents, as well as the social workers were quite amazed. I felt good about myself and for the time I spent with them. It was challenging and very rewarding to be with them, and I only had my tires slashed once, but I don't think it was any of the kids I counsilled.

Why might I have trouble responding to this request?
What flaws can you find in the letter?

September 26, 2000

Jennifer MacLennan

5419 39 Street

Red Deer AB T4N 1A1

Re: Policy# CH-BINDER (AUTO 96 HONDA ACCORD)
        Effective September 16, 2000 to March 16, 2001

Dear Jennifer:

Please be advised that Canadian Home has written us requesting a copy of your
drivers license (front and back). This is because the number we submitted was
rejected by Motor Vehicles.

Kindly send this to our office as soon as possible. Your immediate attention to
this matter would be appreciated. We thank you in advance for your
cooperation.

Trusting this is in order.

Sincerely yours,
LEARNERS INSURANCE LTD.

Agnieska Bustard

Agnieska Bustard
B/pe

---

figure 2.5 Though Lucy has included most of the necessary details, her letter is ineffective. Why?

Lucy Wallersheim
27 Wormsley Road
Airdrie, Alberta
T4X 1U7

November 25, 2001

Contemporary Fashions
Manager, Nancy Schindelhauer
1729 Trutch Street
Vancouver, British Columbia
V6J 7Y8

Dear Ms Schindelhauer:

I am writing to tell you about my new pink sweater which I bought from your catalogue last summer. I have always liked your service in your store and enjoy dealing with you. I am returning the sweater to you.

Your catalogues are always nice and clear and the pictures are beautiful, which is what led me to order this one from you in your Spring and Summer catalogue, on page 26.

I am really writing because the one I got was size 16 and I ordered size 12 in August I think. I need the right one sent back right away because I am planning to wear it over my Christmas holidays. It was $29.95.

Thank you very much for your help in fixing this mistake. If you can't send it to me would you please refund my money I paid you?

Yours sincerely,

Lucesca Wallersheim

Lucesca Wallersheim

PS The sweater is catalogue number JM-3076P

H O T E L   B o n A m i

where good friends meet

19 Sherwood Avenue
Mississauga, ON M2R 7G5

phone: (905) 987-6543
fax: (905) 987-5432
email: hba@inet.ca

Friday, November 10, 2000

Mr. Ray Pronyshyn
Waskasoo College
20015 Laketree Place
Forestville, Ontario
K1A 5X7

Dear Ray:

Further to our conversation of the above-referenced date, please be advised that the following positions are presently available at our BonAmi Airport International Hotel: Room Service Telephone Operator; Waiters/Waitresses; Hostess (November and December); Bartender; Busboys; Dishwashers; Potwashers.

If it should prove to be the case that any one or more of your current students presently in your Hotel Administration Program should be interested in the above-mentioned positions of employment, it is my hope that your staff or faculty will inform them to contact myself at their earliest convenience.

I appreciate your co-operation in this matter and please do not hesitate to contact me if you should be in need of any further information or assistance.

Thanking you in advance for your assistance,

Best regards,

Judy Cheung

Judy Cheung
Assistant Food and Beverage Manager

Business Letters, Memos, and E-mail Messages

LEARNING OBJECTIVES

➤ To master standard business letter and memo format.
➤ To understand the common types of business messages and when to use them.
➤ To learn the parts of a business letter and memo.

Whether they are sent by surface mail, by facsimile machine, or through electronic mail (e-mail), the business letter and the memo are the most common forms of business communication. Although information can be exchanged by telephone, this method isn't satisfactory for all situations. For many practical reasons, written communication may be preferred: it allows a precision not possible in oral exchanges and creates a permanent record for your own files. Whenever someone in a company exchanges written information with someone in another firm, the business letter has traditionally provided the appropriate vehicle. Within the company, formal written communication is usually conducted via the memorandum, while informal messages may be sent by e-mail. If a message must be sent across Canada or to another country, electronic mail or even regular post is still much cheaper than long-distance telephone calls.

Electronic mail provides a quick and inexpensive means of communicating within an organization or with other people and firms in locations around the world; generally, communication by e-mail is less formal than by letter or memorandum. Although its use is widespread, e-mail is still considered largely an informal medium. It is also, as many of you know, not a secure form for discussing personal or sensitive issues. As a result, it has not yet replaced the business letter or the memo as the dominant form of business communication, particularly for the formal demands of business. Still, the principles of business writing that follow are applicable not only to the more traditional forms of written business communication, but also to communications sent by electronic means.

Before you can even begin to communicate what you have to say, you must choose an appropriate method of communication. Here are some general guidelines for choosing between oral and written communication, or between a formal letter or memo and e-mail. Use a letter or a memo rather than a telephone call for any information that might be considered "official" or formal, and for any information that is to be retained on file. A phone call or even a personal note will suffice if the information is for one person only, if no copies will be distributed elsewhere, and if it is not for the record.

E-mail, on the other hand, may be used for a whole variety of communication situations, is handy if you have to send the same message to a number of people, and can be quite casual in its set-up. However, because it cannot as yet carry your signature, it is not usually considered suitable for formal needs. Also, busy people who are inundated with dozens of e-mail messages a day may not give an important piece of communication the attention it deserves.

Nevertheless, despite its casual air, you should remember that anything you send via e-mail may be retained indefinitely by the recipient or forwarded without your knowledge or permission to someone else virtually anywhere in the world. Your personal e-mail files may also be viewed with impunity by your employer. You should not use e-mail communication for confidential messages unless you can ensure that they will be securely encrypted and decoded only by the intended recipient.

Generally, you should use a letter or memo when:

- a copy of the information you are sending must be retained on file;
- the information concerns organization policy;
- the information is important; and
- copies of the document will be formally distributed to someone other than the individual to whom it is addressed.

Because business letters and memos are used so frequently, consistent standards of content, format, and style have evolved to help make the task of writing easier. As electronic mail replaces "snail mail" as the standard for business communication, style requirements are evolving for its use as well. Observing conventional standards in your writing will not only help to make your message more easily understood, but will also create a positive impression and help to establish you as a professional. Both memos and letters — as well as e-mail communication — observe the same rule: get to the point and don't waste the reader's time. To be effective, they must be professional, that is, accurate, clear, and written in an acceptable format.

Types of Business Letters, Memos, and E-mail Messages

Business letters, memos, and e-mail messages can carry both good and bad news and may serve a multitude of purposes, from providing information to selling merchandise. As a general rule, you should use letter or memo format for formal messages and reserve e-mail for more informal purposes. Whether they carry good news or bad news, business letters, memos, and e-mail messages can be divided into two main categories: request and response. Whichever form your message takes — letter, memo, or e-mail — it will follow the same general guidelines.

Making a Request

A *request* may be written for any number of purposes: to order or sell merchandise; to request information (printed materials, catalogues, travel flyers) or an appointment; to reserve a conference or hotel room; to apply for a job; or to ask for favours (a reference, for instance).

Basically, a request is any message that initiates contact with another person; the writer should aim to establish an effective working relationship between correspondents. These days, business contacts may be initiated via e-mail as well as by letter; the following guidelines also apply to these exchanges.

Request messages should observe the Six C's listed in Chapter 1, keeping in mind that a major part of courtesy is making reasonable requests — don't ask the person to whom you are writing to do your work for you. Here are three questions to ask yourself before you write.

1. Am I being specific about what I want to know or what I'd like done?
2. Am I asking someone else to find information or perform a task that I could easily accomplish myself?
3. Is this request going to inconvenience the person in any unreasonable way?

If you can easily find out the information you need from a library or other source, or if you are vague about exactly what you want, you should reconsider your request carefully. Do not ask others to do for you what you could easily do for yourself. Of course, you should also be sure to say please and thank you.

Writing a Response

A *response* is any message written in response to a request, an advertisement, or a situation. These might include letters of recommendation, information, congratulations or condolence, adjustment, refusal, or complaint.

Once again, the Six C's apply, with a few additional considerations. In a letter of response, you should be prompt, as well as helpful. Always give the reader a positive impression and make your letter complete.

Good News and Bad News Messages

Within the two general categories of request and response, there are a variety of situations that require a business letter, a memo, or an e-mail message. The messages arising from common business situations may be broadly characterized as "good news" or "bad news" messages, written for purposes of congratulations, complaint, sales, or refusals. Some of these present special problems for a beginning writer. Business letters, memos, and e-mail messages carrying good news make it easy to establish a positive writer–reader relationship; those that carry bad news — messages of complaint or refusal, for example — demand more careful handling.

It is especially important to watch your tone when delivering bad news. Try to cushion your bad news message with suitable positive language and a positive tone. Be especially careful to avoid suggesting or implying that the other person is somehow responsible for the situation, even if you believe this to be the case. Always assume that you could be mistaken, and give your correspondent the benefit of the doubt if you can. What you really want is to have the problem solved, and creating unnecessary bad feelings will only lessen the chances of this happening. Be pleasant and take care to avoid a sarcastic tone.

Both good news and bad news messages require the same qualities of conciseness, coherence, correctness, and completeness as other business correspondence. Bad news messages also require an especial emphasis on courtesy. In a difficult or challenging situation, especially one in which bad news is being presented, it is particularly important to be courteous to your correspondents in order to make certain that your wishes are complied with.

Following are several common writing situations; messages of congratulations and sales messages are considered good news, while messages of complaint and messages of refusal are considered bad news. Keep in mind that any of these types of messages maybe sent in letter, memo, or e-mail formats, depending on their level of formality.

Congratulations or Acknowledgement

Of the four special types, this good news message is the most pleasant to write. A letter (or memo or e-mail message) of congratulations may be written to an employee, a colleague, or a client on the occasion of achievement or accomplishment. This accomplishment may be an award, the publication of a book or article, a promotion, a significant contribution to a company project, or simply recognition of long or effective service. Whatever the occasion, the message of acknowledgement or congratulations should be positive in tone and to the point. Such messages should be:

- specific (identify the achievement or occasion);
- positive (make sure your tone is warm and your comments flattering);
- sincere (nothing is more insulting than congratulations that sound insincere; avoid being too effusive or ironic); and

- brief (as in any business communication, say what you have to say, then stop — many people ruin effective acknowledgement or congratulations messages by not knowing when to quit).

Figure 3.1 contains a memo of acknowledgement from a supervisor to a staff member who has contributed an extraordinary year's work to the company. Figure 3.2 is an e-mail message expressing congratulations to a colleague who has received the company's Employee of the Year award. Compare the two. Based on your knowledge of business writing, which is the more effective? Why is this so?

Complaints

Although not so pleasant to write, these bad news messages are unfortunately much more common than messages of congratulations. Most businesses do their best to handle orders, requests, and other correspondence in a professional and efficient manner; however, occasionally mix-ups do occur. Orders may be misplaced, cheques lost, wrong merchandise sent, or mailings waylaid.

Most firms will do all in their power to keep such mistakes from happening, since businesses function more smoothly when goodwill is maintained through effective customer relations. If you always make it a rule to assume, at least initially, that the mix-up is an honest error and to treat such incidents as unintentional, your complaints will be dealt with more promptly and positively.

The first rule for letters or memos of complaint is to be especially courteous. No one wants to receive abusive, sarcastic, or threatening letters; phrase your bad news in as positive terms as possible. Problems will be more easily solved if you allow your correspondents a chance to correct the situation without making them look foolish. They will be more interested in helping you and they will be more anxious to maintain your goodwill if you approach them in a friendly, nonthreatening manner.

It is also important that in a complaint you specify the nature of the problem and the action you wish taken. For example, if you have ordered merchandise and after waiting a reasonable length of time have not received your order, you will want to identify the missing items by name, catalogue or item number, colour and size (if applicable), catalogue issue, and page number. You should state the date of your order, the cheque number, if there is one, and the amount of the order. If you have a standing account with the firm, cite your account number. Be sure that all of this information is correct. Be sure also that you tell the reader exactly what you want done about the problem. The reader's idea of a satisfactory solution may differ from yours.

Below are the points to remember for letters of complaint.

- Phrase your comments positively.
- Be sure to identify the exact nature of the problem immediately.
- Provide all relevant details.
- Request specific action.
- Be courteous. Thank correspondents for their help.

Communications Corporation

INTERDEPARTMENTAL COMMUNICATION

DATE: April 14, 1999

TO: Gwynne Nishikawa

FROM: Michael Cea

RE: Appreciation of your contributions during the 1999/2000 fiscal year

Just a note to say thank you for all the work you have done for the Publishing Division during this past year. I have especially appreciated your willingness to aid in the vacation period when I needed someone to fill in for ill personnel, and to take on an extra book publishing project when one of our other editors left the company.

Considering that you also managed to design a new training program for the Staff Development department, your contribution has been truly commendable and beyond any requirements of your job description.

Thank you for all that you have done and for your valuable assistance. Few, if any, members of the division have done more to make this a successful year.

Please accept my heartfelt thanks for a job well done.

Mike Cea

cc. Personnel File
    Daena Tobias

MC:jm

Message Composition

| Send Now | Quote | Attach | Address | | Stop |

Randy Alexander <
Randy_Alexander@commcorp.ca>

Subject: Employee of the Year Award

▽ **Addressing**　　　　　　　　　　　　　　　　**Attachments**

　　Mail To: Peter_Holowaczok@commcorp.ca

　　　　Cc:

January 25, 1993

Congratulations on winning the Employee of the Year Award. It doesn't usually go to somebody who has been in the company only two years – you must really be something special. I have been here for four years and though my work is really deserving, nobody seems to notice. I haven't even been nominated. I suppose I haven't made friends with the right people; I never was much good at lobbying.

I have heard it said that the work you've been doing in Public Relations is really outstanding, especially that slick brochure you produced for the new Business Writing Workshop. Most everybody believes that it's really well designed. I saw it – it is pretty good, but could I give you a little advice? I didn't think that the photo of Daena Tobias and Michael Cea was appropriate for the cover. I have a talent for graphic design, and it's not what I would have chosen.

Please let me know if you want to get together sometime to talk about layout; I took a course in graphic art in college and could probably pass on a few useful hints. Also, I'd like to have a chance to talk with the golden boy from PR.

Congratulations again on winning the award.

Randy

In the letter in Figure 3.3, Lam Huan is making a complaint regarding some student loan payment cheques that have been mistakenly processed too early and have been rejected by his own bank. Note that though the loans officer is at fault, Huan wisely does not cause more difficulty by being sarcastic or abusive.

Sales or Persuasive Messages

Throughout this book, I emphasize the necessity in any business writing of identifying the reader's needs, expectations, interests, and knowledge. Such an understanding of your reader is always necessary if you are to write effective business communications, but is especially important when you move from merely informative to persuasive writing. All persuasive communication must engage the attention and interest of its intended audience and motivate that audience to act as requested. As well, an effective persuasive message will help to guide the reader to the appropriate action through an enabling strategy, a device that makes it easy and convenient for the reader to do what is requested.

Sales letters are the most common form of persuasive writing, although they are not the only ones you may have observed. Though these can be considered good news letters and should, like the previous types, be positive in tone, they are more challenging to write because you are not only asking the reader to accept your message, but inviting the person to respond with action. You want to appeal to your readers, influencing them to purchase your product, employ your service, or provide some authorization or sanction, or donate funding. You need to establish a human connection with the reader through the relational aspect of your message; to do this, you should sound upbeat and personal, and above all, honest and sincere. Outline to the reader the advantages of the item(s) you are offering. Keep your letter personal; don't bully, patronize, or pander to the reader, and avoid obvious gimmicks.

Although sales messages, like other business correspondence, could conceivably be sent in memo or e-mail format, the letter is the usual vehicle for such messages because it suggests, and invites, greater personal connection between writer and reader.

Sales letters may be sent to potential customers or to established clients of your firm; your approach will differ slightly depending on which is the case for you. The following are some of the things your sales letter to a new customer should do.

- Catch the reader's attention immediately. You may do this with a question, an unusual statement, a story, or a quotation, or you may offer a premium or gift for prompt responses.
- Create a desire for the product you're offering. Show your readers the advantages of buying your product; if it will save time, work, or money, show how this will be accomplished.
- Make it easy for the reader to acquire the product. Provide an order form, a postage-paid envelope, or instructions as to how to place an order by phone, fax, or e-mail. Offer instalment payments.

What features make Lam Huan's letter of complaint effective? Compare Huan's letter with the letter in Figure 3.4; which is better?

90 Victoria Crescent
Scarborough, Ontario
M2E 2R4

November 20, 1999

Accounting and Process Control
National Exchange Bank
Student Loan Business
PO Box 12345
Rochester, New York 10098
USA

Re: Returned cheques dated November 1, 1999, and December 1, 1999
         Loan Payment Account #555693737 - 9

I received the above cheques from you, with a letter indicating that they were rejected by my bank due to insufficient funds. However, the cheques were processed by your department on October 20, 1999, and received by my bank on October 25. The reason for their rejection was thus not insufficient funds but postdating. Although American banks may operate differently, Canadian banks do not accept postdated cheques.

I dated the cheques according to their payment dates, and mailed them in advance to make certain that they would reach you on time. Since I would like to prevent such a mix-up happening again, is there some way to ensure that in future my cheques are not processed until the appropriate dates have arrived?

I am enclosing a third cheque to cover both payments. Since the original cheques reached you before the November 1 and December 1 due dates, I would appreciate an adjustment to any additional interest charges. Thank you.

Sincerely,

Lam Huan

Lam Huan

22 Ulethe Crescent
Scarborough, Ontario
M3R 5Q8

March 14, 1999

Manager
The Intimate Moment
222 Bank Street
Toronto, Ontario
M4T 2H6

Dear Manager:

The other night I was in your restaurant. My friend and I just went there for dessert. I don't really know the name of my waiter, but I wish to complain about the immature behaviour he showed toward our group.

I ordered a carbonated fruit drink without ice. I don't like to have ice in my drinks because it makes them go flat. I don't see why you can't train your wait staff better or something. They should know better. When the waiter brought my drink, he brought a water goblet with ice in it and then poured my drink in before I could stop him. When I objected, he went and got another goblet, held his fingers over the top of the glass to hold back the ice, and poured my drink into the second goblet. I don't mean to be rude, but I could catch something! I don't think this could be considered in any way sanitary. I don't know where his fingers have been, and judging from the look of him I wouldn't want to speculate about it either!!

When I objected to his having poured my drink over his fingers, he got huffy and said he would bring me another drink. He eventually did that, but I mean, really! What was I supposed to do? And I thought your restaurant was supposed to be a high-class establishment! You're lucky I'm not suing you or something! I could have caught some disease!

As a result of this incident, I am telling all my friends not to go to your establishment. I want to hear from you about what you are doing about this dreadful situation. I hope you aren't letting this dirty person wait on any other customers in the meantime.

Sincerely,

Ing Jang

CHAPTER 3 / BUSINESS LETTERS, MEMOS, AND E-MAIL MESSAGES   **39**

- Keep an enthusiastic tone. If you can, use the reader's name to make the message more personal.
- Communicate your sincerity. If you don't sound as though you mean what you say, your reader will reject your message, no matter how earnest you feel. Be sure that your sincerity is reflected in what you write. Especially avoid the standard clichés of business writing (see Chapter 2), which will make you sound insincere or even phony.

The sales letter to an established client is nearly identical, with the following additions.

- As an established client, your reader will be more predisposed to read your letter through, so you do not have to work quite so hard to catch attention.
- The established client already has shown interest in the products you're offering; briefly emphasize the advantages of your products and outline any improvements or new lines.
- Be enthusiastic. You should definitely use the reader's name to personalize your letter.
- Be sincere and emphasize the effective relationship you've had in the past.

All sales letters must appeal to the reader strongly enough to make that person respond actively. They should be positive, warm, and persuasive, appealing to the needs, interests, and expectations of the reader.

A Note on "Hard Sell"

Sales writing, as a form of persuasive writing, requires careful identification of reader needs. This is a perfectly legitimate, basic principle of persuasion that underlies all effective business communication. However, there are other bases of appeal that are less respectable: instead of identifying and responding to an existing need, some promotional material seeks to create a need for a product. This kind of advertising appears to be designed to manipulate readers by appealing to their greed or to their fears and doubts instead of to their legitimate needs and interests. Some sales flyers use a hysterically enthusiastic style and tone and as a result, their voices are not as convincing. Modern readers, who are overwhelmed with advertising messages from television, radio, the Internet, and print media, are quite sophisticated about gimmicky "hard sell" approaches. They may be wary and suspicious of such methods, and will reject your message as insincere if they detect such an attitude. Remember to keep your tone positive and warm, not crass or offensive, and to keep your audience's concerns genuinely in focus.

The following example of an effective sales memo (Figure 3.5) encourages personnel in a placement agency to take advantage of the company's Referral Bonus Program by recruiting experienced help. Contrast it with Figure 3.6, a letter circulated in a downtown neighbourhood to advertise a newly opened hair salon.

T E M P - P R O

TO: All Temporary Employees

FROM: Ruth Epstein, Placement Coordinator

DATE: November 18, 2000

RE: Temp-Pro's Referral Bonus Program

Did you know that you could earn cash for every qualified person you send to us? Our Referral Bonus Program pays you $50 for each qualified friend you refer!

Because of our recent growth, we have a real shortage of qualified temporary employees for a variety of assignments. Do you know anyone who might be interested in working temp? Maybe someone you know is new to the city, or has recently left a job; perhaps you know students who are tired of being given the run-around by their service.

You can do a friend — and us — a favour, and at the same time do something for yourself, when you invite someone you know to take advantage of the excellent placements offered by Temp-Pro Services. You have reason to be proud of our record: Temp-Pro's reputation is built on service, to our customers and to our temporaries.

We never forget that our temps — you — have helped to make us the largest and most dedicated company in the industry. And because you make our business the success it is, I want to do my best for you.

A brochure describing the Referral Bonus Program is attached, or you can find out more about it by phoning me at 555 6789 or dropping by the office to chat.

I look forward to seeing you and your friends soon!

figure 3.6

A promotional or sales letter like this one is a good idea for a new business, but these writers could use a little help. What improvements to their letter would you suggest?

Short Cuts

22619 Cowan Blvd.
Lethbridge, AB
(403) 345-2476

Dear Potential Customer:

We are recent graduates of the MacLachlan School of Hair Design here in Lethbridge, and we have just opened our very first shop to offer you the best in up-to-date hair care. We learned just about every technique imaginable in school, and we are anxious to try them out on you.

As the new kids on the block, we are anxious to make a go of this business, and we think it will be good for you to try somebody new for a change. We need to establish a clientele or we won't be able to stay in business for long, so we hope you will try us out.

To make our new salon more attractive to you, bring this letter with you when you come in. We will give you 5% off your first haircut and style. Also, we guarantee all our work, so if we do make a mistake on your haircut, we promise we will do it over again once it grows back. So instead of going to your usual stylist, come in and try us. We're anxious to please you and to have a chance to practise our various techniques.

Sincerely,

Missey

Missey Ivanics

Sutri

Sutrisna Kanagaratnam
Co-Owners

Refusals

These bad news messages are often the most difficult to write. While you do not want to trivialize or underplay a difficult situation, you also don't want to exaggerate it through unnecessarily negative language. Great delicacy is required whenever you must turn down someone's request, whether that request has come from a candidate for employment, a client who wants an adjustment for a used or damaged product, or an employee who has asked for a raise.

Here, as in all bad news messages, tone is important. You must be tactful in refusing to provide the service, and you must preserve the client's goodwill if possible. You must observe the rule of putting the main message first. You should use as positive terms as possible under the circumstances to cushion the refusal, and you should especially avoid sarcasm or accusation. State the message briefly and then politely explain your reasons for the refusal.

It is best to avoid placing responsibility for the refusal on the reader, even in cases where that person shares part of the responsibility. It rarely helps to point fingers at anyone; it is preferable instead to stress your own inability to comply with the request. Keep in mind that your most important goal is maintaining goodwill. For example, if you are writing a letter of refusal to someone who has been turned down for a job, stress that the position was offered to another candidate because that individual more closely suited your needs, not because the person you are writing to is inadequate. Likewise, if you are refusing a reference, it is better to stress your inability to supply it, rather than suggest that the person is flawed. The following are some points to keep in mind when writing a letter of refusal.

- Identify the subject in a subject or "re" line.
- Indicate briefly your inability to comply with the reader's request, using as positive terms as possible.
- State your reasons simply, taking responsibility for your refusal.
- Avoid sarcasm or accusation.
- Be polite and sincere.
- Suggest someone else your correspondent might approach for assistance, if possible.
- Offer the person your best wishes for better success elsewhere if it's appropriate.

In the letter of refusal in Figure 3.7, the bad news has been cushioned with positive comments, and the reader has been invited to submit future work to the magazine. As well, the writer has recommended another publication that might accept the submission. Contrast it with Figure 3.8; both letters have a similar message to relate. Which of the two would you rather receive?

Remember, no matter what kind of letter or memo you are writing, be sure to identify your main point first and communicate your message as clearly and concisely as possible, maintaining a polite tone throughout.

figure 3.7

What strategies did John Moffatt use to soften the news of the magazine's rejection of Molly Crump's article? Contrast this example with the e-mail message in Figure 3.8. Which would you rather receive?

Great Canadian Outdoors

The magazine for those with a zest for living

February 15, 2000

Ms Molly Crump
55 Elwood Close
Calgary, Alberta
T5W 3F6

Dear Ms Crump

Thank you for submitting the article on your wilderness trek through the Northwest Territories. Though the subject matter is interesting and the accompanying pictures attractive, I am afraid that we will not be able to publish your article. Unfortunately, the approach you have taken does not quite coincide with our editorial focus, which is less adventure-oriented than this article.

I would like to encourage you in finding a publisher for your work. You might try submitting it to Hadi Kharagani at *Great Northern Adventure*. I believe that, with some revision, yours might be the sort of material that they use.

However, before submitting the article again, you should really consider some close editing. A well-written article that doesn't require polishing by the magazine is more likely to find favour with a busy editorial staff.

Despite our inability to use the article, we would like to extend our best wishes in placing this article with another magazine.

Sincerely

John Moffatt

John G. Moffatt
Managing Editor

---

934 George Street, Yellowknife, NWT X1A 3X2
Phone 403/787-5545 • Fax 403/787-5565 • www.greatoutdoors.ca

figure 3.8

How might Martin Oordt respond to this note? Suggest some ways David Kaminski's message might be improved.

Message Composition

| SendNow | Quote | Attach | Address | | Stop |

David Kaminski <
editor@collegian.waskasoo.ca>

Subject: poetry submission

▽ **Addressing**   **Attachments**

Mail To: MartinOordt@Inetexpress.com

Cc:

April 1, 2001

Dear Marty:

Thanks for submitting your latest poetry for consideration by the Collegian's editorial staff. As you know, we usually welcome submissions from students and members of the community at large.

We would prefer, however, not to receive any more poems from you. Although I admit that we published one of your poems last year, you should know that poetry is not really our "thing" and we used the other poem only because we had a little bit of space to fill andn your work just fit.

We are more interested in other kinds of submissions – photos, drawings, and fiction written by the college community; I am pretty sure that our readers don't know much about poetry and don't really want to see it in the Collegian. If they did want to read such stuff, they could take an English course! After all, we are interested in things that are relevant to real life and most people agree that poetry is boring. Besides, I'm not even sure how to judge the quality of your poetry.

I Hope you won't be too upset by my note, but I thought you would want to hear the truth. If you decide to take up a more interesting kind of writing, please let us know. We might like to have something else from you.

David Kaminski
Editor

The Parts of a Business Letter

All business letters contain the same parts and may be written in any of three standard formats. All are also single spaced. Whether the letter is sent by ordinary post or via fax, the structure is the same. Before we look at formats, let's consider the parts of a standard business letter. (The numbers correspond to the numbers in square brackets in Figure 3.9 on page 52.)

1. Return Address This is the normal address of the writer of the letter; it does not include the writer's name. In a personal business letter, the return address is your home address; if you are writing on behalf of your company, it is the company's name and address. If you are using company letterhead, you do not need to include a separate return address.

2. Date Though there is a move toward dating letters numerically, it is still better to write out the date; styles of numerical dating vary, and this inconsistency can cause confusion, especially as we move into the new century. There are currently three numeric forms in use:

Canadian	12/06/02	Day/Month/Year
American	06/12/02	Month/Day/Year
"Metric"	02/06/12	Year/Month/Day

Without some further cues for interpretation, it's very difficult to ascertain whether the date shown is December 6, 2002, June 12, 2002, or February 6, 2012. If your employer prefers numerical dating, you should use the format the company uses, but otherwise, avoid this unnecessary confusion by writing out the date in full — in this case, June 12, 2002.

3. Inside Address This is an important part of the business letter; it provides information for the files of the company to which it is sent. It should include the following, in this order.

Name and title	Ms Daena Tobias, Director
Name of company	Communications Corporation
Address of company	555 California Street
	Vancouver, British Columbia
	V1R 7H9

If the person's title is very long, it might be placed on a separate line, but the order of the parts remains the same.

Name	Ms Soo Liang Chan
Title	Assistant Manager, Human Resources
Name of company	Communications Corporation
Address of company	555 California Street
	Vancouver, British Columbia
	V1R 7H9

4. Salutation This is the opening of your letter; traditionally, it's "Dear...." Use the name of the person to whom you are writing, if you know it. If you don't know it, and it is important that you have it (for instance, in a job application letter), telephone the company and ask for the person's name. If you can't bring yourself to do this, you may be able to locate the correct name on the company's web site. If you can't find the name, you may wish to delete the salutation altogether. In modern correspondence, this is permissible. Do not use "Dear Sir" if you don't know the name of the person to whom you're' writing; women who occupy professional positions might reasonably object to the assumption that all such positions are held by men.

If you are corresponding with a person whose given name is not readily identifiable as male or female — for example, R.I. McAdam, Terry Ferguson, Raj Bhanot, Saran Narang, or Mai Li Chiu — you may wish to write the full name in the salutation: "Dear R.I. McAdam" or "Dear Mai Li Chiu." Unless you are on very friendly terms with the person you are writing to, note that it is never proper to address him or her by first name in a business correspondence: "Dear Saran" or "Dear Mai Li" is unacceptable.

5. Subject or "Re" Line This useful device is borrowed from the memorandum. It has become an important part of the business letter, since it forces the writer to observe the rule of putting the main information first and allows the reader to identify the main point immediately. This line should be brief and to the point, and should indicate clearly what the letter is about. It usually consists of a single phrase or two.

6. Body This portion of your correspondence contains the main information you wish to communicate, in as clear a form as possible. Identify the subject matter at the beginning, giving a brief outline of the situation or problem. Follow with some pertinent details, carefully selected and organized so that the reader may easily understand your message. Finish with a specific statement that outlines what you expect of the reader. The body of the letter is single spaced and divided into brief paragraphs for ease of reading. The number of paragraphs can vary, as can the length of the letter, depending on the complexity of the subject matter. Some letters are two or three pages long, but most are one page. Whatever the length of the letter, its message should be easily grasped on one reading. If your reader must reread the letter several times simply to understand it, it is poorly composed and ineffective.

7. Complimentary Closing This can be any one of a variety of forms; the most common nowadays is "Sincerely" or even "Yours sincerely." "Yours truly" is not used very much anymore, though it isn't wrong. Whichever you use, be sure to note its correct spelling. If you are on very friendly terms with your correspondent, you may even wish to use a more familiar closing, such as "Cordially" or "Best wishes" or even (if you are very friendly) "Cheers." Do not use these for formal correspondence, however. If you are in doubt, simply use "Sincerely."

8. Company Name Occasionally, a writer using company letterhead will signify that correspondence is written on behalf of his or her employer by placing the company name, in block capitals, immediately below the complimentary closing, above the writer's signature. This precaution is observed to clarify responsibility for legal purposes. At one time, it was safe to assume that anything written on the company's letterhead was written on behalf of the firm, but frequent use of letterhead for personal correspondence has made this assumption impractical. Modern writers may take this extra measure to emphasize that the contents of the letter are indeed a matter of company business. It is not necessary to include this line in your business letters, but if it is common practice in your company, by all means do it.

Yours sincerely,
COMMUNICATIONS CORPORATION

Daena Tobias

Daena Tobias

9. Signature This is the name of the writer only; it should not include any nicknames, titles, or degrees. A professional should also use a consistent signature, not Jennifer in one letter and Jen or Jenny in the next. Choose one form of your name (preferably not a diminutive, and certainly not a nickname) and use it consistently for your business correspondence.

10. Typed Name and Titles Since many people's signatures are unreadable, a courteous writer types the name in full beneath the signature. If you wish to include any degrees or titles, type them along with your name. (These are not, you will remember, included with the signature.) If your name is gender-neutral or potentially misleading, you may wish to make it easier for your correspondent to reply to you by indicating the honorific you prefer. If you are a woman and sign yourself as J. MacLennan, for example, you should not be surprised or offended if some correspondents make the incorrect assumption and address you as "Mr." Very often you will also wish to include your position in the organization you represent.

Terry Lansdown (Mrs.)	Nancy Black (Dr.)
Chief of Operations	Chief of Staff
Saran Narang (Ph.D.)	Soo Liang Chan (Ms)
Editor in Chief	Assistant Manager, Human Resources

11. Secretary's Notations As with the inside address, this information is useful for record purposes; it is sometimes important to know who typed the correspondence, whether any enclosures or attachments were included, or whether any other people received copies. The notations appear in the lower left of the page and are as follows.

/jml	Secretary's initials — some organizations use this form to indicate that the secretary actually composed the correspondence on behalf of the writer, though this is not the case in every firm.
DFC/jml	Writer's initials/typist's initials — may be written this way to indicate that the secretary typed what was written by someone else.
encl:2	Enclosure notation — indicates that two items were enclosed with the package.
attach:3	Attachment notation — similar to enclosure notation, but items were appended to the letter with a clip or staple. In this instance, there were three.
cc. J. Moffatt B. Ramtej	Correspondence notation — these people received copies of the correspondence. The notation "cc" stands for carbon copy, the method used for creating copies of documents before photocopiers became indispensable office equipment. Although no one now uses carbon copies, the notation "cc" continues to be used whenever copies, however generated, are sent to individuals other than the addressee. This notation might also appear as "pc" for photocopy. In either case, its meaning is the same.

12. File Number A code consisting of a combination of letters and numbers may appear at the lower left or, at the upper right of the page. This is a file number that assists the business in filing correspondence in the appropriate location.

The Parts of a Memo or E-mail Message

Although the letter and memo serve similar purposes and may carry similar kinds of messages, a memo is intended to remain inside the company or institution, and this affects its structure. It has no need of an inside address, return address, or salutation; instead it has a relatively standard heading made up of four parts. The labels To, From, Date, and Re (or Subject) are usually arranged vertically at the top left-hand side of the memo.

Most e-mail programs have adopted the To/From/Date/Subject format of the memo. The program automatically fills in the date and the e-mail address of the sender; the sender inserts the e-mail address of the recipient, along with a brief subject title.

The other sections of the memo or e-mail message are similar to the parts of the business letter, as explained below.

1. To Takes the place of the salutation and identifies, by name and title, the person or persons to whom the memo is directed. In an e-mail message, the

"To" line consists of the e-mail address rather than the name of the recipient. The e-mail addresses of any additional recipients may also be added here.

2. From Identifies, again by name and title, the person who wrote the memo. In the case of a message sent by e-mail, your program will automatically fill in your e-mail address on any messages sent from your account.

3. Date States the date on which the memo was written; you may wish to use a numerical dating style in a memo, but as we discussed above, numerical dating can cause confusion, and you should probably avoid it unless your firm recommends it. You do not need to supply the date in an e-mail message, since the program itself will automatically record the date and the time of the message, which will be displayed when the recipient reads the message.

4. Re or Subject Identifies for the reader exactly what issue the memo or e-mail message addresses and what you wish to say about that issue. This most crucial line of your memo should contain the main point you have identified in your rough draft with the key words, "The main thing I want to tell you is that...." Business people are busy and will not want to scan the entire memo or e-mail message to find the gist of it. Often they decide whether to take the time even to read the message by glancing at the subject line, so make sure yours is specific. This line is especially important in an e-mail message; regular users of e-mail can receive as many as twenty or thirty messages *every day*. Most don't have the time to carefully read all of these, and some even delete those that look unimportant — without reading them at all. If you want to make sure your message gets read, supply a subject line that makes clear to the reader what the message involves.

5. Message The body of the memo, without a salutation, follows the headings. It may be separated from them by a solid line if you wish. Like the body of the letter, it contains the main information you wish to communicate, in as clear a form as possible. It is single spaced and deals with the situation or problem as specifically as possible. The body of the e-mail message is similar to that of the memo, although many people like to personalize this impersonal form of communication by adding a salutation. If your e-mail message is to someone you know well and with whom you're on friendly terms, this salutation may be as familiar as "Hi, Jen." If you are corresponding via e-mail to a business colleague or client, you may wish to use the same form of salutation that is used in the letter: "Dear Franco:" or even "Dear Dr. Berruti:".

Like a business letter, a memo or e-mail message may deal with issues of varying complexity. Memos used for simple issues are usually less than a page long, but the memo format may also be used for a short report dealing with more complex situations. (Reports are covered in Chapters 4 and 5.) Whatever its purpose, the memo or e-mail message, like the business letter and report, provides specifics to support the main point given in the subject or "re" line. However, because these messages are often very short and to the point, they risk sounding curt or abrupt in tone. Be especially careful to observe courtesy in a memo or e-mail message in order to avoid offending your reader.

Finally, you should avoid contributing to the flurry of unnecessary memos. Use a memo only for information that might be considered "official"; a casual message may be better delivered by telephone, by e-mail, or by a brief personal note.

6. Initial or Signature No complimentary closing is required on a memo, but it may be initialled or signed if you wish. Though a signature is not absolutely necessary, it is becoming more common to sign memos. Since your name appears at the top, there is no need to type it again under your signature. An e-mail message, of course, cannot be signed, though you may wish to type your name at the end of the message. For this reason e-mail is not yet used for very formal correspondence or for reports and letters that are legally binding.

7. Notations Since memos serve the same purposes as letters, they make use of the same notations, especially secretary's initials and carbon copy designations. If it is appropriate, copies may be sent to superiors or other interested parties within the company. For example, a supervisor who writes a memo commending an employee for work well done might direct a copy to the personnel file; the head of a departmental committee might direct a copy of a meeting announcement to the department head to let that individual know that the committee is getting on with its work. Memos, like business letters, may also contain file numbers for easy reference. E-mail messages may be sent to several people simultaneously; if so, their e-mail addresses appear in the "to" portion of the message rather than in a copy notation at the bottom of the message.

Letter and Memo Format

Business letters may employ one of three formats widely used in Canada: semiblock, full block, and modified semiblock. (The full block format is the type illustrated in Figure 3.9.) The semiblock style is the oldest pattern and although it is still widely used, it is gradually being replaced by the full block style. Modified semiblock is a transitional form, a blending of the other two styles. Memos, with clear-cut headings at the top of the page, have a simpler format than letters and so are generally easier to construct.

Another feature of an attractive and readable layout is the font you select from those available in your word processor program. In general, a serif font (such as Times or Roman) is easier to read than a sanserif font (such as Helvetica). Script fonts, especially in smaller sizes, are also difficult to read, as are gothic lettering. Most computer fonts are proportionally spaced, which means that thin letters (such as "i" or "t") take up less space on the page than do wide letters (such as "w" or "m"), just as they would if the document were typeset. These fonts

[1]   980 Main Street
        Saint John, NB
        E1G 2M3

[2]   January 21, 2000

[3]   Michael Cea, Manager
        Publishing Division
        Communications Corporation
        555 California Street
        Vancouver, BC
        V1R 7H9

[4]   Dear Mr. Cea

[5]   Re Full Block Letter Format

[6]   This is an example of the full block style; note how all the parts begin at the left margin. Paragraphs are not indented, and lines are skipped between them.

        Also, you will notice that this letter is single spaced, as all business letters should be. Note, too, the optional use of open punctuation in this letter — this means no punctuation at the end of the salutation or the complimentary closing. Of course, if you wish, you may use a colon after the salutation and a comma following the complimentary closing.

[7]   Sincerely
[8]   MEDIACORP LTD

[9]   *Stan Cherniowsky*

[10]   Stan Cherniowsky
        Communications Manager

[11]   cc. Ian Hauen, Ryker Sheepskin Products Ltd
        SC/jm

[12]   00-01-SD

also automatically place an extra space after a period, so that sentences are separated by a slightly larger space than words within a sentence. However, a few fonts (such as Courier, which is designed to resemble a typewritten font) are monospaced, which means that every letter — no matter its width — takes up exactly the same amount of space on the page. If you have selected such a font, you must add an additional space after the period, as used to be the case for documents typed on a typewriter. Compare the following examples for visual appeal:

Times The quick brown fox jumps over the lazy dog. The lazy dog does not respond. The fox disappears through a hole in the hedge.

Helvetica The quick brown fox jumps over the lazy dog. The lazy dog does not respond. The fox disappears through a hole in the hedge.

Courier The quick brown fox jumps over the lazy dog. The lazy dog does not respond. The fox disappears through a hole in the hedge.

Whichever letter format you use, give careful attention to layout. In any piece of business correspondence, you want clarity, and the impression of clarity is enhanced by an attractive arrangement of the letter or memo on the page. Leave generous margins — at least 1" on all sides — and place the printed material as near as possible to the vertical centre of the page. Try not to crowd your letter or memo too close to the top of the page; unless it is very brief, you should space your letter so that approximately half of the print falls within the lower half of the page.

As the Reference Guide in Figure 3.10 indicates, the main difference in letter format is in indentation: in *full block style,* everything, including paragraphs, begins at the left margin of the page. It is the most modern form of letter and the simplest to set up. Paragraph divisions are indicated by skipped lines. In *semiblock format,* the return address, date, complimentary closing, signature, and typed name are indented so that they begin at approximately the centre of the page. The first line of each paragraph is indented one tab stop (which is usually preset at $\frac{1}{2}$" in most word processing programs); paragraph divisions may also be (but do not have to be) indicated by a skipped line if the writer prefers. This format has a more balanced appearance, but is also more difficult to type. *Modified semiblock* is laid out exactly like the semiblock style, except that the paragraphs are not indented. The return address, date, complimentary closing, signature, and typed name are lined up to the right of centre, just as in the semiblock style. All of the text in the body of the letter begins at the left margin, and paragraph divisions are always indicated by a skipped line, as they are in the full block style. Though the full block style is now the most commonly used letter form, you should use whichever format your employer prefers.

The layout of the memo is not as clearly defined as that of the letter. All memos contain the standard four-part heading of To/From/Date/Subject, but the arrangement of these parts may vary, depending on the preference of the

figure 3.10 A handy Reference Guide for memo and letter formats.

Memo Formats

MEMORANDUM	**MEMORANDUM**	**MEMORANDUM**
DATE:	TO: DATE:	TO:
TO:		FROM: DATE:
FROM:	FROM: SUBJECT:	
SUBJECT:		RE:

Letter Formats

Dear _____ :
Re _____ :

Dear _____ :
Re _____ :

Dear _____ :
Re _____ :

Full Block Letter   Semiblock Letter   Modified
                                                     Semiblock Letter

writer. The memo's heading section is normally arranged at the left margin, usually in the order To, From, Date, and Subject, or Re, though there is some variation to this standard order. Several common variations are displayed in Figure 3.10. The paragraphs in the body of the memo may be indented, as in the semiblock letter style, or not, according to the writer's preference. Paragraphs that are not indented should be separated with a skipped line.

You may also have noticed that the examples in this book use different punctuation styles. Some use an "open" style, with no punctuation marks at the end of the salutation or complimentary closing; others use "closed" punctuation, with a colon following the salutation and a comma after the complimentary closing. Either punctuation style is acceptable in any of the formats, but do not mix open and closed styles within a single letter.

weblinks

Writing Memos
http://www.csun.edu/~vcecn006/memo.htm

Writing Business Letters
http://www.aifr.com/26.html

Five Steps To Successful Sales Letters
http://www.so-cal.com/writingbiz/page1.htm

Business and Organizational Writing
http://www.wuacc.edu/services/zzcwwctr/businessorg_menu.html

Netiquette Home Page
http://www.albion.com/netiquette/index.html

points to remember

1. Use a business letter or memo if the information you are communicating must be retained on file, or if the information is of formal importance in the organization.

2. Do not use e-mail for messages that are confidential or for important information that must carry a signature.

3. Apply the Six C's of business writing to all letters, memos, and e-mail messages.

4. Letters, memos, and e-mail messages can either be requests or replies and can contain good news or bad.

5. Make sure your letter contains all the appropriate parts, whether you are sending it by fax or by conventional mail: return address, date, inside address, salutation, subject line, body, complimentary closing, signature, typed name, and notations.

6. In a memo, the To, From, Date, and Re or Subject information appears first.

7. Always be positive in tone and attitude.

8. Provide all relevant details.

9. Recognize reader needs, expectations, and knowledge.

10. Say all you need to say and then stop.

11. Always avoid sarcasm.

sharpening your skills

SECTION A

The following situations require letters; some of them will carry good news and some will carry bad news. In writing them, observe all the elements of style and format we have discussed. Add any details that might make your letters more convincing.

1. You ordered a black sweater, number JM-2706B, from Contemporary Fashions of Vancouver, BC. However, the one you were sent is the wrong size. Write to the manager, Nancy Schindelhauer, to request an adjustment. Invent any other details she will need to respond to your request. Her address is:

   1729 Trutch Street
   Vancouver, BC
   V6J 7Y8

2. You and a friend have recently found yourselves in competition for a plum job in your field. You feel certain that you are the better qualified candidate, since your grades are slightly better than your friend's, and you have a full year more experience in this kind of position. Nevertheless, you have just learned that your friend has been offered the job, while you have received a polite letter of rejection. You are happy for your friend, but disappointed for yourself. Write a letter of congratulations to send to your friend. Invent any details you need.

3. The mayor and city councillors of your city have finally proposed to refurbish the old City Recreation Park, which has been allowed to run down in recent years and which has been all but abandoned. You can recall swimming there as a child, and you hope that it can be restored to its former condition.

Write to the mayor lending your support to the proposal.

4. You have heard that a former professor of yours has just been nominated for the Distinguished Teaching Award at your college. Write a letter of support for her or him (choose a professor of your choice) that may be added to the professor's dossier for the awards committee's consideration.

5. Write to a former instructor or employer, requesting permission to name that person as a reference in a job application.

6. You are the former instructor of Pat Yorgason, who has just written to you asking for a letter of reference. It has been three years since Pat was in your class, and you have taught three hundred students per year since then. You never knew Pat well and after all this time you can't picture a face to go with the name; all you can recall is the impression of an indifferent student. A check of your records confirms that impression: Pat's grade in your communications class was C–, but otherwise nothing much jogs your memory. In fact, you have taught lots of "Pats," and you can't even recall whether this one was male or female! You don't feel that you are the best choice to write a recommendation for this person. Write a letter to Pat politely explaining why another referee might be a better choice.

   Pat Yorgason
   PO Box 75
   Okotoks, AB
   T0K 0K0

7. You are a volunteer at the local food bank. Donations are down this month, and you have volunteered to draft a circular calling for donations to distribute at the local mall. Speedi Print has offered to pick up the cost of duplicating five hundred circulars. Write the circular encouraging people to donate to this worthy cause. Be sure to tell them what, where, and how to donate.

8. Write a letter of thanks, on behalf of the food bank, for the donation of the duplicating costs for the five hundred circulars in assignment 7, above. The address is 1765 Shoreline Drive, Glace Bay, NS B6J 7Y8. The manager's name is Margaret Thomson.

9. Recently you deposited in person $300 into your bank account. A week later, on checking your balance at the bank machine, you discover that the $300 has not appeared. When you visit the bank, the teller, Baghwan Dua, discovers that the money has been placed into another customer's account. The person has the same surname as yours, but the account numbers are significantly different. Dua arranges to correct the error, but he is quite unapologetic and even implies that the mistake is somehow your fault. Write to the manager of your bank, Ramona Chief Calf, to register your complaint.

10. You have recently suffered a fire that destroyed a number of the personal effects in your home. Among the items lost are your educational records, particularly your college diploma. You are currently employed at Communications Corporation, but are considering a career move, and you will need the diploma as proof that you graduated from college. Write to the office of the registrar at your college, giving all of the details necessary to locate your file, and inquire whether the college will be able to replace your diploma.

11. You have recently purchased some equipment for making photo-transfers. The kit came with all the materials you would need to make several transfers, using a photographic process with light-sensitive materials. You have followed the instructions carefully, but so far you haven't been able to produce a single usable transfer. After doing some library research, you've discovered an error in the instructions that came with the equipment; the recommended exposure time is more than double what's required, and as a result you've ruined over half of your raw materials, at a cost of over $50. In your view, the problem is the result of the company's misinformation, and you would like them to replace the wasted materials. For an adjustment, write to:

George Murphy, Customer Service Representative
Melind Marking Products Ltd.
214 Sherwood Street
Markham, ON
L4W 3R2

12. You have worked in Communications Corporation's office in Calgary for five years. You enjoy your job, but your spouse has recently been offered a position in Winnipeg. You too have applied and been accepted for a position in that city and will be moving at the end of June. You have submitted your resignation to the personnel department. You have always been on the best of terms with your supervisor, Elaine Girrior. She has been supportive of you throughout your employment with the firm and has provided you with promotions and recognition for any special achievements you have had. She has also encouraged you to take additional training and has recognized your potential to move into a management position.

    You have just recently done so and are sorry to have to leave the company, even though your new position promises to be very rewarding. You wish to communicate your thanks and respect to Elaine Girrior, and you decide to write her a formal thank-you letter. Without becoming too sentimental, but communicating your warmest wishes to her, write the letter you would give to Elaine Girrior on your departure from Calgary.

13. It has been a longtime goal for you to serve your placement term in the Rocky Mountains in Alberta. Your dream has come true in that you have received an offer of work for next semester from the Waterton-Glacier Resort. Unfortunately, your mother has fallen ill and you won't be able to take the

job. You recognize that delaying your acceptance is unusual, and an alternative arrangement is unlikely, but you very much want to have the experience of working in the mountains. Write to your new employer asking whether you can delay taking the position for six months, until your mother recovers. Your contact is:

Sandra Terry, Manager
Water-Glacier Resort
PO Box 26
Waterton, AB
T2W 1A6

14. You handle adjustments for Contemporary Fashions of Vancouver. Your boss, Nancy Schindelhauer, has forwarded to you a letter from Lucesca Wallersheim (turn to her letter, Figure 2.5, on page 28 in this book, to review her complaint) requesting an exchange on a sweater she purchased from your Spring/Summer catalogue. She was sent the wrong size in error; unfortunately, she did not return the sweater within the six-week adjustment period your company allows. In fact, she has waited for over three months, and now that particular sweater style is out of stock. Because of this, you are reluctant to replace the sweater, but you wish to preserve customer loyalty (a check of Ms Wallersheim's account shows that she is a regular, if eccentric, customer). Recognizing that the original mistake is the fault of your firm, you have two options:

1. You can accept a return of the original sweater, substituting a similar style in the appropriate size;

   OR

2. You may refuse the return on the grounds that the sweater cannot be resold because the style is no longer carried by your firm, but you may offer Ms Wallersheim a voucher good for $10 toward her next purchase.

   Choose whichever course of action you feel is warranted and write the appropriate letter to Ms Wallersheim. Remember that the decision is yours, not hers, to make.

15. You work in Training and Development for Communications Corporation. At the request of one of your clients, Diehard Industrial Consultants, your department has just prepared a workshop on effective report writing that can be delivered on-site by two presenters from your company. The workshop has been designed for twenty people, and can be delivered in two sessions of three hours each, which can be offered in one day or on two consecutive mornings or afternoons. The topics you have identified for study are similar to those in the report chapters of this book; they include:

1. Identifying your main message;

2. Identifying your reader (needs, expectations, knowledge);

3. Parts of a report;

4. Conciseness and clarity;

5. Informal report types and formats;

6. Proposals;

7. Formal report types and formats; and

8. Incorporating support data.

You have prepared a booklet on these topics to accompany the workshop, and you've invited participants to bring samples of their own writing projects for discussion, small group work, and individual attention from the seminar leaders. For two of you over six hours, with materials for twenty participants included, you charged the client $5,000.

Based on the success of the workshop for Diehard, you wish to promote it to other clients who might also find it useful for training their staff. One such client, Jacques Angleterre, has used Communications Corporation workshops in his firm before, and you are quite certain he will be interested. Write the promotional letter you might send to Jacques Angleterre to inform him of the new training workshop.

Jacques Angleterre
Human Resources Development
Blackhawk Instrumentation
1112 Rue Montagne
Montreal, QC
H2P 8U7

16. The following business letters (Figures 3.11 and 3.12) contain weaknesses. Evaluate them according to the criteria you have learned and be prepared to rewrite them more effectively if your instructor directs you to do so.

SECTION B

Write the following memos, bearing in mind all you have learned about business writing style and format. Add whatever details are required to make your memos convincing. If your instructor directs you to do so, submit your memo assignment as an e-mail message.

1. Along with three other members of your class, you are interested in forming a student club for majors in your program. In order to be allowed to hold events on campus, your club has to be ratified by the Students' Union. Ratification requires a membership list of at least fifteen people. Write a memo, addressed to all students in your program, to be posted on the department bulletin board, encouraging students to sign up for your club. Be sure to include a listing of the advantages of such an organization, the deadline for ratification, fees or start-up costs, and a number where you can be contacted. If you plan to post or circulate a sign-up sheet, mention that as well. Send a copy of your memo to the chair of your department.

2100 Allendon Crescent
Peachvale, Ontario
L7B 3Z9

July 30, 2000

Ms Monique Martineau
90 Main Street
Oshawa, Ontario
L6K 3D4

My dearest Monique

I have just heard the news from Tobias Johnson that your book *Adventures in the Red Deer River Valley* has been accepted by Prentice Hall.

I know just how you feel — I wrote a book myself, you know, and I'm sure I'd have publishers just knocking the door down if I finished it. (They can be so tasteless, can't they?) But it seems that nearly everyone you talk to is writing a book these days, it almost makes you think you should find something original to do!

However, it is an accomplishment, dear — and who knows? Maybe someday you'll be shaking my hand as a fellow published author!

Yours very sincerely

Donna Skreyuw

Donna Skreyuw

75 Snayall Drive
Couchgrass, Manitoba
R1A 3C6

October 30, 2000

Professor L.M. Calvin
Science Division
Northwoods College
Box 456
Bruce Mines, Ontario
N0E 0B0

Dear Professor Calvin:

I am writting you this letter to please ask if you would kindly act as a reference for me?

I took your class when I attended the college about 6 years ago. Now I want to go back to school in a similar program at Pineridge College here in Couchgrass.

Could you send your letter directly to them? It would be very much appreciated.

Yours truly,

M. Jones

M. Jones

2. Your department chair has been arranging mock job interviews for the students in your program in order to give them experience in interviewing. The interviews are to be conducted by professionals in your future field who have agreed to come to the college to participate in the exercise. Your program chair has impressed upon all of you how important these practice interviews are. Yours is set for next Thursday at 2:00 P.M. Since you made this appointment, however, you have had a real job interview scheduled for 2:30 P.M. that same day. You can't make it to both interviews. If you are successful in the actual interview, the job will give you experience directly related to your college program. Write a memo or compose an e-mail message to your program chair with a copy to the interviewer, Allan Goren, cancelling your appointment and explaining why you can't be there.

3. Your class is having problems with a particular instructor. You wish to meet with him as a class to discuss the difficulties. On behalf of the class, write an e-mail message outlining the specific nature of the problem and requesting a meeting with the instructor to solve it. If you are actually submitting your message electronically, be sure to direct it to your communications instructor. Watch your tone especially in this one!

4. You are the Parking Supervisor at Waskasoo College. You have received a letter from the transit company in your town complaining of unauthorized parking in the bus zones around the college, which prevents the buses from gaining access to the college stops. This is not the first time such a problem has occurred, and the transit company is threatening to cut off service to the college if it is not corrected. Write a memo to students and staff outlining the problem and requesting their cooperation in correcting it. Direct a copy to Herbert Hoppman, president of the Transit Commission.

5. You are in charge of collecting contributions from your co-workers for the local fire department's Charity Clothing Drive for families who have lost their possessions due to fire. Compose an e-mail message to all employees encouraging them to contribute some of their gently used clothing to this good cause. Be sure to provide your readers with a clear motivation to donate and suggestions for the kinds of donations needed. Add information about the deadline date and the location where readers can drop off their donations for delivery to the Clothing Drive. Submit the message to your communications instructor via e-mail.

6. Recently, in class, a professor you like very much made what you believe is a serious error of fact in one of her presentations: she said that the date of the Riel Rebellion was 1875 (it was 1885). You had heard her make the same error in an earlier class, but at the time you thought it was just a slip of the tongue, and so said nothing. Your class is not actually about the Riel Rebellion, but you think it's important enough to want to set her straight. You want to save yourself, and the professor, the embarrassment of point-

ing out the mistake face to face, so you decide to write an e-mail message to her explaining the mistake and correcting her error. You really like this professor and you want to retain her goodwill. Compose the message in which you politely point out Professor Yvette Bruneau's error. Submit it to your communications instructor via e-mail.

7. After six years as a program designer with Communications Corporation, you have made a number of professional contacts and often hear news from other program designers. A business acquaintance of yours, Wade Grandoni, who manages the program designing section of MediaCorp, has passed on to you some information regarding his firm's plans to update their computer system. He has invited Compu-Consulting to give his staff a day-long, hands-on training seminar to acquaint them with the changes. You are aware that the Director of Communications Corporation, Daena Tobias, is considering implementing a similar computer systems update, but as far as you know, there are no plans for a training seminar. It sounds like a good idea to you, and Wade Grandoni is certainly enthusiastic. Write a memo to your boss suggesting that your firm invite Compu-Consulting to provide similar training to you. Explain that the benefits of the training seminar outweigh the costs. Add any necessary details.

8. You are currently out on a job placement through your college program. The work you are doing is on an unpaid volunteer basis, but you are required to complete this placement successfully in order to graduate. The purpose of the placement is to supplement your classes with as broad an experience of your future job as possible. Unfortunately, your supervisor at placement, Donalda Allen, seems reluctant to give you any real responsibility, and you find yourself limited to doing menial tasks unconnected to your school training. Inventing appropriate details as necessary, compose an e-mail message your program chair explaining your difficulties and requesting that he or she approach Mrs. Allen to arrange for you to be given more responsibility. Submit the message to your communications instructor via e-mail.

9. Read the situation description given in assignment 8. In response to your memo, your program chair has spoken with your placement supervisor about the nature of your placement duties. Your chair has told you that Mrs. Allen was very cooperative, and explains that you can expect to be given additional responsibilities starting this week. However, when you go to placement, Mrs. Allen is distinctly unfriendly to you and instead of giving you more relevant duties, merely assigns the usual drudgery. When you attempt to carry out the tasks, she finds fault and complains about your attitude. When you try to speak with her about what your chair told you, she loses her temper and accuses you of lying and of going behind her back to complain. You attempt to defend yourself, but the situation escalates and she "dismisses" you from your placement. Bearing in mind that the two are

friends, that your program chair believes Mrs. Allen to be reasonable, and that you need to complete a placement to finish your program, write a message to your chair explaining the situation and requesting a new placement assignment. Because of the seriousness of the situation, you decide to send your message as a memo rather than via e-mail. You will need to tread very cautiously on this one.

10. One of your instructors has arranged for five students from your program to attend a conference in your field, where you will be taking part in a panel presentation. This is an exceptional opportunity for you to make some contacts and meet some important professionals in your area of study. Unfortunately, the conference falls during exam week, and conflicts with your final examination in a course from another department. It's not your best course, and your interactions with that instructor have not been altogether pleasant. You'd rather not inconvenience this particular instructor, but at the same time you don't want to miss the chance to go to the conference. In order to arrange an alternate exam time, your college requires that you make your request in writing to the dean. Write a memo to the dean of your college, Dr. Rod Serling, with a copy to both your instructors, explaining your situation and requesting an adjustment to your examination schedule. Be sure to provide justification that will satisfy both the dean and the instructor whose exam you will be missing.

11. It's unbelievable, but your instructor, Maury Huknows, slept in and was late for the final exam in your economics course. As a result, the start of your three-hour exam was delayed for forty-five minutes, and you were unable to finish. You have approached your professor, but he seems unwilling to make any allowances for your difficulties: he insists the exam should only have taken two hours anyway, and points out that several members of the class managed to finish all the questions in the time they had. You believe you should have had the whole three hours, and you are certain you would have finished the examination if you had had the full time allotment. Write a memo to the dean of your college, carefully outlining your situation and recommending a course of action: you can request either that you be allowed to re-take your final exam in a full three-hour period, or that you be graded for the full percentage of the exam on the questions you were able to finish in the time period. Be sure to watch your tone carefully and to justify your case in terms that will satisfy both the dean and your instructor.

12. You are the Chief Executive Officer in Training and Development at Communications Corporation. One of your employees, Rickie Chan, has recently prepared a Training Workshop on Effective Report Writing for Marsha McLuhan of Diehard Industrial Consultants. The workshop, which is in two three-hour sessions, looks really good, and you have agreed that it should be added to the general offerings of the Training and Development

department. However, you would like to see it expanded to include another three-hour session on Report Presentation (briefings). Compose an e-mail message to Rickie Chan to suggest that he add a section on report presentation to his training workshop. Request that he forward a copy of the expanded course description to you when he has finished it. Submit the message to your communications instructor via e-mail.

13. As a long-standing executive of Communications Corporation, you are a member of the Advisory Committee to the director, Daena Tobias. Recently, Ovide Vendredi in Public Relations presented your group with a proposal for an in-house magazine that would address some of the more significant problems of information exchange currently facing the Corporation. The group has discussed the proposal fully and is generally in favour of the project, but the major problem is budget. Ovide has asked for approval to hire two employees, at an annual cost to the company of $45,000; unfortunately, budgetary constraints indicate that only one salary can be managed, in the amount of $24,000. As secretary of the Advisory Committee, write a memo to Ovide Vendredi explaining that you would like him to revise his project to meet the limitations of the budget. Suggest that the committee is generally in favour of his proposal and that it will welcome a chance to discuss a revised suggestion.

14. The following messages (Figures 3.13 and 3.14) are weak for one reason or another. Read them through critically to see what improvements you might be able to suggest. Be prepared to rewrite them more effectively if your instructor requires you to do so.

Communications Corporation

INTERDEPARTMENTAL COMMUNICATION

volunter

To: All Employees

From: Ivana Petrovic, Social Committee Chairperson

Date: July 29, 2001

Re: Arrangements for Annual Company Picnic

This is to inform you that the arrangements for this year's annual company picnic are ~~final and~~ complete ~~at long last.~~ After lots of hard work and planning by this committee, it was decided that it will be on Saturday, August 6.

While planning the event, we were blessed to have many

As you know, we needed to ask for volunteers to lend us various types of equipment *volunteers* for playing sports and games, and we also had to arrange for barbecues to be *donate their* brought to the site. Luckily we have lots of willing volunteers who can help us out *sports,* with these requests and they have agreed to bring their equipment for us all to use. *BBQ, sports + game equipment*

If you are one of those generous people who have agreed to volunteer to us any sports or games supplies or a barbecue or any other kind of item we will be needing, those who have done so are asked by your dedicated committee to arrive one half hour early. The entertainment subcommittee and the food committee, including myself among many other dedicated individuals will be on hand by 10 a.m. to get things rolling right along.

The picnic begins properly at 11, though you can plan to arrive with your family anytime between 10 and 11, unless you are one of our volunteers mentioned above. As has been the case with our many previous successful annual company picnics, this one is to be held as usual at Ellsworth Conservation Park.

If you need directions how to get to the park, just contact me or anyone else on the social committee. Plan to bring everyone in your whole family for a super fun-filled day.

See you all there.

figure 3.14 What common error renders this simple message ineffective?

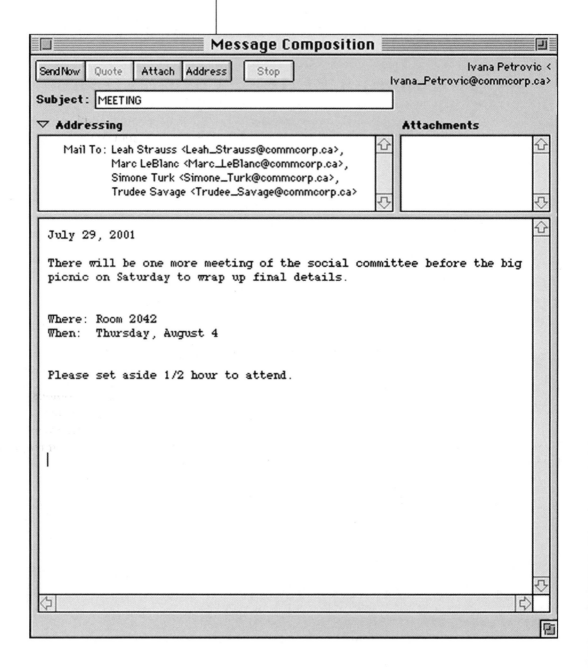

1. One challenge for any business writer is to attract and hold the reader's attention. In "Want Me to Listen to What You Have to Say?" Ernest Nicastro demonstrates how to turn a weak sales letter into a more appealing, positive document. You will find his advice at http://salesdoctors.com/response/respon02.htm. What is Nicastro's main piece of advice to writers of sales letters? How does he apply that advice to improve the weak sample on this web page? Using the same process as the one Nicastro demonstrates, analyze and rewrite one of the weak samples in this chapter.

2. Read Ernest Nicastro's "The 10 Commandments (Plus 5) of Highly Profitable Sales Letter Writing" (http://salesdoctors.com/patients/1write1.htm), and answer the following questions. Submit your responses to your instructor by e-mail.

   a. Why does Nicastro use archaic language for his "commandments"?

   b. Find three pieces of advice that Nicastro provides that are not contained in this textbook. Does he contradict the textbook, or is his advice an expansion of principles found in the book?

   c. Which of Nicastro's "commandments" seems the most striking or surprising to you? Briefly explain why.

   d. Does Nicastro follow his own advice on this web page?

3. Go to the Amazon Books site at http://www.amazon.com/exec/obidos/subst/index2.html/001-5422491-2389731. Use the browser to locate the book *The 3 Rs of E-Mail: Risks, Rights, and Responsibilities,* by Diane Hartman. When and where was it published? What is its ISBN? Locate at least three other related titles, and record the name of the author, the title of the book, the place and date of publication, and the ISBN. Write your list of sources into a bibliography and e-mail the list to your instructor.

Informal and Semiformal Reports

➤ To learn the parts of all reports: Summary, Introduction, Discussion, Conclusion(s), Recommendation(s), and Appendices.

➤ To recognize common report formats and to know how to select the format appropriate for the report you are writing.

➤ To know how to use the Report Writing Planner to plan your report and select appropriate information.

As with the other forms of business communication we have studied, reports generally focus on one issue or set of interconnected issues. Like memos, they can be directed to someone within the organization, or, like letters, they can represent the company to someone outside of it. However, reports are generally more formal than a letter or a memo, lengthier, and more analytical. For this reason, it would be unlikely that you would either send or receive such a document via e-mail, although certain kinds of reports may be posted to a web site. Reports are often commissioned — that is, written at the request of a superior — and are often written in response to a particular problem or situation that has arisen in a company or institution.

Though there are, as you will see, a variety of report formats and styles, all reports share several characteristics with other business writing. First, reports are written with a specific audience clearly in mind, and for a specific purpose. If they are to be effective, they also observe the Six C's of business writing style

— completeness, conciseness, clarity, coherence, correctness, and courtesy. No business communication can be considered effective without these essentials of style, and in your reports as in all of your writing, you must take care to edit accordingly.

Like other forms of business writing, reports can be either informative or persuasive. They usually make recommendations for changing or improving a situation or problem. Reports may also be either formal or informal and are used in a variety of business situations. The writer of a report should be sure to use the focusing statement, "The main thing I want to tell you is that...," in the first draft. Reports, even more than other business writing forms, usually put the main message first. As well, the report writer must have a clear idea of the intended readers — identified, as you will remember, by needs, expectations, and background knowledge.

The Parts of a Report

Like other business writing, in fact like all other kinds of writing, a report must have a beginning, a middle, and an end — an introduction, a discussion, and a conclusion. But along with these three basic parts, all reports (no matter how simple or complex, no matter how short or long) contain a summary, which precedes the report, and may contain an additional two parts: a recommendation or set of recommendations, and one or more appendices. The following are the six standard parts of a report, in order.

Summary

Since reports are longer than most other business communications, and since business people are always busy, the report writer includes a brief statement that gives an overview of the situation or problem dealt with, the general findings, and the specific action recommended. After reading the summary, the reader should know what to expect from the introduction, discussion, conclusion, and recommendations. The substance and the direction of your findings should be clear from the report summary. Further, the language of the summary (along with that of the introduction, conclusion[s], and recommendation[s]), should be straightforward and clear enough to be understood by the least expert of the intended readers. The length of the summary varies with the length of the report, and though there is no set length, you can think of the summary as being approximately one-tenth as long as the report itself. For example, a ten-page report may have a summary of approximately one page, while the summary of a formal report fifty pages long may be five pages. A short informal report using memo or letter format may have a summary consisting of a subject line and a brief initial paragraph.

Introduction

The introduction to a report states as clearly as possible the problem or situation being examined and any necessary background information; it may also set out the writer's approach, assumptions, and the limits of the report. In short, it prepares the reader for the discussion of the possible outcomes or solutions offered in the report.

Discussion

The main body, or discussion, of the report sets out the writer's method (including the criteria used to evaluate possible solutions) and the steps that led to the recommendations and conclusions offered in the report. It may describe those other possible solutions and show why, according to the writer's criteria, they were judged to be unacceptable. Exactly what you include in this section of the report will depend on what situation you are dealing with. However, if you have detailed technical or specialized data, you would place it here. In general, the discussion section of a report is aimed at the most knowledgeable of your expected readers.

The discussion is the longest and most detailed part of your report. It is made up of a number of shorter sections, each with its own heading. The word "discussion" itself rarely appears as a heading; instead, it is a broad term that is used to denote everything in the report between the introduction and the conclusion. The headings that are used in the discussion section are specific to the contents of the report. For example, a report that evaluates a training program offered by a local consultant firm might use these section headings:

Program Description
Prerequisites
Advantages of the Program
Costs
Limitations of the Program
Resources

Conclusion(s)

Depending on the situation you are writing about, there may be several possible outcomes or only one. Your conclusion represents the logical results of the investigation or presentation you have dealt with in your discussion. The conclusion lays out any judgements that can be made based on the facts presented in the discussion. Your conclusion should present no surprises for your reader, who has been led by your discussion to expect what appears there.

Recommendation(s)

In this section you will recommend what you consider to be, according to your evaluation criteria, appropriate action in response to the conclusions you have reached. You may have one or several recommendations to make. Recommendations normally outline the action that the reader of the report should take, and occasionally your recommendation will even list the actions you intend to perform yourself.

Appendices

An appendix is anything that is attached to a report. It is not considered a part of the report itself, but it provides additional support or explanation for points in the discussion. Any relevant supporting information that, for reasons of space or complexity, has not been dealt with in the discussion section of the report may be attached to the report as an appendix. The purpose of the appendix is to assist your reader in fully understanding your information. There may be one appendix or several appendices, and while not all reports have them, any report may do so. Formal reports are more likely than informal ones to have appendices attached.

Reports, like other business communications, should be carefully planned. Before you begin to write, consult the Report Writing Planner (Figure 4.1). Use it to identify the important elements of your message and the probable needs and expectations of your reader. Jot down the main information to be covered in each part of your report, keeping your reader's needs in mind as you plan your writing. Consider carefully the way in which the points in your discussion can be presented, choosing your words with care as you work. Then write your rough draft, beginning with the summary statement. The phrase "The main thing I want to tell you is that..." may help you to focus your rough work, but remember to delete it in the final version of your report.

Report Situations

Reports can be written in response to a variety of business situations and can serve a variety of purposes. However, most reports fit into one of the following categories.

Investigative or Analytical

The investigative report, which is usually commissioned, examines or analyzes a particular problem or question that has been identified by someone in the company. It will probably evaluate causes and effects, and will likely offer solutions to the difficulty. Its conclusions will be based on research, such as results from a controlled scientific experiment or data collected from a survey or questionnaire.

REPORT WRITING PLANNER

Before beginning your report, answer these questions as fully as possible.

1. What is the topic of this report?

2. What is going to be done with this report? Why is it needed? Who asked for it?

3. Who are your readers? What are their interests in this subject? What background information is already known to your readers and what will you have to fill in so that your report may be understood and acted on?

4. What is your main message? What will your summary statement be?

5. Briefly outline your introduction. Remember to provide the appropriate background information.

6. Outline your discussion. Provide any relevant main points and details.

7. Outline your conclusion(s) and recommendation(s).

Evaluation

The evaluation report may be used whenever more information is needed, either on its own to evaluate an existing situation or proposed action or as a follow-up report to evaluate the recommendations made by another report. Rather than analyzing causes and effects, it usually measures a solution or a situation against a set of criteria in order to determine the suitability or unsuitability of that solution or situation. Its conclusions will be based on a careful comparison between the initial criteria (usually the reader's needs) and the suggested action or solution.

Incident or Occurrence

Written in response to an unexpected (usually problematic) incident, this report is primarily an informative one that outlines details of an unexpected event (an accident, perhaps). It may suggest ways in which the event has influenced work currently in progress and outline the steps that are being taken to correct the setback.

Progress

This kind of report details the progress being made on a long-term project and may be one of two types. The first, the *periodic* report, is delivered at regular time intervals — every two weeks, for example, or for very long-term projects, every six months. In a college or school, students receive periodic reports of grades at the completion of each semester. A company's annual report is another example of a periodic progress report. The second type, the *occasional* progress report, is delivered whenever some significant stage in a project is completed, and the time interval between reports may vary. For instance, if I am working on the construction of a building, I may write reports only when significant stages are completed; since each part of the project takes a different amount of time to complete, my reports will be delivered at irregular time intervals.

Research Reports

The research report, like the investigative report, examines a particular question of importance to the field or the company. However, the research report differs from the investigative report in that it does not seek to identify solutions to an existing problem in the firm. Instead, a research report is used to gather information helpful to the company in developing a new procedure, product line, or organizational structure. This kind of report presents the findings from your research; it may or may not offer recommendations for action based on its results. As part of your college program, you may be assigned a research report of this type, in which you consult research sources in order to determine the importance of a particular issue to your field of study.

All reports require some kind of research; however, most business reports rely on evidence drawn from the workplace itself. By contrast, the research report draws on material from outside sources — government documents, books and professional journals, articles in the popular press, Internet sources — in order to assist managers and administrative officers in making informed decisions about the future of the company.

The credibility of such a report depends to a large degree on the thoroughness and authority of your research sources. For this reason, all sources you consult, including Internet sources, should be properly documented, according to the standards appropriate to your field of study. Once you have determined that the information you have collected is reliable and authoritative (an issue of particular importance in dealing with web sites), you should be sure to record all the information your readers would require to locate the cited sources for themselves if they should need to do so.

Documentation information for print sources should include information about author, title, place of publication, publisher, and date. For Internet sources, you should identify the author, the name of the posting or web page, and the date of the posting, along with the electronic address. A style manual will provide you with clear guidelines for recording this information, along with samples of layout. Here are four examples using the documentation format of the Modern Languages Association:

Print Sources
A book:
MacLennan, Jennifer. *Effective Business Communication*. Third Edition. Scarborough, Ontario: Prentice Hall Canada, 1998.

An article or chapter in a book:
David Zarefsky and Jennifer MacLennan. "Achieving Style Through Language." *Public Speaking: Strategies for Success*. Canadian Ed. Scarborough, Ontario: Prentice Hall Allyn & Bacon Canada, 1997.

An article in a book edited by someone else:
Irwin, Lori. "The Real and the Imagined: Students as Teachers in the Rhetoric Classroom." *Public Speaking: Strategies for Success*. Canadian Ed. David Zarefsky and Jennifer MacLennan. Scarborough, Ontario: Prentice Hall Allyn & Bacon Canada, 1997.

Online Sources
A page or entry on an Internet site:
MacLennan, Jennifer. "The Nature of Rhetoric." 19 May 1994. Online posting. Web Site www.uleth.ca/~MACLENNAN/index.htm.

An e-mail message:
Moffatt, John. "Inside Language." E-mail to the author. 10 March 1998.

Proposals

The proposal is usually initiated by the writer and is intended to persuade the reader to do what the writer thinks should be done. It might suggest a change that the writer thinks his or her company should adopt (I might write a proposal anytime I wish to create an innovative program in my department) or it might request additional funding for a project that is already in operation. Because a proposal is intended to solicit authorization or funding for the writer's project, it must be sufficiently detailed and convincing to gain the reader's acceptance and approval. A proposal might also be developed in response to a client's request for a service (I might respond to a client's request for a computer training seminar by submitting a proposal for a seminar designed to fit the client's needs).

Any of these situations can call for a report, and the report you write may be either formal or informal in style, depending on the situation, the audience, and the detail of your investigation.

Report Format

In a business report, format is almost as important as content in communicating your information. Reports may be presented in any one of several formats. Reports may be *informal* or *formal* in their structure, or they may strike a balance between the two as is the case in the *semiformal* report. An informal report resembles a memo or business letter that has run to several pages, whereas a formal report may look more like a book manuscript or a long formal essay, complete with its own cover and table of contents. Length and layout are the most visible differences between formal and informal reports: the informal report is usually shorter than the formal, with an average length of three to five pages; it is also less detailed, has fewer distinct parts, and a less elaborate layout. An informal report may make use of headings to assist the reader in locating information, but because it is frequently under three pages long, such headings are not always necessary.

In writing your reports, remember that format is meant to serve function. Choose a format that delivers your message most effectively. Generally, the longer and more complex the report, the more formal it will be, and the more likely it will be to use headings and other organizational devices to assist the reader in understanding the material presented. The formal report format allows clearer organization of large amounts of material, while short reports may be better presented simply. (We will deal with formal reports in the next chapter.)

As you may already have guessed, reports are not strictly divided into informal or formal types; occasionally you will find that you must write a report that, while important enough to warrant more formal treatment, is not really long enough to require all of the elaborate formatting of the formal report. Since the organizational structure of the formal report, with its table of contents, special headings, and fancy cover can overwhelm a short report of under ten pages, and a memo or letter format could seem an overly casual treatment of your information, you may wish to use a third style of report, called the semiformal report, which combines aspects of the informal report and the formal report styles. Rather than opening with a memo or letter-like format, as the informal report does, the semiformal report usually has the title, author's name, and date at the top of the first page; it is also more likely than the informal report to use headings to separate report sections. The semiformal report is not really a distinct type, but is a variation of the informal report. It is used in place of the memo or letter format when you wish a more formal appearance for your short reports. In this book we will use the term *informal* to refer to letter or memo reports, and the word *semiformal* for short reports that use a more formal style on their first page, and that incorporate some other formal features in a report of under ten pages.

Although your employer may sometimes require a specific format for reports, often you will have to select your own format. How do you know whether to write a formal, an informal, or a semiformal report? Asking yourself the following three questions may help you to decide.

1. *What is your purpose?* If you are addressing a relatively minor issue, your report will most likely be informal; if the situation is important, your report will be semiformal or even formal.
2. *Who is your audience?* The more distinguished or the wider your audience, the more formal your presentation should be. A brief document to your immediate supervisor that no one else is likely to read will probably be informal; a detailed proposal being sent to the company president and advisory board, or outside the company, is likely to be formal.
3. *How detailed is your analysis?* The more complex the problem or issue and the more detailed and thorough your presentation, the more carefully you will have to organize your information, and the more you will require the titles, headings, table of contents, and support materials of the formal report.

In choosing a report format, you should be guided by the complexity of the problem or issue — that is, how much detail or research is required — and the intended audience or readers of the report. Most of the reports you write on the job will be informal or semiformal.

Report Forms

In addition to informal and semiformal reports, some jobs require frequent short reports on a regular basis. Such reports may be handwritten on standardized forms provided by your employer or instructor or word-processed on standard computer forms. These forms are used to ensure consistency in cases where large numbers of reports containing similar information must be kept by many people. For example, if you work for an employment agency, you may have to prepare regular client status reports identifying the applicant's background, qualifications, and record of job interviews. Since you would regularly handle several applicants at once and have to keep track of all of them, and since the other placement consultants would be doing the same, your company would probably find it useful to prepare a standardized form for the information. Insurance claim forms, student grade reports, credit card applications, registration forms, hospital charts, and even job application forms are some common examples. Other types that are commonly standardized include occurrence or incident reports, accident or injury reports, and performance reviews.

Nearly any kind of report that is made out on a regular basis could be composed on a prepared form. Because the information required is always the same, a form guarantees that each person applies the same standards and collects the same details. In this way too, much repetitious work is eliminated. Figure 4.2 shows a sample performance review report form.

Informal Reports

The informal report is the type of report that you will probably write most often. Compared to the formal report, it has a more casual format. For instance, it does not have a title page and table of contents. It may be written without enumerated sections, references, or appendices, although any of these could be included if they were needed. Unless your employer provides a standardized form, the informal report format is commonly used for regular progress reports, incidence reports, evaluative reports, and proposals. If you have been commissioned by your boss to write a short report for his or her eyes alone, chances are you will be writing an informal report.

Informal reports are printed on one side of the page only, observing standard margins: 1" at top, right, and bottom, and $1\frac{1}{2}$" at left. The informal report begins as a memo or a business letter. The standard format of the memo (To, From, Date, Subject) or letter (return address or letterhead, date, and inside address) identifies the primary reader, the writer, and date. The subject or "re" line states the primary recommendation the report makes. If the report is longer than one page, subsequent pages are printed on plain paper. Remember that informal reports, like all other types, may be double or single spaced, according to the practices of your employer.

An informal report, depending on how long it is, may contain section headings. Each new section begins immediately following the previous one, on the same page. Compare the following list of report parts with the sample informal report illustrated in Figure 4.3.

Contents of the Informal Report

Memo or letter opening
Statement of Recommendation(s) contained in subject or "re" line
Brief Summary statement
Introduction
Discussion: Background to Issue or Situation
             Outline of Important Facts and Details
             Possible Outcomes, Results, or Solutions
Conclusion(s)
Recommendation(s)
Appendices (optional):   Charts
                        Supporting Data
                        Diagrams

figure 4.2

A useful report gives clear direction to the writer and ensures a degree of uniformity in subject matter.

Career Progress Report

Evaluation for the period: _____ to: _____

EMPLOYEE'S NAME: _____ Department: _____

Position Duties: _____
_____
_____
_____
_____

Additional Responsibilities Since Last Assessment: _____
_____
_____
_____
_____

Achievements: _____
_____
_____
_____
_____

EVALUATION SUMMARY	Superior	Competent	Development
Overall performance	[ ]	[ ]	[ ]
Job-related goals	[ ]	[ ]	[ ]
Development of others' goals	[ ]	[ ]	[ ]
Relationship goals	[ ]	[ ]	[ ]
Potential for advancement	[ ]	[ ]	[ ]

MERIT INCREASE RECOMMENDED   [ ] yes   [ ] no

figure 4.2 (Continued)

NARRATIVE STATEMENT OF ASSESSMENT: _____

_____

_____

_____

_____

_____

_____

_____

Suggestions for Professional Development: _____

_____

_____

_____

_____

SUPERVISOR: _____ Date: _____

Signature: _____

Employee's Comments: _____

_____

_____

_____

I have read this summary and enclosed comments and discussed them with my supervisor.

Employee's Signature: _____ Date: _____

A Sample Informal Report

The Situation

Thir Huynh is the projects manager of Gwen's Interiors, a decorating firm that has recently been awarded a major contract by Communications Corporation: the firm is renovating the offices of the director, Daena Tobias, her administrative assistants, and all departmental heads. The contract has involved assisting with the selection of new furnishings, choosing new drapes, and installing new carpeting, in addition to wallpapering and painting; it represents several thousand dollars of revenue for the firm. Thir Huynh put in a good deal of time with Daena Tobias selecting the specific furnishings and decorating items she wanted. Tobias was particularly specific about the colour of her carpeting and has chosen an unusual shade — Rose Burgundy — which is available only from the Bill Distix Floor Products Company. Huynh has ordered and received the furniture from Gwen's suppliers, and Gwen's personnel have been painting, papering, and hanging drapes for two and a half weeks. It is Monday and the deadline for finishing the redecoration is the end of next week. Huynh is well within this deadline and has just spoken with Daena Tobias on the telephone to assure her that all will be finished in plenty of time. Tobias and her colleagues are naturally anxious to have their offices finished; they are busy and would like to get their workplace back to normal.

All that is left is to install the new carpeting, and Huynh has been assured by the Bill Distix Company that they will deliver this to the Gwen's Interiors warehouse by the end of this week. On Friday, the carpeting arrives, but instead of Rose Burgundy, Distix has sent Smoky Blue! Huynh telephones the Bill Distix people, but they offer little by way of comfort. They tell her that their Rose Burgundy carpeting, currently out of stock, is on back order from California, and they will be unable to fill her order for at least another month. Huynh decides to return the Smoky Blue carpeting to Bill Distix and approach other firms to see if anyone can fill the order with goods similar in colour and quality to the Distix product.

Huynh's subordinate, Jerry Purcell, does some checking around, and he is able to secure carpeting of equal quality in a similar shade (Dusky Rose) from Fussbudget Carpet Company; it is $5 a square metre more expensive than the Distix carpet, but Huynh will be able to have it by Friday of next week. This means that she will miss the deadline by a few days. Gwen's personnel need three days to lay the carpet, so even if they work over the weekend, the offices will not be completed until Tuesday morning, two working days after the original Friday deadline.

The Report

Huynh's report to Daena Tobias is on pages 83–84 (Figure 4.3). Note how carefully she analyzes the task that faces her: the director is not getting her original choice of carpet, but she will have her offices finished much earlier than would

figure 4.3 Thir Huynh's informal report presented in a business letter format.

Gwen's Interiors

59 Granville Street, Vancouver, BC   V5T 7Y8
Phone: (604) 324-5876   Fax: (604)324-5875

April 8, 2001

Daena Tobias, Director
Communications Corporation
555 California Street
Vancouver, BC
V1R 7H9

Dear Ms Tobias:

Re: Substitution of Carpeting for Corporate Office Redecoration

Due to an unforeseen setback, I would like to recommend a substitution in the carpeting for your office redecoration. The attached carpet sample should assure you that the shade of this new carpet, Dusky Rose, is virtually identical to your original choice, Rose Burgundy, and will match your colour scheme satisfactorily.

When we last spoke about the progress of the project, I informed you that the work would be complete as planned by Friday, April 13. Unfortunately, a problem with our supplier may delay the completion of the project by a few days.

Bill Distix Floor Products Company has indicated that Rose Burgundy, available only from them, is currently out of stock and will be unavailable for at least six weeks. However, after approaching other firms, we have been able to secure carpeting of better quality in a similar shade. We can have this carpeting delivered by April 13, and installed in your office by the opening of business on Tuesday, April 17, well before the earliest delivery date we could expect from Distix. The substitution will involve only a few days' delay in completion of the office redecoration.

. . . /2

The new carpet, Dusky Rose, is a better quality carpet costing an additional $5 per square metre. However, to compensate for the inconvenience to you, Gwen's Interiors will absorb the extra costs. In addition, I am prepared to have my personnel work over the weekend on the installation so that you can be back into your offices by Tuesday, April 17, only two working days later than the original deadline. Given the unavailability of Rose Burgundy, I believe the substitution to be the most satisfactory alternative. If you approve, I will cancel the original order with the Distix Company and complete the project with the new carpeting.

Please accept my apologies, on behalf of Gwen's Interiors, for the inconvenience. I will contact you before Friday to finalize the arrangements.

Sincerely,

Thir Huynh

Thir Huynh
Project Manager

be possible if Huynh waited for Distix. On the other hand, this is an important customer who has been very particular about her carpet. Huynh is disappointing Daena Tobias, but she does also have some good news to offer. She balances the disappointment with the good news, pointing out that her company is putting Tobias' needs first; hence they will absorb the extra costs and work over the weekend to finish by the Tuesday after the deadline. She recommends that Tobias approve the substitution and indicates that she will be cancelling the order with Distix. Note how selective Huynh is about what she includes in her final report. There are many details that she leaves out because her customer does not need to know them. She tells Tobias only what she wants and needs to hear and puts the client's interests — and her main message — foremost.

Figure 4.3 is an informal report; because it is going outside the company, Huynh has written it in letter format. If she wished to, Huynh could present this same information in a semiformal report (as shown in Figure 4.4). The impression that she wants to make on Daena Tobias will influence her choice of style.

Semiformal Reports

The semiformal report format may also be used for regular progress reports, incidence reports, evaluation reports, and proposals. Its primary difference from the informal report is the more formal appearance of its first page: instead of using memo or letter format, the semiformal report displays the company name, report title, author's name, and date at the top of the first page, as shown in the sample semiformal report in Figure 4.4 on pages 87–88. It too is printed on one side of the page only, observing the same standard margins as the informal report, and may be double or single spaced, depending on the preference of your employer.

The semiformal report format is used whenever your reports require a more formal appearance than a memo or letter allows. It is also generally a bit longer than the informal report, running usually between five and ten pages, though it can be used for reports up to twenty pages long. Its contents are usually divided into short sections headed with appropriate titles.

Unlike the informal report, where the summary of recommendations is presented in a "re" or subject line followed by a brief summary statement at the beginning, the semiformal report has a title rather than a subject line and presents its summary in a short paragraph at the beginning of the report.

Because the semiformal report is a variation of the informal report, the distinctions between them are not entirely clear-cut; in some cases, the same material can be presented in either format, as in the example in Figure 4.4. For a very short report, your choice of format should be influenced primarily by your purpose and your audience's needs. The more important these are, the more likely you will choose the semiformal style over the informal one. If the report is longer than ten pages but the issue presented is fairly straightforward and direct, the semiformal format is more appropriate than the formal one. If your report is likely to be more than ten pages long and is divided into many complex sections, you should consider using a formal format.

The parts of the semiformal report are listed below.

Contents of the Semiformal Report

Report title, author's name and title, and date at top of page one
Summary
Introduction
Discussion: Background to Issue or Situation
               Outline of Important Facts and Details
               Possible Outcomes, Results, or Solutions
Conclusion(s)
Recommendation(s)
References or Bibliography (optional)
Appendices (optional):   Charts
                          Supporting Data
                          Diagrams

If Thir Huynh wishes, she may make her report to Daena Tobias regarding her office decorations into a semiformal document (Figure 4.4) instead of an informal one. Changing the structure this way creates a less casual appearance. Note that the headings Huynh has provided shape the reader's perception of the materials she presents. Although the content remains the same, you can see that the change in format creates a very different impression. Compare the appearance of the following report (Figure 4.4 on pages 87–88) with Huynh's earlier version in Figure 4.3.

weblinks

Developing an Outline
http://www.researchpaper.com/writing_center/63.html

Research Papers
http://owl.english.purdue.edu/files/Research-Papers.html

Desktop Publishing: Definition and Links
http://www.pcwebopedia.com/desktop_publishing.htm

points to remember

No matter what kind of report you are writing, you must prepare thoroughly and organize carefully.

1. Identify your main message (the main thing I want to tell you is...).

2. Identify your purpose (to inform or to persuade).

figure 4.4 Thir Huynh's semiformal report. How will her change in format affect the impact on her reader?

Gwen's Interiors

59 Granville Street, Vancouver, BC   V5T 7Y8
Phone: (604) 324-5876   Fax: (604)324-5875

Communications Corporation Office Redecoration
Project Status Report

by
Thir Huynh, Project Manager

April 8, 2001

Summary

Due to an unforeseen setback, I have had to make a last-minute substitution in the carpeting for your office redecoration. The attached carpet sample should assure you that the shade of this new carpet, Dusky Rose, is virtually identical to your original choice, Rose Burgundy, and will match your colour scheme satisfactorily.

Introduction

When we last spoke about the progress of the project, I informed you that the work would be complete as planned by Friday, April 13. Unfortunately, a problem with our supplier may delay the completion of the project by a few days.

Rose Burgundy is Out of Stock

Bill Distix Floor Products Company has indicated that Rose Burgundy, available only from them, is currently out of stock and will be unavailable for at least six weeks.

However, after approaching other firms, we have been able to secure carpeting of better quality in a similar shade. We can have this carpeting delivered by April 13, and installed in your office by Tuesday, April 17, well before the earliest delivery date we could expect from Distix. The substitution will involve only a few days' delay in completion of the office redecoration.

. . . /continued

figure 4.4 (Continued)

Substitution of Dusky Rose

The new carpet, Dusky Rose, is a better quality carpet costing an additional $5 per square metre. However, to compensate for the inconvenience to you, Gwen's Interiors will absorb the extra costs. In addition, I am prepared to have my personnel work over the weekend on the installation so that you can be back into your offices by Tuesday, April 17, only two working days later than the original deadline.

Recommendation

Given the unavailability of Rose Burgundy, I believe the substitution to be the most satisfactory alternative. If you approve, I will cancel the original order with the Distix Company and complete the project with the new carpeting. Please accept my apologies, on behalf of Gwen's Interiors, for the inconvenience. I will contact you before Friday to finalize the arrangements.

3. Identify your reader (needs, expectations, knowledge).

4. Develop your points fully.

5. Observe the Six C's.

6. In choosing a report format, you should be guided by the complexity of the problem or issue — that is, how much detail or research is required — and the intended audience or readers of the report. Most of the reports you will write will be informal or semiformal.

S ECTION   A

Below in Figure 4.5 you will find an earlier draft of the report Thir Huynh wrote to Daena Tobias to inform her of the problems with her carpet. Compare it with either of the final versions on pages 83–84 or 87–88. What changes did Huynh make? Why? Analyze and comment on the revisions, explaining how the final report is an improvement over this draft.

S ECTION   B

The following report situations vary in complexity and requirements. Choose **one** of them and write the necessary report. Whichever report you are writing, observe all of the rules we have discussed and add any specifications you need to make the report convincing. Before beginning to write, you may wish to use the Report Writing Planner (Figure 4.1) to outline your two principal elements: reader and main message.

1. You work for Communications Corporation. Daena Tobias has assigned you to investigate local charities to which the company might make a corporate donation. The members of the advisory board have agreed to make such a donation, but have been unable to decide which charity would be most suitable. You have been asked to make a recommendation to the advisory group on an appropriate organization, keeping in mind the following information. The company wishes to make a single donation in the amount of $10,000; it does not wish to make an ongoing commitment to any organization. The organization must be a recognized charity that can issue receipts for tax purposes, and it should not be of a controversial nature that might damage the corporate image. A well-established, respectable charity, one without political connections, would be best. You may consider standard charities such as the United Way, or you may wish to look into making a donation to a local art gallery or educational institution.

2. You work in the Public Relations department of Communications Corporation. Each year, your director, Daena Tobias, arranges an elaborate and carefully planned company get-together to promote employee involvement

figure 4.5 An earlier draft of Thir Huynh's report to Daena Tobias. What makes this version inferior to either of the other two?

Gwen's Interiors

59 Granville Street, Vancouver, BC   V5T 7Y8
Phone: (604) 324-5876   Fax: (604)324-5875

To: Daena Tobias, Director
        Communications Corporation

From: Thir Huynh, Projects Manager

Date: April 8, 2001

Re: Need for a delay in office decorations

When we last spoke about the progress of the office decorations at Communications Corporation, I informed you that the decorations would be complete by Friday, April 13. Although we have been working well within our deadline, we recently experienced a minor setback that may extend the deadline by a few days.

We have been informed by the Bill Distix Floor Products Company that Rose Burgundy, the carpeting that you requested, is currently out of stock. However, after approaching other firms, we have been able to secure carpeting of better quality in a similar shade (Dusky Rose). You will get this carpeting before the earliest delivery date we could expect from Distix. Attached is a swatch of the new carpeting.

The Dusky Rose carpeting is $5 per square metre more expensive than the Rose Burgundy. However, Gwen's Interiors is prepared to absorb the extra costs. We will receive the carpeting by next Friday, the day of the original deadline.

My personnel will need three days to lay the carpet. We will work over the weekend, and your offices should be complete by no later than Tuesday, April 17. The order from the Distix Company will be cancelled. I hope that this substitution meets with your approval and regret any inconvenience the delay will cause.

and company morale. The evening usually features an informal meeting and an elaborate sit-down dinner, along with an after-dinner presentation that is typically a morale-booster featuring an interesting and inspiring speaker. This year, you were responsible for locating and hiring this speaker and have been able to hire Dr. Dan Ryan, a renowned stress expert from Montreal, to speak on the effects of stress in the workplace. From previewing his presentation, you know him to be a dynamic speaker, and everyone, including Daena Tobias, is looking forward to hearing his presentation. You made the arrangements two months ago; the dinner is one week from Friday. Late Thursday evening, just before you leave the office, you receive a long-distance telephone call from Dr. Ryan's agent in Montreal. Unfortunately, Dr. Ryan has come down with a severe case of strep throat, complicated by laryngitis. He is unable to utter a sound, and his doctor has advised him to cancel all of his speaking engagements for at least a week. He will thus be unable to appear at the Communications Corporation dinner.

Despite the lateness of the hour, you immediately contact an acquaintance who is a member of the local library board; you are aware that the board maintains a "Speaker's Bureau" listing of local experts who will speak to community groups for a nominal fee. Your friend is sure that you will be able to replace Dr. Ryan with another competent speaker. He mentions a speaker who has successfully led seminars for the library board on effective morale-building, another subject of interest to Daena Tobias. Your friend agrees to contact the new speaker, Denise Johnson, and to get back to you sometime the next morning with Ms Johnson's answer; he is reasonably certain that she will accept. Note that because Ms Johnson is local, there would be no airfare to pay to bring her to your city to speak. Also, since you have not heard her speak before, you will want to arrange to meet with her to determine the quality of her presentation.

Write a report to notify Daena Tobias of the situation and of your actions. Keep in mind the importance of the evening to the company, and the fact that Daena Tobias has been looking forward to hearing Dr. Ryan speak. Below is some other information you might need.

TOTAL COST OF PRESENTATIONS:

Dr. Ryan:		Ms Johnson:	
Speaker's fee	$1,000.00	Speaker's fee	$600.00
Return airfare	799.00	Mileage	30.00
Hotel accommodation (2 nights)	210.00	—	—
Meals & expenses	200.00	—	—
TOTALS	$2,209.00		$630.00

3. You are on placement at the West Side Recreation Centre. This afternoon at about 3:00, while you were supervising some children in the gym area, one of the children, ten-year-old Ian Scrundlehaver, tripped while running

across the deck of the pool and fell, knocking loose one of his teeth. Running is not permitted in the pool area, and it is your responsibility to supervise, but your attention was diverted because you were assisting another child, eight-year-old Andrea Hansen, with her flotation device. According to the nurse on duty, Martha Black, to whom you immediately took Ian, the tooth is still rooted (though loosened) and should not fall out. Ian was crying but is otherwise unhurt. You are required to make a report of any accidents or injuries in case of possible legal complications. Write the occurrence report you will file with your supervisor, Burton Urquhart, noting as many of the details of the incident as possible.

4. When you are working, you will frequently be assigned long-term projects, some of which will require periodic or occasional progress reports. In most instances, you will have to evaluate your achievements and your failures along the way, indicating how you plan to overcome any obstacles you have met with. This semester, you are enrolled in a business writing course, and it is now mid-term. Your task for this assignment is to prepare and submit a short (informal) report to your instructor outlining and evaluating your own progress in the course. The report will include such topics as your initial objectives or expectations, your achievements thus far, any failings or obstacles you have encountered and what you have done (or plan to do) to overcome them, the work that has yet to be done, and your expected grade or performance. You will want to supplement your report with evidence such as mid-term or assignment grades, course projects, and topics covered. Keep in mind that you are not evaluating the course *per se,* but your own commitment to and progress in the course. Essentially what you are preparing is a self-evaluation report such as you might occasionally be expected to prepare for annual performance reviews on the job.

    Although the assignment is intended to focus on your business writing course, you may wish to use another of your courses instead. If you want to do this, get the approval of your instructor.

online exercises

1. If you are preparing a research report, you may wish to begin with the "Searching the World Wide Web" page at Purdue University's Online Writing Lab (http://owl.english.purdue.edu/files/128.html). Choose a topic relevant to your studies, and try searching it using two or three different search engines. Compare the results of your search; what differences did you find in the kinds of sources that each engine produced? Did one seem to be better for your purposes than the others? Prepare a short informal report of your findings to turn in to your instructor. If your instructor directs you to do so, discuss your findings with the class.

2. Travel to the web site for *Canadian Business* magazine (http://www.canbus. com/). Search the current issue and the archives to find at least three articles about how the World Wide Web has affected Canadian business. Present your findings to your instructor in an informal report. Your instructor may also direct you to present your findings in an oral briefing.

formal Reports and Proposals

- ➤ To learn the basic format of a formal report and how to select the appropriate format.
- ➤ To understand the purpose and focus of a formal proposal.

A formal report may be used for any number of purposes. Annual reports, research reports, some progress reports, evaluation reports, proposals, and feasibility studies are some types.

Generally the formal report is more complex and detailed than the informal report. It tackles more difficult problems, analyzes them in greater depth, and presents thorough evidence to support its recommendations. It is usually much longer than either of the other report forms, being anywhere from ten to several hundred pages. You should use a formal report format if your subject matter is of great significance to your company, if your readership is likely to be large or important, or if your findings are extensive. Usually a project resulting in a formal report will involve several or all of the above considerations. For example, a lengthy report from your department to the president of the company that makes important recommendations for major department changes will most likely be formal.

The Parts of a Formal Report

A formal report, especially if it is to be sent outside the company, is meant to reflect and maintain the company's professional corporate image. As such, it must be very attractive and professional. It should be error free and printed on one side of the page only, with standard margins of 1" at the top, right, and bottom of the page and $1\frac{1}{2}$" at the left side. It may be single or double spaced, according to your company's practice. It normally has a formal cover that bears the company name, report title, author's name, and date, and it is usually bound. The parts of a formal report are as follows.

Cover

A *cover* usually encloses a formal report. You may used a purchased cover or have one specially designed. If you are buying a cover, don't choose one with a gaudy picture or design. A plain-coloured, good-quality cover is preferable. The cover, like the work inside, should make as professional an impression as possible, and one in grey, black, or white makes a more dignified impression than a wildly coloured one. Avoid cheap, poor-quality report covers. Spending a little more for a good cover will make a better overall impression. If your cover is a specially designed one on which the title of your report appears, choose the title carefully to reflect the content: informative, but not too long or too brief. A subtitle may help to clarify the material presented within the report.

Letter of Transfer or Transmittal

A *letter of transfer or transmittal* should be attached to the outside of the report cover or bound inside the cover just ahead of the title page. The choice is a matter of preference, and in writing your report you should follow your company's practice. The letter is a formal business letter from the writer (you) to the person or persons to whom the report is addressed. It should briefly outline the reason for the report and point out some of its important findings or features. Like all business letters, it is single spaced. If your report is to stay inside your company, you may wish to use a memo form in place of a letter; if it goes to readers outside the firm, write a proper business letter on company letterhead.

Title Page

The title page, containing the name of the company or institution, the title and subtitle of the report, the name(s) and title(s) of the person(s) who commissioned the report, the name(s) of author(s) and their title(s), and the date, comes next. If you are provided with a title page format by your employer, use that; otherwise use the format of the sample title page shown in this chapter. The formal report should contain a title page whether or not the title appears on the cover.

Summary of Recommendations

The summary of recommendations usually precedes the table of contents; it is a brief overview of all of the important parts of the report and should include condensed versions of the introduction, discussion, conclusion, and recommendation(s). After reading your summary, even your least knowledgeable reader should have an idea of your findings and your approach.

Table of Contents

The table of contents, a detailed listing of the sections of the report (which may or may not be numbered) and the pages on which these are to be found, comes next. (Note, though page numbers are customarily listed in a table of contents, some writers may choose not to include them.) The contents page is not considered part of the actual body of the report, and so is not numbered as part of the text. Numbering of the pages of the report usually begins at the introduction.

Introduction

The introduction begins the report proper. It not only introduces the subject matter of the report, but it prepares the reader for the report's particular focus and its findings. It also outlines any necessary background information, states the problem or issue, describes the situation, and sets out any limitations that might have been imposed on the investigation or analysis, as well as giving specifics about the direction that the analysis has taken.

Discussion

The discussion, or main body, of the report follows. It sets out the writer's method (including the criteria used to evaluate possible results, solutions, or outcomes) and presents a detailed analysis of the problem, issue, or situation that led to the conclusions and recommendations offered in the report. It should outline the important facts of the situation, including relevant history, details, and examples. As well, it should itemize any possible outcomes or courses of action, indicating the one that has been recommended and detailing the reasons for rejecting the others. The discussion of the formal report, like that of the informal report, is broken into subsections, each with a specific heading reflecting its contents. The contents of these subsections deal with facts specific to the focus of the report. Exactly what topics you include in your discussion will depend on the situation you are dealing with, but detailed technical or specialized data, aimed at the most knowledgeable of your expected readers, should be placed here. All pertinent facts, arranged in a logical order, are presented. Remember that, as in the informal report, the word "discussion" denotes everything in the report between the introduction and the conclusion, but is rarely used as a heading in the report itself.

Conclusion

The conclusion outlines any inferences that can logically be drawn from the material presented in the report; it shows the outcome of the analysis. It briefly summarizes the findings of the report and should be a natural result or extension of the point of view presented in the discussion. It should not contain any unexpected revelations or outcomes, but should satisfy the expectations created by the rest of the report.

Recommendation(s)

The recommendation (or recommendations) spells out the action that the report writer expects will be taken on the conclusions presented. If a conclusion says "this is what I think about this situation," the recommendation says "here's what we should do about it." The recommendation may include several steps that the reader is expected to follow; if so, these should be listed and numbered individually so that they are easy to identify and follow.

Bibliography

The bibliography (a listing of references or works cited) may also be included since many formal reports involve some sort of research. This list provides the reader with the information needed either to do further reading on the subject of the report or to check the accuracy of the writer's interpretations.

Appendices

Appendices are often necessary in a formal report, since the information presented in such a document is sometimes quite complex. As in the informal report, these attachments may include any supporting data that are either too cumbersome or too complicated to be included in the body of the report. Some examples might include charts, supporting data, or diagrams.

The parts of the formal report are usually arranged in the order listed, and each of the parts (introduction, subsections of the discussion, conclusion, and recommendations) normally begins with its own title on a new page, almost like a chapter of a book. Starting at the introduction, the pages of the report are numbered; depending on your company's policy, page numbers may appear in the upper-right corner, or centred either at the top or bottom of each page.

Remember that part of the effectiveness of a formal report, as of any business communication, depends on its visual appeal, so it is important that your report look professional. Although informal reports may sometimes be handwritten, a formal report must always be typed. Follow an accepted format carefully and take great care that no spelling, grammatical, or typing errors mar the quality of your report. Do not make corrections to a formal report in ink or pencil; instead, reprint the page. Always make corrections using the same font as you used for the rest of the report.

Formal reports also make use of frequent paragraphing and employ headings and subheadings to assist the reader in following the reasoning of the writer. But it isn't simply a neat and professional format that gives a formal report its visual appeal: most formal reports also use visual aids to present their messages clearly.

Using Visuals in a Formal Report

A well-written formal report should contain straightforward, readily under-standable explanations. Sometimes visual aids can make your explanations even clearer. Such visual aids include photographs, line drawings, diagrams, graphs, and charts. Depending on their size and immediate relevance to the text (the written material), they may be placed either within the body of the report or in an appendix at the end. If they are necessary to the reader's immediate under-standing and if they are small and simple enough, visual aids should be posi-tioned close to the appropriate paragraph in the report, preferably on the same page. It is best to number them sequentially (Figure 1, Figure 2, and so on) and to identify them by a title and a brief caption. The report text should refer to the visual aid by figure number or title when discussing the material shown in the visual. If the visual is very complex or if it is not necessary to the reader's im-mediate grasp of the situation, it could be placed in an appendix. If it is very complex but necessary to the reader's understanding, the complex version could be placed in the appendix and a simplified version placed in the body of the re-port. Below is a brief description of when and how to use each of these visuals. The examples illustrate a house design, the Olshansky Model 980, and its sales figures.

Photographs

Whenever you must describe a site, a scene, or a product to give the reader a clear idea of what the item looks like, there is nothing like a good photograph. A photograph may be colour or black and white, as long as it is clear and of good quality, with no fuzziness or unnecessary clutter in its composition.

Professional typesetting and colour separations for high-quality printing are expensive and unlikely to be an option except for items as important as the an-nual report of a large corporation, which is often as much an advertising docu-ment as it is a report. For small reports or for a small number of reports, you will most likely be using in-house laser printing and photocopying. You have sev-eral options, even under such circumstances. Some offices may be equipped with up-to-date equipment for such tasks: high-quality colour photocopiers, scanners, digital cameras, and colour laser printers can make it easy and rela-tively inexpensive to include photographs in your day-to-day reports, provided the results are clear enough to display the information you require. Depending on your needs, you may find it best to have multiple prints of the actual pho-tograph made and paste them into position in each copy of the finished report. You may decide for yourself how many reports you are prepared to assemble by hand like this. An advantage of this hand-assembly is that it may allow you to use colour photographs of high quality in a report that is otherwise simply pho-tocopied. Ordinary black and white photocopying will not produce sufficiently clear prints even of black and white photos.

Line Drawings

When the information a reader needs from the visual is likely to be unclear in a photograph, a simple line drawing may be a useful substitute. A line drawing may be used, for example, to show the design of a company logo or the package design for a product you are about to produce. Such drawings are often used in advertising to illustrate products when photographic illustration would be too expensive. You need not be a professional artist to do a simple line drawing, but your work must be neat and easy to read. It should be drawn with black ink and clearly labelled, and should be as uncluttered as possible. You may prefer to use your computer to produce professional line drawings that are crisper and clearer than most of us can produce by hand. Such illustrations printed on a laser printer can make any document look more professional. Whether your illustrations are hand-drawn or computer-generated, it's important to remember that they are not simply decorative. Be sure that all the illustrations in your report clearly communicate the information that they are meant to provide. Visuals that are complicated or difficult to understand do nothing to help the message, and in fact may even hinder the communication by distracting and frustrating the reader. Below are two line drawings of the Olshansky Model 980, one without shading and one using line shading techniques that will reproduce clearly (see Figures 5.1 and 5.2).

figure 5.1   A line drawing without shading. Line drawings are useful for illustration when photographs are unavailable or unsuitable.

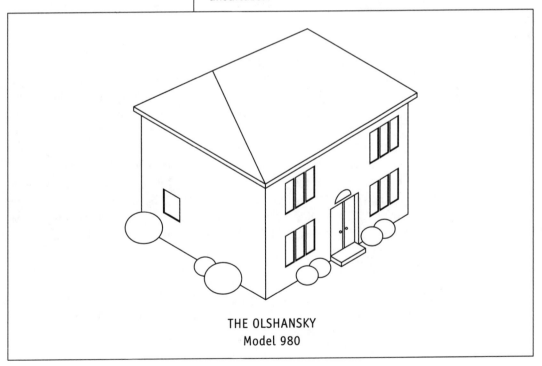

THE OLSHANSKY
Model 980

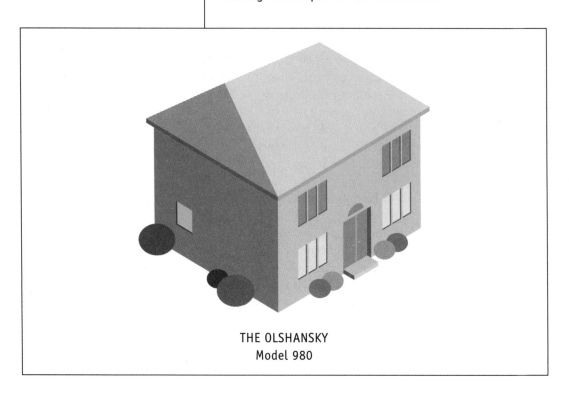

THE OLSHANSKY
Model 980

Diagrams

Diagrams are useful if your report explains how something works or is assembled. Diagrams may break down a process into steps or may show the parts or proper use of a piece of equipment. A diagram may even show the floor plan of the company's proposed new office space. Diagrams, too, should be clearly drawn in plain black ink or produced by computer. As is the case with line drawings, diagrams are meant to assist you in communicating your message clearly. They should therefore be as simple and as clear as possible. You may, if you have easy access to a colour photocopier or printer, use colour in your diagrams. If your report is to be reproduced in black and white, you should substitute shading for the colour in your original, taking care to ensure that any labels are still clearly legible. Figure 5.3 shows the main-floor plan of the Olshansky Model 980.

Graphs

Graphs are used to show the relationship between variables and to display successive change or growth over time. This growth is shown by a line that slopes either upward (for an increase) or downward (for a decrease) inside the graph. The change is measured using a scale that is marked out along the vertical axis (at the

figure 5.3 A diagram such as this floor plan assists your reader in accurately visualizing your meaning and may help prevent misunderstandings.

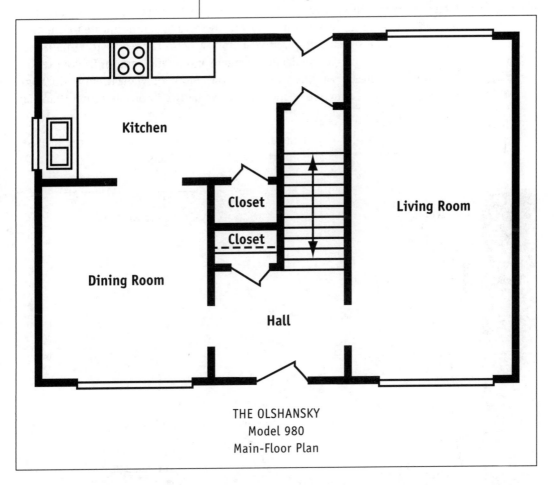

THE OLSHANSKY
Model 980
Main-Floor Plan

left) and along the horizontal axis (at the bottom) of the graph. The notches along the horizontal axis (bottom) of the graph represent time periods (days, weeks, or months), while the notches indicated on the vertical axis (up the left side of the graph) represent growth units (kilograms, number of items, or profits). For example, you could use a graph to track weight gain or loss, showing the time interval along the bottom and the weights along the left side. Graphs may also show a comparison of two or even three growth lines, but any more than three or four is confusing. If, when you keep track of your own weight loss or gain, you also record a friend's progress on the same graph, you are using the graph comparatively. Like line drawings and diagrams, graphs can be produced by computer. In fact, computer-generated graphs are often preferable since for most of us it is usually easier to achieve a professional-looking result on a computer than by hand. Some programs allow for elaborate shading, colouring, and three-dimensional effects, all of which can enhance the appearance and clarity of your report. However, although fancy graphs and diagrams are attractive and can be fun to create by computer, it's sometimes easy to get carried away with visual effects and lose sight of their primary purpose, including them just because they look attractive rather than because they really serve to communicate information clearly. A graph is meant to provide an easy way for the reader to visualize significant information. If you decide to create and include graphs in your report, ask yourself honestly whether they will do the job you want them to do. Some graphs, although attractive to the eye, can actually complicate rather than clar-

f i g u r e   5.4   A graph enables the reader to compare easily the relative success of the three house models.

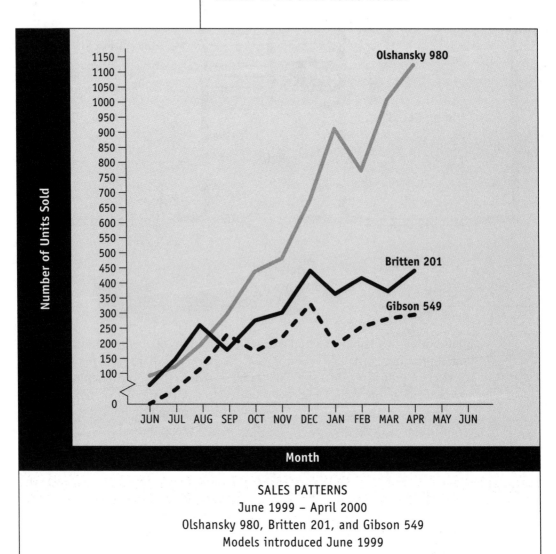

SALES PATTERNS
June 1999 – April 2000
Olshansky 980, Britten 201, and Gibson 549
Models introduced June 1999

ify information the reader needs. Graphs that force the reader to puzzle through complicated information are ultimately detrimental to the impact of the report. Remember that graphs, whether in colour or in black and white, are meant to give the reader a quick overview of information that can be easily compared. Don't try to make a graph do too much. If you use a graph to show comparisons in sales figures, weight loss or gain, profits, absenteeism, or costs of training for example, you should use a different colour line to represent each of the items compared (sales figures for three different sales representatives, absenteeism in four different departments, costs of two different training programs, weight loss for four individuals). To compare items in a graph that must be photocopied on a black and white copier, use lines of varying thicknesses or a combination of broken, dotted, and solid lines. The graph in Figure 5.4 compares the sales of the Olshansky Model 980 with those of two other home models by the same builder.

f i g u r e   5.5   A bar chart can be used to show the sales relationship among the three house models over a particular time period.

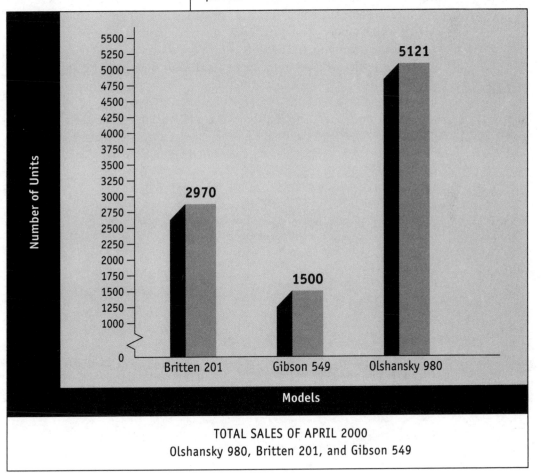

TOTAL SALES OF APRIL 2000
Olshansky 980, Britten 201, and Gibson 549

Charts

Charts come in many different forms, but the most common are bar charts and pie charts. Bar charts are used to compare a single significant aspect of two or more items; each bar on the chart represents one of the items being compared. The length of the bars may be easily compared and give the reader a quick impression of the difference among items. Bar charts may be drawn vertically or horizontally. The vertical bar chart in Figure 5.5 compares total sales, during the first three months of the year, of the three home models shown in the graph in Figure 5.4.

Pie charts (as in Figure 5.6) are used to show percentages or parts of a whole: how a budget is spent, the percentage of employees who have college diplomas, the breakdown of total business expenditures, or the percentage of total sales made up by sales of one item.

Both bar charts and pie charts, like graphs, can be generated on a computer, and are frequently crisper and more professional when generated using software designed for this purpose than they are if produced by hand. If you are reproducing your report using colour, you can use colour to enhance the presentation of the information displayed in the chart. Like graphs, charts are also intended to clarify and support textual materials. If your charts are overly complicated or difficult to understand, the benefits of the devices are cancelled out by the frustration your reader will feel in trying to puzzle out their meaning. It is better to

figure   5.6   A pie chart shows the relationships of the parts to the whole. The reader can see at a glance what percentage of total sales is represented by each model.

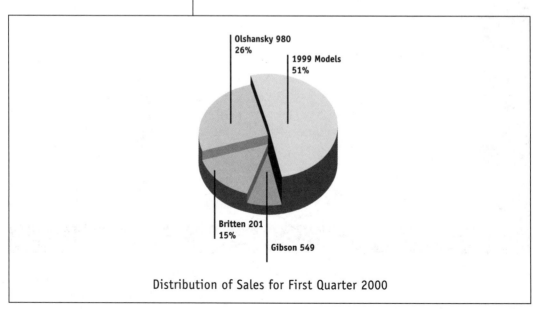

Distribution of Sales for First Quarter 2000

underuse such devices and make sure they are clear than to provide numerous charts that defy interpretation.

Proposals

In reports, as in all business writing, the writer must develop the skill of identifying the reader's needs, expectations, and interests or knowledge. As we saw in the section on sales letters, this skill is especially crucial in persuasive writing. A proposal is a report that "sells" an idea, much as a sales letter does. The main parts — summary, introduction, discussion, conclusion, recommendations, and any appendices — are the same as for any other report, and as in other reports, the headings in the discussion section reflect the specific subject matter of the proposal. All reports are challenging to write, but a proposal is more so, because, as the writer, you must not only provide all necessary information, but also influence your reader to accept the project or suggestion you're putting forth. You must focus on the advantages to the reader of the proposal you are offering.

Proposals may be initiated by you or they may be invited by someone else; your approach will differ slightly depending on which is the case for you. If the idea for the proposal originated with you, you will want to do the following.

- Identify your suggestion immediately (remember, "the most important thing I want to tell you is…").
- Spell out the advantages of the proposed change. If it will save the reader time, work, or money, or if it will increase sales, efficiency, or profits, show how.
- Make it easy for the reader to implement the proposal. Give all pertinent details of the situation and point out any existing resources that can be put to use. Try to anticipate any questions your reader will have and answer them in advance.
- Keep an enthusiastic, positive tone, even when outlining disadvantages. Naturally you feel that the advantages of your proposal outweigh any disadvantages it may have. Your task is to make your reader share this view.
- Indicate as accurately as possible what implementation will cost, but do this after you've presented all the advantages of your proposal. People may be more willing to spend money, time, or effort after they have been convinced of the importance of the project.
- Indicate the steps to be taken to bring about the proposal. Remember that to help your reader accept your project, you must show how it can be done.

Above all, with a proposal, you must demonstrate that you really know what you're talking about and have done your homework thoroughly. You may be convinced that your proposal is sound, but unless you can convince your reader that you have thought the project through and have anticipated any problems, you will not gain his or her confidence, approval, or money. Don't expect the reader to act on faith if your presentation is incomplete or unclear. Do your research.

Occasionally, you will be invited to submit a proposal for implementation of a project someone else has suggested. As with original proposals, you must still present all the information the reader will need to evaluate your suggestions, but in this case the proposal will differ slightly, since you will be responding to requirements that the reader has outlined for you.

- Since your proposal was requested, you are more likely to have your reader's interest at the outset; however, you will still need to emphasize the advantages of your proposal, showing that it is the best means of reaching your reader's desired objectives.
- Because the reader has requested a proposal designed to meet specific needs, you must make sure that the details of your proposal match those requirements.

Remember that a proposal, whether originated by you or requested by someone else, must be especially persuasive to convince a reader to implement the very good idea you've presented.

The sample formal report illustrated in Figure 5.7 is a proposal, but the format is similar to that of any other type of formal report.

weblinks

Proposal Writing
http://www.csun.edu/~vcecn006/propo.htm

A Guide for Writing Research Papers
http://webster.commnet.edu/mla.htm

Report Writing Checklist
http://www.smartbiz.com/sbs/arts/sbs106.htm

Audit Report Writing Guide
http://www.psc-cfp.gc.ca/audit/metod1-e.htm

Proposal Development Information
http://www.govsolutions.com/propmnu.html

SUMMARY

A combination of training modules and individual consultations would be a more efficient method of instructing our personnel in report writing than the group workshops we are now using. Since the quality of employee writing is important to us, we want the best training available, and people learn to write best through individual instruction, regular practice, and feedback. Our method would not only provide each trainee with individual attention, but would free the trainer from the repetition of basic material that would be offered in written form.

The proposed new system will consist of a written self-learning package, complete with concrete suggestions for improving writing effectiveness, supplemented with biweekly consultations over the initial six-month probationary period. This will replace the two-day seminar that is currently provided. Participants will bring work-in-progress to each meeting with the trainer, who will provide ongoing support and suggestions for improvement. Such a process will obviously require a greater time commitment from both trainer and participants, but should produce much more effective and confident writers.

I believe Communications Corporation, as a leader in training and development and a frontrunner in the communications field, should implement such a training program in place of the traditional workshop approach currently in use.

figure 5.7 (Continued)

Table of Contents

Appendices

    A. Cost Breakdown for Manuals/Support Materials
    B. Survey Results

- 1 -

INTRODUCTION

We currently train our personnel in report writing through a two-day workshop in which one trainer works with as many as twenty participants. For material that is primarily content-oriented, this is as effective a means of training as any, but where mastery of a skill is required, this is neither the most efficient nor the most effective means of dealing with staff needs.

Communications Corporation, as a leader in the communications field, needs employees who are competent, efficient writers; obviously they must not only recognize the qualities of good writing, but be able to produce such writing themselves. Many of the new employees we hire have strong basic language skills, but their writing needs polishing. We have long been willing to provide the support that they need in this area, but the current system is not meeting all of our needs as fully as individualized training would.

In present training workshops, for example, participants discuss writing needs and processes, but they actually produce only a single short memo report on a hypothetical situation. There is not room in the workshop for individualized feedback and suggestions, and although participants leave the seminar with basic theory, they are not always able to apply it to their various writing tasks. Many employees feel that though the workshop they attended helped make them aware of some of the weaknesses in their own writing, it did not give them the skills necessary to correct those weaknesses. All agreed that they learn best by doing. Eighty-seven of the one hundred workshop participants we surveyed for this proposal indicated that they would like to have had individual practice and feedback on their writing; only one felt that the present training needed no improvement.

- 2 -

Good writing can be greatly improved by effective editing. To learn how to edit their own writing, our employees need practice and the kind of support that is not available through the present training situation. Though our current method makes employees sensitive to the weaknesses in their writing, it does not offer sufficient help in editing their work to correct these weaknesses. Our proposed training program will offer employees individual editorial appraisal on actual writing projects, and in the process teach them to be better editors of their own work.

- 3 -

PROPOSAL DESCRIPTION

Instead of the two-day seminar currently offered to new employees, the Training and Development department would provide each employee with ongoing support for report writing through two individualized sessions per month. Each employee would meet with one of the trainers for approximately one half hour every two weeks over the first six months of employment. The current workshop system has two trainers each spending sixteen hours in a workshop session, with approximately fifteen employees participating ($16 \times 2 = 32$ hours). The new system would involve a slightly greater time commitment from our trainers (15 participants $\times$ 1/2 hour $\times$ 12 meetings $\div$ 2 trainers = 45 hours), but less from each participant (6 hours as compared to 16). Our proposed training program would take up less of the employees' time than the current system, but at the same time would provide them with more effective instruction in writing.

Our employees themselves recognize the need for improved training. Of one hundred employees surveyed, 36 percent had already attended one repeat workshop within two years of the first one and ten others felt that they would like to do so. Such repetition is costly to the company in time and money, and doesn't guarantee us the best results. Further, 54 percent of respondents indicated that they spend over half their working time on writing, and most (70 percent) felt that they relied heavily on others for editorial guidance. An even greater number (79 percent) felt that they needed more training and experience in correcting the weaknesses in their own writing.

Clearly, training our employees to be their own effective editors would cut down on the time needed to produce written materials and would improve the quality of work.

- 4 -

BENEFITS OF INDIVIDUALIZED TRAINING

This system offers distinct advantages over the current system. The time spent discussing writing theory would be decreased (we would not, of course, eliminate the study of theory; that subject would be dealt with in our self-help manuals) and the time spent assisting employees in the mastery of writing skills would be increased. The advantages for participants, Training and Development staff, and the company are as follows.

PARTICIPANTS:
1. will receive more practical instruction and more individualized attention from the trainers;
2. will receive immediate and relevant feedback on actual writing they are doing for the job, and not on hypothetical examples; and
3. will receive the hands-on experience necessary for mastering complicated writing and editing skills.

TRAINERS:
1. will be in close contact with participants and more intimately involved in the training experience;
2. will be able to address specific individual writing problems that can't be effectively handled in a workshop; and
3. will be able to track more effectively successful training procedures and techniques.

THE COMPANY:
1. will gain better-trained writers who produce more efficient writing;
2. will experience a reduction in the number of staff who repeat the report writing training;
3. will benefit from the general morale boost that is felt across the company as confidence in writing is increased; and
4. will benefit from the improved relationships among staff as they work more closely with the Training and Development department.

- 5 -

CONTENTS OF SELF-TEACHING MANUAL

The bulk of the information needed to produce the training manual has already been prepared by the Training and Development department; supplementary materials are currently being developed. Below is the projected Table of Contents for the manual.

Introduction
    The written message
    The basic principles of writing

Know Your Reader
    Identify needs
    Identify expectations
    Identify previous knowledge

The "Unnatural" Order of Business Writing
    Identify your main message
    The main thing I want to tell you is...
    The business writer's priority list

Style of Business Writing
    The Six C's
    Conciseness and clarity

Inform or Persuade
    Keep it simple
    What's in it for me?

Letters and Memos That Work
    Formats
    Follow your priority list
    Difficult messages

-6-

Report Style
    Focus
    Follow your priority list
    Main report parts

Report Formats
    Informal
    Semiformal
    Formal

Choosing the Appropriate Report Type
    Report situations
    Occurrence or incident
    Evaluation
    Investigation
    Progress
    Proposals

figure 5.7 (Continued)

- 7 -

PREPARATION AND RESOURCES

PRESENT RESOURCES

Oscar Katz, Gwynne Nishikawa, and Heather Scott have already prepared a collection of exercises and tips for use in the Report Writing Workshop that could, with some minor alterations, be used in an individualized learning program. As well, Gwynne and I have been working on a supplementary manual for participants in the workshops, which should be completed within a month. Some additional materials would have to be developed to round out the package as a self-teaching manual, and these should include a series of guidelines for achieving mastery of specific writing skills.

These learning materials are currently stored on disk and could be set up attractively and printed on the Printing department's laser equipment. In-house photocopying and coil binding would enable us to produce economical manuals at approximately $5.00 each (cost breakdown attached as Appendix A), not much more than the present cost of printing supplementary handouts for the workshops. The manuals could be distributed to new employees on their joining the company, in advance of their first meeting with training personnel.

IMPLEMENTATION TIME

Using the existing materials from the Workshop as a starting point, we estimate that the manual and supplementary materials could be prepared within two months, in time to begin the new training procedures for employees hired in the spring.

figure 5.7 (Continued)

- 8 -

CONCLUSION

Though individualized training is not practicable for all of our new-employee programs, we believe it will provide more effective training in professional writing and editing, and ultimately make our employees more efficient and competent writers.

Once the new system is in place for report writing training, we can chart our success by follow-up studies and comparisons with the results of the present method. As well, we might consider making the new manuals and approach available to other companies through our Management Consulting Program. We could, of course, continue to provide the traditional workshop training to other companies who are interested in it.

RECOMMENDATIONS

I recommend that the new approach to report writing training be implemented on a pilot basis as of March 2002, for a one-year trial period. At the end of this time, Training and Development personnel will conduct a study to determine the success of the project and the feasibility of extending it permanently.

APPENDIX A:
Cost Breakdown for Manuals/Support Materials

New Self-Teaching Manual
We recommend having the manuals printed in runs of 50 copies, which would help
to maintain the cost at under $5.00 apiece; manuals will be 48 pages long, printed
on two sides.

First Print Run Cost for 50 Copies

Laser typesetting	$0.10/page	$4.80*
Photocopying	$0.05/page	120.00
Binding	$2.50 each	125.00
Print Run Total		$249.80
Per Copy Total		$5.00

Present Workshop Materials
Currently there are 50 pages of materials provided to participants in the workshop.

First Print Run Cost for 50 Copies

Laser typesetting	$0.10/page	$5.00*
Photocopying	$0.05/page	125.00
Folder	$0.55 each	27.50
Print Run Total		$157.50
Per Copy Total		$3.15

*One-time only cost; subsequent print runs will come in slightly cheaper, since the
same typeset originals can be used again.

APPENDIX B:
Survey Results

We used a questionnaire to collect information from one hundred employees who have taken the Report Writing Workshop over the last four years. The completed questionnaires are available for viewing in Jennifer Varzari's office.

1. How much of your working time is spent writing (including reports, promotional material, copy, correspondence, or other job-related materials)?

    Fifteen respondents spend more than 75 percent of their working time writing; a further thirty-nine spend over half their time on writing activities; thirty-nine said 25 to 30 percent of their time is spent writing, and seven indicated under 25 percent.

2. How soon after joining Communications Corporation did you take the Report Writing Training Workshop?

    One hundred percent of respondents had taken the workshop within four months of being hired.

3. Did the training provide sufficient hands-on experience to improve your writing?

    All one hundred respondents found the training valuable in making them aware of their writing weaknesses, but seventy-nine felt that it did not give them enough experience in correcting the weaknesses that had been identified.

4. How useful was the hypothetical writing assignment?

    Ninety-six felt that they gained some insight from the assignment, but only forty-two felt that there was a direct carryover to their daily work.

5. Would you find it beneficial to do the training a second time? If so, how soon after completing the first workshop?

    Forty-six of the respondents indicated interest in attending the workshop a second time; of those, thirty-six had already done so within two years of the first workshop.

App. B

6. Do you currently rely on editorial guidance from others in your department? To what extent would you say this is so?

> Seventy respondents indicated a heavy reliance — 75 to 100 percent of the time — on guidance from superiors or co-workers; the other thirty indicated a range of reliance from 5 to 50 percent of the time. Most, however, showed that this dependence decreased as confidence in writing ability increased. Usually with more practice, the need for consultation diminished.

7. In your view, should the training include more individual consultation?

> All one hundred respondents said yes. Eighty felt that they would have relied less on peer or superior editorial input if the training had provided more practice with feedback.

8. In what way could we increase the effectiveness of the training?

> Seven suggested making repeat workshops mandatory; five wanted an additional workshop day; one felt the training as it stands cannot be improved; eighty-seven wanted additional individual practice and feedback.

Once again, no matter what kind of report you are writing, you must prepare thoroughly and organize carefully.

1. Identify your main message (the main thing I want to tell you is that...).

2. Identify your purpose (tell or sell).

3. Identify your reader (needs, expectations, knowledge).

4. Develop your points fully.

5. Observe the Six C's.

6. Be sure to format your report carefully and use appropriate headings.

7. Use visuals to clarify, and not complicate, the information in the text.

s h a r p e n i n g   y o u r   s k i l l s

The following sample report situations may require a formal report or a proposal. Using the Report Writing Planner in the previous chapter to outline your approach, follow your instructor's directions to write **one** of these reports.

1. A number of people at Communications Corporation are considering returning to college to enter the program that you are now completing. Daena Tobias has requested a report from you regarding your local colleges' offerings in this area. Investigate the program as offered by three colleges in your region and write up your findings into a formal report addressed to Daena Tobias. You will outline for these prospective students all they will need to know regarding the basics of the program (including admission requirements, duration, courses, any practicum or co-op experience or special courses, and advanced standing), as well as the general facilities offered by various institutions (student services, library facilities, recreational facilities, and any special assistance for mature students). You will also want to draw up a study of costs. Evaluate the programs according to their appropriateness for Communications Corporation personnel and recommend the one you feel is most applicable.

2. As Senior Training Officer in the Public Relations department of Communications Corporation, you have recently been contacted by Daena Tobias, who has received rather disturbing comments regarding the effectiveness of the sales workshops delivered by some of her executive staff. She has had unfavourable feedback from participants in the workshops, and she suspects that many of the executives have had no training in public speaking. At any rate, their workshop participants have identified flaws

in the presentations, such as dull and lifeless delivery, "memorized" spiels, and general lack of confidence. Daena Tobias would like you to investigate the situation and offer some suggestions as to how these individuals can improve their presentations. You have decided to investigate the available resources and have discovered three that seem most appropriate for your people.

- Dale Carnegie Foundation Training;
- the International Communications Training Club (formerly Toastmasters); and
- a public speaking course offered by your local college.

You will investigate the three options, outlining approximate course content, emphasis, duration of the courses, and cost of each. You have considered preparing an in-house training program, as well, and will evaluate the advantages of that program. Daena Tobias has indicated that she wants something done fairly soon and at a modest cost.

3. You work in the Public Relations department of Communications Corporation's Toronto office. Your company has branch offices all over the country, with major locations in Halifax, Montreal, Winnipeg, Calgary, and Vancouver, and several smaller regional offices in other centres. Daena Tobias, Director of the Corporation, is committed to team-building and encouraging employee morale.

One frequent complaint you have heard is that there is little continuity of information between branches. As things stand at present, the company has a fairly efficient computer and courier mail system, and information is distributed within departments through numerous memos and other documents. But there is a gulf between branch offices — few of the individuals in the company have any real understanding of what's happening in other branches, and sometimes even in other departments within their own branch.

You are aware that other large corporations publish in-house magazines as a means of drawing everyone in the corporation into the "team." Articles include topics of interest to people all over the corporation and range from the directly vocational or professional to spotlights on advances in different departments or regions, and profiles on individuals within the company.

You believe that such a magazine would go a long way toward improving the morale of Communications Corporation employees, and you feel that the production of such a magazine would be within the scope of your department. You want to produce a glossy, professional publication, on quality paper, and with lots of attractive photos and illustrations. You are aware that Daena Tobias has been looking for some way to recognize the contributions of employees and you think that your magazine could include a feature on these deserving members of the company. Such a periodical would be immensely more attractive and readable than the high number of memos currently distributed and would provide company members with a sense of community.

Since the Printing department has recently acquired a laser printer and equipment for photo reproduction, the magazine could be produced for approximately 75 cents per copy and effectively distributed through the already extensive inter-office mail system. You envision a bimonthly publication, with a production run of approximately one thousand copies: eight hundred for Corporation employees and another two hundred to be used for promotional purposes.

You calculate that producing the magazine would necessitate the hiring of two more staff members to oversee its production, at an approximate cost of $45,000 per year to the company, but it would encourage higher morale and ultimately mean greater productivity for the company.

Write the proposal to Daena Tobias encouraging her to authorize you to produce such an in-house magazine.

4. Choose any topic in the broadly defined area of business or professional communication as the focus of your formal report. If you prefer, you may work with **one** of the topics on the list below rather than selecting your own. Drawing on all available research sources, survey the current trends in thinking on the topic you have chosen. Write a formal report that answers the following questions.

   a. Briefly, what major trends appear to be current in this area of communication? Is there a particular emphasis that seems to be especially important?

   b. Has there been any significant change in focus or direction of conventional thinking on communication in business or the professions as a result of new technologies?

   c. What impact has this trend or these developments in technology had on the practice of your profession?

   d. What conclusions can you draw from your research into this topic? What are the implications of this information for others who wish to pursue careers in your field?

   Here are several topics that have received attention in the recent past, though you are certainly not limited to these. You may choose your own topic if you find something of greater interest to you.

   Virtual Office/Home Office
   Cross-Cultural Communication in Business
   Corporate Retreats
   "Opting Out"
   Information Superhighway
   "Outsourcing"
   Ethics in Business Communication Practice

Ethics in Advertising

Corporate Coaching and Consulting

Your research should include a minimum of ten sources, and may include interviews or web sites as well as library journals and books.

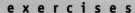

online exercises

1. At the page entitled "Guidelines for Writing an Engineering Report" (http://www.civeng.carleton.ca/Courses/UnderGrad/1996-97/82.497/Report-Guidelines.html), posted by Carleton University's Department of Civil and Environmental Engineering, you will find advice on the preparation and organization of a formal report. Although the advice on this page is adapted specifically to the needs of engineers, formal reports in all disciplines share several common characteristics. Read the advice carefully, and then answer the following questions:

   a. What is the "cardinal principle" of all report writing?

   b. What is the role of the reader in shaping the contents of the report?

   c. Which of the Six C's of Business Writing seem to be most important to the writers of this web page? How do you know? Send your responses to your instructor by e-mail, or submit them in the form of a short report.

2. Among the features of Prentice Hall Canada's web site is a page called "Guidelines for Submitting a Proposal." You will find these guidelines at http://www.prenticehall.ca/general/manu.html. List the ways in which the instructions on this site resemble the instructions given in this chapter, and the previous chapter, for preparing a report. Why do you think the publishing house has made this information available to prospective authors?

Oral Reports and Presentations

➤ To master the four common types of oral presentations: impromptu; manuscript; memorized; and extemporaneous.

➤ To learn how to prepare an oral report and how to deliver your message effectively and confidently.

More and more often, people in business are called upon to present materials orally, whether in workshops, seminars, or staff meetings. Inexperienced speakers often find these public speaking situations unnerving, and may try to avoid them whenever possible. However, anyone who wants to advance in an organization will sooner or later have to face an audience.

An oral report or briefing, like a written report, should be carefully thought out, well organized, and clearly presented. No matter how uncomfortable you are at the thought of public speaking, you can give an effective speech or presentation if you prepare and organize your materials carefully, and practise effectively. You will find that your fear will actually fade if you gain control over your subject matter and focus on communicating your message to your audience.

One big difference between oral presentations or reports and the written variety is the advantage of meeting your audience face-to-face. Though it may be intimidating to stand before a group of your peers or your supervisors, you should remember that it's also a lot easier to establish rapport with someone who is in the same room with you than it is to engage and motivate the readers of a written report. If you can think of the opportunity for oral communication as an advantage rather than a burden, you will find it easier to prepare for the experience. In order to take full advantage of the opportunity to speak directly to your audience, you will need to think about your speech as communication rather than simply a performance. Like all effective business communication, oral communication depends on making a connection with your audience and staying focused on your purpose. When you are preparing an oral presentation you should also think about the context or setting in which your report will be given.

1. Consider Your Audience To whom are you speaking? Are you delivering material to your peers? Your subordinates? A group of visitors? The board? What is the audience's interest in your project? How much information do they already have? What do they want or need to know? How much depth do they expect? As you consider these factors, adapt your report presentation as closely as possible to your audience's expectations. Recognize that some things you consider important may have to be left out if they are not as significant to your audience.

2. Focus on Your Purpose Why are you giving this presentation? What, exactly, are you expected to accomplish? Should you give a quick overview of your project, or should you present an in-depth analysis of your work? Are you expected to outline, support, or justify what you've been doing? Do you have to persuade your audience to accept a new point of view or course of action? Will you be subject to questions from your listeners? What are your own expectations? At the planning stage, you will need to shape your speech to reflect the task it is meant to accomplish.

3. Identify the Speaking Context Oral communication is distinguished from written work primarily because it is presented face-to-face in a physical setting. The size of your audience, the size and features of the room in which you are speaking, and the limits of time are among the factors that will constrain you in planning your speech. How much time will you have to make your connection with the audience? If you have prepared a forty-five-minute presentation only to find that you have been allotted three minutes, you'll have a difficult time — though not as difficult as if you're in the reverse situation! Make sure you know how much time you're expected to fill. Where are you giving your presentation? How big is the room? What facilities are available? How far will you be from your audience? Will you be using a microphone? Overhead cameras? If you're expected to give a three-minute overview of your project, you may have to do that standing next to your desk as the visitors are paraded past; a forty-five-minute comprehensive outline will probably be presented in a meeting room or boardroom.

Types of Oral Presentations

Oral presentations vary not only in length and formality, but also in the style of delivery. There are four main types of speech delivery, but not all are suited to every occasion. Be sure to choose the one that is most appropriate for the requirements of your situation.

Impromptu This kind of speech is given on the spur of the moment: the speaker is called upon to speak without warning and without any prepared notes. This type of presentation is most commonly used as an exercise in public-speaking classes or groups, or it may occur when a party guest who wasn't expecting to be honoured is called upon to say a few words. For obvious reasons, the impromptu speech is usually short (under two minutes); a topic that is suitable for such a speech is one on which most anyone could speak without having to prepare. The speaker isn't expected to provide new information; at best, she may simply give us a new way of looking at something we all know. This style of delivery is not suitable for an occasion where the speaker is expected to be prepared to give a presentation.

Manuscript This presentation is written out and read word for word from the printed document. It is the result of extensive research and thoughtful organization by the speaker, and is most appropriate in situations where there are legal considerations (a lawyer or politician issuing policy would probably use this form) or where exact wording is important. This kind of speech is rarely effective for persuasion, since it is difficult to maintain audience engagement when you're focused on a manuscript in front of you instead of on your audience. If you aren't focused on your listeners, you won't hold their attention, and if you lose their attention, you can't hope to move them. As well, written discourse just doesn't sound like spoken discourse — and reading from a manuscript tends to deaden the speaker–audience relationship. Even if you are very accomplished at reading aloud (most people are not), you may have trouble keeping your audience's attention during this kind of presentation. Despite these warnings, you may be tempted to resort to a written manuscript in your business talks. However, if you have ever had to listen to someone read an essay or a paper aloud, you know how hard it can be for an audience to pay attention. It's just plain boring to listen to such a speaker, and that's not a style you should want to emulate. To keep your audience with you, you need to focus on communicating clearly with them and making a personal connection.

Memorized A speech can also be prepared in advance and memorized, but this is also not good speaking practice, because a memorized spiel will typically fail to engage the audience. If you've written something and then memorized it, it will sound like exactly that — your focus will be on the text in your head as you reach for exact phrasing, and not on the audience in front of you. As well, since you're reaching for exact wording rather than for ideas, a slip of memory will leave you gasping. You may not be able to recover your train of thought without repeating phrases you've already spoken. Finally, as you focus on re-membering word-for-word what you were going to say next, you lose the contact that's vital to the communication exchange. There is little likelihood that you will be using a memorized speech unless you are acting in a play. Otherwise, mem-orization is not the way to achieve the audience connection you desire.

Extemporaneous This is the most versatile and useful form of oral presentation. The speaker works from an outline written on a notecard and expands the details from memory. An extemporaneous presentation is superior for most purposes be-cause it allows you to respond to the immediate needs of your audience and so establish a bond with them. Don't make the mistake of thinking that an ex-temporaneous speech is unprepared or "ad-libbed"; it isn't. It requires detailed planning and organization ahead of time, but the delivery has a natural, spon-taneous, engaging quality. It is by far the most flexible of speech delivery styles, and of the four types listed here, this is the one that you will find most useful. Detailed guidelines for preparing an extemporaneous presentation appear on pages 133–136.

Before turning to the process of preparing the speech and making the note-card, we will spend a little time discussing topics for your speech.

Choosing a Topic

Clearly, one of the first things you must do in preparing for a speech, whether it's in the classroom or the boardroom, is to select and properly focus your topic. In some cases, your professor may assign you a topic, or your choices may be limited by the projects you're working on in your job. Whether you are assigned a topic or are freely choosing for yourself, you should be careful to select a sub-ject or an aspect of the assigned topic that is interesting and important to you. Effective presentations require careful research and preparation, and those tasks will be easier for you if you've chosen a topic that interests you.

Also, if you're fascinated by your subject, your enthusiasm will show in your presentation, making it more dynamic. Speakers who choose subjects that bore them usually bore their audience with dull, lacklustre delivery. Remember: no topic is by nature boring; it becomes so only in the hands of an under-prepared, unenthusiastic speaker.

Let's assume that you have been assigned a speech in a class, but no topics have been assigned. Your instructor has given you the freedom to choose your own topic and approach. How do you choose something interesting for both yourself and your audience? First, you should strive to give your speech a sense of immediacy for your audience; if possible, it should address something that will be important to them right now. The newspaper magnate William Randolph

Hearst once said that a dogfight in your own neighbourhood is more interesting than a full-scale war half a world away. He knew the importance of giving the audience something relevant to their lives. You should keep this principle in mind, too.

Here's an example of immediacy. One of my students gave a speech designed to persuade his classmates not to use the school elevators when it was unnecessary. Because student tuition costs had taken a sharp rise just previous to his presentation, he used the costs of operating the elevators — more than a full year's salary for one extra professor — as his focal point. By avoiding the use of the elevators, he argued, the students may be able to increase the number of course offerings at the school, or prevent an additional scheduled tuition increase. This focus affected all the students in the class, and dealt with something of immediate interest and importance to them. They couldn't help but be interested.

Another student who was looking for a speech topic was walking along the main hallway of the school, past the location of a small snackbar. She noticed with some annoyance the amount of debris that littered the hallway — candy wrappers, chip bags, pop cans, and pizza boxes. As she picked some of it from the floor to put into the trash, she found herself asking silently why nobody else was doing the same. She realized she'd found a subject for a persuasive speech, and she set about to investigate it: how much time did the maintenance staff spend cleaning up garbage that inconsiderate students left behind? What other chores were neglected because the staff was occupied by this task? In what way could her student audience benefit by taking the action she was asking for? The answers to these questions, which she obtained by interviewing the head of Maintenance Services and by doing some library research on the psychology of physical surroundings, provided the basis for a powerful speech persuading her classmates to put their own garbage in the trash cans, and to pick up just two pieces of litter from the floor each time they walked along the hall.

Speech topics are everywhere. As long as there are problems to be solved, new ideas to be communicated, actions to take, there will be subjects for speeches. It's up to you to find one that you care about, are committed to, and can engage your audience with. It's possible to take any approach to your topic that you please, provided it will gain your audience's interest and prompt their action. But one thing is certain; if you can't interest yourself in your topic, you're not going to succeed in holding the interest of an audience. You'll be bored, and that boredom will be evident to your audience. The most important thing you can do for yourself and your audience is to pick something that holds *your* interest as well as theirs.

There's one other rule to picking a topic that you should consider: some topics have been overworked. For example, most speech instructors have heard far too many speeches on recycling and on exercise. Chances are that, if a topic comes easily to your mind, it has likely crossed the minds of everyone else in the class. Try to pick something a little different from the same few tired topics. Unless you can find some brand new information and focus on a specific connection to your audience, you will probably lose your audience in the first few minutes of a speech on an overworked topic. Give them something unusual, original, and exciting. As an additional rule of thumb, if you heard about it on a television talk show, it's probably been overdone, and you should not choose it for your speech.

Finding a Topic When You Can't Think of Anything

Many of us have the most difficult time simply coming up with a beginning idea. Freewriting is a technique you can use to help generate ideas. Simply sit down with pen and paper, or in front of your computer, and start to write — it doesn't matter what you write at the beginning. You can really start from anywhere, from any thought that pops into your head. The trick is to force yourself to keep on writing or typing — no matter what — for at least fifteen minutes without stopping. Don't pause for anything. Even if you have to write something like "this is stupid! I can't think of anything to say!" you will find that pretty soon your thoughts will swing around to the task at hand and ideas will start to flow. Many people find this to be a good generator of ideas for any type of assignment where the topic is left completely open. Once you begin to generate ideas about topics, you can go over them to consider their persuasive possibilities.

You might want to try a somewhat more structured approach. Sit down at your computer, or grab a pen and paper, and make a list of as many topics as you can think of. Don't worry at first if the topics you're selecting seem to be too broad to make a clear speech; narrowing your topic to a specific purpose will come later. As you begin to brainstorm you should write down all the ideas that come to you, no matter how silly they may seem. You can always cross out the weak ones later. The list will likely be things that you already know about. Your list may look like this sample:

school	majors	teachers	sports
music	theatre	movies	books
dancing	art	hobbies	transportation
self-defence	clothes	education	advertising
stress!	exams	time out!	reading

Once you've got a list, ask yourself if any of these subjects contain any possibilities. You will need to find a "hook" that will catch your audience's attention and link the speech to them. Once you've got a list like this one, go through a second time and brainstorm all the subtopics that come to you on each of the subjects. For instance, we might begin with school:

school —	teachers	cost	courses
	grades	requirements	special classes
	exams	library	cafeteria
	gym	clubs	meeting people
	drama/music performances		student newspaper

Select from your second list any topics that might offer possibilities of an interesting topic for you and your class. If you need to, generate a third list, and then a fourth — each time becoming more specific. For instance, let's take the topic of the student newspaper:

newspaper —
volunteer opportunities	movie reviews
articles about school	quality of writing
information about sports teams	weak reporting
interesting editorials	columnists
why do so many people hate it?	costs
journalism experience	

After making such a list, one of my students decided to give a speech encouraging her classmates to read the school newspaper. Another chose to speak about why the class should boycott the newspaper entirely. Another encouraged people in the class, who were communication majors, to join the writing staff at the paper, citing the experience in journalism that could be gained.

This, of course, isn't the only topic that can work this way. Another one of my students gave an excellent speech encouraging her classmates to volunteer for the college's brand new late-night escort program. Another offered a speech encouraging the class to nominate a favourite instructor for a teaching award by pointing out how doing so might help to retain good teachers on staff and would pay something back to someone who had contributed in an important way to their education. Yet another student offered his classmates a method for increasing their reading speed and comprehension. By emphasizing the amount of reading they were faced with in the current semester, as well as the overall reading load in their program, he was able to convince many of them to try the method he advocated.

As a final suggestion for finding a topic, you may find it useful (if you are free to choose your own topic) to think through your experiences in a more structured way. There are three areas of everyone's experience that can profitably be "mined" for topics. First, consider recommending to your audience a product, a book or magazine, or a movie that you have used, read, or seen and liked: I have heard excellent speeches encouraging the audience to subscribe to the speaker's favourite magazine, to incorporate spinach into their diet, or to try a favourite recipe. Any product that you have used that you think is good — perhaps a metal polish for removing rust from your bicycle, or a particular brand of jeans — can be made the basis for a persuasive or informative speech.

Second, you may wish to invite your audience to participate in an activity or join an association that you belong to. The activity may be socially significant, such as volunteering at the local hospital or donating to the food bank , or it may be personally relevant, such as participating in a new sport, joining a particular student club at your college, or trying a new hobby. I have heard some great speeches on rock climbing, juggling, participating in the twenty-four-hour famine program, and joining the rhetoric and communications society at our school.

Once again, this method of topic invention is a good foundation for both persuasive and informative speeches.

Third, it's also possible to make a good and interesting speech out of challenging the status quo. Most of us take certain social attitudes for granted: walk instead of taking the elevator, recycle, get more exercise, wear a certain brand of shoes. You can catch and hold an audience's attention sometimes just by taking an approach contrary to what the audience expects. The trick to this approach is to concentrate your efforts very specifically: not simply global resistance to commercial culture, for example, but a speech on why you should NOT wear a certain brand of shoes or jeans, on why you should NOT take the stairs instead of the elevator, or why you should NOT recycle. Of course, you will still need to do your research and be sure your evidence is convincing. It's not enough simply to disagree with received wisdom; you must prove your case. However, many issues — even ones that everyone takes for granted — can be viewed from the opposite side. This approach can yield a really challenging and interesting speech if you think it through carefully.

Whichever of these methods you use for choosing a topic, or if you use another method, be sure to evaluate your choice in light of the course requirements, your own interests, the demands of the assignment, and the probable interests of your audience. Ask yourself what kinds of angles you could take on each subject, and consider where you might turn to research them further. If your presentation date is a week away, you may not want to pick a subject that will require a trip to a distant library or a lengthy wait for inter-library loans.

Once you have selected a topic and done your research, you are then ready to prepare your presentation.

Preparing an Extemporaneous Presentation

Like all good reports, extemporaneous presentations require meticulous planning, preparation, and practice. When done well, they appear comfortable and natural — so much so that they may fool an inexperienced observer into thinking they are completely spontaneous. One of my students, a very accomplished speaker who has mastered the art of extemporaneous speaking, recently gave a presentation in a senior class. One of her classmates, misunderstanding this highly polished presentation, astonished her by remarking, "I can't believe that you were able to wing it like that, and it came out so well!" This student prepares meticulously, researches thoroughly, and practises repeatedly, but her inexperienced classmate saw only the natural, comfortable delivery of an effective extemporaneous speech. That's what your audience should see also.

When preparing an extemporaneous speech, you must clearly identify your main message and your audience, but to make the presentation really work well, you must create and maintain an effective relationship with your audience. Your oral and visual delivery will help to ensure that your audience responds to your speech, but your real effectiveness as a speaker will rest on the only written material you will bring with you to the front of the room: your notecard.

Instead of reading from a manuscript, or delivering a memorized monologue, a speaker delivering an extemporaneous speech speaks naturally about her knowledge of the topic, gleaned from her research and preparation. Her speech has a clear, explicit structure, and a clearly identified purpose. She carries **one notecard** on which she has written only enough, in a scratch outline form, to jog her memory of the points she wants to make.

An extemporaneous speech is never written out fully, even during the preparation stages; it is developed as an outline only, and that outline is pared down, as you practise through the material, until it is simply a cue to memory. Once you have arrived at your final bare outline, you should jot it lengthwise on a 3" × 5" notecard. Unless your speech is very lengthy, (longer than twenty-five minutes) you should be able to fit sufficient information onto a single card. You may use both sides of the card, but don't be tempted to write down too much detail. Preparing your notecard well is one way of ensuring that your presentation will be successful, since it is the only text you will have with you at the front of the room. You should never read directly from the card unless you are citing quotations or statistics, and these should be used sparingly. Consult the card only as a reminder of your organization: it is a tool but not a crutch.

The words on the card should be written as large as possible, in dark ink; you may wish to use highlighters or coloured ink to colour code your main points. If you wish to include a brief quotation in your speech, or cite statistics, these may also be written on the card. The use of a card will also force you to extemporize.

Why should you use a card rather than a full-size sheet of paper? A card is preferable first of all because its small size forces you to write down only main points, expanding the details from memory (that is, extemporizing) as you speak. The card is meant to prompt you, and give you something to rely on should your memory fail you because of nervousness.

In addition, you can palm a 3" × 5" card quite easily, so that it is inconspicuous in your hand. By contrast, a full sheet of paper is too large to be used unobtrusively and can actually serve as a distraction to your audience. It can rattle and shake if your hands tremble, communicating your nervousness to your audience and emphasizing it to yourself. Do yourself a favour: write your extemporaneous speech outline on a card.

Making the Notecard

Below (Figure 6.1) is a sample outline and notecard for a presentation that I gave on the subject of toy design, a hobby of mine and a subject on which I have written and published three books. I initially gave this presentation at the launch of the first book and have used it since in speaking to other groups on the same topic. Even though I speak in front of classes every day, I was just as nervous in giving this presentation as any speaker is in an unfamiliar situation. Here is how I prepared myself.

Before preparing the outline, I jotted down as many ideas as I could think of that might provide possible approaches to the subject. Here are some of the ideas I came up with.

General topic   toy design
Possible subtopics   sources of inspiration for designs
demonstration of a simple technique
steps in the design process
getting designs published
selling your designs
writing a book on design
how I got started designing

Focus

Once I had jotted down several possible approaches I might take, I thought about the speaking situation. When I first gave the presentation, I was speaking to a variety of prominent people from the college and the community in a large meeting room. The group consisted of about fifty professionals and community members who were not designers themselves, but had come to hear me speak about the book and the design work I was doing. They were interested in learning about the personality behind the work. Their expectations ruled out some of the topics I'd listed; for instance, these people were not interested in getting such a book published themselves. They were not really concerned with learning a technique either, and in any case, the room was too large to allow for such a demonstration, so that was out too. These people were simply interested in learning something about my design work, and my experience had taught me that there are several questions that people often ask about this hobby.

For these reasons, I selected three of the above topics: how I started designing; sources of inspiration and ideas; steps in the design process. I organized my three topics logically, and in my introduction I linked the three by mentioning that these were questions that I was commonly asked about my work in design.

Once you've completed your research, you should prepare a preliminary speaking outline. *Do not write out your speech in full!* Work at an outline level only, and pare that down as much as possible before you turn to your card. Use words that have enough meaning to you to remind you of what you want to discuss. You should aim for mastery of ideas, not memorization of particular words and phrases. Your card should be so pared down that it would be useful only to the person who had done the research for the speech. If it has enough information that someone who had not researched the material could present your speech, it probably contains too much detail. Once you've prepared your initial outline, you should start practising through the speech, adjusting anything that needs to be changed or reorganized. When you have enough mastery of your information, but before you're through practising, you should make up the final version of your card.

Use only **one** 3" × 5" notecard for your speech outline. Remember, your card should contain only a brief outline that will serve to remind you of your main points. Each point you write down is intended to provide a cryptic signal to you to trigger your memory of the materials and help you organize your comments during the presentation. It isn't meant to record details or exact phrasing.

Figure 6.1 is an example of the notecard I used for a twenty-minute version of my presentation on toy design. The words "Three questions," which I used in my introduction, reminded me of what I wanted to say to begin my presentation. Because these were questions that were also likely to be in the minds of my listeners, this introduction helped me capture their interest. The points listed under each section developed my presentation fully, and I showed the actual toys as visual aids (see the discussion of visual aids later in this chapter on pages 141–143).

figure 6.1   The organizational outline for my hobby presentation and the notecard that will serve as a reminder of my main points.

SAMPLE SPEECH OUTLINE

INTRODUCTION: Three Questions

I. <u>How I Started Designing</u>
    A. Childhood interest in toys/crafts
    B. Nephews/nieces
    C. Altering patterns becomes designing

II. <u>Sources of Ideas</u>
    A. Classic children's stories — witches, elves, Santa, gypsies, angels
    B. Unusual names — Madame Sosostris, Pat Hare
    C. Illustrations — birthday cards, colouring/story books

III. <u>Steps in the Design Process</u>
    A. Concept — show birthday card
    B. Sketch — show preliminary sketch
    C. Pattern — show pattern development
    D. Finished toy — show toy

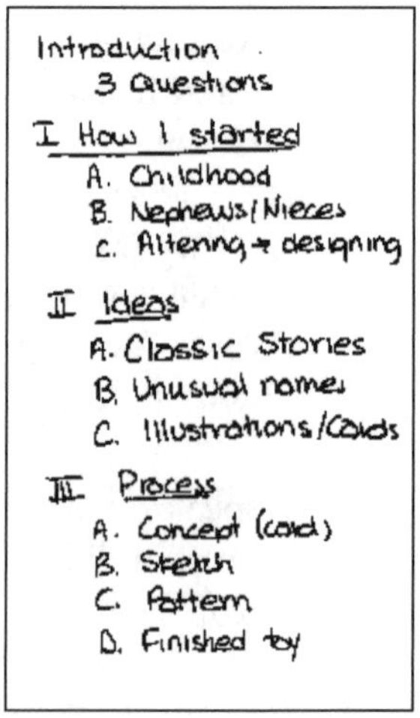

Handwritten notecard:

Introduction
  3 Questions

I How I started
  A. Childhood
  B. Nephews/Nieces
  C. Altering + designing

II Ideas
  A. Classic Stories
  B. Unusual names
  C. Illustrations/Cards

III Process
  A. Concept (card)
  B. Sketch
  C. Pattern
  D. Finished toy

Preparing a Business Briefing

On the job you will not be as free to select your presentation topic as you are in school; instead, you may be required to speak about some aspect of your work. This kind of presentation, often referred to as a briefing, is similar to the kind of presentation outlined above, but may differ in the exact steps you follow to prepare your materials. Let's look at the outline and notecard used by Jennifer Varzari in preparing a briefing for the director's advisory group on the training workshops she outlined in her proposal on pages 107–121 in the previous chapter of this book.

Because Jennifer's presentation is clearly defined by her work, she already knows the kind of approach she must take, and she does not need to jot down ideas for subjects. However, she does need to clearly define her audience, her purpose, and her speaking context, as suggested at the beginning of this chapter.

Audience Jennifer knows that her audience, the director's advisory board, has the power to recommend or veto her proposal. The board is an important group in the company, with greater authority than Jennifer, as manager of her department, is able to command. The board members have already received and read Jennifer's proposal, and have indicated their interest by inviting her to attend their meeting to discuss the proposal and answer their questions.

Purpose Jennifer must convince the advisory group that her proposal is worth implementing. She knows that the board members want to do what is best for the company, so she must show them that this project is to the company's benefit. Because they have already read the proposal, her introductory remarks will be a quick overview of the project, emphasizing the company's need for improved training in this area.

Speaking Context Jennifer has been allotted a half hour at the beginning of the advisory board's regular weekly meeting. The group will be in a small corporate meeting room that holds thirty people. There is no lectern; Jennifer will be seated at a meeting table with the members of the group around her. It will be a relatively informal setting, and Jennifer is expected to present a brief introductory presentation followed by questions from the group.

Jennifer will want to bring support materials with her to the meeting — the survey results, copies of the materials to be used in the training, and an outline of the procedure. She should also prepare a card to help her frame her initial remarks. As a notecard, she can use a shortened version of her proposal, but because her audience has already seen that document, she must not simply read from it or repeat materials they have already read. Given the audience's interests, Jennifer should emphasize the company's need for report writing training, the failures of the current system, and the advantages of the new one. Figure 6.2 presents the outline Jennifer developed for her presentation.

figure   6.2   Outline for a business briefing. Jennifer Varzari focuses on her audience, her purpose, and her speaking context.

BRIEFING OUTLINE:
Jennifer Varzari's Presentation to the Board

INTRODUCTION:
    A. The importance of employee writing competence
I. Value of report writing training
    A. Efficiency
    B. Professional image

II. Problems with current system
    A. Inefficiency
        1) Lost time
        2) Repetition of training
    B. Employee dissatisfaction
        1) Survey results

III. Advantages of proposed system
    A. Employees
    B. Company
    C. Training staff

CONCLUSION
    A. Implementation plan

Delivery

Organization and preparation are, of course, very important in an oral presentation, but the presentation's effect on the audience will also be determined by the quality of your delivery. We all have been bored to near distraction by speakers whose points may have been interesting and even lively, but whose presence was unimpressive or distracting. In order to speak effectively, you need to take account of two major aspects of effective speech delivery — sight and sound. The key is to remember that everything in your speech should enhance and not detract from the overall impact. Often this simply means not calling attention to weak spots, but just as often it means taking special care to create definite strengths in your presentation. Your visual and vocal presence as you claim your place at the front of the room are the most important factors in successful delivery. Here are some of the elements of delivery that can make or break your speech.

Visual Presence: The Sight of Your Presentation

Many people don't realize how powerful a visual impression can be, and in an oral presentation it can be crucial. The speaker may be in front of an audience for anywhere from five minutes to two hours. The attention of audience members is concentrated on the speaker; listeners, without necessarily being completely aware that they are doing so, often take in every idiosyncrasy of the speaker's behaviour and every detail of appearance. (To test the accuracy of this point, ask yourself what small peculiarities you have noticed in your instructors — details of behaviour, expression, or dress. You'll be surprised how much you have noticed without necessarily being aware of it.) While you can't control everything about your appearance as a speaker, there are some details you can take care of consciously that will help you to present a confident and capable visual presence to your audience.

1. Dress for the Occasion Wear clothing that is appropriate to the audience and speaking situation. Don't expect to be taken seriously if you show up in a ragged pair of jeans. Even if your presentation is for a class, dress up a bit. Don't wear clothing you will feel uncomfortable in, however, and avoid pulling at or adjusting your collar, sleeves, waistband, or any other part of your costume. Remember, too, that unless you are speaking about fashion, conservative dress is usually preferable to flamboyant outfits. You want to be memorable for what you say, not for what you wear, and clothing that attracts attention away from your speech will undercut your purpose.

2. Stay Calm Approach the lectern calmly and pause briefly before beginning to speak, so as to give yourself a chance to catch your breath. Don't rush to the podium and immediately begin to speak. Give yourself time to relax and your audience a chance to get used to your presence. Likewise, don't rush away from the lectern just as your last words are leaving your mouth. Give the audience a few seconds to recognize that your speech has ended and allow for questions if it's appropriate to do so.

3. Use Appropriate Movements and Gestures to Show Emphasis You should appear calm and self-possessed. Stand straight, but not stiffly, keeping your body weight distributed evenly on both feet, using gestures to emphasize your points. As well, though you will likely feel vulnerable, don't lean on or hide behind the lectern.

You should not be afraid to move about comfortably in front of your audience, but don't fling your arms about wildly, fidget, or shift uncomfortably from one foot to the other. Such extravagant movements are likely to detract from your presentation (your audience may begin to count your unconscious gestures — Did you notice how many times she pushed her glasses up? Did you see him jiggling the change in his pockets?) If you watch carefully, you will notice that a skilled speaker neither avoids nor overuses gestures and movement.

Such a person knows how horribly dull it can be to watch someone who does not move about at all and how distracting unnecessary movements can be.

4. Maintain Eye Contact The ideal situation is to meet the eyes of every member of the audience at all times or at least to give this impression! Of course this is an impossible ideal, but if you keep it in mind, you will avoid fixing your eyes on a single spot and delivering your presentation to it. Don't, as some speakers do, stare at a point on the back wall (your audience will wonder what you are looking at so intently and turn to stare too) or look too long at your notes. Eye contact is one of the chief means by which a speaker can create a bond with listeners; it helps to maintain their interest. Don't be afraid to meet your listeners' eyes.

5. Employ Appropriate Facial Expressions People who are nervous sometimes betray their lack of confidence by giggling or grinning inappropriately, even when the speech is serious. Try to keep your expression consistent with the material you are delivering. It is perfectly correct to smile when it is appropriate, but you should appear to be in control of your facial expressions.

6. Use Visual Aids Of course, one of the most important of the visual factors of your presentation is your use of visual aids. When used effectively, these can make your presentation. Remember that they should be simple, readable, and well timed. More about these below.

Vocal Presence: The Sound of Your Presentation

Although in these days of television, sound may not be as powerful as appearance, it is still a very significant element in any oral presentation, since your voice is the primary medium through which your information is transmitted. As with visual presence, your vocal presence must be confident and steady; it should not detract from your presentation. There are some common flaws to which first-time speakers are subject, but with awareness and practice you can eliminate them from your presentation style.

1. Maintain a Reasonable Volume Most inexperienced speakers speak too softly to be heard. Without yelling, be sure your voice is loud enough to be heard by everyone, especially those in the back row. If you can, practise your speech in the room where it will be delivered, having a friend sit at the very back to determine whether you can be heard. If you absolutely cannot project your voice that far, try to arrange for a microphone. The members of your audience will not be attentive if they cannot hear you clearly.

2. Watch Your Pitch A common weakness is for speakers to raise their voices at the end of statements as if they were asking questions. In fact, this voice tic is a form of questioning — a plea for the audience's constant support and reassurance. Unfortunately, when used repeatedly, it can make you sound nervous and uncertain. State your points confidently, dropping your pitch at the end of each sentence.

3. Maintain a Pleasant Tone Voice quality is another factor that can influence a speaker's effectiveness. Try to cultivate a voice that is pleasant to listen to: a voice that is piercing or nasal, for example, may irritate a listener and prevent your message from getting through. As well, try to project some animation into your voice. A deadpan delivery in a monotonous voice tone is just as annoying to the audience as a grating, nasal tone.

4. Speak Clearly Enunciate your words carefully. Many speakers swallow the last half of their words or run over them too quickly, making them hard to listen to or to understand. Check your pronunciation too, particularly of words with which you are unfamiliar. Mispronunciations of important words will harm your credibility with your audience.

5. Speak Slowly Enough Although you don't want to pause for too long between words, far more speakers are inclined to speak too quickly than too slowly. Don't rush through your material. Your audience will appreciate a brief pause here and there to allow them time to grasp your points.

6. Avoid Fillers or Speech Tags Don't say **UM**! (Or *okay, like, you know,* or *really*.) These can be so distracting that an audience may actually begin to count them (Did you know she said "um" thirty-seven times in ten minutes?) and thus lose the thread of your speech. Don't be afraid to simply pause if you need a few seconds to collect your thoughts; you need not make sounds all the time. If you find that you tend to use fillers when you give a speech, practise eliminating them in your ordinary speech. Consciously allow yourself to pause and take a breath instead of saying "um." If you can't always hear it in your own speech, ask your family and friends to gently alert you when they hear you saying the offending sound. It takes practice, but it is possible to eliminate fillers almost entirely from your speech.

7. Avoid Any Obvious Grammatical Errors, Profanity, Slang, or Inappropriate Technical Jargon Audiences should be intrigued by your presentation, not put off by it. Slang and profanity are never appropriate, and professional jargon should be avoided unless the audience is made up of people from the same profession. Remember that your most important task is to communicate your ideas to your audience. You cannot do this if your language is inappropriate.

Visual Aids in Oral Presentations

The impact you make on your audience can be enhanced by the effective use of visual aids. People do learn more easily and remember better when they are shown rather than told something. Visual aids are one of the most effective means of demonstrating a point to your audience. Even a large chart or overhead slide with your main points displayed for the listeners will help to fix your points firmly in their minds. Further, visual aids will not only help make your presentation clearer to the audience, but also will serve as an aid to your own memory. There are several different kinds of visual aids that you can use.

1. If you are discussing an object (such as the toys in my example above), bring it with you if it is large enough to be seen and small enough to be carried around. Having the actual object with you will help to attract and hold your audience's attention during your speech.
2. If you can't bring the object itself because of size or unmanageability, you may wish to provide a scale model, for example, a small version of the CN Tower or a large-scale model of the DNA molecule. A scale model will assist your audience in visualizing what you are talking about and make your presentation easier to follow.
3. If the object is impossible to bring and no model is available, other visuals such as pictures, drawings, or sketches may be used effectively.
4. Charts or graphs, large, simple, and colourful, can also support the speaker.
5. You may even use a chalkboard or a flip chart while you speak.
6. Films or videos, slides, and overhead or computer projections may also be useful, but you must be careful not to let them dominate your speech.
7. If your speech discusses how to do something or how something is done, demonstrate the process step by step, using real objects, models, clear diagrams, or a video wherever possible.
8. Avoid using live animals as visual aids, even if your topic involves them. They typically become nervous and uncontrollable in the unfamiliar setting, and will almost certainly undercut the speech.

Guidelines for the Use of Visual Aids

1. Decide on the type of visual aid you will employ (model, demonstration, chart, computer graphics, drawing, photograph, list of main points, etc.) and prepare it in advance. If you are using a chalkboard, you may wish to write most of your material before beginning your speech.
2. Whatever visual aids you choose, be sure that they are clear and understandable enough to be easily followed by your audience. Complex or overly detailed visuals will do nothing to clarify the information you are presenting and may just confuse your audience. Computer programs, such as PowerPoint, can help you generate professional-quality illustrations and charts for your presentation. Attractive visuals can enhance your presentation if they are used effectively. However, whether your visuals are prepared manually or are computer-generated, you should be careful not to overdo the number or variety of visuals in a short speech. Overly complex or detailed visuals may actually harm your speech by distracting the audience from the content of your message.
3. Your visuals should be large enough to be seen by your audience. A 3" × 5" photo from your album may be interesting to you, but is unlikely to be of any

value to your audience members who cannot see it from their seats. It may seem that the solution is to pass the object around during the speech, but this is not a good idea since it is difficult to keep your audience's attention while you pass around small photos or models. You will want to keep their eyes and attention fixed on you.

4. Show your visual aids while you speak about them (believe it or not, some people forget to show their carefully prepared charts, drawings, or models at the appropriate moment because of nervousness or poor planning) and be sure to speak about them once you have displayed them. Nervous or inexperienced speakers sometimes display very intriguing-looking visuals and forget completely to refer to them during the presentation. Your visuals should clearly connect to your speech so that the audience is not preoccupied with puzzling out their meaning, but they should not substitute for a clearly communicated verbal message. Neither let your visuals take the place of your words nor assume that they speak for themselves.

5. Visual aids should be used sparingly — don't overwhelm your audience with so much visual material that your presentation is lost. Remember that these are aids to your presentation and should not substitute for an effective presentation. The speaker remains the focal point in an oral presentation and all visual aids should enhance that presentation. Too much visual material can detract from your presentation, and visual aids cannot by themselves serve as a substitute for an effective presentation.

6. While showing your visuals, remember to speak to the audience and not to the picture or chart you are discussing. Avoid turning your back to your audience as you speak so as to maintain your relationship with the audience at all times through your speech. Be especially careful of this point if you are using a chalkboard or flow chart as you speak.

7. Practise using the visual aid when you practise delivery of your presentation.

8. Be sure to check the accuracy of any posters or charts that will be displayed during your speech. Mistakes in arithmetic or spelling or incorrect facts and details can destroy your credibility and distract the audience from your message. I have seen numerous examples of otherwise impressive visuals that undercut the speaker's message because of a glaring mistake in spelling or arithmetic.

The Importance of Practice

Once you have organized your presentation and selected and prepared your visual aids, the next step is to practise your delivery. If you can, set up conditions as close as possible to those in which you will be speaking. Have a friend or someone else you trust listen to your presentation and give you honest feedback. If you have access to a video camera, have your presentation taped and then watch it for ways to improve. You cannot do a really good presentation without practice.

Actually deliver your presentation several times, out loud, to master your timing, your command of your material, your delivery, and your use of visual aids. You will have enough to worry about as you step up to speak, without worrying about your command of the material. You will feel much less nervous if you are well prepared, and can concentrate on projecting a positive, confident image. Practise delivering your speech out loud until speaking about this topic is as natural to you as breathing, but stop before you begin to memorize particular turns of phrase. Your audience will be able to spot a memorized presentation, and the quality of your speech will suffer for it.

In addition to improving your delivery, practice will also tell you whether your presentation fits the time you've been allowed. Think about how much time you have: a short time limit means you'll have to be selective about the details you include. On the other hand, you will need to make sure that you have enough material to fill the time you've been given. As I write this, I have just awarded the first failing grade to a five-minute speech assignment in my communications class. The time came in at two minutes and twenty-five seconds. The speaker had done practically no research and had chosen a poor topic. Don't let this happen to you. Practise your delivery, to be sure you have estimated correctly how long your presentation will take. You don't want to be in the uncomfortable situation of running out of material, or of being cut off because your speech is too long. If your speech is running long, cut some material out. If it's not long enough, you will need to develop your points with further research. Don't wait until the morning of your speech to find out that you didn't prepare properly — practise in enough time to make any adjustments that are needed.

When you are practising, *do not write out your presentation in full*. If you do this, you will have a tendency to read it during practice, or to memorize it, either of which will deaden your delivery and almost certainly bore your audience. Always practise speaking from the single notecard that you intend to use in the final speaking situation; by the time of the presentation it will be familiar to you and will serve as an additional aid to memory, resulting in a much smoother delivery. Avoid the temptation to make a brand new card as the last step in your preparation. Use the card you have practised with, even if it's beginning to look crumpled. When you get up to speak, you'll find that the familiarity of your practice card will make it easier for you to remember your points and to recover your place if you should falter.

weblinks

Business Presenters' Home Page
http://www.busicom.com/

The Ten Commandments of Client Presentations
http://www1.tagonline.com/~strategy/tencommpres.html

The Key Steps to an Effective Presentation
http://www.access.digex.net/~nuance/keystep1.html

Good Presentations: Hints and Tips
http://www.csun.edu/~vcecn006/hintspre.htm

points to remember

In summary, an oral presentation needs as much care and attention in its organization and preparation as a written report. Here, briefly, are the things to remember when getting ready for a presentation.

1. If you can, choose a topic or aspect of a topic that you are interested in and familiar with; in business you will be speaking about some aspect of your work.

2. Focus your topic to suit your audience, according to their needs, their expectations, and their prior knowledge.

3. Tailor your topic and your approach to the purpose and the setting of the presentation.

4. Prepare your topic so you can cover it adequately in the time you have been allotted for speaking.

5. Select and prepare at least one appropriate visual aid.

6. Practise your delivery, practise your use of visuals, practise your timing!

7. Remember that every element in your presentation should support, and not detract from, your presentation. Avoid inappropriate gestures, mannerisms, or visual items that will distract your audience from your message.

Whether you are presenting your report orally or in writing, you must prepare thoroughly and organize carefully.

sharpening your skills

SECTION A: WARM-UP EXERCISES

Your instructor may wish to use one or more of the following exercises to help you overcome stage fright and gain confidence.

1. Introduce yourself to the class. In a brief impromptu speech, present the following information to the class: My name is _____. My goal for this

course is _____. My biggest concern about public speaking is _____. After everyone in the class has presented, discuss the various concerns that have been raised. How realistic are the fears that people identified? Does there seem to be any pattern to them?

2. Introduce a classmate to the class. Pair up with someone in your class whom you don't already know well and spend a few minutes getting to know that person. Each of you should provide the other with enough information so that you can introduce your partner to the rest of the class in a brief (two-minute) impromptu presentation. Some sample questions might include:

   a. Where were you born? How many brothers/sisters do you have?

   b. What do you think will be the most challenging or difficult thing for you in this class?

   c. How would you most like this group to remember you as a speaker?

   d. What do you most look forward to about giving a speech? What do you most fear about it?

3. Public speaking is just like _____. Take a few minutes to make up a simile that expresses your main concern about public speaking, and present it to the class in a brief impromptu presentation. Briefly explain why you have chosen the comparison you have used. (For example, you might say something like "Giving a speech is like leaping off a cliff in the dark, because..." or "Public speaking is like a trip to the dentist, because...").

SECTION B: PUBLIC SPEAKING ASSIGNMENTS

1. Prepare a briefing on **one** of the following topics, making sure it is no more than ten minutes long and employing at least one visual aid.

   a. Proposal for in-house magazine (see pages 123–124).

   b. Proposal for training workshop in report writing (see pages 107–121).

   c. Your research into your communications program as offered at other institutions (see page 122).

   d. Your research into appropriate charities for a corporate donation (see page 89).

   e. Your research into a topical issue in communication (see pages 124–125).

2. Prepare a ten-minute presentation for your classmates, employing at least one visual aid, in which you provide them with tips on **one** of the following.

   a. Incorporating visual data into a report presentation (briefing or written format).

   b. Applying report writing organization to a specific report situation.

   c. Conducting library research (using print and electronic sources) for a report on any topic (identify a specific topic and show samples).

    d. Distinguishing between a proposal and an ordinary business report in purpose and organization.

    e. Writing a self-evaluation report.

    f. Organizing and presenting a briefing.

3. Choose a topic that you are interested in and knowledgeable about, and prepare a five-minute presentation for your classmates, employing at least one appropriate visual aid and providing some information that your audience is not likely to know already.

4. Prepare a five-minute persuasive speech in which you advocate that your audience read a book or magazine you have read, participate in an activity or hobby you enjoy, join a club to which you belong, or try a product, tool, or study method that you have found useful. Be sure to focus on your purpose (moving your audience to the requested action) and explain the benefits to the audience of doing what you suggest.

online exercises

1. Many people find public speaking very frightening, but there are steps you can take to minimize your fears. Travel to the Cosnett Associates' "Presentation Laboratory" (http://salesdoctors.com/cosnett/index.htm) on the *Salesdoctors* magazine web site, where you will find two postings dealing with presentation anxiety. What strategies do the authors recommend for dealing with the fear of public speaking? Which ones do you think will be most useful for you? Prepare to discuss these suggestions with the rest of the class.

2. Breathing properly can help you to speak with more ease and confidence, but how do you go about practising to breathe? Get some advice on "Proper Breathing for Powerful Speech" from broadcaster and public speaking consultant Steve Ryan. You will find his article at http://salesdoctors. com/ryan/ryan03.htm. After reading the article carefully, practise the breathing exercises Ryan recommends (you will probably want to do this at home!). Discuss your experiences with the rest of the class.

3. One of the most powerful tools you have as a speaker is your visual presence, an element that can be enhanced by effective visual aids. You will find some helpful advice on "Preparing Slides," part of the "Giving a Talk" web site prepared by Frank Kschischang, a professor of Electrical and Computer Engineering at the University of Toronto. Locate Dr. Kschischang's advice at http://www.comm.toronto.edu/~frank/nobots/guide/guide3.html. What is the most important single quality of an effective visual aid? Why?

The Job Package

- To learn the types of résumés, the principles of résumé format, and what to include in your résumé.
- To learn what is included in a letter of application and a letter of recommendation.
- To practise completing an application form.
- To become familiar with typical job interview situations and questions.

As your first step from school into the real world of business or careers, the job application package may well be the most important business writing you will do in college. When you are competing for your first career position in a tough job market, everything depends on the impression your application makes, so it must be as professional — and effective — as possible.

Like all other business communication, the job application has a clear, specific purpose. In it (perhaps more than in any other kind of business writing), you must recognize and respond to the reader's needs. The job application is really a kind of sales document; the product you are selling is your own suitability for a position in the employer's company. You must focus not simply on what you have done or what *you* consider most important, but on what your prospective *employer* wants, expects, or needs to hear, and you must tailor your presentation to suit the job you're applying for. You can figure out what the employer is interested in by taking time to read the job advertisement carefully. You can then use that knowledge to shape your application so that you emphasize the experience and skills that the employer will find relevant.

In writing an application, you normally will prepare a résumé and a letter of application, and often you will be required to complete an application form supplied to you by the employer. As well, you will no doubt have someone write a letter of recommendation on your behalf, so it's important to know what such a letter should contain.

The Résumé

A résumé is a kind of biographical summary that you prepare for an employer. It outlines the information he or she would likely want or need to know regarding your suitability for a job. Think of a résumé as "you" on paper — or at least, the professional "you" — and keep in mind that you want to make the best possible impression. Remember that the résumé and application are the first step in establishing a professional relationship with your prospective employer. In a résumé, even more than anywhere else, all the virtues of business writing are important: understanding your reader and your purpose, and applying the Six C's of business writing — clarity, correctness, conciseness, completeness, coherence, and courtesy.

Visual impact (layout) also makes a big difference as to how you will be perceived. A pleasing balance between white space and print is important; a résumé should display its important information without crowding or obscuring any part. As you have already discovered, effective layout actually assists in communicating your information — it's part of your organization. As you recall from Chapter 3, another feature of an attractive and readable layout is the font you choose. Since readability is especially important in an application, you will most likely want to choose a font that is easy on the eye. In general, a serif font (such as Times) is easier to read than a sanserif font (such as Helvetica), a script-style font, or a gothic font. Choose a serif font for your résumé, and use the same font for your letter of application so that the two will be visually unified. The résumé introduces you to the prospective employer and should make that employer want to speak with you. That is its only function, and you will be called for an interview only if it fulfils this purpose effectively. For this reason, your résumé should make a very good impression.

Types of Résumé

There are three main types of résumé: the *functional* (or skills-oriented), the *chronological*, and the *analytical* (or crossover). The functional résumé is sometimes recommended for people who have little formal education or experience; it emphasizes employable skills instead of positions held or training completed, so it may obscure gaps in an employment or education history.

However, there are a couple of problems with this kind of résumé. First, it contains no dates, names, or locations that can be verified, so its claims appear unsubstantiated. Second, because it is commonly used when the applicant's background is sketchy, what is worse is that employers may assume that a functional résumé is being used to cover up undesirable information and may become suspicious about what is left unsaid. Thus, while this format may serve the writer's needs — to make a lack of experience or gaps in work history less obvious — it doesn't usually provide the details an employer needs to make an informed assessment. As a result, because it does not effectively serve the needs of the reader, this kind of résumé may be set aside without much consideration. A sample functional résumé is included in this chapter as an illustration.

The chronological résumé is more widely used and generally accepted than the functional: it presents your training and experience chronologically, always beginning with the most recent and working backwards. The information is organized under fairly standard headings and focuses on facts and details, without elaboration or interpretation. Employers usually prefer this chronological organization over the functional format because it shows the applicant's relevant experience and provides details of dates and names that may be verified.

Because it accommodates the employer's expectations, the chronological format is usually a better choice than a strictly functional résumé. However, neither of these is perfect. The brief bare-facts outline provided by the chronological résumé alone may not be enough to convince a prospective employer to take a closer look at the applicant. The competition for good jobs is always intense, and many employers want more of a "sense" of the applicant before the interview. For this reason, the analytical or crossover résumé (which is a blend of the chronological and functional approaches) is frequently a better choice. Because it combines the strengths of both forms, the analytical résumé accommodates both the employer's needs and the applicant's background. This is the résumé form you will learn in this chapter.

Parts of the Résumé

Many people assume that a résumé should simply list every job-related experience you have ever had, no matter what it is, but as you know by now, this is not enough. A résumé, like other forms of business writing, is a form of communication with a very specific purpose. It is effective only if it gets you an interview, and since it is the *reader's* needs that will determine who is interviewed, it is very important that the résumé be designed and focused to meet those needs. Although this document, like most business forms, does contain standard sections, the contents of your résumé are to some extent flexible, and what you choose to include will depend partly on your experience and the position you are seeking. All résumés should include sections on personal information, education, employment, and skills, with experience and education arranged in reverse chronological order (that is, starting with the most recent and working backwards in time). A few additional categories, discussed below, may be useful if they are relevant to your background and to the position you are applying for. The following is a list of categories usually included on a résumé.

Personal Information

This section includes your name, your address, and a phone number where you may be reached. You may also wish to include your e-mail address and a web site address if you have one. Do not include an e-mail or web site address that will soon be defunct, however; for instance, if your e-mail and web site are college accounts that will become defunct after you graduate, do not invite your prospective employer to contact you this way if you are close to graduation. You will notice from the recommended examples that this information should be displayed in an eye-catching position on the first page. You may wish to use a desktop publishing program to design an eye-catching personal letterhead to use as the first page of your résumé document. This type of letterhead can be very effective if well designed, but you should avoid cutesy graphics and combined effects such as boldfacing, italics, block capitals, and underlining. A slightly conservative effect is more professional than one that displays a whole range of visual effects in a single heading. Information such as age, height, weight, social insurance number, state of health, marital status, and citizenship are no longer considered appropriate for a résumé, though in the past they were commonly included and are still occasionally recommended by people who are working with outdated information. If, despite these guidelines, you wish to include such information, place it near the end of your résumé — don't take up valuable space on the front page. You definitely should not include such sensitive information as religious affiliations, and racial or cultural origin, unless, of course, they have some direct bearing on the job for which you're applying. As a general guideline, leave out any personal information that has no bearing on your ability to perform the job or that may invite prejudice; if a piece of information is not a strength, don't put it into your résumé.

Career Objective

The career objective statement, a phrase or sentence that states your career aspirations, is an optional part of a résumé. If your cover (application) letter is well focused and your experience is directly related to the job you're seeking, you may want to leave out the career objective, since in that case it would be redundant. Recent graduates of a college program that has specifically trained them for the position they seek may find it unnecessary. However, a career objective statement can be useful if your experience is diverse; an accurate, well-worded career objective can focus your background. Here are some instances in which a career objective statement can prove useful.

- If you are aiming at a *specific* position or type of position and are not interested in any other kind of work, you may wish to focus on this aim in your career objective.
- If you have spent some time out of the workforce — to raise a family or to travel, for example — a career objective can explain the gap in your employment history.

- If you are changing careers, this statement can serve as a link between your aspirations and your previous experience.

If you decide to use a career objective statement, you must be clear and specific; avoid such statements as "I am seeking a challenging position that will make use of my skills and offer room for advancement." Can you think of any candidate in any job competition for whom this would *not* be true? Such a vague statement takes up room without adding anything valuable to your résumé and is better left out.

Education

For a student or a recent graduate, this section usually comes immediately after the personal information, because it is your most recent, and likely most relevant, experience. Once you have been working in the field for a year or two, you will likely want to place your employment history before education on your résumé, because by then it will have become your most recent and most relevant experience.

Your educational history should include the following information, in reverse chronological order: dates attended; name and location of institution; diploma, certificate, or degree obtained; and some brief detail about your particular program of study. Mention grades only if they are outstanding.

List everything back to (and perhaps including) high school, but no further. If you have taken more than one diploma or degree following high school, or if you have been working for a period longer than two years, consider leaving out even high school. Be selective: remember that the employer needs to know only what is relevant and useful in making the decision to interview you.

Employment History

Beginning with your most recent position, in reverse chronological order state dates, place of employment, job title, and duties. Provide a quick outline of the job, emphasizing any skills you could bring to the new position. Again, always be forward-looking, focusing on the skills that will be needed in the job you want rather than on those demanded by your old job. You may cluster similar or related jobs in a single entry if you have had a series of them, or even delete some less important or irrelevant jobs. For example, if I have worked as a sales clerk in three different clothing stores over a period of two years, I may present this work as a single entry because all three positions were similar. I should list the dates from the point I began my first position until I left my last position, then provide the job title (for example, Sales Personnel) and the names of all three employers. This strategy can save valuable space on the résumé if you have a lot of information to include, and is demonstrated on the résumés of Gabe Praskach and Nel Nyhof, later in this chapter. In all cases, emphasize skills or knowledge that are relevant to the job you seek.

Areas of Ability, Areas of Expertise, Special Skills, or Employable Skills

In this useful section you have an opportunity to emphasize your relevant skills, regardless of your past experience. Employers want to know not only that they are hiring someone with the minimum qualifications, but also that this person is the best choice from among applicants with similar training or experience. This part of your résumé may give you the edge over other applicants of similar background. You should take full advantage of this chance to "sell" your unique combination of skills, but make sure this section of your résumé is targeted to the job you seek.

It's a good idea to cluster your skills under subheadings of some type, as demonstrated in the sample résumés that follow. You will notice a variety in the ways that the skills are clustered and presented in the samples; each person has selected a method that shows his or her skills to best advantage and that best suits the job sought. Like the writers of the sample résumés, you should choose the format that displays your skills and experience most effectively. Though you may place your skills section at the beginning of your résumé, most people prefer to put it at the end where it supports the information given in the rest of the résumé. The prospective employer then comes on it after reading the details of your employment and education history.

Skills are generalized abilities that may be transferred with relative ease from one situation to another, and there are three main areas in which any employer is interested: specialized, practical, and interpersonal. These classifications will give you an idea where to start when grouping your own skills. Claim for yourself only those skills that you can demonstrate. As you list your skills, be sure you can provide an example of a situation in which you demonstrated each one. An employer may ask you for such an example in an interview.

1. Specialized Nearly all jobs require some type of specialized skills necessary to the efficient performance of the job duties. These might be highly technical, such as operation of equipment (computers or business machines, for instance), knowledge of specific procedures (such as drafting, surveying, or bookkeeping), mastery of certain kinds of software packages (database, spreadsheet, web design, desktop publishing), or any other specialized ability (public presentation, training skills). Do you have the skills required by the job you are applying for? You should state them clearly on your résumé.

2. Practical General work-related skills can also set you apart from others with similar education or experience. Although all the applicants for a given position may be trained in the field, not all are equally competent. Employers want to be assured not only that you can do what the job requires, but that you can do it efficiently and well. In this category you might include such qualities as punctuality, conscientiousness, organizational ability, problem-solving skills, ability to work to deadlines, and efficiency. These qualities emphasize how you handle tasks in the workplace. Again, be sure you can think of a specific example from your past experience that illustrates this skill if you are asked for one in an interview.

3. Interpersonal The third area of concern for an employer is how well you will get along with your customers, clients, and co-workers. Interpersonal skills include such abilities as tact, diplomacy, leadership, motivational skills, cooperation, and teaching ability. Essentially these skills are concerned with how well you handle your professional relationships with people. Employers do not want sarcastic or complaining people to join their staffs. As with the previous categories, be prepared to provide evidence of your effective interpersonal skills if called upon to do so.

4. Artistic Skills If they are relevant to your line of work, you may wish to include such abilities as drawing, design, painting, and photography. If you will need to demonstrate your skills in these areas, you should prepare a portfolio of your work to bring with you to the interview. Your instructors in art and design courses can show you how to do this.

References

Prepare a list of two or three names of people who are willing to provide references for you. Opinion is mixed about whether you should include these references with your résumé. Some employers I have spoken with are suspicious of an applicant who does not automatically volunteer references, even when he or she promises to supply names "upon request." Others say they are not concerned about receiving the list of references until after the first interview is completed, because they normally do not contact references until that time, and then only if the candidate is to be offered a job. Still others put no stock in solicited references at all.

In light of such divided opinion, what should you do? All of the employers I spoke with agreed that providing references will never hurt your chances, whereas *not* providing them may do so. Thus, it may be safest to provide them if you can.

References should be obtained from former employers or others acquainted with your work, or former teachers. Letters or testimonials from friends, family, or fellow students are not appropriate for a job search. Personal references are not very useful to employers, unless a character reference is specifically requested. You will find more information on references in the section on letters of recommendation (page 190).

These are the common and essential sections of every résumé; however, there are some other useful categories that you may want or need to include in your résumé. Select any of these that seem appropriate for the job you seek, displaying your unique experience to best advantage. If none seem relevant to your experience or necessary for the job, you can certainly leave them out. If you have an accomplishment or experience that is relevant to your job search, but does not fit into any of the listed categories, you can invent your own heading. The résumé is a flexible instrument that you should structure according to your own individual needs and the demands of the job you seek.

Awards

In this section, list in reverse chronological order any awards received in school activities, giving dates, institutions, and titles of awards. If you have never won any such awards, leave out the whole category. If your awards are not school-related, you may want to place them in another category entitled "Achievements" or "Accomplishments" (see below).

Extracurricular Activities

This category is useful only for students or recent graduates; once you have been working for two or more years, the relevance of this information will fade. List here any *significant* contributions to school-related activities; membership in academic or athletic clubs or teams, participation in student council, yearbook, or newspaper activities, and so on. If you did not participate significantly in such events or organizations, leave this category out. College experiences of this nature have greater longevity on a résumé than high school ones; as a general guideline, delete this section if it describes high school experience more than three years old or college experience more than six years old, unless your achievements are especially outstanding or relevant to the job you seek, and have not been replaced by anything else.

Additional Courses or Training

Use this category to list courses or certification that are outside of your main education but that have relevance to the job you seek. Perhaps you are formally trained as a mechanic, but have also taken some night school courses in accounting or business management. Perhaps you are a journalist, but have training in computer programming, or a secretary with expertise in web design. Perhaps you have taken pilot's training, a CPR course, or training to teach swimming or music. If so, include this information on your résumé. You may not wish to include general interest courses unless they are in some way relevant to your job search. Once again, list in reverse chronological order the dates, institutions, and names of the courses.

Volunteer Work

If you have held several volunteer positions and feel that they warrant consideration, you can create a separate category for them; if they are few (and relevant) you might want to include them under your employment history instead. (However, don't include them twice on the same résumé!) If you decide to include such a category, list in reverse chronological order any positions where you would, under other circumstances, have been paid for your work. List volunteer positions only if they contribute meaningfully to your résumé.

Community Service

Include membership in service clubs, participation in community events, or service in civic positions, if these contribute meaningfully to your résumé. It is usually considered best to leave out organizations of a strictly religious nature, unless the job you're seeking is religiously oriented. List dates, name, and location of organization, position title, and any relevant duties. If the organizations to which you belong are professional associations and are not unions (the International Association of Business Communicators, the Canadian Communication Association, and the National [American] Communication Association are some examples), you can retitle this category "Professional Service" rather than "Community Service."

Achievements or Accomplishments

Use this category to feature any relevant accomplishment not covered in any previous section. This section includes awards other than scholastic ones (for instance, Citizen of the Year), certification of some form (pilot's licence or swimming instructor's certificate), publication of a book or article, or a special achievement in your work. Once again, in reverse chronological order, include the date, the name and location of the institution, agency, or publisher, and the nature of the certificate, award, or publication. List such achievements only if they help qualify you for the job you seek, and be sure to title the section appropriately.

Layout

The appearance of the résumé — its visual appeal — is almost as important as its content. The résumé is seen before you are, and it should make a positive impression. Just as you wouldn't dream of going to an interview with a smudge on your face or an unkempt appearance, you should never introduce yourself to a prospective employer with an untidy or unattractive résumé. Few employers will be interested enough to interview an applicant whose résumé is poorly constructed; to them a messy résumé suggests a lazy or unmotivated individual — not, of course, the kind of person they want to hire!

An effective layout builds visual appeal by creating a pleasing balance between white space and printed elements, with reasonable margins on all sides (1" at top, bottom, and both sides is standard). A consistent format also lends a professional appearance, as it does to all business communication: major headings should begin at the left margin, lining up neatly beneath one another. They should all be presented in the same format (all capitalized, for example, or all underlined). Subcategories should be indented so that they too line up consistently throughout the résumé, and they should also be consistently treated (all italicized, for example). Use consistent spacing between sections: for example, you might skip one line between subsections and two lines between major categories. This consistency is not only attractive, but, because the layout is also part of your organization, it actually helps the reader to make sense of the information you are presenting.

Use capital letters, underlining, or boldfacing to set apart important details, but use these features consistently and sparingly. In general, you should not combine underlining with capital letters or with boldfaced or italicized type. Other combinations (boldfacing and block capitals, italics and boldfacing, italics and block capitals) are permissible, though these too should be used sparingly and consistently to help your reader make sense of the information on the résumé. A little of each goes a long way and overuse will destroy the effectiveness of these visual devices. For example, if too much of the résumé is printed in capital letters, it is not only harder to read, but important information no longer stands out. If you have ever tried to read a textbook that someone has attacked overzealously with a highlight pen, you know how quickly any form of visual device loses its effect when overused.

In general, it is also not good practice to combine several different fonts in a single document, and you should especially avoid fonts that are difficult to read — sanserif, gothic, or script fonts are typically harder on the eye than a simple serif font and therefore are not so desirable in a résumé or application letter. Finally, be sure to choose a font in a readable size — 10- or 12-point type may take up more space, but is much easier for the reader to process visually. It is in your interest to design your résumé so that it's easy for the reader to find the information she needs to make a decision.

It should go without saying that visual appeal also means using a good quality printer, with sufficient toner or ink to produce sharp, clear type. Don't send out a résumé with faint print, because if the print is too pale, the employer may simply discard the whole thing rather than struggle to read it. You should also send an original résumé, tailored to the job, with every application you submit. Any photocopies you do provide should be perfectly clean.

There are nearly as many varieties of résumé layout as there are people to give advice, but some are better than others. How can you tell a good layout from one that is not so good? A good résumé format is easy to scan for important information and should be appealing to look at. Here are some characteristics of an effective résumé format. The examples that follow meet these criteria.

1. It maintains consistent margins and uses white space effectively. Nothing is crowded or cramped, and everything is readable.
2. The main items of information are easily available to the eye, and the reader can skim the résumé quickly to get the gist of the applicant's work history without having to read every detail (though necessary details are given too, of course).
3. It is professional-looking, but also flexible enough to be arranged to suit an individual applicant.

Never underestimate the importance of an attractive layout; your business communication instructor may be willing to struggle to read your résumé to the end, but an employer does not have to do so. In fact, many employers can cut down a pile of résumés from two hundred to a short list of twenty by immediately discarding unattractive résumés — without even reading them.

Remember that, at least initially, the reader of your résumé is seeking reasons to *eliminate* your application, not reasons to keep it.

The figures below illustrate the use of white space in the résumé layout. All of the samples of effective résumés use the principles of effective layout. One way to check the effectiveness of a layout is to hold the résumé away from you. A good layout is appealing to look at even if it is too far away for you to read the print, because the print and white space are balanced and the important information stands out from the rest of the material on the page. Study Figures 7.1A and 7.1B and take a critical look at some of the résumé examples that follow to see what makes an effective layout and what looks unattractive.

weblinks

Work Search
http://www.golden.net/~archeus/worksrch.htm

Electronic Résumés and Resources
http://www.eresumes.com/

Résumé Doctor Tutorial
http://www1.mhv.net/~acorn/Bad.html

Employment Opportunities and Job Resources on the Internet
http://www.dbm.com/jobguide/

points to remember

1. Résumés should *always* be word-processed (or, if you do not have access to a computer, at least typewritten). Choose a laser printer or an inkjet printer with sufficient toner or ink to produce a dark, sharp image. Dot matrix printers do not provide a sufficiently clear print for your résumé.

2. Always use good-quality paper, preferably white. A paper that has a textured surface is especially impressive. You should as a general rule avoid coloured paper, except possibly an ivory or grey; even pastels can seem garish in a stack of white or off-white résumés. Strong colours should certainly be avoided, since they will call attention to themselves at the expense of the information on your résumé. Most employers are conservative and cautious in their hiring practices and are more likely to be impressed by a high-quality, well-organized résumé than by a brightly coloured one. Make your résumé stand out for its quality and save your flamboyance for after you've got the job.

f i g u r e   7 . 1 A   This sample shows a common résumé format, using only two main margins. Though it is neatly laid out, its lack of variety and large unbroken blocks of print draw the eye downward rather than into the block, making it difficult to scan the page easily. As a result, important information may be missed.

NAME:	GABRIEL A. PRASKACH
HOME ADDRESS:	2938 West Street Vancouver, B.C. V8H 3D4
TELEPHONE:	(604) 546 7890
BIRTHDATE:	October 4, 1969
EDUCATION:	
Sept. 1998–Dec. 1998	Completed the first half of the Journalism Print Program with advanced standing at West Coast College, 299 Valley Dr., Burnaby, B.C., V5G 4R5. Courses of study included: public relations with the emphasis on promoting corporate images, photography and the use of black and white film, studied the day-to-day operations of municipal government and their role, newspaper layouts and graphics and journalism 3&4 with the emphasis on municipal government, courtroom and local news reporting and headline writing.
Sept. 1996–May 1998	Graduate of the two-year Radio Broadcasting Program at Beothuk College, Murgatroyd Street, P.O. Box 1234, Kamloops, B.C., V6N 4R7. Courses of study included radio announcing, writing effective radio copy, grammar and English composition, writing and producing radio drama, sportscasting news reporting and interviewing and radio documentary production and media law.
WORK EXPERIENCE:	
Dec. 1998–Present	Full-time Radio Announcer at 1370 CKJU, 75 Speedmore Ave., Burnaby, B.C., V8U 9J7. My duties included, producing and voicing radio commercials, doing live reports from the CKJU Van, running the automated music system for CDFG-FM, and operating and announcing CKJU's evening music program.

figure 7.1B This sample makes use of more varied margins and smaller print blocks. Important information stands out easily, especially if it is boldfaced or underlined.

GABRIEL A. PRASKACH

2938 West Street, Vancouver, BC V8H 3D4
(604) 546 7890

EMPLOYMENT

1998–Present	**Evening Announcer**

CKJU Radio 1370, Burnaby, BC

Duties: announce evening music program, produce and voice radio commercials, report live on location, run automated music system.

1992–98	**Disc Jockey**

CHBK 89.2 FM, Beothuk College, Kamloops, BC (1997–98)
Eddie's Lounge, Prince Edward Hotel, Burnaby, BC (1996)
"Sounds by Gabe" (Freelance) (1990–95)

Duties: announced; played music for dancing; took requests; ran light board and videos; played private social events; handled all musical and business duties.

1992–94	**Production Assistant**

Shaw Cable 8, Vancouver, BC

Duties: ran portable and studio cameras, studio lighting, special effects generator, and $3/4$" video recorder; worked as studio floor director; aided in production of regular weekly broadcast of District 10 High School Football.

EDUCATION

May 1998	**Radio Broadcasting Diploma**

Beothuk College, Kamloops, BC

Studied Radio Announcing (sports, news, interviews), Writing/Producing Radio Drama and Documentaries, Copywriting, English Composition, Public Speaking, and Media Law.

ADDITIONAL STUDY

1998	**Journalism Print Program**

West Coast College, Burnaby, BC

Studied Public Relations, Government Operations, Courtroom/Local News Reporting, Headline Writing, Photography, Layouts and Graphics. Completed half the program before taking a full-time position at CKJU.

1997	**Conversational French I & II**

West Coast College, Burnaby, BC

3. Prepare an original résumé for each job you apply for. Since each job is different, ideally you will want to tailor your résumé to each new position. However, if you are applying for a number of similar positions, you may find it more convenient and less expensive to use photocopies. If you must send a photocopied résumé, make sure it is as close as possible to original quality. Don't ever send a blurred or smudged photocopy to an employer.

4. Don't try to cram too much information onto one page. Some experts still steadfastly believe that résumés should not exceed one page; for the most part, however, this old-fashioned principle can impose unnecessary constraints on an applicant. In an attempt to adhere to this standard, some people sacrifice clarity and visual appeal to fit everything in, producing a crowded, unattractive page that is difficult to read. A busy employer may be more inclined to discard such a document than to take the time to muddle through it or strain to read a smaller than normal font. As people change careers with greater frequency and bring more complex and varied experience to the job search, expectations for length and content must evolve. Most people applying for a permanent position nowadays would have difficulty displaying their backgrounds attractively on a single page. In a highly competitive job market, you must sell yourself convincingly, and there just isn't room enough on one page to do this.

    One employer, for example, told me that he had recently rejected an applicant for a permanent position because she had not provided enough detail in her résumé. He said that if he could offer the applicant any advice about the résumé, it would have been, "Put some information into it!" A well laid-out, easy-to-skim résumé of two pages is, of course, preferable to a crowded, unreadable document of one page. You will want to keep your résumé from becoming too long, however; a new college graduate should be able to present a reasonable summary of education and experience in no more than two or three pages.

5. This may seem self-evident, but it bears repeating: a résumé should *display your strengths*, not call attention to your weaknesses. Apart from personal information, education, and experience, the résumé is a flexible instrument that can be shaped to fit your background. Use only the categories you require, retitling them or rearranging them to fit your experience and the job you're applying for. If you find that you have experience or training that does not fit the standard categories listed, invent your own and provide them with a suitable heading.

6. Remember that all dated information in every section of a résumé is always arranged in reverse chronological order, beginning with the most recent.

7. Keep your résumé current. Before computers and word processors were widely available, the job of updating your résumé was onerous because the entire document had to be reformatted and retyped with every change. Computer technology makes revision much easier and periodic updating

relatively painless. You should bring your résumé up to date every six months, even if you are not currently applying for work. Doing so will make the task easier when the time comes for you to seek a new job and will ensure that none of your achievements are overlooked. You should also keep hard copies of your résumé, just in case your computer files are damaged in some way.

Sample Résumés

In the following pages, you will find a series of résumés accompanied by brief critiques (Figures 7.2A to 7.6). The first résumé of each pair is weak and in need of improvement; the second is an improved version.

The first set belongs to Cornelia Nyhof. Look carefully at both versions and at the commentary for each; can you see any additional weaknesses that Nel could improve?

There are several problems with Cornelia Nyhof's first résumé (Figure 7.2A on pages 163–164). Like most strictly functional résumés, it makes a series of claims but provides no way for the employer to verify details. No names or locations are given, and the dates are too vague to be helpful. An employer is more likely to be put off than reassured by this sketchy history and will likely wonder what Nel is hiding.

This résumé was prepared for Nel by an employment agency. It could be more attractively presented and more clearly focused to the employer's needs. For example, Nel's unfocused list of skills should be edited toward the job she is applying for. In addition to its faults in presentation, the résumé also contains errors in spelling, grammar, and sentence structure which reflect badly on Nel, even though she didn't write the résumé herself. Nel was educated in Sydney, Nova Scotia, not Sidney, and her lists should be arranged in parallel grammatical construction (for instance, under "Retail," she should use verbs throughout: "Sold clothing, designed and prepared window...").

Nel's new résumé (Figure 7.2B on pages 165–166) is in analytical format, in the chronological order that employers prefer. The average employer will feel more comfortable about hiring her now; her background can be verified because she's given specific details that provide a basis for her claims. The career objective has been made much more specific and Nel has been selective about the skills she has emphasized, bringing them into line with the job she is seeking. The format is easier to read, with important information prominently displayed. Section headings are boldfaced to make them even more prominent.

Notice also that Nel's name appears to the left of centre on the first page, but to the right on the second page; this keeps her name in front of the employer reading the document and also places it in a dominant position on the page. If she wished, Nel could rearrange this résumé to put "Skills" first. However, such an arrangement risks being mistaken for a functional résumé.

CORNELIA NYHOF

1324 Main Street
Red Deer, Alberta
T4N 2D3

Phone 346 1234

CAREER OBJECTIVE

Seeking a position in a people-oriented environment in which my eagerness to learn and my energetic, responsible nature will be an asset.

EMPLOYABLE SKILLS

Retail
- sale of clothing
- designed and prepared window and counter displays
- controlled inventory
- priced items
- performed waitress duties

Organizational
- oriented and trained new staff
- organized clothing according to styles/sizes
- filed invoices and receipts

Communication
- adept at verbally communicating with people
- able to be persuasive
- assisted people identify personal choices
- helpful and cooperative fellow worker
- assisted in a promotional advertisement campaign

CORNELIA NYHOF

Environmental Activities
- worked on survey crew
- identified tree types and clusters
- determined density and type of trees required for lumber use and environmental beauty
- planted trees

WORK HISTORY

Jean Depot - 1999
Baddeck Lands and Forest - 1998
Ponderosa Steak House - 1997

HOBBIES AND COMMUNITY INVOLVEMENT

Interior design, cooking, sewing, Girl Guide, Air Cadet

EDUCATION

Grade 12 Sidney, Nova Scotia
Computer Programming - 30 hour course

CORNELIA DARLENE NYHOF

1324 Main Street
Red Deer, Alberta T4N 2D3
(403) 346 1234

OBJECTIVE: A permanent retail career position requiring excellent sales and organizational skills and eventually leading to management.

EMPLOYMENT:

1999–Present **Cashier/Sales Clerk**
Consumers Distributing/Fashions Fabric Ltd.; Red Deer, Alberta

<u>Duties</u>: serving customers, handling cash and credit transactions, keeping track of inventory, and making bank deposits. I also was able to do some window dressing and arrangement of creative displays.

1996–99 **Child Care Worker (In-Home)**
Sydney, Nova Scotia

<u>Duties</u>: care of a variety of children, including some with severe handicaps. I was responsible for all aspects of the children's care, including specialized medical treatments, and did light housekeeping as well.

1998 **Land Survey Crew (Summer)**
Lands and Forests; Baddeck, Nova Scotia

<u>Duties</u>: Under a Canada Works Project, I was one of four crew members who plotted and surveyed wooded areas to determine species counts.

EDUCATION:

1998 **High School Diploma**
Cape Breton Adult Vocational Training Centre; Sydney, Nova Scotia
Areas of study included Math, History, English, Geography, and
Science.

Cornelia Darlene Nyhof /2

CERTIFICATES:

1999   **Standard First Aid**
Canadian Red Cross; Red Deer, Alberta

1998   **Introductory Computer Programming Certificate**
University College of Cape Breton; Sydney, Nova Scotia

1994   **Food Handling Certificate**
Royal Canadian Air Cadets, Squadron #693

SKILLS:

Occupational
- handling cash
- creating displays
- inventory
- processing charge cards
- soft-selling
- knowledge of fashion trends
- computer literacy
- training staff

Personal
- honesty
- reliability
- conscientiousness
- neatness
- punctuality
- willingness to learn

Interpersonal
- sales ability
- tact/diplomacy
- cooperation
- sense of humour
- patience
- positive attitude

figure 7.3A WEAK RÉSUMÉ. What tips could you give Gabriel to improve the content and layout of his résumé?

NAME: GABRIEL A. PRASKACH

HOME ADDRESS: 2938 West Street
Vancouver, B.C.
V8H 3D4

TELEPHONE: (604) 546 7890

BIRTHDATE: October 4, 1969

EDUCATION:

Sept. 1998–Dec. 1998   Completed the first half of the Journalism Print Program with advanced standing at West Coast College, 299 Valley Dr., Burnaby, B.C., V5G 4R5. Courses of study included: public relations with the emphasis on promoting corporate images, photography and the use of black and white film, studied the day-to-day operations of municipal government and their role, newspaper layouts and graphics and journalism 3&4 with the emphasis on municipal government, courtroom and local news reporting and headline writing.

Sept. 1996–May 1998   Graduate of the two-year Radio Broadcasting Program at Beothuk College, Murgatroyd Street, P.O. Box 1234, Kamloops, B.C., V6N 4R7. Courses of study included radio announcing, writing effective radio copy, grammar and English composition, writing and producing radio drama, sportscasting news reporting and interviewing and radio documentary production and media law.

Sept. 1993–June 1997   Graduate of the Four-Year Program at Bishop Dell High School, 66 Folklore St., Vancouver, B.C., V1H 4H8.

WORK EXPERIENCE:

Dec. 1998–Present   Full-time Radio Announcer at 1370 CKJU, 75 Speedmore Ave., Burnaby, B.C., V8U 9J7. My duties included, producing and voicing radio commercials, doing live reports from the CKJU Van, running the automated music system for CDFG-FM, and operating and announcing CKJU's evening music program.

| figure 7.3A | WEAK RÉSUMÉ. (Continued) |

Sept. 1992–Present	Part-time service clerk at IGA Markets Ltd. Willow Mall, West Vancouver, B.C., V1H 3S8. My duties included, stocking shelves, building displays, assisting customers, bagging groceries and collecting shopping carts.
Sept. 1997–May 1998	Disc-jockey, copywriter, and news-caster at CHBK 89.2 FM Cable, Beothuk College, Kamloops B.C.
June 1996-July 1998	Disc-jockey at Eddie's Lounge at Prince Edward Hotel, 2 Windymere St., Burnaby, B.C., V1K 4E3.
June 1991–Sept 1991	Senior Camp Counselor at Camp Marital day camp, Vancouver CYO, 90 Stiltser St., Vancouver, B.C., V8N 1S2. My duties include the supervision and care of 15 twelve-year-old boys with one junior counsellor.
Sept. 1988–Aug 1992	Part-time receptionist at St. Joseph's Parish, 409 Blister Rd., Vancouver, B.C., V1H 2R4. My duties included, filing, answering the phone photocopying and other odd jobs.
May 1990–Sept. 1995	Freelance Disc-jockey for weddings, birthday parties and other social events at "Sounds by Gabe", 2938 West St., Vancouver, B.C., V8H 3D4.

ADDITIONAL EDUCATION:

I have obtained affirmation certificates from West Coast College for Conversational French Levels I & II and Data Processing Concepts.

TECHNICAL SKILLS:

From 1992–94, I was a volunteer production assistant in the programming dept. at the Burnaby office of Shaw Cable system Channel 8. During this time, I was trained in the use of portable and studio television cameras, Sony 3/4" video tape recorders, television studio lighting, a Sony special effects generator and as a studio floor director. I also aided in the production of many shows including the weekly co-producer and as an on-air commentator.

Because of my experience from the world of radio broadcasting, I am quite familiar with the setting-up and operating of various reel-to-reel tape machines, microphones, casette machines and public address systems.

figure 7.3A WEAK RÉSUMÉ. (Continued)

HOBBIES AND SPECIAL INTERESTS:

I enjoy reading science fiction and murder-mystery novels and listening to music because I have a rather large and comprehensive record collection. I also play clarinet and bass guitar.

VOLUNTEER WORK:

As I've already mentioned, I did two years at Channel 8 and while I was in high school I got involved with the organization Youth Across Canada with the Mentally Retarded as well as the St. Joseph's Children's Youth Organization.

REFERENCES:

Adam Marks	Leo Moroni
Production Manager	College Instructor
1370 CKJU	Beothuk College
75 Speedmore Ave.	Murgatroyd St., P.O. Box 1234
Burnaby, B.C.	Kamloops, B.C.
V8U 9J7	V6N 4R7
(604) 321 5678	(604) 987 5643

This is very disappointing résumé from someone who is actually extremely talented and good at what he does. The format is rather confusing and hard to read, and it contains irrelevant details and wordy, awkward sentences. Another major weakness in this résumé is its numerous errors and inconsistencies in spelling and punctuation, particularly since Gabe emphasizes that his education has included grammar and English composition. Even minor errors can detract from the impression that Gabe wants to make on a prospective employer; his failure to proofread leaves a negative impression and will likely result in his not being called for an interview. Since most of Gabe's work history and education is in some way related to broadcasting, he should be able to produce a much more focused résumé that will attract the employer's attention. He should de-emphasize or delete the irrelevant information to show how he has prepared himself specifically for a career in broadcasting. Notice also that his work experience, which is more recent than his education, should come first.

GABRIEL A. PRASKACH

2938 West Street, Vancouver, BC V8H 3D4

(604) 546 7890

EMPLOYMENT

1998–Present **Evening Announcer**

CKJU Radio 1370, Burnaby, BC

Duties: announce evening music program, produce and voice radio commercials, report live on location, run automated music system.

1992–98 **Disc Jockey**

CHBK 89.2 FM, Beothuk College, Kamloops, BC (1997–98)

Eddie's Lounge, Prince Edward Hotel, Burnaby, BC (1996)

"Sounds by Gabe" (Freelance) (1990–95)

Duties: announced; played music for dancing; took requests; ran light board and videos; played private social events; handled all musical and business duties.

1992–94 **Production Assistant**

Shaw Cable 8, Vancouver, BC

Duties: ran portable and studio cameras, studio lighting, special effects generator, and $3/4$" video recorder; worked as studio floor director; aided in production of regular weekly broadcast of District 10 High School Football.

EDUCATION

May 1998 **Radio Broadcasting Diploma**

Beothuk College, Kamloops, BC

Studied Radio Announcing (sports, news, interviews), Writing/Producing Radio Drama and Documentaries, Copywriting, English Composition, Public Speaking, and Media Law.

ADDITIONAL STUDY

1998 **Journalism Print Program**

West Coast College, Burnaby, BC

Studied Public Relations, Government Operations, Courtroom/Local News Reporting, Headline Writing, Photography, Layouts and Graphics. Completed half the program before taking a full-time position at CKJU.

1997	**Conversational French I & II**	
	West Coast College, Burnaby, BC	

1996	**Data Processing Concepts**	
	West Coast College, Burnaby, BC	

AREAS OF EXPERTISE

Specialized   **Broadcasting Equipment:** can operate all equipment, including splicing/editing and sound effects equipment.
Photography: familiar with still and video techniques.
Musical knowledge: excellent command of popular music history; also play clarinet and guitar.

Practical   **Communication:** pleasing professional voice; at ease with public speaking; some acting experience (college productions).
Organization/Administration: ran my own business; maintain records of all shows produced at CKJU.
Reliability/Dependability: displayed as both volunteer and employee.
Writing/Editing: regularly produce effective copy.
Keyboarding: type 40 wpm.

Interpersonal   **Interviewing:** both trained and experienced.
Gregariousness: get along well with all types of people.

REFERENCES:

Adam Marks,   1370 CKJU
Production Manager   75 Speedmore Ave.
(604) 321 5678   Burnaby, BC
                          V8U 9J7

Leo Moroni, Chair   Radio Broadcasting Department
(604) 987 5643   Beothuk College
                          Murgatroyd St., PO Box 1234
                          Kamloops, BC
                          V6N 4R7

In his revised résumé, Gabe has changed the format and rearranged or deleted some of the unnecessary information to emphasize his training and experience in broadcasting and related fields. He has also carefully proofread the résumé to ensure that there are no spelling or grammatical errors or inconsistencies.

RESUME

BEREND JOHN REURINK
RR # 2 Black Creek, Manitoba

PHONE: 456 7890

PERSONAL:

Date of Birth-December 23rd, 1978
Marital status-Engaged
Social Insurance No.-765 890 432

-No physical disabilities
-No criminal record
-No sick benefit or worker's compensation claim ever made

Height-5'10"
Weight-175 lbs.

EDUCATION:

Kribsler Public School, 39 Foxx Street, Dundas, Ontario
Graduated from grade eight, 1994
Southfern Secondary School, Southfern Road, Dundas, Ontario
Completed grade nine, June 1995

WORK RECORD:

*Pidgeon Foundry Ltd. 95 Fowler St. Dundas, Ontario
Duties: payloader driving, moulding
Reason for leaving: resigned to move west
Rate of pay: start- $9.51 an hour. finish- $11.84 an hour with piecework incentive to $17.00 an hour
Dates employed: September 5th, 1999 to January 18th, 2001

*Lunarware, division of Rabko Stn. Ltd. 19 Elf Ave. Dundas, Ontario (905) 555 6789
Duties: packing bathtubs and basins, forklift and clamp truck driving, shipping and receiving.
Reason for leaving: shortage of work (laid off)
Rate of pay: start- $8.95 an hour. finish- $9.61 an hour

Dates employed: February 14th, 1997 to August 17th, 1998

*Pidgeon Foundry Ltd. 95 Fowler St. Dundas, Ontario
Duties: filling ladle, pouring iron, forklift driving.
Reason for leaving: shortage of work (laid off)
Rate of pay: $8.91 an hour
Dates employed: August 3rd, 1996 to May 28th, 1997

*Wattles Metal and Covering, Robko Business Park, Black Creek, Manitoba
Duties: making up work orders for heating duct and custom sheet metal work.
Reason for leaving: company went bankrupt (laid off)
Rate of pay: $6.00 an hour
Dates employed: October, 1995 to January, 1996

ABILITIES:

-working quickly as well as accurately; have experience on piecework
-operating lift trucks; have lift truck license
-have St. John's First Aid Certificate

HOBBIES:

-camping, fishing, gardening, horse back riding
-playing guitar, reading novels
-weightlifting

COMMENTS:

I was living in Ontario with my fiance. She was offered an exceptional educational opportunity here in Manitoba which initiated our move west. I am hard-working, energetic, and dedicated to my work. I get along well with my fellow workers and supervisors, although I also excel under unsupervised conditions.

Although it has a few strengths, this really isn't a very good résumé, Berend has a problem background and rather than de-emphasizing the weaknesses (lack of education, series of lay-offs), this résumé calls attention to them. As well, negative issues (mentioning any question of criminal record) and personal issues (his common-law relationship with his girlfriend) should definitely not be mentioned at all. Berend says he does not have a criminal record and counts this as a strength; some employers might wonder why he would even raise the issue! As for his relationship with his girlfriend, it is certainly nobody's business but theirs. The question of marital status should not be raised in any case.

There are other problems here also; since Berend has a weak educational background, and especially since it is not his most recent experience, it should not be placed first on the résumé. If he mentions education at all, he would be better not to mention what grade he has completed, and just note his attendance at the secondary school. No mention of elementary school need be made. In any case, his education should certainly follow, not precede, his employment history. It is also unnecessary (though not wrong) for Berend to mention his rates of pay and his reasons for leaving. He should emphasize his responsibilities more fully and display dates and job titles more clearly too. In addition to these weaknesses in content and arrangement, there are also several errors in spelling and punctuation that detract from the overall impression made by Berend's résumé.

Although Berend is not a college student, I have included his résumé to demonstrate how important it is to tailor your résumé to your reader. Berend will be seeking a manual-labour job and his résumé addresses concerns his prospective employer might have in hiring him. The new résumé (Figure 7.4B) leaves out the irrelevant and damaging material included in the first one, and emphasizes the strengths Berend has as a hardworking employee. By deleting the unimportant information, Berend is able to fit his résumé onto one page, something that is likely to appeal to a busy employer who may not be interested in a lot of paper credentials or minute detail.

Berend John Reurink
RR # 2 Black Creek, Manitoba • 456-7890

WORK RECORD

1999–2001; 1996–97	**Driver/Labourer**	Pidgeon Foundry Ltd. Dundas, Ontario

Duties: Driving payloader; casting and moulding metalwork.

1988–89	**Labourer**	Lunarware Ltd. Dundas, Ontario

Duties: Forklift and clamp truck driving, shipping and receiving.

1995–96	**Order Desk Clerk**	Wattles Metal and Covering Black Creek, Manitoba

Duties: Making up work orders for heating duct and custom sheet metal work.

SKILLS

Work-Related
- Licensed lift truck operator
- Experienced on piecework
- Have St. John Ambulance First Aid Certificate

Personal
- Hardworking, energetic, and dedicated to my work
- Get along with fellow workers and supervisors
- Able to work without supervision

EDUCATION

1995	**High School**	Southfern Secondary School Dundas, Ontario

AVAILABILITY   Immediate

RESUME

Personal   I23 Braemar Way
                  Forestville, Ontario
                  555-9876

Education

September I999   Waskasoo College
to May 2000   Social Service Program
                  Cedar Falls Campus

September I993   Waskasoo College
to January I994   Mini Child Care Course

September I990   Waskasoo College
to May I992   Correctional Worker Program
                  Cedar Falls Campus

September I991   Waskasoo College
to May I992   Upgrading Course
                  Allendon Campus

Field Placement

September 2000   Jersey Youth Services
to May 200I   Inner City Youth Program
Duties: Referrals, I.D. Verifications, Intakes, Councelling, Groups, Reception.

January 2000   Forestville Volunteer Centre
to May 2000   Community Relations, Recognition Projects, Interviewing,
Duties: Church Out-Reach Projects, Recruitment Projects, Office Duties.

figure 7.5A WEAK RÉSUMÉ. (Continued)

Work Experience

May 2000	Ministry of Community and Social Serivces
to present	Valleyview Centre
Duties:	I provide parent relief, caring for an eight year old autistic boy.

September I993	Ministry of Community and Social Services
to I998	Home Provider Program
Duties:	I provided day care in my home for five families and took a child care course through the ministry and received a certificate.

April I992	Sasha Park Community Centre
to July I992	Seniors Outreach Worker
Duties:	I provided a houskeeping service for seniors.

July I99I	Childrens Aid Society
to August I99I	Child Care Worker
Duties:	I took care of 3 children ages I3, 9, II, while their mother was undergoing treatment for alcoholism at the Drire Clinic.

Other

May I997	Board of Directors
to present	I have been serving on a founding Board of Directors, working on the development of a housing co-operative. Excellent referrences upon request.

This is a terrible résumé for a brand new college graduate! First of all, there is no name on it. Since résumés and letters of application often get separated by the employer, the writer's name should be on the résumé. Also, look closely at the layout. The poor use of white space, with little distinction between main points and subpoints, combined with the lack of bold print, underlining, or indentation, make this résumé very difficult to read. The applicant has provided no detail about any of the programs taken, and such a lengthy listing of programs started and abandoned gives the impression of indecision; an employer might feel that this person is a quitter. Note the use of the capital I in place of the numeral 1. Computer keyboards typically feature the numeral "1." Even if for some reason you must substitute another figure for the numeral (for instance, if you were using a typewriter that did not have the numeral "1,"), you should know it's customary to use a lower case L — l — in its place. Also, there are numerous misspellings throughout this résumé, and under "Other," this candidate doesn't even tell us what Board of Directors is referred to. Employers like to see evidence of genuine knowledge of the field, something that is lacking here. Originally, this résumé was printed on a dot matrix printer with a faded ribbon. Needless to say, faced with résumés from highly qualified candidates who have put some real thought and effort into their applications, no employer will bother to puzzle through this messy and ill-conceived résumé. It's headed straight for the trash can.

Luchia Gaschler
123 Braemar Way
Forestville, Ontario K0R 3R5
555-9876

EDUCATION

1999–2000	**SOCIAL SERVICE PROGRAM**	Waskasoo College Forestville, Ontario

Program covered both theory and practice in counselling, client support, and enabling, including extensive field placement.

1993–1994	**MINI CHILD CARE PROGRAM**	Waskasoo College Forestville, Ontario

Five-month course covered basic Child Care practices and theory and certified me as a Child Care Worker.

FIELD PLACEMENTS

2000–2001	**COUNSELLOR** (Displaced Youth)	Jersey Youth Services Inner City Youth Program

Handled referrals, I.D. verifications, intakes, and group counselling.

January– May 2000	**COORDINATOR**	Forestville Volunteer Centre

Handled community relations and interviewing; ran various projects including Recognition, Church Outreach, and Recruitment. I was also responsible for office duties.

EMPLOYMENT

2000–Present	**CHILD CARE WORKER** (Valleyview Centre)	Ministry of Community and Social Services

Provide extensive care for an eight-year-old autistic boy.

1993–1998	**CHILD CARE WORKER** (Home Provider Program)	Ministry of Community and Social Services

Provided ministry-certified home day care for five families.

1992	**SENIORS OUTREACH WORKER**	Sasha Park Community Centre

Provided housekeeping service for seniors.

figure 7.5B IMPROVED VERSION. (Continued)

Lucy Gaschler /2

1991 **CHILD CARE WORKER** Children's Aid Society
I took over the care of three children, aged 9, 11, and 13, while their mother underwent treatment for alcoholism at the Drire Clinic.

COMMUNITY SERVICE

1997–Present **BOARD OF DIRECTORS** Allendon Community Association
(Founding Member) Forestville, Ontario
Participated in numerous projects, including the development of a housing co-operative.

AREAS OF SKILL

Specialized I am experienced in therapeutic counselling, client support, group dynamics, and enabling. As well, I am familiar with the procedures and requirements of both the Ministry of Community and Social Services and the Children's Aid Society.

Personal I learn quickly, am enthusiastic and dedicated. I am also organized and disciplined, and work effectively to deadlines.

Interpersonal I have skill in active listening, supportiveness, and questioning techniques. I can interact effectively with clients of diverse backgrounds and with other professionals.

This is a much better résumé. Lucy has given herself a better chance to be considered by her prospective employers, not only because she has corrected her errors and improved the organization of her résumé, but because she has incorporated some of the language of her profession into her presentation. This is something you should try to do whenever you can; employers of new graduates like to see the applicants making correct use of the terms associated with the profession because such usage suggests both knowledge and confidence. Note that Lucy's listing of duties and activities has also been improved, and that she has deleted the long list of programs that made her sound like a quitter.

Our final résumé, Michael Fedaj's, is also chronologically organized, but see how Mike has handled his skills area: it is written in paragraphs, but individual skills are boldfaced to make them stand out. He has used boldfacing throughout the document to make it even more readable and easier to follow. Once again, notice the layout of Mike's background; he has not included a career objective because his training has prepared him specifically for one kind of position. Note that on this document, the education, as Mike's most recent experience, comes first.

Mike doesn't have a lot of experience, but he has just graduated from a specific career program, and he will impress an employer with his well-developed and professional résumé. It is in such a case that this résumé format really comes in handy: Mike's background might appear sketchy if he had merely listed it in a strictly chronological format.

figure 7.6 Evaluate Mike's résumé to show how it displays the qualities of an effective résumé: visual appeal and attention to the reader's needs.

MICHAEL MURRAY FEDAJ

PO Box 1234, Forestville, Ontario K0B 4L0
(519) 632 2791

EDUCATION

| Feb. 2000– Apr. 2001 | **Pharmacy Technician** | Tomahawk College Forestville, Ontario |

Program covered all aspects of Pharmacy operation, including both laboratory techniques and retail business operations, and included an extensive placement component.

| 1999 | **Grade 12 Diploma** | Forestville High Forestville, Ontario |

EMPLOYMENT HISTORY

| Feb. 2001– Apr. 2001 | **Pharmacy Technician** | Benjamin's Drugs Forestville, Ontario |

Duties included assisting the pharmacist in the dispensary, and involved all other aspects of retail pharmacy work. My three-month employment was work experience for the Pharm. Tech. program at Tomahawk College.

| Apr. 1996– Aug. 2000 | **Clerk/Stock Person** | IGA Groceteria Forestville, Ontario |

This position was part time during school year, and full time during summers. I unpacked and priced stock, maintained shelf inventory, packed orders, and assisted customers.

| June 1996– Sept. 1996 | **General Labourer** | County of Pine Hill, Ontario |

On construction sites I did painting, shingling, general carpentry, and some demolition.

figure 7.6 (Continued)

Mike Fedaj /2

AREAS OF SKILL

Technical As a trained Pharmacy Technician, I am familiar with all related **laboratory techniques**, including aseptic, IV admixture, TPN, compounding, prepackaging, and **dispensing techniques**, as well as **inventory control** procedures such as ordering/receiving, invoicing, and third-party billing.

Personal In both my education and my previous work experience, I have always shown myself to be an **honest**, **reliable** worker who takes **pride in a job well done**. I take an **organized** approach to my work and perform it to **exacting standards**. I am able to **take initiative** and work effectively to deadlines.

Interpersonal I am able to function effectively in a **leadership** role or in **cooperation** with others. I maintain a cheerful outlook and am **flexible** in dealing with other people.

REFERENCES: A list of referees is attached.

The Letter of Application

Two Types of Application Letter

A résumé is always accompanied by a letter of application, also called a covering letter. Like all business correspondence, a job application letter must follow the Six C's: it must be complete, concise, clear, coherent, correct, and courteous. It also follows the format of a standard business letter — preferably the full block style. There are two types of application letters, solicited and unsolicited; both, in a sense, are sales letters. As in the résumé, the product you are "selling" is your suitability for the job you want. Both types of letter put the reader's concerns foremost.

The *solicited* letter is written in answer to an advertisement for an available position, while the *unsolicited* letter is written to a firm in the hope that a suitable position is currently, or is about to become, available. The advantage of the second, if your timing is right, is obvious: there will be less competition than for an advertised position. Figures 7.7 and 7.8 are effective examples of the solicited and unsolicited application letter.

Both letters perform essentially the same task, however, and may be broken down into steps. How many paragraphs each step takes will depend on the background of the individual and the nature of the job applied for.

Remember that the application letter, like all business writing, must be carefully directed to your reader's needs and expectations. What you might want to say is not as important as what the employer wants to hear, and what you choose to put into the letter should be conditioned by the information the reader needs. To help determine the reader's expectations, study the job advertisement or position description carefully, and ask yourself what questions an employer will want your application to answer. The following steps can serve as a guideline; you could plan to allow one paragraph for each step, though each step may be shorter or longer than a paragraph.

Step 1 The first question an employer will have upon receiving your letter is "What is this about?" You should begin by identifying your reason for writing. In a letter that answers an ad, state the title of the position you are applying for, quoting the competition number if there is one, and the source and date of the advertisement. For an unsolicited letter, state clearly the type of work you desire and enquire whether such a position is currently open or soon to become available. You may wish to use a "re" or subject line for both types of letters, identifying by title or type the position sought.

Step 2 An employer's second question will likely be, "What qualifications does the applicant have for the job?" For both solicited and unsolicited letters, provide the employer with a very brief outline of the highlights of your background and your reasons for applying for this position. This need not be elaborate, since

figure 7.7

This solicited letter of application focuses on the employer's needs, making it more likely to be successful.

1324 Main Street
Red Deer, Alberta
T4N 2D3

January 12, 2001

Ms Nancy Schindelhauer, Manager
Contemporary Fashions
1729 Trutch Street
Vancouver, British Columbia
V6J 7Y8

Dear Ms Schindelhauer:

RE: Assistant Manager, Red Deer
      Competition #12-D-465

Please accept my application for this position in your new Red Deer store, as advertised in *The Edmonton Journal* January 11, 2001. I believe I have the experience you are seeking for your new location.

As my résumé explains, I am experienced in customer service and stock control and am familiar with most aspects of retail operations, including handling cash and credit transactions, maintaining stock levels, serving customers, and handling complaints and returns. My work as a waitress has also given me experience in dealing effectively with client complaints. As well, I have completed a course in business-related computer programming and have knowledge of basic bookkeeping procedures.

I am very interested in meeting with you to discuss my future with your company, and would be available for an interview at your convenience. I may be reached at (403) 346 1234.

Sincerely,

Nel Nyhof

Cornelia Nyhof

PO Box 1234
Forestville, Ontario.
K0B 4L0

April 21, 2001

Dr. Iqbal Zafar, Pharmacist
Value Drugs
34 Centre Street
Cedarton, Ontario
K7Y 2F6

Dear Dr. Zafar:

Re: Pharmacy Technician Position

I am a recent graduate of the Pharmacy Technician Program at Tomahawk College in Forestville and am very interested in finding employment in the Cedarton area. I believe you will find my background of interest if you are currently looking for an enthusiastic and competent technician.

I completed the pharmacy program with first-class honours overall, and high marks in all pharmacy-related courses. The program covers all aspects of retail pharmacy work, including laboratory and inventory procedures. As you may already know, the program also includes a three-month work experience component, which I spent with Benjamin's Drugs in Forestville. A letter of recommendation from Dr. Norman Benjamin is attached, along with a résumé of my experience and abilities.

Though I am relatively new to the pharmacy field, I am a conscientious and hard-working employee. I am interested in speaking with you about a possible position with your firm. I will be available mornings at 632 2791. Thank you for your consideration.

Yours truly,

Mike Fedaj

Mike Fedaj

your résumé will take care of the details, but should provide some legitimate reason why you would be a suitable candidate for the position. Remember that the purpose of the letter is to convince an employer to read your résumé, which will be attached. In this paragraph, you may wish explicitly to refer the employer to the résumé.

Step 3 An employer's third concern will be what makes you the best candidate for the job. Here you will want to be specific about why you are more suitable than the other applicants for the position. You may choose some particularly relevant skills and details from your résumé, qualifying these with brief examples appropriate to the job you seek. This is where you really sell your appropriateness for the position; show the employer what you can do for him or her and emphasize your strengths.

Step 4 If you have not yet referred the employer to your résumé, do so now; mention also that you have attached letters of recommendation or other documentation (if you have done so) or invite the employer to contact the references you have listed.

Step 5 Close with a strong statement of confidence in your abilities; thank the employer for considering you and ask for an interview. You might say that you will call the employer on a specified date to set up an interview. This is a good move if you can carry it off. However, if you really can't imagine yourself making such a call, don't say that you will do so. Instead, request an interview at the employer's convenience. Provide a telephone number where you may be reached or where a message may be left.

The Application Form

The application form is relatively easy to complete once you have written a résumé. Though it may seem unnecessary, some firms require that you both submit a résumé and complete an application form. Some prefer only a form, because it makes comparison between applicants easier. In any case, it's a good idea to know how to complete one in case you are asked to fill one out at the interview.

Forms may vary considerably in their thoroughness. The example below is exhaustive. Though a longer form may seem difficult, it is generally to your advantage because it allows you room to communicate any special skills and abilities that might be overlooked on a shorter form. It can thus help you to make a stronger impression.

Your instructor will likely provide you with a full-size version of the application form shown in Figure 7.9. In filling out the form, complete all areas as fully as possible, taking special care to fill in areas asking for elaboration on the form's standard questions. On this form, you will find such areas under the headings

"Career Goals" and "Areas of Expertise." It is important to take advantage of these sections, not only because they allow you to distinguish yourself from other applicants, but also because one of the most common employer complaints about applicants is failure to fill out forms completely.

The "additional information" questions are especially important; they are areas that you can use to your advantage, elaborating on strengths that may not have shown up clearly in the rest of the application form. Read the form carefully before completing it fully.

The Letter of Recommendation

At times, employers will ask for references from people who have known you professionally, either as employers or instructors; sometimes you can simply provide a list of names, but at other times you may need or want to provide a written record of the person's impressions of you.

For a number of reasons it is a good idea to request a letter of recommendation whenever you leave a job or an educational institution. If you apply for a job in an area far away from your previous location, a prospective employer might not bother to phone long distance to speak to your references and may instead hire someone whose references are easier to check. A letter might be sufficient to allay this concern. As well, people who have been familiar with your work move on, retire, or get promoted, or just plain forget you. A letter written when your performance is current and fresh in the person's mind is more desirable than a vague recollection written long afterward, which is unlikely to be as enthusiastic.

You should know what a letter of this type should include because you will probably be asking people to write them for you; eventually you may even be writing them for others.

A letter of recommendation is usually written by someone who knows you in an employment or educational context; these two types of reference are considered most appropriate for a job hunt. Most employers prefer them to personal references. However, if for some reason you wish to include a personal letter of reference, it should be written by someone who can evaluate you objectively and who will be viewed by the employer as a credible source. (From the employer's point of view, credibility may be at least partly a function of the person's status in the community.) A teacher, a physician, a member of the clergy, or a business person would be a suitable choice; a relative or friend would be considered biased in your favour, and therefore unreliable as a reference for a job. Remember, prospective employers want information regarding your ability to do a job; they will want this information from as reliable and objective a source as possible.

APPLICATION FOR EMPLOYMENT

Name: _____
            (last)   (first)   (middle)

Address: _____

_____

_____

_____

_____

EMPLOYMENT HISTORY: List in chronological order, beginning with most recent and working back.

From: _____ To: _____ Position Held: _____ Name of Firm: _____

_____

Duties: _____

_____

_____

_____

From: _____ To: _____ Position Held: _____ Name of Firm: _____

_____

Duties: _____

_____

_____

_____

From: _____ To: _____ Position Held: _____ Name of Firm: _____

_____

Duties: _____

_____

_____

_____

figure   7.9   A typical application form. (Continued)

From:_____   To:_____   Position Held:_____   Name of Firm:_____

Duties: _____

_____

_____

_____

Do you type? _____ wpm speed _____

Do you drive? _____ Licence class _____

Do you speak French? _____ fluently _____ well _____ some _____

Do you write French? _____ fluently _____ well _____ some _____

Are you computer literate? _____ If yes, explain _____

_____

_____

CAREER GOALS: Briefly describe the nature of the work you are interested in and the origin of this interest: _____

_____

_____

_____

_____

_____

_____

_____

_____

_____

_____

_____

_____

figure 7.9 (Continued)

EDUCATIONAL HISTORY: List in chronological order, beginning with most recent and working back.

From: _____ To: _____ Program: _____ Institution: _____ Diploma: _____

_____

Details: _____

_____

_____

From: _____ To: _____ Position Held: _____ Name of Firm: _____

_____

Duties: _____

_____

From: _____ To: _____ Position Held: _____ Name of Firm: _____

_____

Duties: _____

_____

RELATED ACTIVITIES: Describe any school- or community-related activities in which you have taken part, including offices held:

_____

_____

_____

_____

_____

_____

_____

_____

_____

figure 7.9 (Continued)

AREAS OF EXPERTISE: Elaborate on the above factual material by outlining briefly any skills you have developed from your experiences, any strengths you can bring to your position, or any information not already covered above.

_____

_____

_____

_____

_____

_____

_____

_____

_____

_____

_____

_____

_____

_____

_____

_____

_____

_____

_____

_____

_____

To my knowledge, all of the above information is true and accurate.

Date _____ Signature _____

Whether the writer is providing an employment or an educational reference, the contents of a letter of recommendation are approximately the same. The writer of a letter of recommendation, just like any other writer of business letters, should consider the needs of the reader and provide answers to the questions the employer is most concerned about.

1. *How long, and in what context, have you known the person you are writing about?* The writer must indicate his or her relationship (supervisor? employer? instructor? academic advisor?) to the job applicant, and the length of time that he or she was the person's employer, teacher, or advisor.

2. *What is your estimation of this person as an employee or a professional* or, if it's an educational reference, *as a student?* The writer should provide some specific examples — mention grades, work completed, duties of the position, record of advancement, quality of work, or outstanding achievements.

3. *What is your estimation of the subject's personality?* Employers want to know what kind of person they are considering for a position. Will he or she get along with others? Is he or she flexible? Cooperative? Personable? Outgoing?

4. You should make a strong statement of recommendation for the person and may invite the employer to contact you for further information. If the person writing a letter of reference can't strongly recommend the applicant, he or she should not be writing the letter in the first place.

The format for a recommendation letter is like other business letters. Naming the person in a "re" or subject line will help the reader more easily identify who is being described in the letter.

points to remember

If you ask someone for a recommendation, keep these points in mind.

1. Be sure that the person approached will give you a positive recommendation; a lukewarm or unenthusiastic letter is as bad as a negative evaluation.

2. Many people are uncertain about what to include in a letter of recommendation. If the person is unsure of what to say, don't be afraid to make suggestions! Ask the person to comment upon the three major areas above and emphasize any qualities that are important to the job you will be seeking.

3. Provide your writer with the correct name and address of the person to whom the letter is addressed, if it is to be sent directly; if not, ask for a general letter addressed "To Whom It May Concern."

The examples below demonstrate effective letters of recommendation (Figures 7.10 and 7.11).

Benjamin's Drugs

1430 Speedvale Road
Forestville, ON K7O 4T6
Phone: (416) 381 9459   Fax: (613) 329 2369
e-mail: norman_benjamin@ben.com.ca

April 12, 2001

To Whom It May Concern:

Re: **Michael Fedaj**

As pharmacist with Benjamin's Drugs, I had the pleasure of supervising Mike during his placement from the Pharmacy Technician program at Tomahawk College.

Throughout his placement with us, Mike showed himself interested and diligent. He undertook with care all tasks assigned him and completed them efficiently. He performed well above the recommended standard for placement students and offered some valuable suggestions for streamlining our prescription process.

I had not even a moment's concern over Mike's performance of his duties or his professionalism. Mike impressed me as very personable, and he interacted effectively with customers and staff alike. His conscientious good humour was appreciated by all who worked with him, and he made himself a valued member of the Benjamin's team.

I can without hesitation, therefore, recommend Mike as a reliable and conscientious employee.

Sincerely,

N. Benjamin

Norman Benjamin (Dr.)
Pharmacist

 **Beothuk College**

Murgatroyd Street, PO Box 1234 • Kamloops, BC V6N 4R7
(604) 987 5643 • www.beothuk.ca

Mr. Wayne Chiu, Director of Admissions
School of Journalism (Broadcasting)
Tyrrell University
Lypsinc, Saskatchewan S9R 1F3

April 2, 2000

Dear Mr. Chiu

Re: Gabriel Praskach

In response to your letter of March 25, I am happy to provide you with what information I can about Gabe's suitability to your program in Journalism.

Throughout his two years in our program I have been impressed with Gabe's liveliness and enthusiasm for the business, and with his sincerity and warmth both on-air and off. I also have a great deal of confidence in his mastery of the technical aspects of the business; some of the productions he made for us were among the best student work I've encountered in ten years in the program.

My only hesitation has to do with Gabe's tendency to suffer anxiety when he is under stress. However, this has never affected his performance, which has invariably been outstanding. Although I feel that this tendency deserves mention because you may detect something of his anxiety during his interview, I sincerely do not feel that it will adversely affect Gabe's capacity to do further study in the broadcast area.

In light of my knowledge of Gabe's work and his disposition, I am pleased to endorse him as a suitable candidate for your program.

Sincerely,

Leo Moroni, Chair
Radio Broadcasting Department
moroni@beothuk.ca

Taking Your Job Search Online

Posting Your Résumé to a Web Site

If you have a web site of your own, you may wish to display your résumé on it. If you do decide to post an electronic version of your résumé, you should make sure that the page is readable and attractive, just as you would do for a print version, using visual devices to help organize the information. One major difference, however, between the print version and the electronic version of the résumé is the potential for violation of your privacy. An employer to whom you have sent a hard copy does not have a legal right to distribute or divulge the information on your résumé to anyone else without your explicit permission. By contrast, a résumé on a web site is vulnerable to anyone who has access to the Internet. Once you have "published" online, your work history and educational experience, along with every other piece of information contained in your résumé, are no longer private. This can be a good thing if it brings you to the attention of a prospective employer; however, you should realize that very few serious employers will seek prospective candidates in this fashion. As long as potential candidates outnumber available jobs, there is little incentive for a busy employer to cruise the Internet seeking qualified entry-level candidates; generally they will wait for candidates to come to them. In any case, placing private information on public view can have potentially disastrous consequences, so you should exercise some caution about what you place online. In my view, more harm than good is done by such a posting because of the potential risks involved with supplying so much information to possibly unscrupulous readers. If you decide that, despite these concerns, you would like to post your résumé to your web site, I strongly suggest that you remove your home and work addresses and supply only your e-mail address and perhaps a telephone number (a good idea is to provide a hotlink to your e-mail address). For your own safety and security, you should not provide any information that might make you vulnerable to unwanted harassment.

Searching the Job Market Online

Although posting your résumé to a web site and waiting for prospective employers to come to you is risky and most likely futile, the same cannot be said for using the Internet as a tool for your job search. Businesses large and small now operate web sites, and many of these maintain a listing of position openings, as do both provincial and federal governments. Most newspapers also operate web sites, and many make their classified advertisements, including job ads, available online. Another possibility for an online job search is professional and trade journals and magazines, many of which regularly feature job ads for career-specific positions. There are also databases to which you can be invited to subscribe online, which feature current job listings in a given field (not all of these are completely reliable; you should probably make it a policy not to pay for access to job listings).

One very nice advantage of using the Internet to look for job opportunities is that you can locate openings not just locally but also in other cities or provinces, or even in the U.S. or other foreign countries. Once you've found a position that interests you, you may even be able to submit your application online by sending your résumé and application letter as document attachments to an e-mail message. If you are looking for a position in another province or country, you should probably remember that some employers may still be reluctant to consider applicants who have to travel a long distance to the interview and may for this reason prefer local candidates. Nevertheless, the access to job listings provided by the Internet can be a major convenience for the applicant. While the Internet should probably not be the only resource you use for searching out employment opportunities, it is a useful source of information that can aid you in your job search. Even if you use it only as a research tool for gathering information about potential careers, the Internet can be a valuable addition to your job-seeking strategies.

The Job Interview

If your application has been successful, the employer will be interested in talking with you about the position and will invite you for an interview. The interview is the employer's chance to get to know you in person, to determine if you are the right person for the job. In the interview, you will want to maintain the positive impression you created with your résumé and application.

A Tip on Answering Machine Messages

The employer will initiate the interview process by contacting you on the telephone. The professionalism displayed in your résumé should also extend to your telephone manner, and to the message on your answering machine. Take a minute to think about how your answering machine might strike a busy employer who calls to offer you an interview. An employer I recently interviewed had just telephoned a job applicant, only to find herself confronted with a long and inane answering machine message. Like most busy employers, she found this exceedingly annoying and unprofessional, and she resented the waste of her time. In her opinion, and that of many other business people, a number left for business purposes should not waste the caller's time with "humorous" messages. In this instance, the employer left no message; instead, she offered an interview to the next candidate on her list.

At least while you are job hunting, keep the message on your answering machine simple and businesslike. Silly messages, especially if they are long, may form a negative impression on an employer who has not yet met you. Don't risk losing an interview by frustrating someone who calls for business reasons.

Remember that the employer's first impression of you strongly influences any decision to hire you. This decision is made in many cases within the first minute of the interview, during the employer's first reaction to you; if this impression is negative, the employer may spend the rest of the interview looking for faults to justify this dislike. It's obviously in your best interest to make the employer's first response to you a positive one. You should do all you can to prepare yourself, and thus give yourself an advantage.

A successful interview, like other effective business communications, depends partly on your preparation. Before your interview think carefully about the needs and interests of your audience — the person who may be paying your salary. What does that person want in an employee? What will he or she be looking for?

Although you cannot completely predict the interviewer's response to you, there are three aspects of that initial impression that you can control so as to make it a good one: your appearance, your attitude, and your background knowledge.

Appearance

1. Wear appropriate clothes. For an interview, you should wear slightly more formal attire than you would wear on the job. For business or professional jobs, wear relatively conservative business clothes: a suit is fine for both men and women, though for men a sports jacket and dress pants may serve the purpose, and for some jobs a woman may want to wear a dress and jacket. If you are applying for a labour or other blue-collar job, dress accordingly; in this situation, a suit might be considered overdressed. Your clothes should also be comfortable enough that you don't have to repeatedly adjust or fiddle with them. No matter what you're wearing, be sure you're neat and clean; avoid splashy colours or unusual hairdos, and leave the chunky jewellery at home.

2. Be punctual. Arrive at the interview with a few minutes to spare, but not more than fifteen minutes early. Know how long it will take you to arrive by whatever means you're travelling and allow yourself enough time for delays. Be sure to take a watch. Occasionally, there may be a legitimate reason why you have to be late — car trouble, an accident, illness. If this happens to you, telephone the interviewer immediately to explain the situation and politely request a later interview. If you miss your interview, you should not expect automatically to be given a second chance; sometimes the employer will be unable or unwilling to reschedule, and you will just have to give up on that job. You should also be aware that even legitimate lateness may create a negative impression that damages your chances, so plan to be on time. Sleeping in or misjudging how long it takes to get to the interview are *not* acceptable reasons for being late.

3. Go alone to the interview. An interview is a business meeting, not a social event, and bringing someone with you may cause the interviewer to question your maturity or your awareness of appropriate professional behaviour. A

confident applicant is more likely to get the job, and you won't look confident if you bring someone else along.

4. When you shake hands, use a firm, confident grip. Don't let your hand hang loosely, but be sure not to grip too tightly either. As silly as it sounds, it's a good idea to practise your handshake with a friend before going to your first interview.

5. Don't chew gum or smoke, though the interviewer may do either. If the interviewer smokes, don't do so unless you are invited to. Even then you may wish to refuse. And if you are a smoker, don't smoke just before going in to the interview. Non-smoking interviewers can be put off by the reek of second-hand smoke on a candidate.

6. Make eye contact while you speak. Though some people avoid eye contact simply because they are nervous, this habit can make a very negative impression on an interviewer. It can suggest uncertainty or even dishonesty, neither of which will further your chances. Don't stare at the floor or ceiling or avoid meeting the interviewer's eyes; instead, make eye contact frequently and comfortably. Look away occasionally to avoid appearing overly aggressive.

7. Speak clearly and use correct grammar. Employers do judge applicants' intelligence and education by the way they speak, and poor grammar is one of the indicators of weaknesses in either of these areas. Avoid such pitfalls as "I seen," "I done," "I did good in that course," or "between you and I" and keep away from slang expressions.

8. Watch your body language. Sit comfortably without slumping in your chair or hooking your feet around the chair legs. Don't fidget, tap your fingers, or fiddle with your clothes. You should appear controlled and any of these is a clear message that you are overly nervous or inexperienced. If you are carrying supporting materials in a briefcase, place the case on the floor beside you rather than in the way on the desk. Don't block your view of the employer, or the employer's of you, with a large briefcase or other unnecessary props.

Attitude

Many interviewers agree that a good attitude is one of the most important things an applicant can bring to the interview. You should appear confident and positive. Although you will most likely feel, and the employer will expect, a little nervousness, you should try to be as relaxed and comfortable as you can. Be yourself — at your very best.

1. Avoid bragging or overstating your abilities. Employers, like everyone else, dislike arrogance. Be alert and attentive to questions, enthusiastic and sincere in your answers. Show a willingness to learn and grow with the company; no matter how much you feel you already know, there is always something else to learn.

2. Avoid one-word responses. At the same time, don't take over the interview with long, impossibly complicated replies. Watch the interviewer for cues that will signal when to stop speaking.

3. Show some interest in the company and don't be vague about what you want from your career. Employers like someone who has thought about his or her future and can show some direction. Indicate a willingness to work hard and start at a reasonable level. You may display ambition, but don't give the impression that you expect to run the company.

4. Don't appear obsessed with money, benefits, or vacations. Don't stress how you can benefit from the position or how much you need it. Remember that the goal of the interviewer is to find out what you can do for the company, not to hear what it can do for you.

5. Be courteous at all times. Don't do or say anything that could be considered rude or discourteous. Remember this especially when you enter and are met by a receptionist or a secretary: rudeness to these people can cost you the job offer, since they often are part of the screening process. Among other things, the employer wants to know how well you will get along with other people in the company, and one measure of this is how you treat people you meet on the way in. Always remember that first impressions count!

Knowledge

Employers are interested in discovering just how well you know the duties of the position you've applied for; they will want you to demonstrate the skill that you have claimed on your résumé. You should naturally be prepared to discuss your experience, always remembering to show how it is relevant to the position you are looking for.

But there's much more on the employer's mind. Although primarily interested in what you know about the duties of the job, your prospective employer will be impressed if you can demonstrate knowledge of the company. Try to learn as much as you can about the firm before the interview, for example, how large it is and what products or services it offers. You can find out a little about the company by looking in your local library or checking with the Chamber of Commerce. Here are some questions you might consider answering for yourself before the interview.

1. What is the exact nature of the business — what do they make or do?
2. Is it a local company or is it a branch office or plant?
3. How extensive is their business?
4. How long has the company been in business?
5. What is their management style?

An annual report will give you this information and more that might be useful. If you know someone who works for the company, try to talk to that person before your interview. If the company has a web site, visit it when you are preparing for the interview. It will provide you with important information about how the company sees itself. Find out as much as you can. Though you may not be asked such questions in the interview, the more you know when you go in, the more confident you will be and the better impression you will make.

Employers' Questions

Employers also want some indication that you are self-aware, that you know yourself and have thought about your goals, and that you have realistic expectations. They will also be interested to see if you can effectively solve the problems you are likely to face on the job. They will try to determine this information through careful questioning. Though every interview is different, and interviewers have different focuses, there are some questions that occur regularly in one form or another. If you think about these before you go to any interview, and about some potential answers, you will have a better chance of handling the questions effectively. As you answer, you should try to tailor your response to fit the job you're applying for. Don't memorize a prepared answer and don't try to be something you're not. Answer fully and sincerely. Here are some samples of favourite employer questions, with suggestions for answering them.

1. *Tell me about yourself.* Employers often like to begin the interview with this one, because it not only provides information about you, but it also shows something of your priorities. What you choose to discuss will tell them what you think is important. Be aware that the employer is interested primarily in information relevant to the position you've applied for. Avoid the temptation to deliver the epic of your life. A brief summary of educational and employment highlights, as they have prepared you for the job in question, will work best in answering this question.

2. *What are your strengths?* Don't be falsely modest. Take some time to identify the things you do really well; go back over the skills section of your résumé and be ready with some examples. A mature person knows what his or her strong points are and can state them briefly without either bragging or understating them.

3. *What are your weaknesses?* We all have weaknesses, and a mature adult is aware of his or her own. However, be careful when you're answering this question. Don't identify weaknesses in such a way that they are likely to make an employer think twice about hiring you: such comments as "I never finish what I start" or "I can't get motivated in the morning" won't endear you to an employer. If you have such weaknesses, of course you should be trying to correct them, but an interview is not the place to highlight them. Identify weaknesses that show you are human, but not ones that will reveal you as unemployable. For example, you might (if this is true) tell the employer something like "I sometimes take my work too seriously, and don't leave myself enough time for leisure." Or you may identify a not-so-serious flaw and immediately balance it with a positive: "I sometimes find it hard to take criticism, but even though I find it difficult I usually benefit from constructive comments." Avoid confessing really serious or negative traits, but don't say "I don't have any weaknesses" or "I don't know," and above all make sure you are sincere in your answers. An experienced interviewer can recognize phony or insincere answers and will reject an applicant she believes is misrepresenting himself.

4. *Why do you want to work for this company?* or *Why do you want this job?* Your research into the company will give you some information to use in answering this question; don't, however, identify pay or benefits as a primary reason for choosing this company. Emphasize the position itself, and don't, as an acquaintance of mine did, answer by saying, "because I'm unemployed." Employers want some evidence that they are getting the best, not merely the most desperate, applicant. This question might also appear as "What do you think you can do for this company?" accompanied by "What can we do for you?" You can best prepare for these questions by thinking them through beforehand and planning how you will answer. Don't memorize an answer though; it is bound to sound false or insincere.

5. *What made you choose [corrections, editing, corporate communication, recreation administration, nursing, etc.] as a career?* There are many acceptable answers to this question, and you will have to choose your own. However, "My father [or mother] is [a corrections officer, an editor, a public relations officer, a recreation manager, a nurse, etc.]" is not one of them. Neither is "I knew I'd earn lots of money." The employer wants to know that you've made a thoughtful choice, not just an expedient one.

6. *What was your favourite subject in college/university/school?* You may wish to identify one or two subjects, but watch out for the other half of this question, which asks you to identify the subject(s) you disliked. You may indicate that there were some subjects you liked better than others, but you should avoid sounding like a complainer. Instead of identifying courses you couldn't stand, indicate that you learned something from all of them, even the ones you didn't particularly enjoy.

7. *How would your friends describe you?* This is another way for an employer to find out a bit about your self-awareness. You should not be overly modest. Again, try to identify real strengths, but don't sound arrogant.

8. *What would you like to be doing in five years? ten?* Employers can find out how much thought you've given to your career with this question. They may also be looking for evidence of a commitment to the company. If you say that you're not planning to stay in this job, or in this field, an employer may not want to spend the time or money on training you for the position. Answering "I don't know" isn't a good idea either; an employer might consider it a sign of indecision or immaturity and it could cost you the job. Try to show that you have given some thought to the future, but that you are flexible and able to adjust your goals as well.

9. *Do you have plans to further your education? Would you be interested in doing so?* Your answer here could depend on whether the employer is wondering if you're open to more training or afraid you'll quit the job in six months to return to full-time study. You should never close any door on yourself. You could indicate that you are willing to take further training if necessary. Even if you don't think right now that you would ever go back to school, remember that with time you might change your mind. On the

other hand, you might also want to reassure the employer that you're not going to quit this job as soon as you're trained in order to return to school.

10. One type of question that is often favoured by employers is the situation question. The most common type is one in which the interviewer gives an example of an incident that might happen to you on the job and asks for your solution. There isn't any way to prepare for this question; it's designed to test your awareness of the job's requirements. You might try going over your experience in your memory. Think of difficult situations you have faced and how you handled them; analyze how you might have handled them better than you did. If you consider in advance how you might answer such a question, you will be better prepared for it. The question may also appear in another form, such as:

Give me an example of a situation in which you showed leadership.
Tell me about a situation in which you resolved a difficulty.
Tell me about a situation in which you initiated change.
Tell me about a situation in which you handled criticism.
Describe an achievement you are proud of.

11. These questions might also be phrased evaluatively. Instead of asking for an example, the interviewer might simply ask you to outline your capabilities using such questions as:

How well do you handle pressure?
How do you handle criticism?
Are you able to handle change?

You should always support your answers with brief, specific examples from your work or educational experience.

12. The employer might also probe your attitude toward others with such questions as: *Are you usually right? Are other people's ideas as important as yours?* Of course, you will want to show some openness to others' views and not indicate that you believe only you are ever correct. Provide some balance in your answer: you're not always right, naturally, but you are not always wrong either. You must show that you are capable of making decisions, but that you can also recognize good ideas that others put forward and can compromise. You might also be asked:

Do you make mistakes?
How do you handle those?
Can you give me an example?

Naturally you will want to show that you are aware that you can make mistakes, but also that you can learn from them. If you say you do not make mistakes, the interviewer will reject you outright, because of course we all make errors from time to time, and the measure of us is in how we handle the errors we make.

13. *How would you describe a good [manager, teacher, electrician, engineer, etc.]? What will make you a good [manager, teacher, electrician, engineer, etc.]?* An

acquaintance of mine, unnerved by the interview situation, once answered the latter question with, "I don't know; I just do it!" By now, of course, you know that's not an appropriate answer; a good answer should be thought out beforehand in a way that's relevant to your program or profession.

In answering any of these questions, keep in mind the probable needs and interests of all employers: they will be looking for someone who is confident and capable, but not arrogant or self-absorbed. Admit to mistakes, but show that you have learned from them and can handle criticism effectively. Be honest and not overly modest; be confident but not arrogant. Show that you have both strengths and weaknesses, but that your weaknesses are not serious and can be overcome. Don't cite weaknesses or flaws in character that are likely to damage your employment chances.

Some Reasons Why People Don't Get Hired

Of course, there are many reasons why people aren't hired, some of which you may not be able to control; however, there are some elements that you can control. The following are some of the reasons employers have given for turning down applicants.

Arrived late to the interview.
Dressed inappropriately.
Poor personal grooming.
Was rude to the receptionist.
Seemed unduly nervous.
Fidgeted; did not appear relaxed or confident.
Didn't answer questions fully; rambled on too long.
Could not provide examples to support claims in the résumé.
Attempted to dominate interview.
Was over-confident, arrogant, or self-important.
Criticized former employers.
Appeared more interested in pay and benefits than in work.
Chewed gum.
Was unable or unwilling to provide references.
Spoke poorly, with poor grammar or diction.
Had a limp handshake.
Knew nothing about the company.
Was unfamiliar with current trends in the profession.
Had exaggerated on the application or résumé.
Had ambitions far beyond abilities.
Had no clear goals or professional interests.
Appeared whiny or unmotivated.
Could not admit to weaknesses or mistakes; tended to blame others.
Was defensive when answering questions.

Was unwilling to start at the bottom.

Lacked courtesy; was rude or ill-mannered.

Had a poor school record.

Appeared insincere or glib.

Lied on the application or résumé.

What to Expect

Interviews can vary not only in the type and number of questions that employers ask, but in other ways as well. There is no set pattern for interviews and no right way to conduct them in terms of length or number of screenings. Employers tend to decide for themselves what selection process best suits their needs, and the more interviews you go to, the greater variety you will see.

For example, the length of time you spend in an interview may be anywhere from twenty minutes to two or even three hours, depending on the type of position and the number of applicants. (An acquaintance of mine recently attended an interview that lasted seven hours!) Often the person who telephones you to set up the interview will indicate how long it will take; if she or he doesn't volunteer the information, ask for an estimate of how long the interview will last. If you're not sure, allow yourself at least two hours, just to be safe.

You may be interviewed by one person, by two or three together, or even by a committee of five or more. Again, you may be told this ahead of time. But whether you are told or not, be prepared; the more responsible the position, the more likely there will be more than one interviewer. In some companies or institutions, two or three people interview you separately, then compare impressions. This may be done on the same day (you may spend twenty to forty minutes with three different people successively) or on subsequent days. This is neither a good nor a bad sign; it merely shows the employer's personal preference.

In any of these cases, don't be thrown off by interviewers taking notes while you speak. Remember that they have seen several different people in a short space of time and are merely interested in keeping track of what was said. It's really for your benefit — you wouldn't want an interviewer to forget you or confuse you with someone else.

Sometimes, depending on the employer and on the position, you may be asked to complete some form of testing. Occasionally these tests will be vocationally specific — secretarial applicants may have to take a keyboarding test, drivers may be asked to operate a vehicle, or trainers may have to give a sample lesson. In these cases, the interviewer is interested in knowing that you really do have the level of skill needed for the job.

But there are other kinds of tests that you may be asked to take: general aptitude or even psychology tests. These are tests you can't really prepare yourself for; they are thought to reveal your general intelligence, attitude, or aptitude for the position you are interested in. Like all trends, aptitude testing goes in and out of favour, and is used more in some fields than in others. Even when they are popular, such tests are not universally employed by all companies. However, employers who choose to use aptitude testing generally believe it is useful. Your best bet if you are asked to write one of these is to be as honest and forthright as you can. Most of the tests are designed to double-check your responses by asking several questions aimed at the same information, so keep in mind that it's difficult to try to second-guess the tests. Fudged answers can usually be identified by the cross-questions. Simply try to relax as much as possible and do your best. There is nothing to be frightened of, and you will do better if you can keep from being too upset.

There is much talk these days about poor writing skills among college and university graduates, and many employers have expressed concern over such weaknesses. As a result, occasionally an employer will ask applicants to write a piece of business correspondence — a letter or a memo — right on the spot, in response to a situation such as the ones given in Chapter 3. You should be prepared to write if necessary; you might review Chapters 2 and 3 before you go to the interview. In this case, the employer will be looking not only for proper letter or memo format, but also more importantly, for correct grammar and sentence structure, and the other Six C's of business writing.

You should also know that not all interviewers will be equally skilled. In some companies, interviewing is typically conducted by skilled human resources specialists, but this isn't always the case. Frequently, in fact, you may be interviewed by the immediate supervisor or even by the person who is vacating the position you are applying for. Since interviewing people is not their area of specialization, they may be inexperienced at the task, sometimes enough that you will be able to detect their uncertainty. However, if you find yourself in such a situation, maintain your cheerful, positive demeanour and answer each question to the best of your ability. Don't let the interviewer's lack of experience make you overconfident or arrogant. Unskilled interviewers are likely to be more sensitive to such nuances than an experienced interviewer would be, and possibly more easily offended. They will not appreciate challenges to their authority, however subtle. Maintain your poise and do your best with the questions you are given.

Problem Questions

Employers are no longer permitted to ask an applicant questions that will solicit information about age, marital status, religious affiliation, ethnic background, or family relationships. It is illegal to do so, but occasionally you will encounter an interviewer who asks you such questions anyway, either because of inexperience or because of deliberate disregard for the law. You are obviously not obliged to answer such questions, but refusing to do so may be awkward and could cost you the position.

The decision to answer such queries or not is a personal one, based on your own comfort level. If you don't mind a question about marital status, you may wish to answer it even though, strictly speaking, it's not appropriate for the employer to ask. Sometimes such questions are unthinking expressions of other employer concerns; when this is the case, you will sometimes be able to determine the employer's train of thought from the context of the remark. An employer may really be thinking about overtime and may ask about your marital status because he or she feels overtime might be more difficult for a married person. You may choose to phrase your response to address the employer's concern directly. For example, a prospective employer may ask if you are married. You could answer: "If you're concerned about my willingness to work overtime, I am willing to put in all the time the job requires."

If, on the other hand, the interviewer's questions seem a bit too personal or make you very uncomfortable, you may wish to decline to answer. Doing so is tricky, though. If you simply refuse, saying that you don't see the relevance of the question to the job, you will probably turn the interviewer against you. You may try restating the question as in the example, but you should be prepared to balance your need for the job against your willingness to field inappropriate questions. This is entirely a judgement call, and it's important to know for yourself how much is too much. Most interviewers want to see you at your best and will try very hard to put you at ease. However, if you do run into a difficult situation, know how much of such behaviour is tolerable to you, and don't be afraid to leave if you have to. If the interview is that unpleasant, it's unlikely that you would want to work for this company anyway.

Interviewing, like everything else in this book, is a skill you can learn and polish. You can do this best by practising. Go to as many interviews as you can, even if you're not sure you would want the job. You can never get too much experience, and every interview you go to will make the next one easier. You might even find that a job that didn't appear so attractive on paper turns out to be just the position you were seeking.

points
to remember

1. The job application, and the interview, are opportunities for you to display your suitability for the job.

2. Be sure to identify your reader's needs, values, and expectations in order to "target" your application effectively.

3. Prepare your résumé and application letter carefully to display your strengths, not reveal your weaknesses.

4. Always proofread and apply the Six C's of business writing.

5. Word-process your application materials and use a printer cartridge with sufficient ink or toner to produce a dark, sharp image. If you must use a typewriter, make sure it has a new ribbon.

6. Take the goofy messages off your answering machine.

1. Collect as many job advertisements as you can find from newspapers, flyers, web sites, or the placement office of your college. You can look at only jobs related to your field or scan a broad cross-section in all fields. Study the ads carefully and circle key words — that is, those that appear most frequently and that seem to be most important. Based on your survey, what are the skills that employers seem to value most? Which ones are in greatest demand in your field? Compare your findings with those of others in your class; what implications can you draw for preparing your own job application?

2. Write your own Job Package, including a complete application letter, a résumé of your experience and education, a completed job application form, and a letter of recommendation.

   Letter of Application: Use the job descriptions provided by your instructor or answer an ad from the newspaper, placement office, or an Internet site. Type the letter in one of the formats you've learned.

   Résumé: You may complete this as though you have finished your current year of study. Review the section on résumé writing in this chapter and remember that your résumé must be correct, legible, and clear.

   Application Form: There is an application form on pages 191–194. Photocopy it, or use the copy that your instructor provides for you, and fill it out completely either by hand (in ink) or on a typewriter. Be sure to sign it.

   Recommendation Letter: Pretending to be a former employer or instructor, write a letter either for yourself or for someone else in your class. In either case, you will be graded for the letter you have written, not for the one someone else has written for you.

3. You work for the Public Relations department of Communications Corporation. Your boss, Daena Tobias, has struck a hiring committee in your department for a position advertised as follows in the paper and on the company's web site.

ADMINISTRATIVE ASSISTANT
PUBLIC RELATIONS

Major corporation in the Communications field seeks an administrative assistant for its Public Relations department. Primary duties will include writing correspondence to other communications leaders and the general public, as well as some general office duties. The successful applicant will have:

- superior writing/composition ability, with thorough knowledge of techniques of business writing
- good interpersonal skills
- ability to work without supervision
- strong organizational ability

- keyboarding speed of 60 wpm
- pleasant telephone manner

Experience in a secretarial position would be considered an asset, but is not the most important qualification for this position. Applicants with strong demonstrated skills in communications, particularly writing, will be considered for training. Submit résumés in confidence to:

Ellen Koyata, Human Resources Manager
Communications Corporation
555 California Street
Vancouver, British Columbia
V1R 7H9

The initial screening has been done by Ellen Koyata's department. It is up to your committee to make the final decision from the résumés she has forwarded. You should look at the sample résumés in this chapter and then evaluate the following submissions (Figures 7.12 to 7.17) according to the criteria you have learned. See if you can identify specific weaknesses of these résumés and letters in content, format, and style. Have they clearly identified purpose and placed the reader's needs first? Make a list of the weaknesses you have found and compare them with those identified by your classmates or instructor.

4. After screening the résumés and making your selection of the person you think is best qualified, turn to the weaker applications. Rewrite them so that they are more effective. Compare your rewritten versions with those of your classmates.

online exercises

1. Before starting your job application, you may find it useful to think about the kind of work environment you prefer. Just for fun, go to http://www.aboutwork.com/quiz/workstyle/ and complete the multiple-choice quiz entitled "What's Your Work Style?" Do you think the quiz results accurately reflect your approach to work? Compare your results with those of your classmates and instructor. How useful was the quiz in preparing to develop your résumé?

2. For a workbook approach to preparing your résumé, travel to Resumania! Online! at http://www.umn.edu/ohr/ecep/resume/step1.htm. The whole site is dedicated to developing a résumé suitable to your background and skills; the personalized workbook page will help you get started. If your instructor directs you to do so, complete the workbook according to the directions on the site, and submit it to your instructor before you complete your résumé assignment.

3. It's important to list relevant job skills on your résumé; sometimes, however, it's hard to identify all the skills you may be able to bring to a new job. Travel to the Purdue University Online Writing Lab (http://owl.english. purdue.edu/Files/59.html) for a checklist of job-related skills. Use the list as a prompt for your own list of relevant job skills; be sure you can think of an example from your own background that shows how you demonstrated each of the skills you select for your résumé.

4. Many Canadian newspapers now have web sites on which they post their career and classified ads. Go to the Canadian Newspaper and Magazine Zone at http://www.storm.ca/~gerald/news.shtml for hotlinks to the major newspapers in your province or region. Go to the newspapers' career listings and find an advertisement for a job for which you would like to apply. (You may also wish to check out job listings in other regions.) If you wish, you may use one of these ads as the target for your job application package in assignment 2 on page 210. If so, be sure to include a copy of the advertisement with the package when you submit it to your instructor.

The application letter is meant to encourage an employer to read the attached résumé. What impression does Leola Bitango's letter make on you?

15 Cedar Avenue
Greyfowl, BC
V8G 1S4

Dear Sir:

Enclosed please find a copy of my résumé for your perusal. I have experience as a secretary.

I look forward to hearing from you at your earliest convenience.

Sincerely,

Leola Bitango

Leola Bitango

figure 7.13 Compare this résumé to the advertisement for the position. How well has Leola targeted her résumé to the job she wants?

-1-

RESUME - LEOLA BITANGO

ADDRESS: 15 Cedar Avenue   SIN: 987 654 321
            Greyfowl, BC
            V8G 1S4

PHONE: 678 9087

PREVIOUS WORK EXPERIENCE:

— Clerk Typist Position at British Columbia Social Services for a temporary 6 months.
  From September/00 to February/01
  Supervisor: Greta Grey Phone: 234 5678 (8:15-4:30 p.m.)

— Bartender/Server at "Steer's Neighbourhood Pub". Worked from April/94 to
  September/00.
  Supervisor: Dave Pickard Phone: hm 231-2234 wk 345-2876

— Various Server positions in Swan Valley, BC. between the period of 1995 to 1999.
  Along with cashier positions also.

— Volunteer at St. John's Hospital in Swan Valley, BC. In the Geriatric ward.

EDUCATION:

— Attended Northeastern High School in Strickland, BC as an Adult Student for a grade
  12 general diploma. (1996)

— Correspondence Course for a Medical Receptionist Diploma through Drucker Career
  Training Centre situated in Vancouver, BC.

— General courses taken in high school were: Office Procedures, Typing (3 yrs.), English,
  Business Education and also Accounting.

-2-

PERSONAL INFORMATION:

BIRTHDATE: 15/05/74

STATUS: Single Parent

SKILLS & KNOWLEDGE:

— Typing at 50 w.p.m.
— Ability to operate all office machines in general.
— Can operate a Word Processor and a dicta-phone machine.-S
— Spelling/75% average, Math/75% average.
— Know most aspects of bartending and bar service.
— Handle cash well, change register tapes and do cash-outs.

EXTRACURRICULAR ACTIVITIES:

— Presently enjoy all indoor and outdoor sports and activities.

REFERENCES:

— Dave Pickard Phone: 231-2234 (hm)   345-2876 (wk)

— Linda Crumb Phone: 453-9876 (hm)   219-0987 (wk)

— Denise Gorland Phone: 573-0287 (hm)

— Mrs. Roest Phone: 2   938-3847 (wk)

2001 03 10

Ellen Koyata, Human Resources Manager
Communications Corporation
555 California Street
Vancouver, British Columbia
V1R 7H9

Dear Ms Koyata:

Please be advised that I am interested in the position of Administrative Assistant at your firm in Vancouver.

Enclosed is my résumé documenting my experience and education.

Yours truly,

Marya Bumanis

Marya Bumanis

figure 7.15 Check the job requirements listed in the advertisement. How well has Marya addressed the needs of her potential employer?

Marya Bumanis

5555-44 Street, Westock, New Brunswick E4F 2R5
Res. (506) 345 7946
Bus. (506) 344 1230

History

November 1999 to Present	Personal Secretary to District Agriculturist, New Brunswick Agriculture, Westock, New Brunswick
July/August 2000	Attended Sproxler H.S., Saint John to obtain Grade 12 English
February 1997	Administrative officer, Tartan River Further Education Council, Box 980, Tartan River, New Brunswick

- worked out of own home
- planned and directed all phases of Council business
- received and processed all correspondence
- prepared copy and arranged for printing of twice-yearly, twelve-page advertising brochure
- prepared financial reports, payroll for 40 instructors, accounts receivable and payable and bookkeeping
- taking and transcribing minutes of general and executive meetings
- set up and maintained filing system
- worked independently at all times
- attended seminars and workshops re position

June 1994 to January 1996	Owner-Manager of retail fabric store, "Sew-You-See", Tartan River, New Brunswick
March 1990 to May 1994	Clerk-Stenographer, Quinpool College, Tartan River, New Brunswick

July 1987 to August 1992	Secretary to Regional Manager, Agricultural Development Corporation, New Brunswick Agriculture, Tartan River, New Brunswick
February 1982 to September 1988	Secretary to Regional Dairy Specialist and Regional Livestock Specialist, New Brunswick Agriculture, Tartan River, New Brunswick
February 1984	Graduated from Keystone Secretarial School with Business diploma, Eastlock College, Eastlock, N.B.
June 1983	Graduated from High School with Commercial diploma from Tartan High School, Tartan River, New Brunswick
Volunteer Work	Elected to Post Secondary Education committee for Westock - council to investigate development of community college in Westock
Personal Information	Married - three children, two living at home Birth date - February 2, 1962

References available upon request

Evaluate this letter for content and format. How effective will it be in meeting the employer's needs?

General Delivery
Brookfield, Alberta
T0M 9I9

March 11, 2001

Ellen Koyata, Human Resources Manager
Communications Corporation
555 California Street
Vancouver, British Columbia
V1R 7H9

Dear Ms Koyata:

Re: Administrative Assistant Position

I am a recent graduate of the Secretarial Science program at Modern City College in Modern City, and am very interested in relocating to the Vancouver area; I would like to be considered for this position, advertised in *The Edmonton Journal*.

I completed the Secretarial program with first-class honours, achieving top marks in Office Management and Writing courses. The program provided experience in a variety of skills related to successful office operations, including a model office experience component in which I was particularly successful.

An intensive course in Business Writing, covering memos, letters, reports, proposals, and promotional writing is also part of the program. I earned grades of 9 (+90%) in all courses involving major writing components and have been commended for my organized and disciplined approach to my work.

You will find me thorough, conscientious, and committed to producing high-quality written work. I am very interested in joining Communications Corporation and look forward to speaking with you about this attractive career opportunity. I will be available at (403) 555 5106 mornings. Thank you for your consideration.

Yours truly,

Sharma Salaam

Sharma Salaam

figure 7.17 Considering the qualities that your firm is looking for, how effectively has Sharma Salaam focused on the job requirements?

Sharma Salaam

HOME ADDRESS: General Delivery
Brookfield, Alberta
T0M 9I9
(403) 555 5106

CAREER OBJECTIVE:

After several years raising a family, I have prepared myself for a career in Secretarial Science. I am primarily interested in employment as an administrative assistant in a setting where my life skills as well as my specialized training will be of most benefit.

EDUCATION:

Sept. 1999–
Apr. 2001

Secretarial Science Modern City College
Modern City, Alberta

The program covered all aspects of Secretarial Science, including office procedures, machine transcription, word processing, spreadsheets, and data entry, as well as written and interpersonal communication and public speaking. The course also included hands-on experience in a model office situation.

May 1999–
Aug. 1999

High School Modern City College
Equivalency Modern City, Alberta

In order to round out my High School courses and prepare myself for entry to the Secretarial Program, I completed English, Business Math, and Social Studies.

Sharma Salaam /2

EMPLOYMENT HISTORY:

Nov. 1998– Apr. 1999	**Resort Worker**	Coyote River Golf Resort Coyote River, Alberta

As occasional help, I assisted in the running of the resort, handling a variety of duties from customer service and banquet set-up to convention bookings.

June 1991– June 1995	**Partner/Manager**	Morton Janitorial Service Brookfield, Alberta

Under contract with Alberta Natural Gas Ltd., I operated a successful janitorial service with one other individual. Our business was so successful that we won additional contracts and hired additional staff to meet the demand. I handled all aspects of the cleaning business, including training new staff.

SKILLS:

Technical

As a trained secretary, I am familiar with related office procedures and techniques, including word processing, filing, and reception, as well as business procedures such as ordering/receiving, invoicing, accounting and third-party billing. I can type accurately (60 wpm), and am familiar with WordPerfect, Microsoft Word, Lotus, and Microsoft Publisher. I can also write clearly and effectively.

Personal

I am an honest and meticulous worker and strive to do my best whatever the task. I am organized and punctual and work hard to meet deadlines. I am also able to assume responsibility when necessary to get the job done.

Interpersonal

I genuinely like people and am able to interact effectively in cooperation with others; I maintain a cheerful outlook and am flexible in my approach to situations. I understand that people are sometimes difficult to handle and am able to show tact and patience in my dealings with them.

figure 7.17 (Continued)

Sharma Salaam   /3

REFEREES: **Mrs. D. Malvolio**   Coyote River Golf Resort
                       Owner/Manager   PO Box 1378
                                                Brookfield, Alberta
                       (403) 555 6050   T0C 2H0

                       Ms Maureen Vapid   Modern City College
                       Secretarial Science   PO Box 5005
                       Instructor   Modern City, Alberta
                       (403) 342 3286   T4W 5K5

Grammar Review

Writing effectively means choosing your words carefully and putting them into an understandable order so that your reader receives the message clearly and without ambiguity. Part of this process involves using correct grammar. Incorrect grammar can sometimes result in unclear or unintended meanings being communicated, and in a business or career situation this can mean lost revenue. It quite literally pays to give some attention to what you're really saying in your work.

As well, people will judge you as surely by the quality of your writing as by your appearance, and though you may consider this unfair, you must recognize that it's a fact of life. You may, like some people, believe that correct spelling and grammar are things that matter only to an English teacher, but this is far from the truth. Even people who are weak in these areas themselves notice someone else's mistakes, and they may be just as unforgiving — in some cases more so — than the average English teacher.

For example, one of the most common complaints that colleges hear from employers, no matter what the field, is that graduates can't write. Much of the problem they see is with grammar; of all writing problems, it is the most visible.

Though this is not intended to be a grammar book, the subject is important enough that this appendix is included to provide you with a handy guide to avoiding the most common grammar errors. If you feel you need a more thorough review, there are plenty of excellent books available. Ask your English professor to recommend one.

Though there are many ways to mangle the language, the following six errors in grammatical structure seem to occur with frequency.

subject–verb agreement
sentence fragments

run-on sentences
pronoun, tense, and person agreement
modifier errors
faulty parallelism

Before we deal with these, however, it is important to have a clear understanding of what makes a sentence.

Word Groups

Language is constructed principally of words, which can be grouped according to some pretty basic rules. By following these rules we can make three types of word groups:

clauses
sentences
phrases

A CLAUSE is a group of words that contains a subject — a "do-er" or "be-er" of something (this word will usually be a noun or a noun substitute) — and a verb — what the subject does or is.

<u>Joe</u> teaches.	subject: Joe verb: teaches
<u>Birds</u> fly.	subject: birds verb: fly
<u>Babies</u> cry.	subject: babies verb: cry
The <u>class</u> learns.	subject: class verb: learns

If these are the only elements contained in the word group, it is considered to be an INDEPENDENT CLAUSE. This means that it is able to stand by itself, and its meaning is complete. Independent clauses are important, because they are the fundamental units from which sentences are made.

Clauses may also be made DEPENDENT by the addition of a joining word called a *subordinate conjunction*. This word reduces the clause to a lesser (or subordinate) role in a sentence; it is no longer the fundamental unit within the sentence. Some subordinate conjunctions are:

although	because
if	when

whenever	which
before	after
who/m	that
though	since

Let's see what these do to our independent clauses from above:

When Joe teaches...
If birds fly...
Because babies cry...
After the students learn...

Suddenly they are no longer complete; they merely set the stage for the really important information that is to follow. In other words, they must now be joined to something else, in fact another independent clause, to make a complete thought.

When Joe teaches, he uses many examples.
If birds fly, people should too.
Because babies cry, they can get attention.
After the students learn, they may be tested.

When you begin to join clauses in this way, you are really building sentences. The rule for a SENTENCE is simple: each sentence *must* contain at least one independent clause; though it may contain other things, the independent clause is an absolute necessity. A SIMPLE SENTENCE contains only an independent clause. You can see that our first grouping of clauses, though made up of only two words each, is also a grouping of sentences. A COMPOUND SENTENCE contains two or more independent clauses joined by *coordinate conjunctions (and, but, or, nor, yet,* and *so)*. A COMPLEX SENTENCE contains a combination of at least one independent clause with one or more dependent clauses. The examples above are complex sentences.

REMEMBER: if there is no independent clause, you do not have a sentence.

The third classification of word groups is easy: anything that is not a clause or a sentence is a PHRASE. To put this another way, anything that does not contain a subject or a verb is a phrase. This is true no matter how long the group of words may be.

climbing up the hill
across the street
beside the store with the big sign out front
over between the drive and the garage
with my dad

Because these groups of words contain neither a subject nor a verb, they are phrases, even though some may be quite long.

Joining Clauses

Independent clauses may be combined into longer sentences in any of several ways. The following are two related independent clauses.

Dave frequently dribbles. He plays basketball.

These may be joined by:

■ using a coordinate conjunction (*and, but, or, nor, yet,* and *so):*

Dave frequently dribbles, so he plays basketball. (compound sentence)

■ using a subordinate conjunction (such as those listed above):

Because Dave frequently dribbles, he plays basketball. (complex sentence)

■ using a semicolon (;):

Dave frequently dribbles; he plays basketball.

The following are common *incorrect* ways of joining two independent clauses.

■ no joining method, simply running two clauses together:

X Dave frequently dribbles he plays basketball.

■ using a comma:

X Dave frequently dribbles, he plays basketball.

Be sure to use only one of the correct methods at a time. It is, for example, also incorrect to use the semicolon *and* a conjunction to join two clauses:

X Because Dave frequently dribbles; he plays basketball.
X Dave frequently dribbles; and he plays basketball.

Six Common Sentence Errors

1. Subject-Verb Agreement

Subjects ("do-ers" of an action or "be-ers" of a state) agree with their verbs in person and number. Singular subjects always take singular verbs, and plural subjects take plural verbs. Singularity of the verb is determined by its subject.

he walks	but	*they* walk
sings		sing
does		do
is		are

Regular verbs are made singular by the addition of "s" to the end. Irregular verbs change form depending on the person (first, second, third — that is, "I/we," "you," or "he/she/it/they") of the pronoun.

I am   you are   he/she is

Luckily, there aren't many irregular verbs in English, and you will be familiar with them from your speech. Just make sure you match them up in your writing. This is easy enough to do when subject and verb come together, but if they are separated by phrases or other words it is more difficult. Here are some quick rules to remember.

a)   Subjects compounded with "and" take plural verbs.

Bob and Devon <u>were</u> with me when it happened.

b)   Subjects compounded with "either…or," "neither…nor," and "or" take verbs that agree with the subject *closest* to the verb.

Neither the Kennedys nor Sheila <u>is</u> happy with the result.
Neither Sheila nor the Kennedys <u>are</u> happy with the result.

c)   Words ending in "-one," "-thing," and "-body" are always singular.

Everybody <u>was</u> present at last night's meeting.
Everything <u>is</u> all right.

d)   Phrases such as "together with," "in addition to," "along with," "apart from," and "as well as" are not part of the subject and do not influence the choice of verb.

Joyce, along with her friends, <u>is</u> going to the movie.

e)   Collective nouns may take singular or plural verbs, depending on their context. If the group, family, committee, or class acts in unison, it is singular.

The committee <u>has made</u> a decision.

If they act individually, the verb is plural.

The committee <u>have argued</u> about this issue for months.

f)   The word "each" is always singular; "both" is always plural.

Each of these <u>is</u> perfect for my sister.
Both of them <u>have</u> advantages.

2. Sentence Fragments

Complete sentences always contain at least one independent clause. Do not punctuate phrases or dependent clauses as sentences. A fragment is a part of a sentence that has been treated as a complete sentence.

X Running down the street and around the corner.
X The thing being that I don't like him.
X After I had finished the laundry and the cleaning.
X For example, scrubbing, polishing, and waxing.

To fix these, either:

- join them to an independent clause; or
- add whatever is missing.

In the case of the second example, the word "being" is not a complete verb; therefore this cannot be a sentence. Change the present participle ("being") to the simple present "is."

John was running down the street and around the corner.
The thing is that I don't like him.
After I had finished the laundry and the cleaning, I took a nap.
I hate household chores, for example, scrubbing, polishing, and waxing.

3. Run-on Sentences

This mistake is created by trying to cram too much information into a single sentence; to correct it, break the elements up in some way. The most common run-on sentences are created by putting two independent clauses together with only a comma.

X I slept in, I missed the bus.

This is incorrect. As is explained above, the only permissible ways to join clauses are with a coordinate conjunction, as in the first example sentence, below; with a subordinate conjunction, as in the second example; and with a semicolon, as in the third example.

I slept in, so I missed the bus.
Because I slept in, I missed the bus.
I slept in; I missed the bus.

4. Pronoun, Tense, and Person Agreement

Always strive for consistency in pronouns, person, and tense. Jumping from one to another person or tense is confusing; using ambiguous or inaccurate pronouns is likewise.

X Ted asked the neighbour to move his car. (Whose car? Ted's or the neighbour's?)
X A person should mind their own business. ("A person" is only one; "their" is plural. Pronouns should always agree with their antecedents in number [singular-plural] and gender [he-she-it].)
X His piece of cake was bigger than hers, which made her angry. ("Which" must refer to a single noun antecedent; a pronoun should not be used to refer to a whole idea.)

Maintain consistent tense. Generally, there are three kinds of time you may refer to in writing: past, present, and future. We tend to write about events in the past or present, and the rule is the same for both. If you're writing in the past, stay in the past unless the meaning changes. The same applies to writing in present tense, and future tense, too, if you happen to be using it.

X So he came up to me and says, "Who do you think you are?" (This is incorrect due to the switch from past "came" to present "says.")

Keep person (I, you, he/she, we, you, they) consistent. The most common problem with person agreement is to move from the first person "I" to the second person "you"; if you stop to think about the sentence, it really doesn't make sense.

X My apartment faces a busy highway, so when I'm trying to sleep in, the noise of the traffic keeps you awake. (Why would the traffic keep you awake if I'm the one sleeping?)

The second common error in person agreement is switching from the use of third person "one" or "a person" to second person "you."

X One should always keep your eyes open. (Use "you" or "one," but don't mix them in the same sentence.)

5. Modifier Problems

Modifiers are words or groups of words that describe, explain, intensify, or negate other words or groups of words. The two kinds are *adjectives,* which modify nouns or noun substitutes, and *adverbs,* which modify verbs, adjectives, or other adverbs. Modifier errors occur when the modifier is either misplaced or "dangling." The best rule for correcting both of these problems is to place the modifier as close as possible to the thing it modifies; if that item is not in the sentence, rewrite the sentence so the meaning is clear.

Misplaced Modifiers
In the case of this error, the modifier is in the wrong position in the sentence. Put the modifier as close as possible to the thing modified.

X I only ate half my dinner. (I only ate it; I didn't dance with it or take it to a movie! Probably I intend the "only" to modify the "half.")
I ate only half my dinner.

Dangling Modifiers
The modified element, though implied, does not exist in the sentence. Rewrite the sentence so that the modified element is clear.

X Running alongside the river, a treasure chest lay in the bushes. (Since the treasure chest can't run, this sentence doesn't make sense. Who saw the treasure chest? Who was running?)
Running alongside the river, Mark spotted a treasure chest lying in the bushes.

6. Faulty Parallelism

This error occurs when you are using lists or series of items. Whenever you are speaking of more than one item, place them all in the same grammatical form. Use nouns with nouns, adjectives with adjectives, "-ing" words with "-ing" words, clauses with clauses.

X Professionals include doctors and people who practise law.
X I like running, jumping, and to sing.
X She's pretty, but has ambition too.

Replace such faulty parallelism with corrected forms:

Professionals include doctors and lawyers.
OR
Professionals include people who practise medicine and people who practise law.

I like running, jumping, and singing.
OR
I like to run, jump, and sing.

She's pretty, but ambitious too.
OR
She has beauty and ambition too.

This coverage of grammar is necessarily a brief overview. There are many more subtleties to good grammar than there is room to cover in this book. A good grammar handbook will give you more information, should you require it.

sharpening your skills

The following sentences contain errors of the types explained above. See if you can correct them. The answer key follows.

1. I only lived in Ottawa for four months.

2. Doing his homework, the TV was distracting.

3. The thing being that I really enjoy their company.

4. Take me with you, I'll miss you too much if I stay here alone. In this scary place with no phone.

5. Give me a bite of your sandwich, I haven't had lunch.

6. Darlene's answer almost was right.

7. Genevieve, but not the others, are going camping.

8. I nearly told you a hundred times! Don't call me!

9. A person should mind their own business.

10. One should always keep your eyes open.

11. Doing a test is better than explanations, you can see the rules in action.

12. I didn't want his sympathy, I sent him away forever.

13. If a mosquito bites your face, it should be squashed.

14. On the table was his hat and gloves, so I knew he was home.

15. I only mailed half the letters after lunch.

16. In college I took English, History, and a course in people and society.

17. If I want to do a good job, you should never overlook details.

18. There was three people on the bus: a student, a mail carrier, and a man who worked on cars.

19. I love lasagna. Even though it's fattening.

20. I don't want to go to the party with him. The reason being that I had a lousy time when I dated him before.

21. Jeff looks familiar to me; because I have a friend who looks just like him.

22. There are lots of things you can do in winter. Skiing, skating, and hikes are only three of them.

23. Running up the stairs, someone tripped Erika and she fell on her arm, breaking it in two places.

24. Where is Rebecca's dictionary, she'll be lost without it.

25. Neither Bryce nor his friends is willing to help.

26. If the dog sleeps in your bed, it should be disinfected.

27. Being too large a sandwich, she declined to eat it.

28. It really made me laugh. The day she told us about Ted.

29. He is a kind person who has generosity too.

30. If a person is nervous, they should try to relax more.

31. Suzanne likes to wear soft sweaters, eat exotic food, and taking bubble baths.

32. My sister's boyfriend is stingy, sloppy, and doesn't have much ambition.

33. I noticed a crack in the window walking into the house.

34. Eating a hot dog, mustard dropped onto my shirt.

35. What do you think of this, Red Deer is the fourth largest city in Alberta.

36. When you're stuck. You can use your dictionary for help.

37. Hallowe'en is my least favourite holiday, I'm afraid of ghosts.

38. Although I like Christmas, since I love all the sparkle and magic.

39. I nearly earned a hundred dollars last week.

40. Jerry invited only Buffy and me, I guess you can't come.

answer key

1. I lived in Ottawa for <u>only</u> four months.

2. <u>As he did</u> his homework, the TV was distracting.
   OR Doing his homework, <u>Marshall found</u> the TV distracting.

3. The thing <u>is</u> that I really enjoy their company.
   OR I really enjoy their company.

4. Take me with you<u>;</u> I'll miss you too much if I stay here alone in this scary place with no phone.

5. Give me a bite of your sandwich<u>.</u> I haven't had lunch.

6. Darlene's answer was <u>almost</u> right.

7. Genevieve, but not the others, <u>is</u> going camping.

8. I told you <u>nearly</u> a hundred times! Don't call me!

9. A person should mind <u>her or his</u> own business.
   OR <u>People</u> should mind their own business.

10. One should always keep <u>one's</u> eyes open.
    OR <u>You</u> should always keep your eyes open.

11. Doing a test is better than explanations, <u>because</u> you can see the rules in action.

12. I didn't want his sympathy, <u>so</u> I sent him away forever.

13. <u>A</u> mosquito <u>that</u> bites your face should be squashed.

14. On the table <u>were</u> his hat and gloves, so I knew he was home.

15. I mailed <u>only</u> half the letters after lunch.

16. In college I took English, History, and <u>Sociology</u>.

17. If I want to do a good job, <u>I</u> should never overlook details.
    OR If <u>you</u> want to do a good job, you should never overlook details.

18. There <u>were</u> three people on the bus: a student, a mail carrier, and a <u>me-chanic.</u>

19. I love lasagna, even though it's fattening.

20. I don't want to go to the party with him. I had a lousy time when I dated him before.
OR I don't want to go to the party with him, because I had a lousy time when I dated him before.

21. Jeff looks familiar to me because I have a friend who looks just like him.

22. There are lots of things you can do in winter. Skiing, skating, and <u>hiking</u> are only three of them.

23. Running up the stairs, <u>Erika tripped</u> and fell on her arm, breaking it in two places.

24. Where is Rebecca's dictionary<u>? S</u>he'll be lost without it.

25. Neither Bryce nor his friends <u>are</u> willing to help.

26. <u>Your bed</u> should be disinfected if the dog sleeps in <u>it</u>.

27. <u>Because the sandwich was too large,</u> she declined to eat it.

28. It really made me laugh the day she told us about Ted.

29. He is a kind <u>and generous</u> person.

30. If <u>people are</u> nervous, they should try to relax more.
OR <u>People who are nervous</u> should try to relax more.

31. Suzanne likes to wear soft sweaters, eat exotic food, and <u>take</u> bubble baths.

32. My sister's boyfriend is stingy, sloppy, and <u>unambitious</u>.

33. <u>Walking into the house,</u> I noticed a crack in the window.

34. <u>As I was</u> eating a hot dog, mustard dropped onto my shirt.

35. What do you think of this<u>?</u> Red Deer is the fourth largest city in Alberta.

36. When you're stuck, you can use your dictionary for help.

37. Hallowe'en is my least favourite holiday, <u>because</u> I'm afraid of ghosts.

38. I like Christmas, since I love all the sparkle and magic.

39. I earned <u>nearly</u> a hundred dollars last week.

40. Jerry invited only Buffy and me, <u>so</u> I guess you can't come.

Punctuation

This review is designed to remind you of the basic uses of the most common punctuation marks. Students often find punctuation confusing, but it is important. It is a convention designed to help your reader understand the meaning and intention of your written work. Like road signs on a highway, punctuation marks help the reader find her or his way in the journey through your written work. Though style guides differ somewhat, the following general rules should see you through most basic punctuation needs. For more detailed information, consult a style manual. Remember, no matter which style guide you decide to follow, you must follow a consistent style throughout your document.

Reviewing Common Punctuation Marks

There are three common forms of "full stop" punctuation: the period, the question mark, and the exclamation point.

The Period (.)

1. Use a period to mark the end of a sentence.
2. Use a period following an abbreviation: etc., Dr., Alta.
   Some common abbreviations (TV, VCR) don't require periods. Neither do the two-letter provincial abbreviations used by Canada Post: NS, NB, PE, NF, QC, ON, MB, SK, AB, BC, YT, NT.
3. When an abbreviation falls at the end of the sentence, use only one period, omitting the abbreviation period.

   Since Jerry completed dentistry school, he loves to be called Dr.

The Question Mark (?)

1. Use a question mark only after a direct question.

    Where are you taking that box?
    Why did you bring him with you?

2. Never use a question mark for an indirect question.

    I wonder whether Shirley has a copy of this book.
    I asked him where he intended to take that box.

    A question mark is end punctuation and should not be directly followed by any other form of punctuation — period, comma, or semicolon.

The Exclamation Point (!)

1. Use an exclamation point after an exclamatory word (interjection) or phrase:

    Wow!
    Hey!
    How about that!

3. Use an exclamation point for emphasis when a statement or question is meant to be read with force.

    What did you do that for!
    I just won the lottery!

    In formal writing, and most business writing, you should avoid the exclamation point. Occasionally it is useful in sales letters, for emphasis, but too many exclamation points will create an overly loud or hysterical impression.

    You can win!
    Act now and save!
    No Down Payment! No Interest!

The Semicolon (;)

1. Use a semicolon to separate two independent clauses that are closely related in meaning.

    I am tired of Shawn; I really wish he would go away.
    I built my first model two years ago; now I'm hooked.
    I have a sinus infection; I went swimming without nose plugs.

2. Use a semicolon before conjunctive adverbs such as "however," "therefore," "thus," and "consequently" when they are used to join two related clauses.

    I don't want to deal with those people ever again; however, they are my relatives.

Ernesto didn't prepare well enough for his presentation; consequently, he felt like a fool in front of the class.

3. Use a semicolon to separate items in a series, but only if the individual items in the series already contain commas.

I have invited Madhu, my cousin; Nancy, my best friend; and Ian, Nancy's brother. I have to replace my VCR, which is ten years old; my television, which is twenty years old; and my stereo, which is practically an antique.

The Colon (:)

1. Use a colon to introduce a list on two occasions: when the list is vertical, or when the introductory clause is independent.

Please bring the following supplies with you:
camera;
film;
flash attachment;
batteries; and
lenses.

I can't believe how many things I have to do this week: prepare my presentation for English, organize my project for Business Practices, finish shopping for my vacation, and get my hair cut.

2   Use a colon after an independent clause if what follows (a word, phrase, or another independent clause) explains or enlarges upon the first one.

Wait until you hear what he gave me: a machine for making rubber stamps.
Cameron got the highest grade in the class on that test: A+.
Vernon is the perfect place to stay away from: my in-laws live there.

3. Use a colon to introduce a formal quotation.

In *Second Words,* Margaret Atwood says: "A voice is a gift: it should be cherished and used, to utter fully human speech, if possible."

If the quotation is lengthy (over three lines), begin it on a new line following the colon and indent it.

4. Use a colon after the salutation of a business letter.

Dear Dr. Ingham:
Dear Ms Ramtej:

5. Use a colon between a title and a subtitle.

A Gift of Voice: The Role of Self-Projection in the Rhetorical Appeal of Margaret Atwood's Nonfiction

The Comma (,)

1. Use commas to separate items in a list.

   Betty, Elaine and Debbie are close friends.
   I can bring my cat, my dog, or my fish.

   The comma before the coordinate conjunction is optional; it may be used to avoid confusion.

   X Be alert for inclement weather, falling rocks and wildlife. [Was the wildlife falling or only the rocks?]
   Be alert for inclement weather, falling rocks, and wildlife.

2. Use a comma following someone's name in a direct address to that person; do not use a comma when the name is the subject of the sentence.

   Bill, will you hand me that book on economics?
   X Bill, handed me the book.

3. Use a comma after an introductory dependent clause.

   Because I was late, I missed the pizza.
   Whenever he participates, we have problems.
   If I want you for anything, I'll call.

4. Use a comma after a lengthy introductory phrase.

   After the best night of my life, I was exhausted.
   Before the graduation dance, Ely came down with the measles.

5. Use a comma before a coordinate conjunction (and, or, nor, but, yet, so) that joins two independent clauses.

   I went downtown, and Bea joined me.
   I went for the interview, but somebody else got the job.

   You can omit the comma if the two clauses have the same subject.

   I went for the interview and I got the job.
   I went for the interview and got the job.

6. Use a comma after conjunctive adverbs such as "however," "therefore," "thus," "moreover," and "consequently."

   I like him very much; moreover, I think he is an outstanding accountant.

7. Use commas to set apart phrases or clauses that interrupt a sentence between its subject and verb.

   David, who has the office beside mine, has accepted a job with another firm.
   Feral, the little rascal, didn't finish her homework.

8. Use a comma before a short, direct quotation.

    Paul said, "I'd like to nail that guy."

Don't use a comma for indirect quotations.

    Paul said that he'd like to nail that guy.

9. Use a comma to separate parts of an address, if they appear on the same line.

    19 Sherwood Blvd., Lethbridge, Alberta

10. Use a comma to separate the day and month when identifying a date.

    Saturday, November 13

The Apostrophe (')

1. Use an apostrophe to indicate possession in nouns, but not in pronouns.

    Paul's book
    David's minutes
    Maureen's comments
    whose book (NEVER who's book — that's *who is*)
    its colour (NEVER it's colour — that's *it is*)

    Singular nouns, as above, add an apostrophe and an "s"; plural nouns or others ending in "s" usually don't need an additional "s".

    the Inghams' house
    the students' grades

    However, when the possessive word is pronounced as though it had an additional syllable, you may wish to add the second "s."

    Chris's test results
    Iris's new gloves

    For plural nouns not ending in "s" add apostrophe and "s."

    children's coats
    criteria's validity

2. Use apostrophes in contractions.

    can't
    won't
    they're
    wasn't
    he's

Quotation Marks (" " or ' ')

1. Use quotation marks for indicating direct speech, but not indirect speech.

   David asked, "Do you need a ride to the airport?"
   David asked if I needed a ride to the airport.

2. Quotation marks within quotation marks are usually indicated by single marks within double ones.

   She said, "You know what Joseph Campbell says: 'Follow your bliss.' "

3. Use quotation marks to indicate that a word is slang, an inappropriate usage, or someone else's wording, but be very careful not to overuse them in this way.

   I don't think "intimacy" is quite the right word for this concept.
   I should have realized the truth when he said he was "cool."

4. Use quotation marks for the titles of short works, such as poems, short stories, essays, articles, songs, or chapters in a book.

   "The Rime of the Ancient Mariner"
   "Home on the Range"
   "Chapter Seven: The Job Package"

   Enclose commas and periods within the quotation marks; semicolons and colons are placed outside the quotation marks. Other end punctuation (question marks and exclamation points) falls outside unless the original phrase was a question or exclamation.

Title Treatments

1. Italicize (or underline if you can't italicize) the titles of book-length works wherever they appear in your writing.

   Hamlet
   Lovable Soft Toys
   Effective Business Communication

2. Place the titles of short works (essays, book chapters, poems, short stories, songs, recipes, or articles) into quotation marks.

   "Chapter Seven: The Job Package"
   "Introduction: Are You a Designer?"
   "Stopping by Woods on a Snowy Evening"

3. Do not underline the titles of your own reports or essays, or place them in quotation marks, on the title page of your paper.

The Agony and the Exigence:
A Rhetorical Analysis of Two Presentations

Innovations in Training:
A Proposal for Improving Our Report Writing Workshops

4. If your title contains the title of another work, you should treat the title of the other work appropriately, depending on whether it is a short or long work.

    Method or Madness? An Analysis of Motive in <u>Hamlet</u>
    OR
    Method or Madness? An Analysis of Motive in *Hamlet*

Miles to Go Before I Sleep:
Hypothermia in Frost's "Stopping by Woods on a Snowy Evening"

This brief refresher is not intended to be a comprehensive guide to punctuation usage, but should provide enough detail for everyday usage. For a more comprehensive guide to punctuation conventions, you may wish to consult a good English handbook or manual of style such as *The Chicago Manual of Style* or Strunk and White's *The Elements of Style*.

Index

LICENSE AGREEMENT AND LIMITED WARRANTY

READ THE FOLLOWING TERMS AND CONDITIONS CAREFULLY BEFORE OPENING THIS DISK PACKAGE. THIS IS AN AGREEMENT BETWEEN YOU AND PRENTICE HALL CANADA INC. (THE "COMPANY"), BY OPENING THIS SEALED PACKAGE, YOU ARE AGREEING TO BE BOUND BY THESE TERMS AND CONDITIONS. IF YOU DO NOT AGREE, WITH THESE TERMS AND CONDITIONS, DO NOT OPEN THE DISK PACKAGE. PROMPTLY RETURN THE DISK PACKAGE AND ALL ACCOMPANYING ITEMS TO THE COMPANY.

1. GRANT OF LICENSE: In consideration of your adoption of textbooks and/or other materials published by the Company, and your agreement to abide by the terms and conditions of the Agreement, the Company grants to you a nonexclusive right to use and display the copy of the enclosed software program (hereinafter "the SOFTWARE") so long as you comply with the terms of this Agreement. The Company reserves all rights not expressly granted to you under this Agreement. This license is not a sale of the original SOFTWARE or any copy to you.

2. USE RESTRICTIONS: You may not sell or license copies of the SOFTWARE or the Documentation to others. You may not transfer or distribute copies of the SOFTWARE or the Documentation, except to instructors and students in your school who are users of the adopted Company textbook that accompanies this SOFTWARE. You may not reverse engineer, disassemble, decompile, modify, adapt, translate or create derivative works based on the SOFTWARE or the Documentation without the prior written consent of the Company.

3. LIMITED WARRANTY AND DISCLAIMER OF WARRANTY: Because this SOFTWARE is being given to you without charge, the Company makes no warranties about the SOFTWARE, which is provided "AS-IS". The COMPANY DISCLAIMS ALL WARRANTIES, EXPRESS OR IMPLIED, INCLUDING WITHOUT LIMITATION, THE IMPLIED WARRANTIES OF MERCHANT ABILITY AND FITNESS FOR A PARTICULAR PURPOSE. THE COMPANY DOES NOT WARRANT, GUARANTEE OR MAKE ANY REPRESENTATION REGARDING THE USE OR THE RESULTS OF THE USE OF THE SOFTWARE. IN NO EVENT, SHALL THE COMPANY OR ITS EMPLOYEES, AGENTS, SUPPLIERS OR CONTRACTORS BE LIABLE FOR ANY INCIDENTAL, INDIRECT, SPECIAL OR CONSEQUENTIAL DAMAGES ARISING OUT OF OR IN CONNECTION WITH THE LICENSE GRANTED UNDER THIS AGREEMENT INCLUDING, WITHOUT LIMITATION, LOSS OF USE, LOSS OF DATA, LOSS OF INCOME OR PROFIT, OR OTHER LOSSES SUSTAINED AS A RESULT OF INJURY TO ANY PERSON, OR LOSS OF OR DAMAGE OF PROPERTY, OR CLAIMS OF THIRD PARTIES, EVEN IF THE COMPANY OR AN AUTHORIZED REPRESENTATIVE OF THE COMPANY HAS BEEN ADVISED OF THE POSSIBILITY OF SUCH DAMAGES.

SOME JURISDICTIONS DO NOT ALLOW THE LIMITATION OF IMPLIED WARRANTIES OR LIABILITY FOR INCIDENTAL, INDIRECT, SPECIAL OR CONSEQUENTIAL DAMAGES, SO THE ABOVE LIMITATIONS MAY NOT ALWAYS APPLY. THE WARRANTIES IN THIS AGREEMENT GIVE YOU SPECIFIC LEGAL RIGHTS AND YOU MAY ALSO HAVE OTHER RIGHTS WHICH VARY IN ACCORDANCE WITH LOCAL LAW.

ACKNOWLEDGMENT

YOU ACKNOWLEDGE THAT YOU HAVE READ THIS AGREEMENT, UNDERSTAND IT AND AGREE TO BE BOUND BY ITS TERMS AND CONDITIONS. YOU ALSO AGREE THAT THIS AGREEMENT IS THE COMPLETE AND EXCLUSIVE AGREEMENT BETWEEN YOU AND THE COMPANY.

Should you have any questions concerning this agreement or if you wish to contact the Company for any reason, please contact in writing: Editorial Manager, Prentice Hall Canada, 1870 Birchmount Road, Scarborough, Ontario M1P 2J7.